INTRODUCING

FEMINIST THEOLOGY

INTRODUCING

FEMINIST THEOLOGY

Anne M. Clifford

ORBIS BOOKS

Maryknoll, New York 10545

Ninth Printing, December 2009

The Catholic Foreign Mission Society of America (Maryknoll) recruits and trains people for overseas missionary service. Through Orbis Books, Maryknoll aims to foster the international dialogue that is essential to mission. The books published, however, reflect the opinions of their authors and are not meant to represent the official position of the Society. To obtain more information about Maryknoll or Orbis Books, please visit our website at www.maryknoll.org.

Queries regarding rights and permissions should be addressed to:
Orbis Books, P.O. Box 308, Maryknoll, NY 10545-0308.

Published by Orbis Books, Maryknoll, NY 10545-0308.

Manufactured in the United States of America

Library of Congress Cataloging-in-Publication Data

Clifford, Anne M., 1944-
    Introducing feminist theology / Anne M. Clifford.
      p. cm.
    Includes bibliographical references and index.
    ISBN 1-57075-238-9 (pbk.)
    1. Feminist theology.   I. Title

  BT83.55 .C57 2001
  230′.082 – dc21

                        2001018525

In memory of Karen Marie Clifford (1946–1999),
and in honor of the retirement of
Jacinta Van Winkel (Carlow College) and
Marilyn Schaub (Duquesne University),
with gratitude and love.

Contents

Acknowledgments

In thinking through the questions and issues addressed in this book, I have been assisted by many women and men who have contributed to Christian feminist theology and by the students whom I have been privileged to teach. Although I am responsible for the book's content, I am grateful to colleagues who gave their time generously to read a first draft of one or more of its chapters and provide me with helpful critical feedback: Maureen Crossen (Carlow College), Carol Dempsey (University of Portland), Sally Kenel and Pamela Kirk (St. John's University, New York), Moni McIntyre (Duquesne University), Mary Ann Zollman (Clarke College), and Kathleen Contini Borres (my former teaching assistant at Duquesne). Thanks also to Anthony Godzieba (Villanova University) for his supportive interest in this project.

Many of the ideas in this book, especially its final chapter on Christian feminism and ecology, were first developed in papers that I gave at a Duquesne University theology department seminar and at annual conferences of the College Theology Society and the Catholic Theological Society of America. Without the thoughtful responses of colleagues, my work would be much impoverished. My life, and this book in particular, would be greatly impoverished without the loving encouragement of my mother, Julia Goodwin Clifford, my sister, Mary J. Clifford, my brother and my sister-in-law, J. Robert and Cherie Fike Clifford, and my godmother, Beth Clifford Cosgrove. The same can be said of my religious community, the Sisters of St. Joseph of Baden, Pennsylvania, especially of Jeanne Rodgers and Marguerite Coyne, and the other members of the Sophia Corporate Reflection group. Among the great consolations in my life are my family of birth and my community of choice because I find in both support for my Christian feminism. My sincere thanks to each of you.

Thanks also to Orbis Books for inviting me to write this book. My heartfelt gratitude goes to its editor, Susan Perry. Due to a series of pressing family concerns, the book took longer to complete than both of us had hoped. Throughout the process, Susan Perry was patient and supportive. What began as a "contractual relationship" evolved into an opportunity for me to get to know a highly intelligent and compassionate woman who clearly embodies the mission of Orbis Books and its sponsoring community, the Catholic Foreign Mission Society of America.

I dedicate this work in memory of my sister, Karen, an exceptionally courageous and generous woman, and in honor of the retirement of Jacinta Van Winkel from Carlow College and Marilyn Schaub from Duquesne University, both of whom have been pioneers, paving the way for new generations of women in biblical and theological studies.

Introduction

On occasion I teach a course entitled "Women and Christianity." Every time I happily receive the course assignment, I am immediately faced with the quandary: What readings and book(s) will I choose that will enable my students to leave the course with a representative and meaningful overview of what feminist scholars are contributing to Christianity, especially to Christian theology? Although there is no shortage of fine theological works by feminists in every area of Christian theology and ***spirituality,**[†] an introductory overview that provides a sense of the bigger picture has not been available. This book is intended to fill that gap. It addresses basic questions about what feminist theology is and what Christian feminists are contributing to biblical studies, talk about God, relationship to the church, spirituality, and concerns about ecology.

This introduction to theology, which is at once feminist and Christian, is written for college and university students, particularly upper-level undergraduates and beginning graduates. The book is written by a woman with women interested in Christianity and ***feminism** in mind, but also in the hope that it will be of benefit to men who share these interests. It is also my hope that this book will be a resource for the person seeking a single source that has compiled a lot of information about major breakthrough areas and important trends in Christian feminist theology. Although an introduction, it presumes some familiarity with Christianity but not necessarily with Christian feminist theology as an academic discipline.

At the outset it is important to provide a working understanding of theology in the Christian ***tradition** as it is treated in this book. Christian theology has long been viewed as a communal process of bringing faith in the God revealed in the life of Jesus, the Christ, to understanding (*fides quarens intellectum*) through a listening openness to the Holy Spirit. "Understanding" here refers to far more than a rational exercise; although it is that, it brings together the mind and heart in an expression of felt knowledge, born of relationship with God. It is, therefore, a knowledge that ideally flows from and to love of God revealed in Jesus Christ. This love tends to impel a person to envision her or his life differently, for such is the nature of the Spirit's transformative activity.

Bringing faith in God to understanding is not a generalized process. The process is initiated again and again by questions of importance that rise in the experiences of culturally situated human persons. "Experience" features strongly in feminist theology. Experience has a commonsense meaning and yet it names a complex and varied reality. In this book any tendency to essentialize a concept of

---

[†] Terms included in the glossary are indicated by an asterisk and bold type.

1

"women's experience" is avoided. Instead, the experience of women is attended to within specific frames of reference that are both cultural and historical.

For a feminist engaged in doing theology, the effects of history and culture on women are an important starting point. Feminist theologians bring questions "of the moment" — questions rising in contemporary women's lives — to specific biblical texts and church teachings, the primary sources of Christian faith. In an era of heightened awareness of women's consciousness of themselves as women, sources of and about women that have long gone unnoticed or were at best pushed to the periphery are moved to the center and are the focus of Christian theology to which the important adjective "feminist" is attached.

One such source is a *New Testament baptismal formula. A baptismal text is a logical one to highlight in the introduction to an introductory book on Christian feminist theology. One obvious reason is that most Christians begin their life journey with the God of Jesus Christ with *baptism. Another reason is what is explicitly affirmed in the text chosen, the baptismal formula in Gal. 3:28. Likely written by Paul in 54 or 55 C.E., this formula posits a theological claim very important to women's experience as Christians: "All of you who were baptized into Christ have clothed yourselves with Christ. There is neither Jew nor Greek, there is neither slave nor free person, there is not male and female; for you are all one in Christ Jesus. And if you belong to Christ, then you are Abraham's [and presumably also Sarah's] descendant, heirs according to the promise."

This statement provides a feasible reason for arguing that Christianity, at least at the time in which Paul wrote the letter to the Christians of Galatia, is a religion that affirms *gender equality or, at the very least, glosses over gender differences of inequality where full participation in the community of Christians is concerned. Persons regarded by the broader society as insignificant, subordinate, and even unworthy of inclusion — slaves and women — are incorporated with full communion in a community inspired by Jesus' good news of love. Why? Because Jesus Christ makes a difference and because the Holy Spirit impels the community of nascent Christianity to embrace a discipleship of equals in the name of Christ. Surely, this must be part of the promise into which Christians are initiated. With the waters of baptism comes a new vision for a new humanity, an inclusive community.

If this text had been the only biblical text on women, or if it had been the one that became normative for all Christian texts on women to follow, the need for a feminist theology would be minimal to non-existent. Yet the equal treatment of women and men was apparently a source of annoyance to the surrounding society in which Christians lived. During a probable time of persecution, Christians were treated as social outsiders, even deviants from cultural norms, especially where the role of women was concerned. Christian social deviance contributed to the threat of martyrdom. This reality, along with the maleness of Jesus and the assumption that God also must be male, proved to be obstacles to the Galatian vision of an inclusive Christian community. Christian leadership, perhaps anxious to establish a positive reputation among their non-Christian neighbors in the broader society, distanced themselves from the Galatians' doctrine of females and males being equally one in Christ.

A few years prior to the letter to the Galatians, in the first letter to the church at Corinth (circa 51), Paul affirms the equality of men and women in a different way: "Woman is not independent of man or man of woman in the Lord. For just as woman came from man, so man is born of woman; but all things are from God" (1 Cor. 11:11–12). Yet later in the letter a seemingly contrasting message appears. It is improper for a woman to speak in the church. Women are to be silent: "for they are not allowed to speak, but should be subordinate, as even the law says" (1 Cor. 14:34). Scholars are divided about whether this is Paul's own position or the quoting of one adopted by the leaders at Corinth in the interest of order. Some years after the first letter to the Corinthians, in the letter to Timothy (63–110), attributed to Paul, one of his followers brings Paul's authority to bear to change women's behavior. It was not fitting for a Christian community to "permit a woman to teach or to have authority over a man. She must be silent" (1 Tim. 2:12). The reason given focuses on *Eve, who was not only the first woman but also the first human to be deceived and to sin (1 Tim. 2:13–14). Eve voiced her temptation to Adam and caused disruption in God's created order. Apparently, the women who were raising their voices in the churches were seen as "tempting" men to allow women to have authority over them, thereby disrupting what was perceived to be God's proper order for male-female relationship. Therefore, "Woman must receive instruction silently and under complete [male] control" (1 Tim. 2:11). What is conspicuously absent from this text is any mention of Jesus Christ, the crucified and risen Savior, with whom every Christian is equally "clothed" at baptism. A possible conclusion is that women participate more fully in Eve's role in the "fall" than they do in Jesus Christ and his mission. Yet such a conclusion is not the only reasonable explanation. In chapter 2 of First Timothy the writer may have cited the familiar story of Eve's "fall" (Genesis 3) because it lent itself to support behaviors that more readily matched what was acceptable in the society at large. This passage may be a capitulation to the status quo in order to preserve the reputation of the churches during a precarious time.

How one interprets Gal. 3:28, 1 Cor. 14:34, and 1 Tim. 2:8–15 has a great deal to do with what body of experiences one brings to these texts. I have developed interpretations that reflect my own experiences and commitments as a Euro-American woman who continues to find in the Christian sources a treasure that captures my heart (Luke 12:34) and in feminism a call to have this treasure make a difference where discrimination against women is concerned. Early on, the Christian movement accommodated itself to the culture of its members, yet it also maintained its capacity for prophetic witness in the cherished memories of Jesus Christ that it preserved. This perspective on Christianity is shared by many theologians who identify themselves as Christian and feminists, perhaps 75 to 80 percent of feminist theologians writing today. These authors continue to find something genuinely good about the good news of Jesus Christ, yet also seek to correct a myriad of injustices tolerated and even supported in the name of Christ: subjugation of women, oppressive racism directed to persons of color, and exploitation of nonhuman creatures for human ends. There is a treasure in the Christian message, but it is in earthen vessels, vessels that Christian feminist theologians believe can be remolded in ways that are in keeping with the core of Christian truth.

Not all feminist theologians agree that Christianity contains a treasure to be found. These women have concluded that although a promise for a new humanity, a fully inclusive community, may have been made early on in the Christian movement, the promise was an empty one, a mere anomaly in a long history of Christian institutional bias against women. The church all too quickly and willingly conformed to the social norms of the broader society and even willingly contributed to them where the oppression of women and their gifts were concerned. Male church leaders not only demanded that women be silent in the assembly, but also effectively masculinized God. For these women, therefore, there is something inherently contradictory about a Christian feminist anything, especially a Christian feminist theology. The exclusion of women from decision-making processes in the formation of the Christian tradition and the dismissal of even the possibility of God being imaged as female make Christianity bankrupt in their eyes. These systemic ways of discounting the experiences of women cause irreparable harm not only to women, but also to all persons seeking the face of God. Some of these women now identify themselves as "post-Christian." Some of you reading this introduction may find yourselves in a similar position. You are distressed at the negative treatment of women and the discounting of women's experiences of God by the Christian churches. Feminist critics of Christianity illustrate in a poignant way that Christianity and feminism are emotionally laden realities and not merely objects awaiting detached academic commentary.

The emotionality of feminism is further illustrated by women and men who reject feminism outright today. Reasons for this rejection are myriad. A common one voiced by some women who fit the "generation X" or "generation Y" demographics is that the feminist movement for liberation may have been needed in the 1960s and 1970s, when our mothers "came of age," but it is no longer needed now. Women of the "post–baby boom" generations have no need for feminism: "We are able to do whatever we want regardless of gender. The sky is the limit." Yet, as I reflect on this recent statement by one of my former students as I write this introduction, images from the evening news of women being indiscriminately accosted in New York City's Central Park on a warm June afternoon fill my head and bring a great sadness into my heart. At least forty-five to fifty young women were injured in a moblike and indiscriminate attack by at least twice as many young men. Video clips taken by tourists in the park show some of the women lying on the ground in fetal positions, protecting their denuded and wounded bodies from the further frenzy of male sexual assault. Others, in tears, are running for their lives, clutching their torn clothing to their chests. News commentators draw analogies to the "wilding" incidents that women of the previous generation experienced in this same locale in the 1980s. A century ago, during the period known as the ***first wave of feminism,** sexual assault on women was explained as an inevitable explosive acting out by men in a highly repressive sexual atmosphere. Now it is explained as an inevitable effect of a permissive sexual environment. Yet, at least on the surface it would seem that where women are concerned, the more things change, the more they remain the same.

This example is cited because of the discrepancy between talk about women not needing feminism and women's daily realities around the globe. This problem is addressed in chapter 1, "The 'Why' and 'What' of Christian Feminist Theology." The assumption governing the content of that chapter is that it is not possible to talk about theology that is feminist and Christian unless the reader is first engaged by the related questions, Why feminism? and What is feminism? The answer to the first question is developed in relationship to the experience of the global reality of women. The answer to the second question surveys the many forms of feminism that have existed since the mid-nineteenth century. It takes into account the three major waves of feminism that projected different social visions of women. The first wave, of the mid-nineteenth through the early twentieth centuries, envisioned women as capable of participating in the public *polis* by voting responsibly. The ***second wave of feminism,** of Euro-American women in the 1960s and 1970s, sought civil rights and equality for women. The ***third wave of feminism,** which began in the 1980s, takes seriously the differences in women's experiences around the globe and envisions justice for all women. In all three waves, feminists have emphasized equality and mutuality in relationships as the basis of the world as it ought to be.

Since there are many definitions of feminism available today, a definition well-suited to the Christian feminist theology addressed in this book is proposed in the first chapter. Additional groundwork is also provided. Feminism has long been a social vision and a movement advocating liberation for women, but it is also a form of academic study, as is constructing Christian theology. Providing an overview of major developments in the theology of Christian feminists in the academy is a major purpose of this book. Academic Christian feminist theology is profoundly affected by the social vision and advocacy for change of fellow feminists, but it also incorporates feminist theories. Since the mid-1980s academic feminism has diverged in two very different directions: feminist theory that draws heavily on French philosophy and psychology, especially that of Luce Irigaray and Julia Kristeva, and feminist thought that takes into account the many voices of women of color, such as Audre Lorde, bell hooks, and Rosario Morales. In this book the first, although offering many important insights, is "the road not taken." The second, with its attention to the difference that social location makes in women's lives, is the road of choice because the majority of Christian feminist theologians find clear links between their beliefs about the mission and message of Jesus and the difference that social location makes where the injustices of gender discrimination, racial prejudice, and colonial oppression are concerned.

At the end of the chapter, the reader will find a sketch of the methodological steps often used by Christian feminist theologians today. These steps incorporate important insights on gender experience from the second wave of feminism, while being attentive to third-wave concerns about the difference that social location makes in the lives of women and subjugated men.

The application of the method for doing theology presented in chapter 1 immediately follows in chapter 2, "Feminist Perspectives on the Bible." Focus on the *Bible in the second chapter is a logical topic because the Bible is an important primary source for theology. This chapter begins with the most important first-wave feminist work on the Bible, *The Woman's Bible,* edited by Elizabeth Cady Stanton, also known for her work on behalf of women's suffrage in the United States. *The Woman's Bible* was actually a biblical commentary, composed by a group of female-suffrage sympathizers at a time in which a new translation of the Bible was being done by an all-male group of Protestant scholars. *The Woman's Bible* presumes a certain understanding of what the Bible is. Therefore, the question "What is the Bible?" is explored by surveying a spectrum of views, both on the process of the Bible's creation and on the finalization by church leaders of the books that were included in the Bible. In each of the steps of the process of the Bible's formation, questions are raised about where and how women do and do not play a role. These are important questions for what follows, namely, a survey of perspectives that women contribute to biblical translation and interpretation. Here the reader will encounter a sample of the various ways in which second-wave and third-wave feminist biblical scholarship interpret the Bible, particularly those texts about women.

"Feminist Perspectives on God" is the title of chapter 3. In its pages is addressed a question of paramount importance, not only for the future of feminist theology, but also for Christianity as a religion: What are the most meaningful and appropriate ways to speak about God? The question is of such import because God is the ultimate reality whom Christians worship. How the communities of Christian believers speak about God represents what the community affirms as its highest good, greatest beauty, and most authentic truth. God-talk — theological symbols, images, and narrative metaphors — functions to mold the corporate identity of the Christian churches, reflecting its values and directing its lived realities. While making no claim to exhaustively treat the subject, the chapter critically examines major problems associated with the masculinization of divine symbols for Christianity and explores the Bible for alternative female symbols. What appears in the biblical discourse about God coalesces and continues to develop in the Christian affirmation that God is One, yet Three. Although Christianity is monotheistic, its revelation of God is unique in the triune revelation of the divine. The *Trinity, a core symbol for Christian feminist theology today, is explored with an eye on what it presents as the highest good for Christian women and men. Finally, examples of the unique and rich diversity in talk about God voiced by Christian women from around the globe are surveyed.

"Feminist Perspectives on Women and the Church" is the title of chapter 4. This chapter takes as its focal question, How can we differentiate between the "core of Christian truth" and the cultural influences on how that truth has been interpreted where women's participation in the Christian churches is concerned? The focal question lends itself to abstract speculation if it does not deal with women's real concerns. One of the real concerns is the issue of women's **ordination** to the priesthood or official church ministry. Weighing the pros and cons of women's ordination is undertaken as a "testing of the spirits," with openness to the guidance of the Holy Spirit. This testing addresses a plethora of positions. Ordination, although an important concern for Christian women, is not the only concern related to the position of women in their churches. Christian ministry is important to many women. Therefore, perspectives on the ministerial activity of women in their churches are surveyed. In this survey, attention is given to differences among Christian *denominations and cultures.

Chapter 5, "Feminist Spirituality, God, Mary, and Her Sister Saints," describes Christian spirituality in general terms and then revisits some elements of feminist theology about God addressed in chapter 3. Here the interest is on what difference female God images and God as a Trinitarian community make to feminist spirituality. God, although important to Christian feminists, is not the only subject of fruitful development in spirituality. In recent years, feminist scholars have contributed important research on *Mary and her sister *saints, retrieving and reconstructing images and stories of "women of spirit." Samples of this important research are surveyed with interest in the variety of ways in which these women, often in spite of difficult circumstances, felt themselves empowered to be all that they could be as persons who uniquely image God.

Chapter 6, the final chapter, entitled "Feminist Perspectives on Ecology," provides an introduction to *ecofeminism, the twofold feminist advocacy for women and nonhuman nature that first emerged in the mid-1970s. Ecofeminists argue that *patriarchy not only negatively affects the lives of women, but also affects everyone and everything, including the Earth. In the drive to dominate, patriarchy forgets that humans, including those in power positions, have a natural biological connectedness with all of Earth's life forms. Ecofeminism is at once a vision of reality, a movement promoting change, and an academic theory. Since information about all three aspects of ecofeminism is important for understanding Christian ecofeminist theology, this information is provided in the first half of the chapter. In the chapter's second half, major contributions of ecofeminist theologians from the United States and the *Third World are presented.

To help to make this text well-suited for classroom use, the end of each chapter provides questions for reflection and discussion, and suggestions for further exploration to stimulate further engagement with the issues and ideas raised in the text. A bibliography to help direct further reading has been selected to provide the reader with a spectrum of positions. Most of the works selected complement the content of the chapter. Each chapter also provides blocked inserts with information about theologians featured in the chapter and additional background about topics of importance. At the end of the book is a glossary of terms that provides information not readily available in most general dictionaries.

Chapter 1

The "Why" and "What" of Christian Feminist Theology

There is not the slightest doubt that women belong to the people of God and the human race as much as men and are not another species or dissimilar race. — CHRISTINE DE PIZAN[1]

Christine de Pizan (1365–1430), poet, author, and invited member of the court of Charles V and Jeanne de Bourbon, king and queen of France, wrote these words of passionate conviction six hundred years ago. Why does she find it necessary to affirm that women are human beings? Apparently, the humanity of women was a question because being male was equated with being human. The prevailing thinking of the time regarded woman as "another [dissimilar] species."[2] To the reader today, Pizan's words are a simple affirmation of the obvious: women are human. Yet, the implication of her affirmation that women too belong to the "people of God" has profound implications, especially where the life of a Christian is concerned. Christine de Pizan lived in an era in which to be educated was virtually equated with being well read in the texts of Western antiquity. In the writings of the ancients, particularly in the most frequently cited classics, some of which were written by highly revered, male Christian saints, women were judged to be deficient as human beings. That there could be a different conception of woman was beyond questioning. Women's deficient nature was even attributed to God's plan for creation.

Why was this so? The answer is simple: the judgment about what counts as the criteria for humanness was drawn exclusively from male experience. What was associated with being male was the standard for being human. Women were substandard humans, even, perhaps, a species different from men. Simone de Beauvoir's book title captures the position aptly: women were the *Second Sex,* not quite deserving of the word "human."[3] This judgment prevailed until women stepped forward and raised their voices in protest.

Pizan's words of protest draw attention to how long it is that women who were unwilling to accept the limits their societies prescribed for them have struggled to claim their full participation in "the human race" and the "people of God." Nearly six hundred years ago, Pizan listened to her own experience of being a woman and questioned deeply ingrained opinions about women's inferiority. This self-educated woman was exceptional for her time. Pizan herself was conscious of being an anomaly where women were concerned. Unlike her

9

female contemporaries, not only could she read, but also she could write well enough to attract an audience, including the royal court of France, for what she had to say.

In *The Book of the City of Ladies,* Pizan engaged in a debate of great importance for women. Were women by nature more prone to vice and evil than were men? This was a serious question in an era in which women were blamed for a spectrum of evils, from sterility to deadly illnesses. Another common question was, Were the female descendants of Eve, the evil temptress of Adam, capable of thinking clearly and acting ethically? The common response was no. Was it not fitting, therefore, that men rule over women, the sex weaker in mind, body, and morality? Pizan pondered these questions and the arguments of many highly regarded male experts who claimed that women by nature were inferior in every way to men. After thinking intensely about these matters and praying for divine guidance, she decided to trust herself over male authorities. She notes,

> I began to examine my character and conduct as a natural woman, and similarly I considered other women whose company I frequently kept, princesses, great ladies, women of the middle and lower classes.[4]

What did Pizan conclude from her reflection on the experiences of these women? Without qualification, women are fully human and not in need of the protection and guidance of men. To prove her position, she drew on stories about women from the Bible, from history, and from her own time. She argued that women are not inferior to men because of their sex. It was women's inferior education and training that created the illusion of male superiority. If women were as well taught as men, they would understand the subtleties of the arts and sciences as well as men do.[5]

Long before the term "feminism" was coined, many characteristics commonly associated with contemporary feminist authors are found in Christine de Pizan's writing:

1. She gave attention and credence to her own experience. Listening to her experience and to the experiences of other women rather than uncritically accepting the opinions of male authorities is a hallmark of feminism today.

2. She critically analyzed attitudes about women. Like so many feminist authors today, her critique of prevailing attitudes that define woman as less than man was highly negative. This type of thinking conflicted with her own experience of being a woman.

3. Positively, Pizan did research on women from a variety of sources that enabled her to uncover the constructive contributions of women. She engaged in the type of research that feminists today often call a "search for a useable past." Her search pointed out stories and traditions that gave her a basis for envisioning in new ways what it means to be a woman.

4. The steps that Pizan took in uncovering the contributions of women also had a goal beyond mere research: she was committed to ending men defining "woman" in male terms. Women should begin to define what it means

to be a woman for themselves. To achieve this, she wanted women to have the same educational and professional opportunities that learned men could enjoy.

Christine de Pizan never used the term "feminism" in reference to her work. It was not until the late nineteenth century that the term was coined. Another woman who made her home in France, Hubertine Auclert, is credited with first using the word "feminism" in 1882 to name the struggle of women to gain political rights.[6] The term "feminism" had a long period of gestation associated with history-making women. A century before Auclert penned the word "feminism," Mary Wollstonecraft wrote *A Vindication of the Rights of Woman* in England in 1792.[7] In the United States, women began to lift their voices to challenge the inferior status of women at the end of the 1830s. This chorus rose in the midst of women's active participation in the pre–Civil War *abolitionist movement.

The Female Anti-Slavery Society, founded in 1833, was a natural setting for connecting the oppression of slaves with the subordination of women.[8] History records the emergence of a woman's movement in the United States in the words and actions of women such as the Grimké sisters, Sarah (1792–1873) and Angelina (1805–79).[9] The Grimké sisters spent their childhood in the South on a slave-owning plantation and their adulthood in the North as Quaker abolitionists. They not only condemned the evils of slavery, but also championed why it was appropriate for women to speak publicly about this dehumanizing evil in Christian churches. Certainly, few women of this period are better known than the former slave Sojourner Truth (Belle Baumfree [1797–1883]), who, in her famous "And Ain't I a Woman" speech, drew attention not only to the degradation of being owned by another, but also to the burden of grief borne by female slaves who were separated from their children when they were sold and sent to unknown destinations. Elizabeth Cady Stanton (1815–1902), an active abolitionist, brought attention to the ways in which the Bible contributed to the subordination of women. She gathered female colleagues to create a biblical commentary, *The Woman's Bible*. Stanton, along with Lucretia Mott (1793–1880)[10] and Susan B. Anthony (1820–1906),[11] are the best-known champions for the legal and economic equality of women with men in the United States of this first wave of feminism. Due largely to the persistence of these women, women in the United States won the right to own property. These women paved the way for the success of women's suffrage. Carrie Chapman Catt (1859–1947)[12] and many others aided women in getting the right to vote through the passage of the Nineteenth Amendment to the U.S. Constitution in 1920. Elsewhere, women had already attained this right. New Zealand was the first country on record to give women the vote; the year was 1893, and Finland followed in 1906. Women in Russia and Canada were permitted to vote in 1918. In the same year, women over thirty could vote in Great Britain. A decade later, women in Great Britain over twenty-one were fully enfranchised. That same year (1928), Ecuador became the first Latin American country to permit women to vote. Gradually, many other countries granted women voting rights.

Providing an answer to why feminism emerged in Western Europe and the

United States during the nineteenth century is complex. Prior to the nineteenth century, women in most societies were regarded as subordinate to and dependent on their male relatives. Like the women of Christine de Pizan's time, they were excluded from equal access to education and participation in public life. As men created new political and economic structures, they assigned to women the role of producing and raising male citizens who would lead society. Men exercised sovereignty in the city square, while women were charged with making a home for them and their children. In the nineteenth century, women were commonly said to be morally superior to men, yet too weak and delicate to be active in the public world of business and politics. This widely accepted cluster of attitudes, known as "the cult of true womanhood," was something that the women of the first wave of feminism used to their own advantage. They selectively conferred on the "cult of true womanhood" a significance that suited their cause, attributing a special status to women because they cared for children and were the guardians of Christian moral values, while rejecting that women were unsuited for politics.

The momentum for the cause of women's equality did not continue in the United States after voting rights were acquired by women. Since the first wave of feminism was so closely associated with getting access to voting booths, once women could vote, the feminist movement virtually ended in the United States. The worldwide economic depression and the many adjustments in societal life during and immediately after World War II also contributed to the movement's decline. It was not until the 1960s that a second and broader women's liberation movement emerged in the United States and Western Europe. In the United States, this new wave of feminism once again converged with the struggles of African Americans.[13] Women participants in the civil rights movement realized that not only were the black men and women not equal to white men and women, the women championing their cause were not equal to white males. A glaring disparity existed between the lofty ideals of the civil rights movement for blacks and women's own lived realities. Women such as Betty Friedan,[14] Gloria Steinem, Susan Brownmiller, and a host of others began to call for the expansion of women's rights. These women revived earlier dreams of political and economic equality of women with men. Some of these same women would also lend their voice in protest of the Vietnam War, forming or joining demonstrations for peace. At approximately the same time, women in Great Britain, France, and West Germany also were actively criticizing the gap between public rhetoric about women's roles and their own experience, between, in the words of Bonnie S. Anderson and Judith P. Zinsser, "what they were told they had achieved and their private perceptions of their own situation."[15]

In the late 1970s a new development in feminism arose, one that drew attention to differences in race and social class of women. Historians of feminism now call this the "third wave" of feminism. It emerged in the United Sates with "women of color" taking that name to expose the whiteness of the interests of second-wave feminism. Difference was given center stage at an international feminist conference held in New York in 1979 with these challenging words from the African American poet Audre Lorde:

If white American feminist theory need not deal with the differences between us (black women and all women of color), and the resulting difference in our oppressions, then how do you deal with the fact that women who clean your houses and tend your children while you attend conferences on feminist theory are, for the most part, poor women and women of color? What is the theory of racist feminism?[16]

In response to challenges such as Lorde's from women of color, many Euro-American feminists became attuned to the difference that race and class make to feminist identities, challenges, and goals.

Why Feminism?

Having briefly surveyed major watershed points in the history of feminism in the West, it is important to delve more deeply and concretely into the question, Why feminism? Our response to this question cannot be separated from the reasons for the many forms of Christian feminist theology that exist today. The major reason for any feminist movement is to end oppression, discrimination, and violence directed to women and to acquire full equality and human dignity for every woman. Some women in the United States and Western Europe may wonder "Why feminism?" at the dawn of the twenty-first century. In the past forty years women have made many gains. Some may wonder if feminism has not already accomplished its goals. After all, women and men think about their family and societal roles differently today than they did in the 1960s and 1970s. This leads some women to believe that feminism is passé. In the 1920s many women apparently had the same thought, only to be proved wrong forty years later.

Although progress has been made by some European and Euro-American middle- and upper-class women, there are valid reasons for arguing that this is the exception rather than the rule. In every part of the globe women are still discriminated against because of their sex. Many women continue to be relegated to a secondary status and even actively oppressed by men. Therefore, feminist women and men committed to change continue their advocacy for women in every society. The persistent commitment of feminists from North America and Western Europe to improve the lives of women everywhere continues the legacy of the second wave of feminism while engaging in a global encompassing third wave that attends to the difference that social location makes in the lives of individual women.

The third wave of feminism self-consciously seeks to attend to differences among women from different parts of the globe. The international scope of the third wave has been a long time in the making. A survey of United Nations initiatives on women illustrates this well. As early as 1947 the United Nations established the Commission on the Status of Women (CSW). Twenty years later the U.N. brought women from around the globe together to surface areas of common concern. To draw attention to these concerns, the U.N. adopted the "Declaration of the Elimination of Discrimination against Women." This groundbreaking document was followed in 1972 by proclaiming 1975 as

"International Women's Year." The events of this year included a planned conference on women, in Mexico City, that launched the "UN Decade for Women." In conjunction with this meeting, the United Nations adopted a "Plan of Action." Major conferences on women followed: in Copenhagen in 1980 to mark the midpoint of the decade and in Nairobi in 1985 to mark its end. At Nairobi the sense was that badly needed work to end discrimination against women was only beginning. Another conference was called and held in Beijing in 1995. At Beijing, delegates adopted a "Platform for Action," signed by 189 countries — 120 of which adopted action plans of their own — that called for changes in twelve areas of critical importance to women. Those included poverty, education and training, health, violence, armed conflict, the economy, power and decision-making, institutional mechanisms for advancement, human rights, media portrayals, the environment, and "the girl child." In 2000, women representatives from 180 nations converged on the United Nations headquarters in New York to begin to assess the progress or lack thereof of these initiatives, in a conference entitled "Beijing+5."

United Nations research gathered in preparation for the Beijing conference (1995) included statistics on the economic status of women compared with that of men. Women constitute 70 percent of the world's poor. Women make up slightly more than 50 percent of the population, but do two-thirds of the world's work, paid and unpaid. Yet, women earn between 5 and 10 percent of the world's wages and own only 1 percent of the world's property. Women in the poor countries of the Third World put most of their earnings directly into the survival needs of their families. In addition, it is a woman who is most likely to head a household in which she and her children suffer from homelessness and malnutrition.[17] In a "progress report" prepared by the United Nations Development Fund for Women for the Beijing+5 Conference (2000), global statistics were not provided.[18] The report does note that women's share of wages is increasing, with the exception of parts of Eastern Europe. But the quality of employment for women around the globe has not increased in the same way and has even deteriorated. Women's jobs have less social protection and employment rights than do men's jobs. A critically important point in the "progress" report is that conventional economic indicators of national governments fail to look at economies through women's eyes. There is a need for a different analysis of economics that takes into account the real costs of people's time and effort. Costs that are monetized show up in government records, but domestic costs, not monetized, are ignored. It is women who bear these real human costs. This report points to the need for a more holistic approach that directs attention beyond financial statistics.[19] This insight points to the limitations of abstract statistics. So much depends on how the data are compiled and whether a country has the means and the commitment to gather statistics in a way that even includes data from women's experiences.

Another even more pressing concern is the problem of violence directed against women. The First World Conference on Women in Mexico City in 1975 did not even discuss the issue of violence. A decade later in Nairobi, domestic violence was mentioned, but in Beijing in 1995 the elimination of violence against women was a central theme, with the plea to look at the cruel abuse of women through women's eyes. Attention was given to educating women about their rights, training officials in the protection of these rights, and bringing the perpetrators of violence against women to justice.[20]

The "why" of feminism becomes especially obvious when one considers the global problem of violent behaviors directed against women and girls. Assault by domestic partners, rape, murder, infanticide, cruel neglect, and the international trafficking in women and girls, along with harassment in the work place, make violence against women the most pervasive human rights problem in the world.[21] Whether a woman lives in a wealthy *First World nation, the poorest of Third World countries, or a country torn apart by war, the threat of violence is a reality with which women must contend. According to a report compiled by the United Nations Development Fund for Women (UNIFEM) in 2000, more than one out of five women (22 percent) are victims of physical violence from an intimate partner in the United States. In Turkey, that figure is 58 percent; in Kenya, 42 percent; in Canada, 29 percent; in Mexico, 27 percent.[22] Although it is unclear whether there is an actual increase or that the silence is being more frequently broken because of heightened awareness about the problem, these figures are distressing. None of this data, however, can begin to capture the human misery that is the life story of so many women and their children around the globe.

Worldwide, domestic violence is the leading cause of death among girls and women ages fourteen to forty-four. In India, young brides are frequently burned by their husbands' families in so-called kitchen accidents. When parents fail to provide sufficient dowries for their daughters, these women pay with their lives. *Femicide is not limited to adults. In countries like Nepal and South Korea, female babies die of neglect because parents value sons over daughters.[23] China has a population of over one billion. A strict population control policy limiting the size of families to one child is enforced in most Chinese cities. In the past, giving birth to a girl was regarded as bad luck. Now, having a baby girl often results in her abandonment by the family. Many female infants are placed in orphanages and are adopted in the West. Others die of neglect. In rural China, bride-trafficking is also rampant. Marriage brokers buy young women from impoverished peasants; others they kidnap. Many women who are bought live a life of virtual slavery. From 1991 through 1996, Chinese police freed eighty-eight thousand kidnapped women and children, and arrested 143,000 people for engaging in slave trading.[24] In Eastern European countries women in rural areas are being duped by employment brokers into signing contracts that require them to be prostitutes in deplorable conditions. In sub-Saharan Africa, women and their infant children are contracting AIDS at a higher rate than are men, so much so that HIV is called "the women's disease" in some tribal languages. Many women with HIV/AIDS are either prostitutes trying to feed themselves and their children or spouses of men who have visited prostitutes. Once diagnosed with the disease, many of these women and their children are abandoned by their families.

In these instances females are the recipients of violence, neglect, and abuse

because of their sex. None of this is random. The risk factor is being born female. The implication is that women are still not viewed as being fully human.
Mistreatment and even violence can therefore be justified. The oppression of
women is not limited to economic inequality and violence. In many countries
women are given far less academic education than men. Two-thirds of the illit-
erate people in the world are women. In countries where literacy is high, such
as the United States, teenage females quitting school because of pregnancy is a
serious problem. The causes of early pregnancy are complex, but what is clear
is that when children have children and do not complete school, the mothers,
their infants, and society as a whole suffer.

Another problem is the subtle social conditioning that reinforces women's
reluctance to develop a sense of personal worth. Studies show that women, far
more than men, tend to have low self-esteem. Its extremes are manifested in
women's inability to take adequate care of themselves, whether physically, emotionally, psychologically, or spiritually. Many women spend much of their time
trying to figure out what other people want of them, especially what male "significant others" want. These same women are likely to believe that whatever
goes wrong in their relationships is their fault and therefore their responsibility
to resolve.[25] Such women have mastered the strategies of those in subordinate
positions: pleasing and enduring, no matter the personal cost.

This survey of problems is not a complete depiction of the experience of
women, but it does draw attention to some urgent reasons for feminist advocacy
for change. Progress toward ending the oppression and inferiority of women is
being made, but not as quickly as the advocates for change would like. Feminists around the globe are putting new thinking and creative energy into how
to diagnose societal problems and transform the lives of women for the better.
Education in particular is playing a vital role. Feminist scholars are challenging previously unquestioned assumptions about women and men that restricted
people's lives for centuries. In every field, scholars are rethinking old modes
of explanation and are formulating new ones to take into account feminist research and insights. These accomplishments are a source of hope and a reason
to celebrate. More, however, waits to be done.

Before addressing what Christian feminist theology is, exploring another
foundational question is important: What is feminism? In responding to this
question we will examine the ways in which feminists analyze the root causes
of the subordination and subjugation of women; but also, we will explore some
of the diverse ways in which women are acting to bring about changes that
honor the full human dignity of women and of men who carry heavy burdens of
oppression due to their race and/or class.

What Is Feminism?

Feminism is a worldwide phenomenon that has taken many forms and that
means different things to different people. Feminism is a social vision, rooted in
women's experience of sexually based discrimination and oppression, a movement seeking the liberation of women from all forms of ***sexism,** and an

academic method of analysis being used in virtually every discipline. Feminism is all of these things and more because it is a perspective on life that colors all of a person's hopes, commitments, and actions. Feminism has been given a variety of broad and narrow definitions since the 1960s. Of the many broad definitions available, Joann Wolski Conn's is particularly helpful. She defines feminism as

> both a coordinated set of ideas and a practical plan of action, rooted in women's critical awareness of how a culture controlled in meaning and action by men, for their own advantage, oppresses women and dehumanizes men.[26]

Wolski Conn's broad definition depicts feminism as a set of ideas or ideology. As a "practical plan of action," it makes those persons who share the feminist ideology agents for change. Very importantly, Wolski Conn's definition draws attention to problems for women associated with sexism — the overt and sometimes more subtle claims to male control of females on the basis that males by nature are superior to females. These claims are not rooted simply in sexual differences. Sex is a biological given, determined genetically by the presence or absence of X and Y chromosomes. Recognition that roughly half the population is female and the other half male says nothing about how our lives as women and men are lived. The "hows" are related to societal perspectives on gender.

Feminism explicitly rejects biological determinism as a reason for assigning specific roles to either males or females. As Wolski Conn's definition highlights, a critical awareness of cultural attitudes and values is extremely important. Roles for women, such as domestic work or "homemaking," which was long treated as if biologically determined, are actually rooted in attitudes about gender, which are socially constructed. Gender definitions are culture bound. They reflect beliefs about clusters of behaviors and roles designated as appropriate to either males or females by a society at a particular time.

A simple example of gender as a cultural construction is the nursery rhyme that responds to the question "What are little girls made of?" with "Sugar and spice and everything nice." In contrast, the reply to the question "What are little boys made of?" is "Slugs and snails and puppy dog tails." What really makes sugar and spice a more apt description of girls and puppy dog tails of boys? Beyond seemingly innocent nursery rhymes, a visit to a toy store communicates loudly and clearly societal gender stereotyping. Consider, for example, the phenomenon of the "Barbie doll," which for generations has promoted an image of the ideal woman that very few women can fill. Although Barbie has her Ken, note how many different Barbie likenesses exist. A whole industry is focused on her and the clothing — often quite provocative, considering that this is a toy meant for young girls — to outfit her. How many women are platinum blond, blue-eyed, tall, and svelte? It is not much of a leap to question whether or not Barbie is a contributing cause for the eating disorders that are plaguing so many girls and young women in North America today.[27] Feminism brings to bear its vision of woman by raising questions about blatant and subtle gender stereotypes that inhibit women's healthy self-determination. Feminism is by nature critical of the values and attitudes about women that cultures tend to unreflectively promote.

An important critical question that feminists ask concerning gender stereotypes is, Who is responsible for definitions of what is masculine and what is feminine? The answer: those who have the most power in the institutions of influence in the society. Traditionally, the persons who hold that power in institutions such as federal and state governments and in major corporations have been men. For example, in 2000 only 13 percent of the members of the United States Congress were women: fifty-eight women in the House of Representatives and nine in the Senate, out of a total of 535 elected positions.[28] Statistics in corporate America are similar: 12 percent of the Fortune 500's corporate officers are women.[29] These data are part of the reason why the definition of feminism above explicitly draws attention to the control of culture by males to the advantage of males and the disadvantage of females.

Academic feminism emphasizes the importance of paying attention to our habits of information gathering and analysis. It provides methodological tools for exposing and analyzing male advantage, especially white male advantage over women and men of color. In academic feminist literature, male advantage exercised as power over women and disadvantaged males is called patriarchy. Literally, the word "patriarchy" means rule by a father or fathers. It should not be confused with ***paternity** or ***paternalism,** although they have the same linguistic root. Paternity refers to a man parenting his minor children. It does not assume that a father will dominate them or relate to his adult children in ways that do not respect their autonomy. Paternalism usually means treating or governing people in a fatherly manner, especially by providing for their needs. But paternalism also often includes the denial or at least diminishment of adult responsibilities and rights. If a man exerts power over his children or other people in ways in which he assumes his superiority and their inferiority, then that is paternalism.

Patriarchy refers to systems of legal, economic, and political relations that legitimate and enforce relations of dominance in a society. It functions as an ideology that affects every aspect of societal life. In patriarchal societies the status of women and children is one of inferiority. To the advantage of men, women are not treated as equals. The rule of men neglects the rights, freedoms, and hopes of women. Men, however, are not the only ones who can exhibit patriarchy. Women can also dominate their children and other persons who are more vulnerable to domination than they are. For example, professional women who hire less-educated women to clean their homes, cook their meals, and care for their children can display patriarchy if they dominate these women and fail to respect them and honor their human dignity.

Although women can display patterns of domination, in patriarchal cultures the organization of patriarchal societies is initiated by men in positions of power, continues to be maintained primarily by men, and has men as its principal beneficiaries. Gerda Lerner, a historian who has done groundbreaking research on patriarchy and its long history, points out a basic gender assumption in a patriarchal society:

> Men and women are essentially different creatures, not only in their bio-
> logical equipment, but in their needs, capacities and functions. Men and
> women also differ in the way they were created and in the social function
> assigned to them by God.[30]

It is against reasoning like this that Christine de Pizan argued that women
are not a distinct species or race essentially different from men. Women are
every bit as human as men and completely capable of full participation in "the
people of God." There is no good reason, therefore, why the lives, activities, and
achievements of women and men of color should be devalued or disregarded.

The devaluing of women has a very long history bound to the rigidly defined
patterns of patriarchy. These patterns are built on a social structure that held that
only the free, propertied male could be a citizen. We can trace them to the influential Greek philosopher Aristotle (384–322 B.C.E.),[31] who described the natural
organization of society as a hierarchy of graded subordinations. He argued that
according to nature it is fitting for the soul to govern the body, the master to govern the slave, and the male to govern the female. In each case, "one [the first]
is superior, the other is inferior, for one governs and the other is governed."[32]
Although such an argument may be offensive to the reader, Aristotle's thinking
was uncritically adopted in Western societies. Until very recently his patriarchal
hierarchy was given a validity beyond question.

The hierarchy of patriarchy in Aristotle's analysis is highly dualistic. His
thinking supports a dualistic pattern that divides reality into opposing spheres
and assigns more value to the first of each pair. All that is associated with being
the ruling male is judged to be superior to all that is associated with being the
ruled female. Feminists point out that patriarchal hierarchical ***dualisms** of male
and female, mind and body, intellect and emotions, white people and people of
color, and humanity and nonhuman nature are closely linked. For example, in
Western language patterns it is common for woman to be regarded (or treated)
as emotional, whereas man is rational. Woman is identified with nature, referred
to as "Mother Earth," and man is identified with science that seeks to control
and dominate her. Such hierarchical dualisms must be challenged because they
easily result in oppositional relationships and oppressive behaviors. Historically,
the elevation of what is associated with the stereotypical upper-class, white, well-
educated male has been at the expense of females, the body, the emotions, people
of color, and nonhuman nature. Patriarchy, therefore, is a root cause not only of
sexism, but also of racism, ethnic prejudice, colonialism, economic classism, and
naturism (the destructive exploitation of nature for human ends).

Gender discrimination manifests itself not only in the patterns of patriarchal
male domination, but also in behaviors that make the experience of males central
in every area of life. The name for this pattern is ***androcentrism,** meaning
what is associated with being male is the norm and what is associated with being
female is the exception. Or to express it somewhat differently, the male norm is
the human norm. Recognition that maleness is but one kind of experience is
minimal, if nonexistent. The reality of androcentrism is captured graphically by
philosopher Simone de Beauvoir:

In the midst of an abstract discussion it is vexing to hear a man say: "You think thus and so because you are a woman," but I know that my only defense is to reply: "I think thus and so because it is true," thereby removing any subjective self from the argument. It would be out of the question to reply: "And you think the contrary because you are a man," for it is understood that the fact of being a man is no peculiarity. A man is in the right in being a man; it is the woman who is in the wrong.[33]

The collapse of any distinction between maleness and humanity results in femaleness being viewed as the exception. De Beauvoir succinctly captures this in the statement: "woman is the Other."[34] In its extremes, androcentrism envisions that man is the free, determining being who defines the meaning of his existence. Woman is the "other," the object whose meaning is determined for her by men. Androcentric bias reveals itself in prevailing cultural attitudes that assign more significance to the dreams, hopes, and values of men than to those of women. To overcome androcentric bias, women want to occupy the center along with men and have their dreams, hopes, and values taken just as seriously.

Androcentrism manifests itself in more subtle ways: when English-speakers are told that the generic term "man" includes woman, or when researchers in various fields, including medicine, fail to include women in their studies. The result of subsuming women under the collective term "man" is that it ignores women as part of humanity. The result in research that ignores women is that most studies in any given discipline have universalized male concerns. Women's questions, concerns, and very lives have been rendered peripheral if not invisible. This has been true for all disciplines, including Christian theology.

A third and very subtle form of androcentrism recognizes that the generic masculine does not cover the feminine. This form of androcentrism argues that women do deviate from the male norm, but they do so in a complementary fashion. In such cases specific women are studied in relation to specific males, especially as these women complement what is important or of value to males. In gender complementarity, however, it is usually the female that completes some aspect of male reality and not the reverse.

Women and men in academic circles who identify themselves as feminists seek to make others aware of how patriarchy and androcentrism function as a pervasive ideology in society. This requires careful diagnosis of the causes and effects of patriarchy on women and men. Diagnosis in scholarly journals, however, does not necessarily lead to remedies. Although some scholars are reluctant to make the necessary changes to accommodate the full humanity of women, many feminist scholars do work for change. Guided by a vision for practical action, these feminists seek not only to liberate women from oppression and discrimination, but also to be of benefit to men in their pursuit of wholeness. They do this because, as Wolski Conn points out in her definition of feminism, the humanity of men is also diminished in a society that tolerates violence and discrimination directed to their mothers, wives, daughters, and female friends and colleagues. All men are dehumanized in a society in which abusive and oppressive behaviors toward women are tolerated, not just those men who engage in such behaviors.

Patriarchy, therefore, puts burdens on the shoulders of men. Some men attuned to critical feminist analysis recognize this. James B. Nelson, a Euro-American theologian, draws attention to the deprivations that men experience in patriarchal societies:

> We who are male have lost touch with our vulnerability, our deepest human capacities for tenderness, our need for dependence — in short, a whole range of emotions. We simply do not feel very well. We are more alienated from our bodily existence, and our sexuality, instead of being a richly diffused sensuousness and invitation to intimacy, has taken a narrow genital focus. We lose touch with the concrete particularity of pulsing life and instead are seduced by abstractions, confusing them with reality. We seem to live with a constant need to prove self-worth through achievement and winning. We relate competitively with other men and find it easier to have buddies than deep friendships. Predictably, we males will die younger than women — about seven years at latest count.[35]

Patriarchy, with its dominance and submission dynamics, is a barrier to an interdependence and mutuality that can guide the vision of a holistic and egalitarian society in multiple ways. It limits the capacity of society to call forth the gifts of women. It also brings needless suffering into the lives of men of color for reasons that are part of patriarchy's history. But not only are women and men of color deprived of opportunities for developing and expressing their gifts, white men also are deprived of the gifts of both groups and of developing their own in relationship to them. The androcentrism that accompanies patriarchy sentences men to a myopia that sees the white male point of view to be the only view of a situation. When this is the case, every group is diminished.

Second-Wave Feminisms

The second wave of the women's movement not only revived women's political struggles for civil rights and equal pay, but also brought forth feminist studies as a new academic discipline. Scholarly research shows that feminism is not a monolith, however. Many perspectives on feminism exist. Why are there different types of feminism? The most direct answer is that women have different experiences of patriarchy and androcentrism, and therefore different ways of analyzing their causes and remedies. Analysis of the perspectives of the different manifestations of the feminist movement has resulted in many categorizations of feminism by scholars. Maria Riley's analysis is helpful in its straightforward way of mapping the complex feminist terrain of second-wave feminism.[36] Riley groups the forms of feminism into four major types, each of which makes unique contributions to understanding societal attitudes about gender roles: ***liberal feminism, *cultural feminism, *radical feminism,** and ***socialist feminism.** It is important to take note of them, because the different types of feminism affect and intersect with theology done by Christian feminist theologians.

1. Liberal feminism is the most logical form of feminism with which to begin because the other forms of feminism have been defined in reaction to this most widely familiar form of feminism. The guiding question is, If you were to meet a liberal feminist, how would you know that she or he is one? If you met a person whose overriding emphasis and motivation are achieving full equality of women with men in every facet of societal life, then it is likely that you have met a liberal feminist. Liberal feminism's defining characteristic is its stress on social equality, especially achieving equal economic and political rights for women. A liberal feminist seeks: (1) the removal of the barriers that deny women full legal, political, economic, and civil rights as autonomous adults; and (2) equal access to all structures of society — political, economic, social, and cultural.[37]

In the United States, liberal feminism has been the most pervasive form of feminism. It first emerged in the first wave of feminism in the suffrage movement of the mid-nineteenth through the early twentieth centuries. True to its nineteenth-century liberal political roots, it is concerned with securing the rights of the individual and promoting the equality of all persons. Since the 1960s, the struggle for full equality has expressed itself in a variety of ways, including passing legislation that ensures equity in pay for women, and gaining equal access for women to leadership roles that have been traditionally closed to them, such as holding political office, being CEO of a major corporation, or being president of a large university. Liberal feminism also emphasizes individual freedom for women. The most pointed manifestation of this trait is the claim that each woman has the right to privacy that ensures that she can make decisions about her own body, especially about childbearing. Liberal feminism champions the right of women to decide matters related to their own sexual and reproductive health.

2. Cultural feminism, sometimes also called "romantic feminism" or "reform feminism," focuses on the contributions and values traditionally associated with women, like nurturing and compassion, and the difference they can make to the betterment of society. Cultural feminism is rooted in two premises that can be traced to "the cult of true womanhood": (1) the presumption of the moral superiority of women, associated with their maternal role; and (2) the need for that moral superiority to make societal life more humane.[38]

Having roots in the nineteenth century, cultural feminism was a reaction against attitudes associated with the industrial revolution, especially competitiveness and the ruthlessness associated with it. Cultural feminism envisions women as less ambitious and driven, and more likely to be egalitarian, nurturing, and peacemaking than men. Riley points out that the influence of cultural feminism is evident not only in the women's movement but also throughout society.[39] Forms of it can be found in progressive and conservative groups. It exists wherever women and men emphasize the notion of complementarity to define masculine and feminine roles as distinct, while positively disposed to female partnership with males.

In contrast to liberal and cultural feminism, which focus on social reform agendas, radical and socialist feminism seek more extensive revolutionary change. Radical and socialist feminists not only challenge women's subordinate

---

MAJOR TYPES OF FEMINISM OF THE SECOND WAVE

1. Liberal Feminism. Emphasizes civil rights, interprets the right to privacy to include the right of women to freely make decisions about their own sexual and reproductive health.

Seeks the full equality of women with men in all facets of societal life, especially in economic and political life.

2. Cultural Feminism, also called "romantic feminism" and "reform feminism." Emphasizes the moral superiority of women over men and the values traditionally associated with women, such as compassion, nurturance, and peacemaking.

Seeks the betterment of society by stressing the contributions made by women.

3. Radical Feminism. Emphasizes the pervasiveness of male domination, which is the cause of all societal problems, and the importance of "women-centered culture," characterized by nurture, closeness to nature, and compassion.

Seeks to eliminate patriarchy in order to liberate women from male control in every facet of life, including family life.

4. Socialist Feminism. Emphasizes white male dominance in the economic class struggles of capitalist societies. Believes that this dominance is the reason for the division of labor according to sex and race and the devaluing of women's work, especially the work of raising children.

Seeks to end the economic dependence of women upon men and to achieve major social reforms that will end class divisions and enable all women and men to have the same opportunity to be gainfully employed and to be actively involved in parenting.

---

position in society, but also dispute the legitimacy of the societal structures that contribute to it.

3. Radical feminism is a twentieth-century development that envisions feminism to be concerned with more than social equality for women; it seeks to eradicate every form of male domination. For the radical feminist, the most important element of social analysis is the awareness of how patriarchy has structured society. The influence of radical feminist analysis of patriarchy has become pervasive in feminist literature, even among feminists who do not consider themselves radical. What makes radical feminism radical is the belief that male domination is the root of all societal problems. This is the case because radical feminists hold that the male-female relationship is the ***paradigm** for all power relationships.

Radical feminists, therefore, do not limit their criticism of patriarchy to societal structures and institutions. Their goal is the liberation of women from all male control in every facet of life. Radical feminists argue that in patriarchal societies male dominance not only dictates the hierarchical structure of society, but also influences personal relationships. For example, some radical feminists are critical of traditional romantic love because the man is the initiator, and the woman is expected to be submissive or at least passive. Some radical feminists are also critical of traditional attitudes about motherhood. They identify women in a patriarchal family primarily in terms of reproduction, a function that they believe lends itself to female dependence on males and to women's subordination to men.

Radical feminist analysis is particularly critical of pervasive violence tolerated in a patriarchal society. Male domination is overtly violent in acts such as rape, pornography, woman battering, war, and ecological destruction. It is covertly violent in its support of economic dependency, psychological diminishment, and imposed limitations on roles judged to be suitable for the "weaker sex." To counter the violence of patriarchal culture, some radical feminists propose creating a "women-centered culture." They argue that women need this to give women new space to create a lifestyle characterized by nurture, closeness to nature, and compassion. To achieve this, these radical feminists have created separatist-oriented communities, sometimes self-identified as lesbian, where they can celebrate and develop women's culture together, apart from men.[40] These radical feminists believe that if women would only absent themselves from patriarchal culture altogether, then the power of patriarchy would be overthrown.

4. Socialist feminism agrees with radical feminism that patriarchy is a major problem. Socialist feminists fault, however, the tendency of radical feminists to attribute women's oppression solely to patriarchal males. They also regard the movement among some radical feminists to create a separate woman's culture to be fundamentally flawed. Influenced by Marxist principles, socialist feminists locate women's oppression within the broader context of an economic class struggle. They emphasize that we cannot ignore the impact of economic class on women's oppression.[41] Society is fundamentally structured in terms of the relations persons form as they work to produce things needed for people to survive humanly. Work is a social process; class is its economic structure.[42]

Socialist feminists stress that in capitalist societies those who control the means of production also define the division of labor according to sex and race. In the capitalist structure, white males are responsible for production in the public sphere and females are responsible for reproduction in the private sphere. The patriarchy of capitalism manifests itself in the undervaluing of the work of women in childbearing and childrearing because it is not considered economically productive. Comments like "My wife doesn't work; she's home raising the children" are criticized because they devalue women. Socialist feminists argue that capitalism results in the subordination of women due to the division of labor, the valuing of the public sphere over the private, and the economic dependence of women upon men.

Because socialist feminist analysis focuses so strongly on economic class struggles as the most fundamental struggle for liberation, it is highly critical of the equal rights agenda of liberal feminists. In the judgment of many socialist feminists, liberal feminists too often focus only on goals that match the position of privilege of well-educated, middle- and upper-class women.[43] For the poor woman who works in a domestic job in the home of a woman of privilege, liberal feminism's focus on equal rights and the abstract ideal of individual freedom mean little, if not nothing. Women struggling for economic survival do not have the means to enjoy the rights and freedoms championed by liberal feminists.

Although socialist feminists embrace Marxist economic analysis, they fault it for its failure to focus sufficiently on the pervasive effects of patriarchy. Socialism does not automatically liberate women. Although in socialist societies women are as free as men to work outside the home, and in this regard are men's equal, the vast majority of working women continue to do most of the domestic work in their homes.

It logically follows, therefore, that the goal of socialist feminism is change while socializing women and men to certain roles that have a strong bearing on the economy. It is committed to liberating women by major social reform. Women and men of all classes should have the same opportunity to be gainfully employed and to be actively involved in parenting.

Third-Wave Feminisms

The analysis of the four major types of feminism associated with feminism's second wave is one helpful way to map the landscape of feminism today. It fails, however, to capture the complex contours that take into account the great variety of women's experiences. For example, in the United States during the early years of the second wave of the women's liberation movement, the vast majority of its spokeswomen were well-educated, white, middle-class women. Most uncritically presumed that their perspectives on women's reality were true to the lived experiences of all women. Women of color have been critical of white feminists for universalizing their experience and thereby ignoring the experiences unique to them. Social location plays a significant role in the liberation of women. No true liberation exists unless the difference that race, class, age, and sexual orientation make in people's daily lives is heeded.

To draw attention to the fact that the struggles of black women are different from those of white Euro-American women, many African American women today identify themselves as *womanist.* Alice Walker, author of *The Color Purple,* is credited with coining the term in the 1970s.[44] In its most elemental sense, a womanist is a black feminist. Nevertheless, the linguistic roots of the term point to a meaning that is more complex. Walker asserts that "womanist is to feminist as purple is to lavender."[45] "Womanist" is a wordplay on the popular folk term "womanish," which in African American culture refers to women, especially young women, who display self-assertive or willful behavior, behavior judged unsuitable for black women because of the place society has assigned them. The term "womanist" turns the pejorative tone of "womanish" on its head and pointedly affirms the African American woman who is courageous, responsible, and mature. When an African American woman identifies herself as a womanist, she proclaims who she is as a woman and as black in a world

THE REALITIES OF NORTH AMERICAN
HISPANIC AND LATIN AMERICAN WOMEN

Struggle to overcome the oppression of poverty and *machista* cultural attitudes is part of the daily lives of the majority of North American Hispanic and Latin American women. There are, however, noteworthy differences to be found among them. Some, usually those of the upper class, have a cultural heritage and ethnicity more closely tied to Spain or Portugal. Others, the vast majority of the poor class, are the product of three different cultures: Amerindian (Native American), African (slaves), and Spanish/Portuguese. Mexican, Central American, and South American women are more influenced by Native American and the Spanish/Portuguese cultures. Women from the Caribbean are more influenced by African and Spanish cultures. Some women reflect the heritage of all three groups; this is particularly common among Puerto Rican women.

In the case of the *mestiza* woman of Amerindian and Spanish origins, her female ancestors gave birth to mixed race offspring, often due to rape at the hands of the Spanish conquistadors. Abusive patterns continued as male Spanish colonizers enslaved Amerindian women and forced them to bear their children. The pattern of women's oppression in their families and in the broader society continues a long history of control exercised by men over women's sexuality, reproduction, and work.

that places little value on either status. She also affirms her gifts and talents as a black woman who has something of value to contribute to the well-being of her people, female and male.

Other groups of women are also being formed in the United States. Mindful of the uniqueness of their struggles and their special strengths, Ada María Isasi-Díaz coined the term *mujerista* to name the theologizing being done by Hispanic women whose roots are in Central and South American countries, but who now live in the United States.[46] Other women of Hispanic origins prefer to use Latina when speaking of their theology. Still others prefer something that reflects their country of origin, such as Mexican American or Chicana, because each Latin American country has its own unique history that has affected the experience of the women who live there. Those whose Spanish or Portuguese ancestors intermarried with Africans and Native Americans may prefer *mestiza*, since they are persons of mixed race. Asian American women and Native American women also are developing their own agendas for liberation reflecting their unique experiences and their desires for positive transformation and are developing their own theologies.

African American author bell hooks has expressed well why attending to these differences is important: "Much feminist theory emerges from privileged women who live at the center, whose perspectives on reality rarely include the knowledge and awareness of the lives of women and men who live in the margin."[47] The experience of being a woman is inseparable from being the kind of woman one is. An African American woman experiences being a woman differently from a first-generation Hispanic woman, an Asian American woman, and an educated white woman, even though all of them may live in the same city.

hooks's explanation of the need for black women to develop a womanist stance is applicable to other ethnic groups. On every part of the globe, more contours on the feminist map are being drawn by women. These women are struggling to express their goals from the perspectives of their distinct cultures and in response to the forms of oppression that are unique to their societies. Among these women are new voices from the Third World who struggle not only against sexism and racism, but also against the effects of classism. In addition, women from various locations on the globe are bringing insights from feminist analysis to bear on the ecological crisis. To draw attention to the connection between women's struggle in patriarchal systems and the ecological crisis, Françoise d'Eaubonne coined the term "ecofeminism."[48] Women who identify themselves as ecofeminists call for an end to all forms of oppression, especially the exploitation of the Earth, the home that human and nonhuman forms of life share. This growing group of women argues that the domination of women and of nonhuman nature is intimately connected and mutually reinforcing. No attempt, therefore, to liberate women or any other oppressed group of people is truly liberating without an equal attempt to liberate nonhuman nature from the threat of ecological disaster.

The movements that embrace previously overlooked racial and cultural differences and interconnections between human behavior and the plight of the Earth constitute a third wave of feminism. The third wave of feminism is well underway. The world conference on women sponsored by the United Nations in Beijing in 1995 and its smaller-scale sequel held in New York City in 2000 gave ample testimony that women's concerns cannot be reduced to one feminism. Women of different countries and ethnic groups, different classes and races, different religious and cultural backgrounds have different issues and visions for their resolution. In this latest emergence of feminist awareness, attention is given not only to the effects of sexism on women, but also of racism, ethnic prejudice, economic classes, and the exploitation of nonhuman nature.

Sandra Schneiders, a Catholic feminist theologian, draws together all of these elements in her summary description of third-wave feminism as a movement of liberation:

> This movement is concerned not simply with the social, political, and economic equality of women with men but with a fundamental re-imagination of the whole of humanity in relation to the whole of reality, including nonhuman creation. In other words, the feminist consciousness has gradually deepened, the feminist agenda has widened, from a concern to right a particular structural wrong, namely, the exclusion of women from the voting booth, to a demand for full participation of women in society and culture, to an ideal of recreating humanity itself according to patterns of eco-justice, that is, of right relations at every level and in relation to all of reality.[49]

THIRD-WAVE FEMINISMS

1. Attention to Difference. European and Euro-American feminism continues the legacy of second-wave feminism, while setting new directions in response to women of color outside of their limited group. Womanist, *mujerista,* and other feminists of color emphasize that they have unique experiences and concerns that are connected with their special social locations.

Each group seeks to develop its own agendas for liberation that respond to its unique experiences and desires for positive transformation. Dialogue and solidarity play a role in forming alliances that extend across the lines of difference.

2. Ecofeminism. Brings together a plurality of voices that connects the domination of women (and other subjugated groups of people) with exploitation of nonhuman nature, arguing that the two forms of domination are intimately connected and mutually reinforcing

Guided by a vision of ecojustice that encompasses all realms of life, ecofeminists seek to bring to an end all forms of discrimination and exploitation, because no attempt to liberate women or any other oppressed group will be successful unless it is connected to the liberation of nonhuman nature.

This has been a lengthy response to the question "What is feminism?" Yet, a more simplified response would be neither adequate nor appropriate to the complex reality of women's experiences, especially their struggles and hopes. The pluriformity of feminism is evident also in responses to questions that seek to probe the "why" and "what" of Christian feminist theology. It is to these questions that we now turn.

Why Christian Feminist Theology?

Christianity is a major world religion that externalizes its beliefs about the God revealed in Jesus Christ in a myriad of symbols, stories, rituals, and moral teachings. Christian theology rises out of a believing community's desire to more fully understand its faith relationship with God by interpreting its beliefs in ways understandable in its own time and place. Theology done by Christian feminists is no exception to this broad description. Christian theology also presupposes a faith that is at once personal and shared with other Christians. This presupposition also affects Christian feminist theologians as they seek to contribute to Christian belief. Christian feminist theologians do theology with appreciation for many elements in the Christian tradition, particularly its prophetic and liberating elements.

In the biblical prophetic tradition, God's messengers drew attention to the community's neglect of God's saving truth. A distinguishing feature of Christian feminist theology is its attention to the neglect of women's full incorporation into the people of God. The prophetic naming of this truth sets the direction for liberating Christian theology from a centuries-long pattern of patriarchal myopia where women and their experiences of God are concerned. Myopia is an appropriate description, because the vision of Christian theologians was deficient. What is included under the gender-blind term "Christian theology" is actually male theology, done with an almost exclusive focus on questions of interest to European or Euro-American, well-educated, middle-class males. Therefore, when someone uses the term "Christian theology," what that person is usually talking about is faith in God being brought to understanding from the perspective of male experience. Christian theology was and often still is presented to Christians as if it represented everyone, but the generic "Christian theology" incorporates only the lived experience of relationship to God of Christian men. Its authors may intend their theology to be in service of the faith-life of both male and female Christians, but women's experiences of God-relatedness are excluded. As a result, prior to feminist awareness of the masculinization of theology, women's unique Christian faith perspectives were absent from Christian theology.

Even in the first wave of feminism, among its leaders were women who recognized the absence of women's perspectives in Christian theology. Mary Baker Eddy and Elizabeth Cady Stanton challenged the use of select biblical texts to justify limitations imposed on women. It was not until the second wave of feminism, however, that Christian women began to successfully draw attention to the shortcomings of the "maleness" of Christian theology. Not only was Christian theology male, and therefore not universally applicable, but also, like every religion, it was profoundly affected by the culture in which it developed. Christian male theology is marked by patriarchy, a cultural ideology that favors male experience, thinking, and values.

Second-wave feminist theology was initiated by Euro-American women who did something novel for the time: they pursued advanced degrees in theology, sometimes in seminaries previously attended only by males, to provide new lenses to correct the myopia of male theology. Through the 1970s and most of the 1980s the experience claimed as a source for Christian feminist theologians was more often than not that of white, Euro-American and European, middle-class women. However, many of these women began to recognize that their theologies were also myopic. Heeding the challenges of womanist, *mujerista,* Latina, and Asian American women, many Euro-American and European Christian feminist theologians recognized in the tendency to universalize their own experience a not-so-subtle form of patriarchal ideology. Therefore, many of these feminist theologians expanded their focus to encompass women from social locations different from their own and those men who are subjugated by patriarchy. European and Euro-American feminist theologians began to speak increasingly about being in solidarity with Second World women of Eastern Europe and Third World women and men of the southern hemisphere in their struggles against patriarchal oppression. Some have also contributed to ecofeminism by developing feminist ecological theologies that draw attention to the connections between the struggles against the subjugation of women and the exploitation of the earth's creatures. During the 1990s, women from almost every social location around the globe began to pursue education in theology and feminist theory, thereby drawing attention to how the manifestations of patriarchy particular to their societies affect Christian theology and ethics.

Although each feminist theology is unique, feminist theologies share in common the commitment to bring faith in God revealed by Jesus Christ from the perspective of women's experience to understanding. Feminist theologians recognize that this understanding will never be complete; God is a mystery. However, the desire to deepen and grow in relationship to God as women of faith compels women to engage in doing theology for their own benefit and the good of the people of God. Normally, feminist theologians use a variety of scholarly methods to bring women's experience of the presence and absence of God and Christian sources into dialogue. Absence is included here because some Christian theologies are an obstacle to women's relationship to God and therefore beg for critique.

All Christian feminist theologies share a distinguishing principle: patriarchy and androcentrism in their many forms conflict with faith in a God whom Christian revelation proclaims to be love itself (1 John 4:8). Ideally, theologians serve God by serving the people of God by bringing the *gospel to bear on every facet of human life. Yet, an examination of the history of the Christian churches in Western Europe and the Americas reveals unmistakable manifestations of patriarchy in how theologians and church authorities failed to bring the gospel to bear on the subjugation of women, the enslavement of people of color, and the abuses of colonialism. Christianity is not exempt from criticism where sexism, racism, and classism are concerned. Criticism, however, is not limited to a failure to challenge the evils of patriarchy; church leaders and theologians have sometimes used the Bible to support these societal evils, interpreting relevant texts as "proof" that these practices were sanctioned by God.

In the case of women, simplistic interpretations of Genesis 2–3, for example, resulted in Christian theologians depicting women as "the daughters of Eve" and therefore the temptresses of men. A feminist reading of this important text is explored in chapter 2, "Feminist Perspectives on the Bible." It is important to note here, however, that influential Christian theologians, in spite of their personal search for holiness and the richness of many of their insights, contributed to negative stereotypes about women based on their interpretations of Genesis 2–3 and other texts about women. Over the centuries many Christian theologians have treated women as not only a "dissimilar species," but also as a defective one. Tertullian (ca. 160–225) characterized women as "the devil's gateway."[50] Augustine (354–430) argued that man alone can fully image God; a woman images God only with her husband.[51] Thomas Aquinas (1225–74), influenced by Aristotle, spoke of women as "defective" and "misbegotten."[52]

The prevalent androcentrism in the writings of Christian theologians is systemic in church life as well. Theological positions such as those cited above have shaped Christianity's thinking about women and resulted in their exclusion from church leadership. This topic is addressed in some depth in chapter 4, "Feminist Perspectives on Women and the Church."

Most people experience "being church" at Sunday service. All too often these are occasions in which the secondary status of women is symbolically reinforced. Preaching rarely focuses on readings that present women of the Bible in a positive light. Biblical texts on women are not included in the lectionary of Sunday readings. In addition, in the language of prayer and song in ***liturgy,** phrases such as "faith of our fathers," "men of God," and "the "brotherhood of believers" frequently are heard without any parallel inclusion of "mothers," "women," or "sisterhood." Men are treated as if they represent the whole of humanity before God.

Patriarchy has legitimated many forms of oppression in addition to sexism. Among them is the enslavement of human beings, perhaps the cruelest negation of the dignity of a person. Slavery, like sexism, was once treated as if a part of God's scheme of things: (1) Africans could be enslaved because they were under Noah's curse upon his son Ham; (2) Israel held slaves; (3) Christ never preached against slavery; (4) slavery was merely the lowest level in a divinely created social order; (5) enslavement of Africans actually improved their lives, because with access to the gospel they were transformed from savage heathens to civilized Christians. It was not uncommon for preachers to use the Bible to legitimate this cruel form of human domination by insisting that the Bible required that slaves accept their enslavement (2 Cor. 11:20) and obey their masters (e.g., Eph. 6:5; Col. 3:22). The use of such texts to justify slavery, however, ignores the historical context in which these passages were written and the belief of early Christians that the second coming of Jesus Christ was close at hand. After Jesus' death and resurrection, many early Christians believed that the end of the world was approaching; therefore, there was no need to make major societal changes. A message intended for a radically different time and situation was abused centuries later to legitimate slavery.

During the era of slave trading by Western Europeans and Euro-Americans, Christian theologians did not question the morality of slavery but only debated whether slavery was a matter of faith. Some popes drew attention to the evils of slavery, but it was not until 1839 that Pope Gregory XVI condemned slave trading. Unfortunately, many Catholic bishops in the southern United States interpreted the pope's condemnation as applying only to the transatlantic slave trade and not to the domestic slavery that was already well established in the South.[53] Protestant Christian leaders in the South also considered slavery a political and economic issue, not a religious and moral one. Most, therefore, did not champion the cause of enslaved Africans. Divisions over slavery led the three major Protestant denominations to split during the two decades prior to the Civil War, as some Christians of the North, including some very vocal women, began to champion abolition.[54]

European colonialism is also a form of patriarchy that has had long-term damaging effects. The most pronounced is the phenomenon known as the "Third World." Peoples and nations in the southern hemisphere continue to deal with the aftermath of colonial conquest by Western European nations. Christian missionaries compounded the problem by presenting the gospel in ways that showed little or no respect for the existing religious traditions of the people they baptized. They presented to the people an imperial God, brought to them by a superior people. Some Christian feminists are seeking to redress these problems. Certainly, additional manifestations of patriarchy exist; I have drawn attention to three that have had a long-term impact on the lives of women and men around the globe.

Feminist theology recognizes that theology cannot be done without working to overcome those things that conflict with the core of the Christian message, which affirms the dignity of each person. In addition, Christian feminist theology affirms that theology cannot be merely an exercise in speculation. Any theology inspired by Jesus Christ and his mission must have practical implications and applications. What could be more practical than promoting the full human flourishing of women and oppressed people in the Christian churches and civil society? This is the overarching "why" for the existence of Christian theologies committed to the full humanity of women and subjugated men, whether they are called feminist, womanist, *mujerista,* or Latina, or are known by any other name, representing other social groups around the globe. Achieving this goal is important for the integrity and vitality of Christianity.

Types of Feminist Theology

Attentive to experiences, which are personal yet profoundly affected by social location, feminist theologies are not privatized exercises. Feminist theologies have a public and communal character. Obviously, there are many publics and communities from which and for which theologians do their work. Part of the public situatedness of feminist theologians is their relationship to the secular feminisms that exist today. These relationships account, in part, for the different types of feminist theologies. At the risk of oversimplification, the major forms of feminist theology can be grouped under three major headings: revolutionary, reformist, and reconstructionist.[55] In the treatment of each that follows, it is important to keep in mind that this analysis is intended to sketch the landscape of the major forms of feminist theology. The shortcoming of this sketch is that it does not sufficiently address the many differences in feminist theologies. No categorical analysis can fully account for the enormous diversity in feminist theology today.

*Revolutionary feminist theology** is affected most by radical feminists, especially by those who advocate woman-centered culture. Many radical feminist theologians can accurately be described as post-Christian. Many of these women originally participated in Christian churches, but their own feminist consciousness led them to conclude that Christianity is irredeemably patriarchal, even anti-woman. We can trace the beginnings of this line of argument in the United States to Matilda Joslyn Gage (1826–93), a suffragist closely associated with Susan B. Anthony and Elizabeth Cady Stanton. Her considerable research on the cultures of the Near East and Egypt led her to propose worship of the Goddess as a key to female ascendancy in families and in religious and secular societies.[56] She insisted that if women ever hoped to be liberated, they must cast aside Christianity and the patriarchal legal codes influenced by the Christian Bible.

Gage remained a little-known figure until feminists involved in the second wave of feminism discovered her work and reprinted her *Woman, Church and State*. Her theory of matriarchy resonated with the positions of radical feminists. We can rightly call many of these women post-Christian feminists. Their major problem with Christianity is the centrality given to the revelation of a male God, whom they believe is used to legitimate the patriarchal oppression of women by Christian churches. In addition, they point out that Christians continue to subordinate women in their churches and in their marital relationships. Thus, these theologians have abandoned Christianity as oppressive to women. Many have turned to ancient Goddess traditions for their theology. They envision the Goddess to be an appropriate symbol for the creative power of women.[57]

*Reformist Christian feminist theology has virtually nothing in common with the revolutionary model. The reformist theologian is not looking for sweeping changes that totally revolutionize Christianity. Reformist theologians do not want to replace the God revealed by Jesus Christ. They do not want to be part of a community that worships goddesses. They are looking for far more modest changes within existing church structures. Although unanimity among reformist feminist theologians does not exist, they do share in common their commitment to the Christian tradition. Their positions show commonalities with cultural feminism. Reformist feminists can be found in Protestant denominations and in Roman Catholicism.

In the Protestant denominations, the more conservative of the reformist feminists are the evangelicals or fundamentalists who are committed to the inerrancy of the Bible and to a literal interpretation of its texts, yet are also opposed to gender bias in the treatment of women in their families, churches, and civil societies. Proponents of this form of feminist theology believe that they can solve the problems of women's secondary status with measures such as better translations of the Bible and more emphasis on egalitarian passages in the Bible.

Roman Catholic women and men who espouse a deep respect for the Roman Catholic tradition and its institutional authority, yet hold that women need to be more included in the life and leadership of the church, are another example of reformist feminists. They are, for the most part, uncritical of the structures of the institutional church and are supportive of church teaching, such as limiting ordained ministries to males, yet they also champion having women involved in other church ministries and in theological education.

*Reconstructionist Christian feminist theology, the third major type, shares with reformist feminism a commitment to Christianity, but does not find the positions of reformist feminism to be an adequate response to the subjugation and secondary status of women. Permitting women to hold church offices and do church-related ministries is not sufficient. Reconstructionist feminist theologians seek a liberating theological core for women within the Christian tradition, while also envisioning a deeper transformation, a true reconstruction, not only of their church structures but also of civil society. In company with the revolutionary feminist theologians, reconstructionist feminists share a critical appraisal of patriarchy, but they believe that reinterpreting the traditional symbols and ideas of Christianity without abandoning the God revealed in Jesus Christ is possible and desirable.

What makes a reconstructionist feminist theology Christian? The short answer is Jesus. The somewhat longer answer is the gospel vision of release from bondage for a new creation — the realization of the reign of God, proclaimed by Jesus, the Christ, in word and deed. Jesus' powerful social vision was incarnate in the inclusive community of women and men, drawn together and empowered by him to preach the good news of God's coming reign. Like the Jesus of Mark's Gospel, there is an urgency about the mission of this inclusive community for feminist theologians: "This is the time of fulfillment. The reign of God is at hand. Repent, and believe in the gospel" (Mark 1:15). The time of fulfillment is an age of shared commitment to the loving God of Jesus Christ in the Holy Spirit, the giver of life. The shared commitment in a discipleship of equals, embraced by Christian feminist theologians, transcends particular denominational affiliations. Christian feminist theologians, whether they are Episcopalian, Lutheran, Presbyterian, or Roman Catholic, may have doctrinal differences, but these usually take a distant second place to their shared partnership and liberating social vision. Interdenominational partnership emerged in the second wave of feminism and continues as new directions that constitute the third wave continue to unfold.

A powerful theme of the feminist theology of the second wave is that the reign of God, when rightly understood, liberates and empowers women for the fullness of life. Feminist theologians participating in the third wave seek to bring this theme to bear on the difference that social location makes in their theologies. Many reconstructionist feminist theologians envision feminist theology to be a form of *liberation theology, a term first coined by Gustavo Gutiérrez in 1968, when he called for a theology that speaks from the life experience of the poor of Latin America and engages in *praxis that liberates them from economic poverty and political oppression.[58]

The liberation sought by reconstructionist feminist theologians is not one dimensional, nor is it a "cheap grace" easily incarnated. It calls for repentance by righting wrongs. The wrongs of primary concern are the life-denying effects of patriarchy, a panoply of "isms": sexism, of course, but also racism, classism, and any other societal distortions of patriarchy — ageism, heterosexism, and naturism (the exploitation of the creatures of the earth). In the third wave of Christian feminist theology, partnership transcends more than denominational lines; it stretches across the lines of race, class, sexual orientation, and religion. Christian feminist solidarity envisions these lines not as ones of demarcation, but rather as respectful acknowledgment of difference. This extension of hands across the lines of race, ethnicity, and class honors difference, while creating a space for listening to the heartaches and hopes of persons who speak from diverse cultural and religious experiences. European and Euro-American feminists, womanists, *mujerista,* Latina, and Asian feminists are engaging in conversations — "hearing each other into speech" — becoming attuned to each other's experiences. For many European and Euro-American feminists, such conversations have been painful because they have meant facing the legacy of patriarchy from which they have benefited simply by being born white. Yet, without facing this truth, talk about respecting difference and commitment to a common struggle to resist subjugation can be merely hollow-sounding words.

What makes a theology reconstructionist from the standpoint of feminism? The term "reconstruction" rarely appears as a subtitle in feminist theological writing. Although the related term "revisionist" is used at times for this third type of feminist theology, "reconstructionist" is preferred because I believe that third-wave feminist theologies are doing more than revising and adjusting an already existing tradition by calling for renewed vision of Christianity. They are incorporating women's experiences of God in dialogue with primary theological sources. They recognize that male theologians in patriarchal societies have spoken about justice and peace, love and mercy, sin and forgiveness in meaningful ways. Yet, the application of these words to women and subordinate men has all too often been deficient. Therefore, a reconstructionist theology praises some theologies, critiques others, and draws into discussion the voices of women long ignored to forge not only new feminist theologies but also transformed societies marked by equality and mutuality of women and men. They are, in a sense, constructing a theology from multiple bricks and fresh mortar needed for our time.

To forge this construction in the era of the third wave of feminism, the methodology of Christian reconstructionist feminist theologies often incorporates these three basic steps:

1. Attending to experience(s) of patriarchy and androcentrism by listening attentively to one's own experience and that of other women and/or subjugated men;

2. Bringing these experiences into dialogue with a feminist reading of the Bible and/or other Christian texts;

3. Developing strategies for transformative action or praxis that are liberating.

1. Attending to experience is the first step in developing a reconstructionist feminist theology. This stage flows from a feminist recognition of the particular and the experiential. A feminist theology true to the word "feminist" cannot start from abstract theory about God and the things of God. Concrete experiences must be listened to and learned from. Human experience is particular because it is always embodied experience. It is profoundly affected by the life situation or social location in which one finds oneself. The effects of patriarchy on some women are far less extensive and debilitating than on others. To be born in certain countries immediately makes it more likely for a woman to struggle with poverty, experience violence, or enjoy only a limited number of civil rights.

In this first step of feminist theology, attention is given to one's own experience. Since most people engaged in doing reconstructionist feminist theology are in an academic setting, a location of privilege, to this personal reflection is added an important additional component: being receptive to women's experiences different from one's own, especially of women who have been abused, exploited, and impoverished. Patriarchy negatively affects all women's life experience, but its effects cannot be abstracted from social location.

The term often used for this type of attending to experience, especially by *mujerista* and Latina theologians is ***conscientization.**[59] The purpose of conscientization is to encourage people to listen to and validate their experiences, especially experiences of subjugation, and to probe their causes. Why is conscientization needed? Experiences are usually interpreted in thought patterns that prevail in a given culture. Ideology created by the dominant voices in a society tends to be heard as if it is the way things are and are meant to be. Persons whose life choices are limited by patriarchy unthinkingly internalize the interpretations of them given by persons in power. They do this usually with an attitude of passive resignation. Burdened by patriarchal definitions and androcentric attitudes, subjugated persons tend to uncritically accept their "lot in life" as inevitable and unchangeable. Most of the history of women, with very few exceptions, is characterized by this picture to a greater or lesser degree. Patriarchy, like any reigning pattern of thought or ideology, uses distorted images to promote the internalization of inferiority in the group that is being dominated. This is key to those in power maintaining dominance. Androcentrism works with this distortion, assisting the domination of women by pushing their experiences to the periphery.

Reconstructionist feminist theology not only brings to consciousness the experiences of discrimination and subordination that patriarchy and androcentrism promote, but also unmasks them as not of God and therefore sinful. Suffering visited upon people because of their sex, race, class, age, sexual orientation, or disability can never be of God. Attending to culturally shaped interpretations of diminishment is an important hermeneutical strategy and a necessary first step in developing a recontructionist feminist theology.

It logically follows, therefore, that when you read a feminist theological work, the social location of the author and the people for whom she or he is writing is always significant. Third-wave feminist theology presumes that it is neither possible nor desirable to universalize women's experiences. There are enormous differences in experience in North America among white, black, Hispanic, and Asian American women. The differences are even more pronounced when North American experiences are examined in relationship to those of women in Latin America, Africa, and Asia. Reconstructionist feminist theologies, therefore, are not "value-neutral" thought experiments. They promote new thinking and forge societal patterns of action. An important guiding question to ask while reading them is, What experiences of patriarchy and androcentrism is the author of this text trying to remedy? Apart from remedying patriarchal abuses, reconstructionist feminist theologies also seek to broaden the theological horizon of their communities by attending to religious experiences, especially those relevant to the lives of women, that have been ignored.

2. Feminist interpretation of the Bible and church teachings requires that attention be given to what does and does not liberate women and men from the effects of patriarchy. If a biblical text, church teaching, or an interpretation of either does not liberate, then it either must not be true or has been misinter-

preted. This insight is rooted in the words of Jesus, "You will know the truth, and the truth will set you free" (John 8:32). Getting at the freeing truth where the Bible, church teaching, and their interpretations are concerned is not an easy task. All three present some messages about women that are obviously patriarchal, but many more are ambivalent where women are concerned. Yet, for centuries women have drawn inspiration and guidance from biblical texts and the teachings of their churches, finding in them a freeing truth.

Feminist theological ***hermeneutics** requires detecting patriarchy and androcentrism in biblical texts, church teachings, and their interpretations. Any talk about texts draws attention to the issue of language and the power of symbols. Words not only enable communication, but also condition our thinking. For a Christian feminist theology to be truly liberating for women and for subjugated men, the language of biblical texts and of church teachings that interpret them must be examined from the standpoint of whether they contribute to the diminishment of persons. Such examinations require carefully conceived criteria. One obvious criterion is whether a particular text promotes male advantage at the expense of women's dignity or of a certain group of men. The language in some texts makes them "period pieces," suffering under the limitations of historical patriarchal influences in form and content.

An additional strategy is to focus on biblical texts and Christian sources that illumine the struggles of women and subjugated men and provide a reason for hope in the God of life. Like the watchful sister of ***Moses** in Exod. 2:3–4, feminist theologians guard these texts, many of which heretofore have received very little attention, lest the fragile baby of freeing truth perish in powerful currents of patriarchy. Part of this strategy is to develop interpretations that are liberating and empowering for women and for anyone whose life has been diminished by patriarchy. These components converge in the construction of guiding visions for liberation from those things that diminish the human dignity of any person. But it is important that there not be a gap between the language of liberation and the reality. Taking responsibility for bridging gaps is the final major step in a reconstructionist feminist theology.

3. Liberating action is the final step in a reconstructionist feminist theology. Reconstructionist feminism has a strong sense of the importance of concrete action that effectively embodies religious language that gives voice to truth and wisdom. It is therefore interested in more than raising awareness of the manifestations of patriarchy and of constructing a liberating interpretation of biblical revelation and church teachings; it seeks to make a difference in the Christian community and civil society. Creating societies that are more just and more in keeping with the reign of God proclaimed by Jesus in word and deed is the most important goal of Christian feminist theologies. This requires "transformative praxis." Since theology is a process in service of the faith-life of the people of God, Christian feminist theologies take up the love command of Jesus, recognizing that actively loving one's neighbors, especially those most in need, cannot be separated from love for God (Matt. 22:39; Mark 12:33; Luke 10:27). It is only through praxis, rooted in theological reflection, that the gap that has often existed between theological language and concrete reality can be closed.

The feminist theological talk must be walked, taken into the churches, the market place, the school, the courtroom — everywhere. The theological insights articulated by feminist theology flow into and out of action that seeks an end to sexism, oppression of subjugated people in any form, and damage done by humans to the earth.

Conclusions

This first chapter has laid the groundwork for the chapters that follow. It was designed to address some very basic questions: why and what feminism is, as a prelude to why and what Christian feminist theology is. In responding to these questions I have endeavored to address them with attention to historical and social context. Rather than summarize here what is already in summary form, I offer a brief reflection that I hope will assist the readers for the rest of the book. I recognize that what is presented here on the three waves of feminism and Christian feminist theology is a sketch, a sketch with some detail, yes, but a sketch nonetheless of a much larger picture. The responses to each question provided here are in keeping with my own experience of feminism as a Christian theologian with an education in Christian theology that is unique to me and values that I have gradually made my own over a lifetime. I suspect that some of the readers of this chapter will be in agreement with at least parts of what it proposes. Others may have uneasy or negative responses to some or perhaps all of the major arguments developed. Still others may leave this chapter with more questions than answers. If this chapter sparks considered and reasoned responses about Christian feminism, whether positive or negative, it will have accomplished my intention for it.

A Look Ahead

The methodology for third-wave reconstructionist feminist theologies has been presented in some detail in this first chapter because of its promise for transforming the lives of people and theology as an academic discipline. Consequently, reconstructionist feminist theology will be the lens through which Christian feminist theology will be focused in the remaining chapters of this book. Since the first step of the methodology, "attending to experience," commonly shared by reconstructive feminist theologians has been treated in some depth in this chapter's section "Why Feminism?" chapter 2 will proceed with an exploration of feminist perspectives on the Bible that takes into account how they have been affected by feminism's three major waves.

NOTES

1. Christine de Pizan, *The Book of the City of Ladies,* original edition published in 1405, trans. Earl Jeffrey Richards (New York: Persea Books, 1982), 187. Christine de Pizan (also sometimes spelled "Pisan"), the daughter of an Italian astrologer brought to France to be a member of the court of King Charles V and Queen Jeanne de Bourbon, was a prolific writer who made her living from her works. She was the first woman known to have participated in literary and philosophical debates about women (*querelle des femmes*).

2. Prior to the late eighteenth century, the educated opinion was that women were a separate species. Gender differences were viewed in absolute terms.

3. Simone de Beauvoir, *The Second Sex*, trans. and ed. H. M. Parshley (New York: Alfred A. Knopf, 1952; reprint, New York: Random House, 1974).

4. Pizan, *City of Ladies,* 4.

5. Ibid., 153–54.

6. Bonnie S. Anderson and Judith P. Zinsser, *A History of Their Own: Women in Europe from Prehistory to the Present,* vol. 2 (New York: Harper & Row, 1988); on p. 492 n. 1 the date for the first appearance of the word "feminism" is given as 1882.

7. Wollstonecraft argues in the introduction of this work that the whole of society suffers under the burden of a false education gathered from books written on the subject by men who consider "females as women rather than as human creatures"; apparently, Pizan's argument for the humanity of women had not yet taken hold! See Mary Wollstonecraft, *A Vindication of the Rights of Women* (1792; reprint, London: J. M. Dent; Rutland, Vt.: Charles E. Tuttle, 1995), 9.

8. Margaret Hope Bacon, *Mothers of Feminism: The Story of Quaker Women in America* (San Francisco: Harper & Row, 1986), 103–5.

9. Angelina became a persuasive orator, and Sarah published influential works on abolition (1836) and the equality of the sexes in the church (1838).

10. Mott was a Quaker lecturer for temperance and abolition. She aided fugitive slaves and helped form the Philadelphia Female Anti-Slavery Society. When the World Anti-Slavery Convention in London (1840) refused to recognize women delegates, she joined Elizabeth Cady Stanton in organizing the first Women's Rights Convention, held in Seneca Falls, New York, in 1848.

11. Anthony organized the first women's temperance association, the Daughters of Temperance, and with Elizabeth Cady Stanton secured the first laws in New York guaranteeing women rights over their children and control of property and wages (1848). In 1863 she was coorganizer of the Women's Loyal League to support Lincoln's government, but after the Civil War she opposed granting suffrage to freedmen without also giving it to women. She was president of the National American Woman Suffrage Association (1892–1900).

12. Catt, an American suffragist, was the president of the National American Woman Suffrage Association (1900–1920). When the Nineteenth Amendment to the U.S. Constitution was passed, she organized the League of Women Voters. A woman of wealth, she traveled widely to network for women's rights.

13. Not only were some of the women who supported civil rights for African Americans feminist in their leanings, but also the Civil Rights Bill of 1964 prohibited discrimination on the basis of sex. "Sex" was added to a list that included race, color, religion, and national origin by Howard W. Smith, an eighty-one-year-old representative from Virginia and chair of the rules committee of the House. No feminist, this defender of the "Southern way of life" had voted against bills guaranteeing equal pay for equal

work regardless of sex. He made the addition of the word "sex" as a joke — one that backfired. The bill passed on 9 February 1963. In April 1964 Senator Everett Dirksen, Republican majority leader, led a drive to have "sex" stricken from the bill, but was unsuccessful. See Caroline Bird, *Born Female: The High Cost of Keeping Women Down* (New York: Pocket Books, 1971), 1–15.

14. Betty Friedan wrote *The Feminine Mystique* (New York: Norton, 1963), in which she criticized the traditional notion that women find fulfillment only through childbearing and homemaking. This work is widely regarded as the book that launched the second wave of the women's movement. Instrumental in founding the National Organization of Women (1966), she served as its first president and also helped to organize the National Women's Political Caucus (1970).

15. Anderson and Zinsser, *A History of Their Own,* 407.

16. Audre Lorde, *Sister Outsider* (Trumansburg, N.Y.: Crossing Press, 1984), 112.

17. This information is cited in Dorothy Ann Kelly, "The United Nations Fourth World Conference on Women," *Cross Currents* 46 (1996): 34. The fact that women experience poverty to a greater extent than men has been called the "feminization of poverty" by Diana Pearce. See her "The Feminization of Poverty: Women, Work and Welfare," *The Urban and Social Change Review* (1978): 18–29.

18. United Nations Development Fund for Women (UNIFEM), "Progress of the World's Women 2000, a Biennial Report" (*http://www.unifem.undp.org/beijing+5* [31 May 2000]).

19. Ibid.

20. Kelly, "Fourth World Conference on Women," 30. A 1990 FBI report cited by the Center for the Prevention of Sexual and Domestic Violence (*http://www.cpsdv.org* [1 May 2000]) indicates that one in three women in the United States experiences some form of sexual assault in her lifetime; half of these assaults come from a domestic partner.

21. For a collection of thought-provoking theological essays on violence directed toward women, see Elisabeth Schüssler Fiorenza and Mary Shawn Copeland, eds., *Violence against Women,* Concilium 1994/1 (Maryknoll, N.Y.: Orbis Books, 1994).

22. Ann McFeatters, "Women Still Are Victims of Violence," *Pittsburgh Post-Gazette,* 7 June 2000, sec. B, p. 1.

23. Lori Heise, "The Global War against Women," *Washington Post,* 9 April 1996, sec. B, pp. 1, 4.

24. Dorinda Elliott, "Trying to Stand on Two Feet," *Newsweek,* 29 June 1998, 49.

25. See Anne Wilson Schaef, *Co-Dependence: Misunderstood and Mistreated* (New York: Harper & Row, 1986).

26. Joann Wolski Conn, "New Vitality: The Challenge from Feminist Theology," *America* 165 (5 October 1991): 217.

27. On a personal note, a female college student who has struggled for several years with an eating disorder shared with me an important breakthrough in her disease symbolized by a ritualized burning of her Barbies. She found the action very liberating!

28. Jonathan D. Silver, "Working Women Have More Clout, but Pace Is Slow," *Pittsburgh Post-Gazette,* 7 June 2000, sec. B, p. 2.

29. Ibid.

30. Gerda Lerner, *The Creation of Feminist Consciousness: From the Middle Ages to Eighteen-Seventy* (New York: Oxford University Press, 1993), 4.

31. In keeping with current style in academic writing, I am using the more general terms B.C.E. ("before the Common Era") and C.E. ("Common Era") rather than the Christian terms B.C. ("before Christ") and A.D. (*Anno Domini,* Latin for "in the year of the Lord") to designate dates.

32. Aristotle, *Politics and Economics,* trans. Edward Walford (London: George Bell and Sons, 1885), part 1, "Politics" or the "Treatise on Government," book 1, ch. 5, 12–13.

33. De Beauvoir, *The Second Sex,* xv.

34. Ibid., xix and passim.

35. James B. Nelson, *Between Two Gardens: Reflections on Sexuality and Religious Experience* (New York: Pilgrim Press, 1983), 46–47.

36. Maria Riley, *Transforming Feminism* (Kansas City, Mo.: Sheed and Ward, 1989), 46. I am indebted to Maria Riley for the opportunity to participate in a seminar in which drafts of this book were discussed.

37. Ibid., 48.

38. Ibid., 50.

39. Ibid.

40. Ibid., 55–56.

41. Ibid., 57.

42. Catherine A. MacKinnon, "Feminism, Marxism, Method, and the State: An Agenda for Theory," in *Feminist Theory,* ed. Nannerl O. Keohane, Michelle Z. Rosaldo, and Barbara C. Gelpi (Chicago: University of Chicago Press, 1982), 1.

43. Riley, *Transforming Feminism,* 57.

44. Although Alice Walker coined the term in the late 1970s, the first extensive explanation of it appeared in print in her *In Our Mother's Gardens: Womanist Prose* (New York: Harcourt Brace-Jovanovich, 1983), xi–xii and passim.

45. Ibid., xi.

46. For a more detailed description of *mujerista* theology, see Ada María Isasi-Díaz, "The Bible and *Mujerista* Theology," in *Lift Every Voice: Constructing Christian Theologies from the Underside,* ed. Susan Brooks Thistlethwaite and Mary Potter Engle (Maryknoll, N.Y.: Orbis Books, 1998), 273–74.

47. bell hooks, *Feminist Theory from Margin to Center* (Boston: South End Press, 1984), preface, n.p. bell hooks prefers to spell her name without capital letters.

48. Françoise d'Eaubonne, *Le féminisme ou la mort* (Paris: Pierre Horay, 1974), esp. 213–52.

49. Sandra M. Schneiders, *With Oil in Their Lamps: Faith, Feminism, and the Future* (New York: Paulist Press, 2000), 8.

50. Tertullian, *On the Apparel of Woman,* ch. 1.

51. Augustine, *On the Trinity,* book 12, ch. 7, no. 10.

52. Thomas Aquinas, *Summa Theologiae,* part 1, q. 92, a. 1.

53. Cyprian Davis points out that Catholic bishops such as Carroll of Baltimore, Flaget of Bardstown/Louisville, and Portier of Mobile owned slaves, as did religious orders of women and men. The Jesuits of Maryland owned at least three hundred slaves in the 1830s. See "God of Our Weary Days: Black Catholics in American Catholic History," in *Taking Down Our Harps: Black Catholics in the United States,* ed. Diana L. Hayes and Cyprian Davis (Maryknoll, N.Y.: Orbis Books, 1998), 22–24.

54. Bishop Leonidas Polk, Episcopal bishop of Louisiana and a strong supporter of slavery, put aside his episcopal duties to join the Confederate army. Bishop James O. Andrew of Georgia was a slave owner. In the years prior to the Civil War, as divisions about slavery deepened, the Methodist, Baptist, and Presbyterian churches divided into separate denominations. See Mark A. Noll et al., eds., *Eerdmans Handbook to Christianity in America* (Grand Rapids: William B. Eerdmans Publishing Co., 1983), 257–62.

55. Carol Christ and Judith Plaskow, in their introduction to *Womanspirit Rising: A Feminist Reader in Religion* (San Francisco: Harper & Row, 1979), analyzed feminist theology under the headings "revolutionary" and "reformist" (p. 4). In the introduction

to a more recent collection of essays edited by Christ and Plaskow, *Weaving the Visions: New Patterns in Feminist Spirituality* (San Francisco: Harper & Row, 1989), they draw attention to the limitations of these categories where the enormous variety of feminist theology is concerned (p. 3). I am using them with the addition of the typology "reconstructionist" to account for the major development since 1979. In making this addition, I realize that the three typologies do not completely account for the many distinctive nuances in the growing body of feminist theological literature. Some feminist theologians might prefer "revisionist" to "reconstructionist"; I have chosen the latter because I believe that it more adequately names what feminists are doing in their theologies.

56. Matilda Joslyn Gage, *Woman, Church and State* (1893; reprint, Watertown, Mass.: Persephone Press, 1980). Because of her negativity about Christianity, Gage lost most of her friends in the suffrage movement and her name was deleted from its annals.

57. More attention will be given to Goddess "thealogy" in chapters 3 and 6.

58. Gustavo Gutiérrez, *A Theology of Liberation: History, Politics, and Salvation,* trans. and ed. Sister Caridad Inda and John Eagleson (Maryknoll, N.Y.: Orbis Books, 1973; rev. ed. 1988). See also Leonardo Boff and Clodovis Boff, *Introducing Liberation Theology,* trans. Paul Burns (Maryknoll, N.Y.: Orbis Books, 1987), for a fine introduction to Latin American liberation theology.

59. Paulo Freire coined the term "conscientization" in *Pedagogy of the Oppressed* (New York: Herder and Herder, 1970).

QUESTIONS FOR REFLECTION AND DISCUSSION

1. Can you think of any everyday situations in which you are, or someone you know is, advantaged or disadvantaged by gender, race, or class? How does recognition of advantage or disadvantage enlighten you about privilege and oppression?

2. Were you surprised to learn that a woman, Christine de Pizan, was addressing sexism directed against women over half a millennium ago? Do her words still have relevance for today?

3. Summarize in your own words the issues associated with the emergence of the three waves of feminism. What do you associate with the word "woman" in each of the three waves of feminism?

4. In the section of this chapter entitled "Why Feminism?" some major reasons for feminism are delineated. What is your response to them? Are there additional reasons for feminism that could have been included in this section?

5. Do you find the distinctions between sex and gender helpful ones? Can you think of roles that society seems to say are inappropriate for a woman? for a man? In your opinion, aside from childbirth, are there any roles for women that are biologically determined?

6. What is your response to the following statements about gender roles?

   A. Males and females are significantly different.

   B. Men reason with their heads; women's reasons are matters of the heart.

C. Competitiveness is natural for men; vulnerability is natural for women.

D. Men are interested in accomplishments; women are interested in relationships.

E. There are really no gender-specific roles for men and women in the church and civil society today.

F. In marriage, it is the woman's role to nurture, cherish, and love her husband and children.

G. In a marriage, it is up to the man to be the primary financial provider for the family.

H. In the workplace, a woman should be able to make as much money as a man does for comparable work, but should never have decision-making power over a man.

I. In the professional world today, for women the sky is the limit; all the talk about a "glass ceiling" is really only an excuse for women who don't have what it takes to succeed.

7. Write your own definition of feminism. How does your definition compare with Joann Wolski Conn's definition cited in this chapter? How does your definition relate to liberal feminism, cultural feminism, radical feminism, socialist feminism, and feminism attuned to difference in social location?

8. Do you find yourself either strongly drawn or highly resistant to any of the major types of feminism surveyed in this chapter? Why?

9. What does "unmasking the ideology of patriarchy" mean? Why is doing this important? What are some of the strategies that have kept women subordinate in patriarchal societies?

10. Do you believe that it is important for African American women and other specific groups, such as Hispanic women, to develop their own strategies for advocating change? Would it be better for them to work closely with other feminists, since there is strength in numbers?

11. Christian feminist theology is categorized under three major headings in this chapter: revolutionary, reformist, and reconstructionist. Make a chart in which you express in your own words your understanding of each. To which of these three do you find yourself most drawn or most resistant? Why?

12. In the final section of this chapter, the methodology for reconstructionist feminist theology was presented in three major steps.

A. What are the pros and cons to using a method in doing theology?

B. What are the strengths and weaknesses of each of the three steps as explained in this chapter?

AREAS FOR EXPLORATION

1. Do some research on the lives and contributions to the first and second waves of the women's movement of one or more of the following:

Sarah and Angelina Grimké	Carrie Chapman Catt
Sojourner Truth	Betty Friedan
Lucretia Mott	Gloria Steinem
Susan B. Anthony	Susan Brownmiller
Joslyn Gage	Audre Lorde
Mary Baker Eddy	Alice Walker
Anna Julia Cooper	

2. Find out more about the fourth United Nations conference on women in Beijing (1995) and the Beijing+5 conference (2000) in New York. The twelve planks of the Beijing "Platform of Action" do not include any explicit references to religion, nor does the progress report. Do any of the planks of the platform have religious implications?

3. Do some additional research on the worldwide problem of violence directed to women. What does this violence say to you about the reality of patriarchy and the need for feminist advocacy for change?

4. Ask two or three persons of different ages and racial or ethnic backgrounds this question: In what ways are you aware of changing gender roles? In your opinion, which changes have been positive for women and men and which have been problematic?

5. Explore the history of women in your own family. Try to discover any unusual events that might indicate that your female ancestors were not up to "business as usual" where gender roles for women are concerned.

RECOMMENDED READINGS

Feminist/Womanist/Mujerista Sources

Cone, James H., and Gayraud S. Wilmore. "Womanist Theology." Part 4, pp. 257–351 in *Black Theology: A Documentary History*. Vol. 2: *1980–1992*. 2nd ed. Maryknoll, N.Y.: Orbis Books, 1993.

Copeland, M. Shawn. "Toward a Critical Feminist Theology of Solidarity." Pp. 3–38 in *Women and Theology*, ed. Mary Ann Hinsdale and Phyllis H. Kaminski. Annual Publication of the College Theology Society 40. Maryknoll, N.Y.: Orbis Books, 1995.

Donovan, Josephine. *Feminist Theory: The Intellectual Traditions of American Feminism*. New York: Continuum, 1985; expanded ed., 1992.

Hayes, Diana. "The Vision of Black Women: Womanist Theology." Pp. 135–60 in *And Still We Rise: An Introduction to Black Liberation Theology*. New York: Paulist Press, 1996.

Isasi-Díaz, Ada María. *En la Lucha/In the Struggle: Elaborating a Mujerista Theology*. Minneapolis: Fortress, 1993.

Japinga, Jan. *Feminism and Christianity: An Essential Guide.* Nashville: Abingdon Press, 1999.

Neft, Naomi, and Ann D. Levine, eds. *Where Women Stand: An International Report on the Status of Women in 140 Countries, 1997–98.* New York: Random House, 1997.

Riley, Maria. *Transforming Feminism.* Kansas City, Mo.: Sheed and Ward, 1989.

Russell, Letty M., and J. Shannon Clarkson, eds. *Dictionary of Feminist Theologies.* Louisville: Westminster John Knox Press, 1996.

Schneiders, Sandra M. *With Oil in Their Lamps: Faith, Feminism, and the Future.* New York: Paulist Press, 2000.

Tong, Rosemarie. *Feminist Thought: A Comprehensive Introduction.* Boulder, Colo.: Westview Press, 1989.

Feminist Goddess Religion

Christ, Carol. "Why Women Need the Goddess: Phenomenological, Psychological, and Political Reflections." Pp. 273–87 in *Womanspirit Rising: A Feminist Reader in Religion,* ed. Carol Christ and Judith Plaskow. New York: Harper & Row, 1979.

Downing, Christine. *The Goddess: Mythological Images of the Feminine.* New York: Crossroad, 1988.

Sjöö, Monica, and Barbara Mor. *The Great Cosmic Mother: Rediscovering the Religion of the Earth.* San Francisco: HarperCollins, 1991.

Violence and Women

Adams, Carol, and Marie M. Fortune, eds. *Violence against Women and Children: A Christian Theological Sourcebook.* New York: Continuum, 1996.

Burns, Maryviolet C., ed. *The Speaking Profits Us: Violence in the Lives of Women of Color — El decirlo nos hace bien a nosotros: La violencia en las vidas de las mujeres de color.* Seattle: CPSDV, 1986.

Mananzan, Mary John, Mercy Amba Oduyoye, Elsa Tamez, J. Shannon Clarkson, Mary C. Grey, and Letty M. Russell, eds. *Women Resisting Violence: Spirituality for Life.* Maryknoll, N.Y.: Orbis Books, 1996.

Chapter 2

Feminist Perspectives
on the Bible

From the inauguration of the movement for women's emancipation the Bible has been used to hold her [woman] in the "divinely ordained sphere," prescribed in the Old and New Testaments. The canon and civil law; church and state; priests and legislators; all political parties and religious denominations have alike taught that woman was made after man, of man and for man, an inferior being, subject to man. Creeds, codes, Scriptures and statutes, are all based on this idea.   — ELIZABETH CADY STANTON[1]

These statements by Elizabeth Cady Stanton (1815–1902), active suffragist and major spokesperson of the first wave of feminism,[2] provide a clear rationale for the earliest book-length challenge to male interpretations of the Bible. Angered by the exclusion of women from the company of scholars preparing a revision of the Authorized Version of the Bible, also known as the King James Bible, Stanton initiated *The Woman's Bible* project. If men could take it upon themselves to revise the Bible, women could also.

Although Stanton believed that there were problems associated with translations of the Bible, she recognized that the issues involved were much deeper than rendering words from ancient languages into more readable English. The Bible itself contained texts used as sanctions against change for the conditions of women. Whenever women tried to make advances in education, employment, or political rights, the Bible was cited, usually by men in positions of authority, to argue that such advances contradicted the Word of God, and therefore God's will for women. To remedy the situation, she undertook "to revise only those [biblical] texts and chapters directly referring to women, and those also in which women are made prominent by exclusion."[3]

Even though she was a principal organizer of the first Women's Rights Convention (1848) and president of the National Woman Suffrage Association (1869–90), Stanton found it difficult to persuade her fellow suffragists to write commentary for *The Woman's Bible*. Most of her suffragist colleagues chose to distance themselves from her project, believing that it would hurt support from the National Woman's Christian Temperance Union, most of whose members were evangelical Protestants committed to interpreting the Bible literally. Stanton, convinced of the merits of her venture, could persuade only seven women to collaborate with her on the first volume.

Elizabeth Cady Stanton
Courtesy of the National Portrait Gallery,
Washington, D.C. Art Resource, New York

At a time when most women in the suffrage movement were setting their sights exclusively on the right to vote, Stanton cast a critical eye on a broader "divinely ordained sphere" dictated for women on the basis of selected biblical texts. She believed that the secondary status of women involved far more than women's exclusion from voting. In her mind, the issues were all-encompassing. She was convinced that interpreting the Bible from their own perspective was important for women if they hoped to be truly and totally emancipated.

Stanton was especially critical of the ways in which the Bible spoke of marriage, making it what she called "a condition of bondage" for women.[4] She believed that Christians used certain biblical texts to promote women staying at home, thereby excluding them from the public sphere. Her caustic words challenged attitudes common at the time. She was highly critical of the "cult of true womanhood," which depicted the American woman as the provider of a tranquil home, set apart from the tensions and temptations of secular society. Woman's role could not be reduced to making a home where her husband could find cheer and comfort, and her children nurturance. Stanton grasped well the implications of woman being spoken of as the "ideal" human, for then men are the "real" humans, the real agents of progress in society.

Stanton's stance placed her in diametrical opposition to other suffrage leaders, such as Frances Willard, a temperance activist, who urged women to struggle for voting rights so that they could fulfill their duty as protectors of the sanctity of the home. Willard believed that voting women could influence government for its betterment, especially where its morality was concerned. Stanton believed that women needed not only to participate in the public arena as voters, but also to have access to the professions that were the preserve of men. Interestingly, most of the founding women of the second wave of the women's movement in the 1960s were or had been housewives who believed that the role of homemaker was far too limiting. They therefore sought positions that put them into the public realm.

After the first volume of *The Woman's Bible* was completed, the National Woman Suffrage Association passed a resolution at its 1896 convention disavowing any connection to it and to Stanton. This was a heavy price for her to pay for her convictions. Although many dismissed *The Woman's Bible* as irreligious, both volumes won a wide popular readership. The first volume had seven printings in six months, and later both volumes were translated into several languages.[5]

If evaluated against today's standards of biblical scholarship, *The Woman's Bible* has some serious shortcomings. Stanton's training in biblical studies was minimal. She had attended the Emma Willard Female Seminary in Troy, New York, graduating in 1832, but had no knowledge of biblical languages. It seems that this lack of knowledge was shared by her colleagues who contributed to *The Woman's Bible*.[6] This was a major problem, but we must be mindful that women in the nineteenth century were generally excluded from educational opportunities that would have enabled them to gain mastery of biblical Hebrew and Greek. Some specialized knowledge of the ancient languages would likely have resulted in a commentary of better quality. In addition, the method employed in writing the commentary had some shortcomings. In the preface of the first volume Stanton describes her methodology:

> Each person purchased two Bibles, ran through them from Genesis to Revelation, marking all texts that concerned women. The passages were cut out and pasted in a blank book, and the commentaries then written underneath.[7]

In their comments on the chosen texts, the authors attack both male bias and *****misogyny.** Unfortunately, at points they also uncritically repeat anti-Jewish stereotypes common in the United States at the turn of the twentieth century. Throughout, however, these women do not deny that the Bible presents truth. They accept God as a benevolent Creator concerned with the orderly operation of the world. This fundamental stance led them to believe that it was the will of God that women, like men, have liberty and pursue happiness. Any passages in the Bible that degrade and subordinate women are surely subject to divine judgment. The outcome is an uneven work, with some sections insightful, others regrettable, and a few even laughable.

Stanton and the women who worked with her were white, middle-class, Protestants from the United States and Great Britain. As a group, they did not represent very much diversity in life experience. They gave no thought to a broader inclusion of women of different races and classes. In addition, Stanton herself wrote most of the essays and did the final editing. Because of this, it is all the more appropriate that "woman" appears in the title rather than "women."

In spite of the many shortcomings of *The Woman's Bible,* no discussion of Christian feminist perspectives on the Bible would be complete without giving some attention to Stanton's project. Stanton paved the way for a reconstructionist feminist theology of the Bible, which would begin roughly three-quarters of a century later. Feminist biblical scholars, anticipating or marking the centenary of *The Woman's Bible,* published major works in its honor. The first, *The Women's Bible Commentary,* written by North American women from the Catholic, Protestant, and Jewish traditions (thus "women" in the title rather than "woman"), treats chosen texts from each book of the Bible from a feminist perspective.[8] The second, *Searching the Scriptures*, is a two-volume collection of essays of biblical research written by women from different parts of the world and represents the attention to diversity that characterizes the third wave of the women's movement.[9] Although the editors of these two volumes give *The Woman's Bible* mixed reviews, they acknowledge the debt owed to Stanton for calling women to read the Bible from the perspective of women's experience. Therefore, although the editors of these recent works do not regard *The Woman's Bible* to be a scholarly resource, they do honor its contribution to the woman's movement and feminist thought.

A Spectrum of Viewpoints on the Bible

A great deal of controversy surrounded *The Woman's Bible* after its publication. Controversy continues to swirl around feminist biblical scholarship today. How a person regards feminist biblical scholarship has a great deal to do with one's views of feminism. It also has a great deal to do with a person's own perspective on the Bible. Some people have read the Bible since they were small children, and know many of its texts well. Often, people who have some familiarity with the Bible know what they know not from academic study but from either communal worship or popular preaching, the two principal ways in which the biblical message has been handed down from generation to generation. Not all texts of the Bible are read at church services. Consequently, many people who are familiar with the Bible know certain texts far better than others. Some people look forward to particular liturgical seasons during which their favorite texts are read. Many know specific biblical stories by heart, or turn to familiar passages in times of distress and suffering and in times of joy and gratitude.

Some Christians believe that questioning critically any biblical text is inappropriate because it is "the Word of God." Among these Christians are those who believe that what is written in the Bible is totally beyond human reasoning, and is therefore to be accepted without question. For these people, the mere thought that anyone would actually cut up a Bible, even to write a commentary, is offensive. They are also likely to feel uncomfortable with modifications in translations of the Bible. Such people judge the inclusion of "woman" where only the generic term "man" appears in their English-language Bibles to be an arbitrary tampering with God's sacred Word.

Other Christians have thoughts and feelings about the Bible that are vastly different from the first group. Among these people are those who, without

AMERICAN CATHOLIC WOMEN AND THE BIBLE
AT THE TURN OF THE TWENTIETH CENTURY

During the long life of Elizabeth Cady Stanton, the population of the United States multiplied sevenfold, due largely to the arrival of millions of immigrants, many from traditionally Roman Catholic countries.[10] Most of the newly arrived Irish Catholic women found employment as domestics in the homes of wealthy Protestants. The newly arriving women from Southern and Eastern Europe who worked outside the home were usually hired in sweatshops and factories. Most of these women, because they were poor, had minimal education. There were a few Catholic women, such as Vassar-educated Lucy Burns (1879–1966), who were prominent in the suffrage movement, but most were more occupied with survival in a new country in which anti-Catholic Protestant *nativism often put them on the defensive.

The Roman Catholicism that the immigrant women brought with them was shaped by the *Council of Trent (1545–63), which reacted against the teachings of Martin Luther, whose emphasis on the Bible was expressed in his axiom *sola scriptura* — the Scriptures alone are the source of Christian faith. Luther and other Protestant reformers set about providing translations of the Bible in vernacular languages so that people could have access to the Bible. In contrast, the Roman Catholic Church made the Latin Vulgate version its official translation of the Bible. To guard against what the Roman Catholic hierarchy perceived to be erroneous teaching, dangerous to the faith of Catholic people, the study and interpretation of the Bible were limited to the clergy, or more specifically, in the words of Pope Leo XIII, to "the living and proper magisterium of the Church."[11]

During this era the Catholic hierarchy did not encourage the laity (which includes all women, since none are clergy) to read the Bible. Attendance at Mass, devotional prayer, and memorization of the *catechism were encouraged instead.

It was not until 1943, the same year in which Pope Pius XII called for Catholic scholars to use the modern methods of biblical criticism in their study of the Bible,[12] that the first Roman Catholic program of theology open to women was founded by Sister Madeleva Wolff, a Holy Cross sister, at St. Mary's College in South Bend, Indiana. These factors account for why Roman Catholic women were not actively engaged in a project on the Bible such as that undertaken by Elizabeth Cady Stanton.

In the years following the *Second Vatican Council, which closed in 1965, Roman Catholicism has become much more Bible conscious. The "Dogmatic Constitution on Divine Revelation" promoted Bible study among Catholics. It encouraged all Catholics to make reading the Bible and praying with it a part of their religious practices.

denying that the Bible is divine revelation, regard it to be a human record written by people in the distant past who were struggling with life issues and faith questions not totally dissimilar to their own. In this view, the Bible is also accepted as the Word of God, but a different meaning is invested in the term. They believe that human authors, influenced not only by God's guidance but also by their communities and cultures, shaped the biblical passages. These people turn to the Bible for inspiration, comfort, and instruction, but do not interpret the Bible literally. They are also not opposed to the inclusion of "woman" in translations that formerly excluded females.

Still others feel considerable ambivalence about what the Bible is, and why and how it was written. They are troubled about how women are treated in some biblical stories and laws, and the ways in which the Bible has been used to legitimate wrongs like slavery and the destructive exploitation of Earth's creatures. These people are searching for answers about the role of the Bible in their lives. There are also people who are simply indifferent where the Bible is concerned. Some in this group may regard the Bible to be merely a historical artifact from an earlier age. Its stories and teachings have relevance for their lives only insofar as the Bible has affected Western culture and its values.

Where one locates oneself on this spectrum of attitudes about the Bible has a lot to do with one's reluctance or willingness to accept feminist biblical scholarship. Since the range of viewpoints is so broad, the discussion of contemporary feminist perspectives here is preceded by addressing some basic preliminary questions: What is the Bible? Why are biblical translations important? In the responses to each question, feminist viewpoints are explored. These questions provide important groundwork for an exploration of feminist interpretation of key texts related to women.

What Is the Bible?

"Bible" is a word of Greek origin, *biblia,* which simply means "books." The Bible is not one book, but a collection. When *biblia* was translated into Latin, it became singular and remains a singular noun in its English rendering. In the ancient world at the time in which the Bible was composed, books were scrolls. Collected over a span of many centuries, the Bible was an evolving library of scrolls written in different languages — Hebrew, Aramaic, Greek, and others — and literary styles, all of which represent a variety of cultures and theological viewpoints. With the development of the codex, this library of religious texts could be bound together into one volume.

This straightforward answer to the question "What is the Bible?" does not begin to capture the Bible's complex nature and complicated history. Judaism and Christianity share some books of the Bible, while others are unique to Christianity. The part that they share is the Hebrew Scriptures that Judaism divides into twenty-four books. In this collection are found faith-filled stories of experiences and memories, prophetic admonitions, hymns of praise, wisdom sayings, and much more. The Hebrew name for this collection is the ***Tanakh,** an acronym drawn from the first letters of the Hebrew title for each of its three sections: Torah (Law),[13] Nebi'im (Prophets), and Ketubim (Writings). Although some events to which the Hebrew Bible refers may have occurred as early as 1750–1500 B.C.E., the religious leaders of the Jewish community did not decide what would be accepted into the Tanakh until near the end of the first century C.E.

This is the same time in which the Christian New Testament was being composed. All Christian groups agree about the composition of the New Testament. It consists of the ***Gospels, *Epistles** (also called Letters), Acts (the Lukan account of the early Christian movement), and Revelation (a book filled with ***apocalyptic** imagery).

Biblical Translations

The books later included in the Bible were being translated and edited even before the final decisions about its composition were made. The Bible continues to be translated. Since none of the original books or scrolls of the Bible is extant, the translations are from copies. Although painstakingly done, the hand copying of texts resulted in some variations creeping into the early manuscripts. This has contributed to textual corruptions and variations in translations. Also, every translation involves making word choices because no language is fully translatable into another. Most words have more than one meaning. The problem of translation is even more complex because the Bible is an ancient text written in different centuries, in different locales, and by different authors. When the biblical authors were writing the biblical texts, no dictionaries were available. Therefore, scholars doing translations of biblical texts must carefully examine patterns of word usage in their context to discern their meaning in a passage. Translations also must be updated almost constantly to incorporate new insights found by biblical philologists. Archaeologists also have made important discoveries that served as an impetus for new translations.

In addition, the modern languages into which the Bible has been translated have fluidity; meanings of words change over time. The Bible, therefore, has undergone many translations in the light of changes in the meanings invested in particular words. There are many issues at stake for feminists in translating the Bible. One is male-biased language that renders women invisible or introduces men where the original writers meant human beings collectively. It is important to keep in mind that Hebrew and Greek have different words for "man" (a male person) and for "human being" (males and females). In English, both words historically have been translated into the one word "man." The New Revised Standard Version (1989) distinguishes between the two. Wherever possible, it changes the generic use of "man" to an inclusive word such as "people," and changes masculine singular pronouns to plural pronouns — for example, "he" to "they." Other revised versions of the Bible, such as the Revised English Bible and the New American Bible, also reflect attention to this problem. Why? The answer is simple: women scholars participated in the translating and editing of these new editions and have drawn attention to this important problem, whereas a century ago, translation committees were comprised entirely of men.

BIBLICAL TRANSLATIONS

A good translation is not necessarily a literal translation, but one that perceptively renders meaning from one language to another in a way that is attuned to the life context of both. A comparison of translations of 1 Cor. 11:3 illustrates the extent to which every translation is an interpretation. A word-for-word literal translation from the Greek to English by Elisabeth Schüssler Fiorenza, a Catholic feminist biblical scholar with a long list of written contributions to feminist conversations about the Bible, reads,

> However, I want you [plural] to know that the head of every man is the Christ, however, a head of woman is the man, however, head of Christ is the God.[14]

This literal translation is awkward and unacceptable.

The New English Bible renders this verse in a way that is close to the literal translation, and yet overcomes its awkwardness:

> But I wish you to understand that while every man has Christ for his head, woman's head is man as Christ's head is God.

The Good News for Modern Man translates this passage in a way that makes it far more patriarchal in tone than the literal rendering:

> But I want you to understand that Christ is supreme over every man, the husband is supreme over his wife and God is supreme over Christ.

The New American Bible incorporates a marital relationship in its translation, as does the New Revised Standard Version:

> But I want you to know that Christ is the head of every man, and a husband the head of his wife, and God the head of Christ.

The New Revised Standard Version:

> But I want you to understand that Christ is the head of every man, and the husband is the head of his wife, and God is the head of Christ.

It is likely that "head" means "source" and does not connote a rank of authority. This is feasible because in 1 Cor. 11:8–9, the argument is developed in terms of source.[15] Thus, a possible translation is,

> But I want you to know that Christ is the source of every man, and a man is the source of woman, and God the source of Christ.

This translation is possible if Paul is speaking of the relationship of men and women on the basis of the story in Genesis 2 of the creation of Eve from the rib of ***Adam.**

Clearly, then, translating the Bible involves making judgments that are extraneous to the literal meaning of each word in a particular passage. Those extraneous judgments are affected by attitudes imbedded in the culture of the translators.

The translators of the New Revised Standard Version provide this rationale for the gender-inclusive rendering of "man":

> During the almost half a century since the publication of the RSV [Revised Standard Version], many in the churches have become sensitive to the danger of linguistic sexism arising from the inherent bias of the English language towards the masculine gender, a bias that in the case of the Bible has often restricted or obscured the meaning of the original text. The mandates from the Division [of Christian Education of the National Council of Churches] specified that, in reference to men and women, masculine-oriented language should be eliminated as far as this can be done without altering passages that reflect the historical situation of ancient patriarchal culture.[16]

The question of gender pronouns for God in English translations, however, is more problematic. Jews and Christians know that God has no gender; God does not have a bodily form. Nevertheless, the writers of biblical texts used the male form of the Hebrew and Greek pronouns when referring to God. These continue to be literally translated into English. Thus, we have God consistently called "he." We give this important problem attention in chapter 3.

Contemporary Feminists and the Bible

Some feminists who identify with the radical feminism addressed in chapter 1 reject the Bible for its androcentrism and its contributions to the persistence of patriarchy. For many in this group, the Bible is a hopelessly misogynist book that has been a cause of the subordination and oppression of women for centuries. Among these women are the revolutionary feminist theologians of Goddess movements (noted in chapter 1). Revolutionary feminists dismiss the Bible, yet, ironically, in doing so they also accept male interpretations of it and capitulate to the patriarchy that they vigorously protest. On the opposite end of the feminist spectrum are the reformists, who choose to maintain their commitment to the Bible by distinguishing between divine inspiration and human interpretation. Among these are Protestant evangelical feminists who believe that the Bible itself is liberating, but fault patriarchal interpretations of its texts.[17] There are also reconstructionist feminist theologians, like Elisabeth Schüssler Fiorenza, who argue that although the Bible originated in a patriarchal culture in antiquity, it has elements that are potentially liberating not only for women but also for any person experiencing oppression in patriarchal systems today.[18]

Reconstructionist feminist biblical scholars embrace a great variety of methodologies in interpreting biblical texts. As a result, there is considerable diversity in their theological writings. What they share in common is the commitment not only to expose the patriarchal biases in biblical texts and their traditional interpretations, but also to put forward constructive alternate interpretations that draw attention to liberating elements that have been ignored or overlooked. Written texts have a way of taking on a life of their own, apart from their authors' intentions. This is true for biblical texts as well, which is why feminist interpreters of the Bible can retrieve elements from these texts that are sources of liberation from patriarchy, even though these texts were formed in patriarchal cultures.

An important quality of the Bible is its variety of literary genres. It especially abounds in poetry and story. Since story is one of its most recognizable literary forms,[19] it is fitting to think of the formation of the Bible in terms of the process in which its many stories were formed. Focusing on the story element of the Bible is important for several reasons. As Phyllis Trible points out, "Stories are the style and substance of life. They fashion and fill existence."[20] People enter readily into and remember stories. In addition, in many ways the Bible is the unfolding story of people's relationship to God shared in communal settings in ways that attend to new experiences of God's self-disclosure.

The formation of the Bible as a story of a divine-human relationship is open to more than one explanation. Any reconstruction requires careful historical research about the chronology of biblical events that appear in biblical stories and a time line of the stories' editing and final writing. But this is not all. Imagination applied with empathy for the persons in the story and the story's writer is also important. An imaginative reconstruction is necessary because the biblical communities did not keep a record of the process that resulted in the collection of books in the Bible. To understand the formation of the Bible requires an analysis of the steps that contributed to the Bible as we know it today. A logical and helpful analysis, especially true for biblical stories, is to divide the process of the Bible's formation into four stages:

Stage 1. Insight into the divine-human relationship experienced as God's self-disclosure

Stage 2. Oral repetition of memories of these experiences shared in stories that were told and retold, sometimes for several generations

Stage 3. Writing the stories, gradually forming passages and editing them into book form

Stage 4. Acceptance of some books (and rejection of others) into the Bible by church authorities as being inspired by God's Spirit.

To assist us here in a feminist interpretation of these stages, feminist hermeneutical methodology, as explained by Schüssler Fiorenza, is used. Feminist hermeneutics refers to the theory, art, and practice of interpretation of biblical and other ancient extrabiblical texts in the interest of women.[21] Schüssler Fiorenza's purpose for developing feminist hermeneutics is to enable women to engage in the critical construction of religious meaning from the standpoint of women's experience, especially the experience of struggle against dehumanization and oppression. Among the strategies she proposes that are widely used by feminist biblical scholars are a "hermeneutics of suspicion" and a "hermeneutics of remembrance."[22] A feminist hermeneutics of suspicion is first and foremost a consciousness-raising activity that requires one to take into account the influence of culturally determined gender roles and attitudes on the Bible. It often also includes systemic analysis that seeks to uncover its causes in biblical society, church, and academy. Its starting point is the assumption that patriarchy deeply affects biblical texts and their interpretations in the Christian tradition.[23] Therefore, they must be examined for their possible androcentric assumptions and positions. This includes how biblical texts treat women in stories and laws, and neglect women's experiences completely. Hermeneutics of suspicion, therefore, is concerned not only with what is said about women but also with the silences.

Hermeneutics of suspicion is but one side of the feminist interpretative coin; a hermeneutics of remembrance is the other side. The two belong together. Hermeneutics of suspicion is in service of a feminist hermeneutics of remembrance. Feminist hermeneutics is not satisfied with unmasking patriarchy because it causes human suffering. A hermeneutics of remembrance reclaims the past suffering of women and of all persons subjugated through enslavement, exile, and persecution, and treats it as a "dangerous memory," one that invites us today to solidarity with all persons past and present who struggle for human dignity. Many of its memories are also "subversive" because even in the midst of crisis, biblical figures of the distant past found in their relationship with God reasons for hope and reasons to be agents for liberation.[24] In short, a hermeneutics of remembrance does not negate the dehumanizing effects of patriarchy on biblical history, but neither does it give that the final and definitive word. The Bible and many extrabiblical sources that are contemporaneous with it provide rich resources for constructing a theology for our time that heals suffering and liberates from struggle.

Feminist Hermeneutics and the Bible's Formation

An application of a feminist hermeneutics to the lengthy process of the Bible's formation seeks first of all to use a hermeneutics of suspicion to unveil the underlying effects of patriarchy and account for the androcentrism in many biblical texts. In the treatment of the four stages of the Bible's formation, a hermeneutics of remembrance also comes into play, but is less evident. It features more strongly in feminist interpretations of specific biblical texts.

Stage One: Experiences of God's Self-Disclosure

The first stage underlying the written Bible as we know it today is people having experiences, usually personally transformative ones, in which the presence of God was manifested to them in some memorable way. Rudolf Otto, in his highly regarded study of religious experience, suggests that the origin of religious stories (myths) is people's apprehension of the numinous, an inexplicable experience of divine presence that evokes feelings of awe.[25] Biblical stories often include memories of events that persons interpreted as revelatory of God, as unveiling something of significance for their relationship with God that had previously been hidden. From these experiences some special sense of God and

---

FEMINIST BIBLICAL HERMENEUTICS

The word hermeneutic comes from "Hermes," the messenger of the ancient Greek gods. Today, hermeneutics refers to theories of interpretation of anything that might be the material for study, from body language to ancient texts. Feminist biblical hermeneutics specifically focuses on biblical texts and on ancient writings not accepted into the Bible. Contemporary hermeneutical theory presumes that new understandings, not only of the text but also of its reader, emerge through a reader's encounter with a text. Hermeneutical method accounts for its conclusions about texts, such as those found in the Bible, on the basis of reasonable hypotheses and logical arguments. Persons engaging in hermeneutics also employ the use of imagination to discover the possible meanings and applications of texts in people's lives.

These generalized qualities of hermeneutics are further specified in feminist hermeneutics by making women (1) the subjects of interpretation, and (2) the constructors of religious meaning. The first is important not only because of the extensive institutionalized silencing of women in biblical religions, but also because it is vital that women, and not male attitudes about women, be central. The second brings the interest of women, especially the desire for liberation from all manifestations of patriarchy that dehumanize women and men, to bear on the interpretation of biblical and extrabiblical ancient texts.

In *Bread Not Stone,* Elisabeth Schüssler Fiorenza explains why she uses the technical term "hermeneutics" in her speaking and writing. After one of her public lectures, some men in the audience counseled her against using such difficult theological terms, because "women do not have the sophistication to understand them."[26] Schüssler Fiorenza adamantly disagrees with this assessment of women's intelligence (as do I). There is so much to be gained by women, and by men as well, in the use of hermeneutics when reading the Bible.

---

some memorable insights into God were gained when the persons involved reflected on them and shared them with others. For some people who live in a highly scientific and technological society, experiences of God are difficult to talk about. Yet, people today do speak of sometimes having a sense of God's nearness and of experiencing God's unconditional love in the midst of other life experiences. Such persons are attuned to recognizing the presence of God in the midst of the events of life.

In the **Old Testament,* stories of revelatory moments are most often associated with leaders such as Abraham, Moses, David, and Solomon, and prophets such as Amos, Hosea, and Jeremiah — all males. In the New Testament, the Gospel stories focus on Jesus, who, although proclaimed by the early Christians to be divine and therefore not subject to the limitations of humanity, is embodied

as a first-century Nazarene male. Also, Gospel stories feature more men, especially Jesus' male ***disciples,** than women. A feminist hermeneutics of suspicion
raises this question: Does the predominance of males in biblical stories mean
that women are less able to experience God in their lives than men, or is this
predominance due to the patriarchal nature of the ancient Middle Eastern societies in which these communal memories of God's self-disclosure were formed
and shared? A feminist hermeneutics of suspicion holds that the dominance of
the presence of males in biblical stories is the result of cultural factors that are
part of the deeply embedded patriarchal structure of biblical societies, not the
inability of women to have relationships with God and to recognize the presence
of God in their lives. A hermeneutics of remembrance is therefore drawn upon
to look behind the stories about men's experiences of God, told by men, in order
to unveil women's experience in the unrecorded silences.

Stage Two: Oral Repetition of Communal Stories

Before any text incorporated into the Bible was written, it was passed along
orally. In the case of the Old Testament this oral process lasted for generations,
in some cases possibly even for hundreds of years. Stories were told and retold
in communal settings. Some of these stories may have been related in slave
quarters as people shared their longings for freedom. Others emerged during
a long trek across a desert as people defined themselves and their relationship
with God in the midst of a common struggle to find their way. Stories were also
formed during times of exile as people grappled with the impact of slavery in a
foreign land by trying to keep their hope for freedom alive. Before the Gospels
of the New Testament were written, memories about Jesus were shared orally as
his followers traveled extensively to proclaim the good news he had revealed.

Many interpretative reflections on experiences revelatory of God became special, identity-forming memories for Jews and/or Christians — for example, the
Passover in Exodus or Jesus' crucifixion in the four Gospels. Narratives such as
these reaffirmed the communal identities of the people hearing them. A feminist
hermeneutics of suspicion might raise the question, What role did women of the
Jewish and Christian communities play in the creation of the communal memory? Reconstructing what role, if any, is difficult. Did women have any input
into the oral stage of the formation of the Old and New Testaments? In forming the basic story line of the book of Exodus, for example, it is likely that the
communal reflection on these identity-forming experiences took place around
campfires in the evening. The oral recitation of these stories continued for many
generations. While the men were gathered at the campfires at night, were women
also there, sharing in the storytelling? It is not likely. They were probably busy
readying the tents for sleep and putting their young children down for the night.
One can only speculate about whether or not the bedtime stories they told in the
tents to their daughters and sons had any relationship to the stories men shared
around the fires outside.

We must consider this likely pattern because the life of the community was
ordered not only by the content of the stories but also by who told them. They

regarded the very activity of retelling stories as revealing the way things are in God's plan for the universe. But in reality, what stories were told and who told them reflects the patriarchal structure and androcentric attitudes of the societies in which these stories became the communal memory. As a result, the experiences of men were usually given a position of privilege in the communal memory, while the experiences of women are downplayed or ignored.

Stage Three: Writing and Editing

After some time, one or more writers wrote down these oral stories, often at a time far removed from the original experiences. In a sense, the written texts are the result of the stories of the revelatory moments being filtered through the matrix of the oral stage of repetition and the present-day experience of the communities for which the authors were writing. Just as we interpret the events in our past in the light of our present situation, the writers interpreted the oral stories handed on to them in ways that responded to questions and concerns in their own communities at the time they were writing. Gradually, these stories were integrated with other stories and wisdom sayings, with poetry and hymns sung at liturgical services, and with collections of prescriptive teachings and laws. Sometimes these texts were subsequently edited to incorporate additional oral and written traditions. Over time, books were formed. Identifying with any precision the writer or writers of a particular book of the Bible is therefore impossible. Since there are few Jewish or Christian texts known to have been written by women before the modern period, most likely the quills used for the actual writing of the sacred texts were in the hands of men, not women. Although we cannot simply equate male authorship with patriarchal suppression of women, the fact that women could not have taken pen in hand to write the books of the Bible reflects the patriarchal influences and androcentric biases on those who wrote the biblical texts. This application of a feminist hermeneutics of suspicion draws attention to the fact that the principal actors, preservers of communal memories, and writers were men, most of whom occupied positions of privilege in patriarchal societies. But not only were the writers of the books of the Bible male, so also were those who decided which books were included in the Bible. This brings us to the fourth stage in the formation of the Bible, the decisions about what would be included in the biblical *canon.

Stage Four: The Biblical Canon

The formation of the Bible, the official list of books known as the canon, has long been an emotionally charged issue that impels people to consider related questions about the inspiration of the Holy Spirit and biblical authority. We can trace the beginnings of the canon of the Christian Bible to the early Christian communities' consensus about which sayings of Jesus and which stories about his mission, ministry, crucifixion, and resurrection should be preserved. Although the books that would become regarded as authoritative were written by the end of the first decade of the first century C.E., debates about what books were worthy of canonicity continued well into the fourth century, at which time the New Testament canon was closed.

The canon of the Old Testament is a far more complex issue. The nascent Christian communities accepted the Jewish Scriptures, but since most members were Greek-speaking, they used the Greek language collection of the Jews' holy books known as the *Septuagint. Christians, however, could not fully agree on which books to include in the Old Testament canon. Eastern and Western churches used different lists. Much later, during the Reformation, Martin Luther's preference for the Hebrew Testament over the Greek Septuagint led to further divergence. He decided that only the texts available (the Tanakh) should be accepted into his reformed Christian Bible. As a result of these differences of opinion, to the present day there is no universal agreement about the composition of the Christian biblical canon. The *Apocrypha, books then available only in Greek, were gathered by Luther as inappropriate for the canon but profitable for reading. Roman Catholics decided to retain these books in their canon, as did the Eastern Orthodox, who also included additional books of Jewish-Christian antiquity.

From the perspective of feminist biblical scholarship, why is this information about the composition and history of the biblical canon important? For one thing, it makes the depiction of the Bible as resulting from God directly breaking into earthly history and dictating messages to specially chosen emissaries all the more unreasonable. The biblical canon resulted from a lengthy and complex human process. If one searches the Scriptures for the words of God, one finds the words of humans. Were they words from religiously committed persons? Yes, but they were human nonetheless. In the books accepted into the biblical canon there are inspiring stories, words of peace and consolation, and poems with beautiful imagery. We also find stories of war and murder, of violence directed against women, and of rape. Among the psalms are those that call for vengeance against one's enemies and even brutality directed against the enemies' children.

What is at stake in the decisions about the composition of the canon emerges in sharp relief when one reflects on the power that the Bible has had as a source for the liturgical and moral life of Jewish and Christian communities for thousands of years. For these communities, readings from the Bible, and prayers and hymns based on its texts, have been the source of religious identity. The canonical status of a biblical book has meant that its texts became the standard or norm for other theological writings and teachings. Many passages in the biblical books, as well as the theologies that draw on them, have supported the inferiority of women to men on the grounds that this is God's plan. Arguments for women's subordination on biblical grounds have also further strengthened patriarchal patterns in the social, political, and economic realms. And yet, this is not all that the Bible does. Where women are concerned the Bible also has a positive side. It contains rich memories of consolation and empowerment. Its message certifies that suffering is not of God. Its dangerous and subversive memories motivate women and men to come together to promote social change for the poor and oppressed.

The history of the biblical canon's formation shows that not all of the early texts available in the Jewish and Christian communities were accepted as authoritative. Books like the *Gospel of Mary,* the *Gospel of Thomas,* the *Protevangelium of James* (also known as the *Nativity of Mary*), and the *Acts of Paul and Thecla* were excluded. These writings, and others as well, may also have strong claims to authority but were not given canonical status by the Christian hierarchy. It is sometimes difficult to determine why individual books were judged canonical and others were not. What criteria were used and by whom? Because the answer to this question is not clear, a new controversy has arisen regarding the biblical canon. This controversy was raised not by the institutional leadership of the Roman Catholic and Protestant churches, as in the past, but by Roman Catholic and Protestant feminist scholars who propose criteria that incorporate an explicit feminist perspective.

An important criterion for the biblical canon proposed by feminists has already been noted in the introduction of reconstructionist Christian feminist theology in chapter 1. That criterion is rooted in the principle that the Word of God both liberates and empowers people with freeing truth. When this principle is applied to the biblical canon, it follows that if a biblical text fails to liberate women (and subjugated men) from patriarchy to the fullness of life, then it must not be true or has been misinterpreted (cf. John 8:32). One of the feminist theologians responsible for this criterion is Elisabeth Schüssler Fiorenza. She has applied it to the question of how the biblical canon and divine inspiration can be appropriately understood. In her book *In Memory of Her* she stresses that the biblical canon, long held by the Christian tradition to be the sacred collection of books inspired by the Holy Spirit, must be distinguished from the living inspiration of the Spirit who gives life. In her reconstruction of divine inspiration as traditionally applied to the biblical canon, Schüssler Fiorenza applies a hermeneutics of suspicion to how the Holy Spirit's inspiration has been directly connected to the existing biblical canon. She argues that the inspiration associated with the work of the Holy Spirit does not reside directly in the specific collection of books, compiled gradually centuries ago and declared by male church authorities to be inspired. The Holy Spirit's inspiration resides primarily in communities of faithful persons who engage in individual and collective discernment of the Spirit's presence and absence.[27] It is in this communal discernment that the inspiration of the Spirit is experienced. Consequently, the meaning of the canon as the measure of divine inspiration should be reconstructed in a way that honors the freeing truth of Jesus Christ's message with its call to act in solidarity with others to end the oppression of women and subjugated men. The Christian community is not well served by limiting the inspired canon to the limited library of texts we know as the Christian Bible.

One might ask, Is Schüssler Fiorenza proposing that feminists abandon the biblical canon all together? The answer is no. Although some of the texts of the Bible do bear the marks of patriarchy and do promote androcentric thinking and values, the biblical heritage also provides inspiration for women and men in the struggle to overthrow these dehumanizing things. It is in this heritage, the heritage that liberates, that the Holy Spirit's inspiration is to be found.

ELISABETH SCHÜSSLER FIORENZA

A key contributor to feminist theology, especially biblical hermeneutics, Elisabeth Schüssler Fiorenza is a German-born, American Catholic scholar who was the first woman in Würzburg, Germany, to complete the full academic program in theology that male students for the priesthood were required to take. The year was 1962. She was also the first woman president of the Society of Biblical Literature in 1987. She has spent most of her academic career in North American institutions, teaching at the University of Notre Dame, the Episcopal Divinity School in Cambridge, Massachusetts, and at the Harvard Divinity School, where she is the Krister Stendahl Professor of Divinity. To date, she is best known for her groundbreaking book *In Memory of Her: A Feminist Reconstruction of Christian Origins* (1983). She has written at least eight other books and edited several more. She is the co-editor of the *Journal of Feminist Studies in Religion* and an editor of *Concilium,* an international journal. She is married to Francis Schüssler Fiorenza, also a professor at the Harvard Divinity School, and the mother of one daughter, Christina.

From the time of the appearance of her first book in German in 1964, one of the major focuses of her work has been on women in the church. In this book she sought to reflect on her own experience as a laywoman in the Catholic Church. Since that time she has consistently argued for a reformulation of *ecclesiology that would give proper attention to the ministry women have done and are doing in the church.

In her writings she has taken the stance of a critical historian. She has developed and applied feminist hermeneutical theory to biblical sources and ancient texts of the biblical period. In all of her writings critical appraisal of cultural understandings of gender and the role of patriarchy in all facets of church and civil life feature strongly. Throughout her career she has been critical of a male-dominated academy that has marginalized women and the contributions of women to the history of Christianity. Therefore, she not only is committed to recovering the voices of women in Scripture and the Christian tradition from the silence of neglect, but also actively encourages women to continue this type of work as theologians.

She therefore entreats feminists to engage in a consensus-building process about appropriate sources for their theology and to derive their own canon from the biblical heritage, one that inspires liberation from oppression and affirms an authentic discipleship of equals.[28] In the case of passages inimical to women and dehumanizing of men, such texts should be abandoned. She further stresses in *Bread Not Stone* that "the [official biblical] canon [of particular Christian churches] should not be viewed as negative judgment [excluding] all of the other early writings that were not included" in the Bible.[29] Ancient texts of the biblical period not incorporated into the official biblical canon can also be authentic resources for a feminist canon if they express a message of freeing truth that is of God.

How will one recognize this freeing truth? Schüssler Fiorenza's emphasis on a biblical heritage that liberates is related to a position on divine revelation expressed by the Roman Catholic Church at the Second Vatican Council that states that the Bible is given by God "for the sake of... salvation."[30] In her emphasis on a canon that features liberation she presents an understanding of salvation not limited to life with God in heavenly bliss after death, as it has sometimes been narrowly conceived, but rather that envisions salvation oriented to concrete actions that embody Christ's freeing and saving message on Earth now.[31]

Addressing the authority of the canon, another feminist biblical scholar, Letty Russell, a Protestant, stresses, like Schüssler Fiorenza, that divinely inspired revelation is not identical with the collection of books found in the Christian canon. While not denying that patriarchal views deeply affect the Bible, she points out that the Bible also presents "a story of God's love affair with the world," which leads her to "a vision of New Creation that impels her life."[32] Therein lies its authority. She astutely draws attention to the importance of how a person views authority when addressing questions about the authority of the Bible. Patriarchy, with its hierarchically ordered perspective on reality, envisions authority as dominance. In this perspective the Bible too easily becomes a means for church leadership to exert power over individuals in the community, promoting compliance to a certain position or rule. In contrast, in the feminist perspective, authentic authority is partnership. It is exercised in, not over, community, especially "in service of building a community of human wholeness that is inclusive of women and men."[33] The inclusive community of human wholeness is what she means by "the New Creation" that is of Christ. Whatever denies this intention, which she believes is God's, does not compel assent.

In company with Elisabeth Schüssler Fiorenza and Letty Russell,[34] a growing number of feminist theologians are proposing a reconceptualization of the canon and biblical authority. They argue that texts do not have authority independent of faith communities committed to and struggling for the full humanity of women, and also of men subjugated by patriarchy.

Feminist Hermeneutics Applied to Biblical Passages

Since the nineteenth century a major trend among biblical scholars has been to engage biblical passages by doing research into the historical situations in which biblical texts were written and by attending to their literary genres. Knowing something about how biblical texts were written, for whom they were written, and why they were written in a particular literary style can help one to discern the text's message.

Feminist hermeneutics differs from traditional historical criticism on several scores. One is the claim that historical criticism is objective and value-neutral research. When it was first developed, in the nineteenth century, historical criticism was deeply affected by the rationality associated with the natural sciences. Like the science of that era, it claimed to be objective and value-neutral. Also like the scientists, most of the biblical scholars were white, First World, educated men. The claim to value-neutrality in historical biblical research ignored the influence of cultural attitudes about gender that privileges those men over women and over most men of color.

The application of a feminist hermeneutics of suspicion to the claim that an interpretation of the Bible can be objective and value-neutral results in the judgment that this is an illusion. The dynamics of human understanding and the fact that personal experiences influenced by cultural attitudes affect the understanding of any text indicate that no type of biblical interpretation can be completely objective and value-neutral. A feminist hermeneutics of suspicion recognizes that interpreting the Bible is unavoidably influenced by human subjectivity. Persons engaged in biblical interpretation bring their conscious concerns and unconscious biases to the activity of interpreting biblical texts. This is evident both in the questions interpreters bring to biblical passages and in the use of their imaginations in formulating conclusions from the information available. For reconstructionist feminist biblical scholars, whether their goals reflect second-wave or third-wave feminist concerns, the foremost conscious interest is advocacy for women.

As already noted, feminist hermeneutics is possible because the Bible and the history of its interpretation are more than a product of patriarchy. The Bible has long functioned to inspire and authorize women and men in their daily lives. Biblical interpretation can, and many reconstructionist feminists would perhaps add the word "should," serve as a resource for the construction of religious meaning and empowerment. This is where a feminist hermeneutics of remembrance comes into play when interpreting Scripture.

For many feminist biblical scholars, a hermeneutics of remembrance applied to biblical passages is an activity comparable to that of the woman in the parable in Luke's Gospel who sweeps the whole house in search of a lost coin and shares her joy with her neighbors when she finds it (Luke 15:8–10). Encompassing two related activities, a feminist hermeneutics of remembrance engages in (1) sweeping the house of biblical history in the search for the "lost coins" of a "useable past" for women in the Bible, and (2) celebrating the recovery of the "coins" that are liberating for women and other oppressed persons. We gave attention to the feminist search for "a useable past," for a "her-story" that has gone unnoticed in the prevailing "his-story" in chapter 1 in conjunction with the work of Christine de Pizan. A feminist hermeneutics of remembrance engages in the search for a "useable past" by probing the Bible for texts that depict women in roles uncommon for females in the culture of the ancient Near East. It draws attention to women, most of whom have been given very little attention in the long history of the Christian tradition, who made a significant difference in the unfolding story of Israel or of the early Christian movement. It searches the Bible for traces and fragments of women's stories and recovers the "faint echoes" of women's voices from the historical silences that have rendered them mute or, at best, unnoticed in the margins of history.[35] The stories and faint echoes of women provide far more than interesting trivia about women long since dead. Remembering these women and their stories is an activity that empowers women for their own liberation in the present.

A hermeneutics of remembrance also seeks to retrieve from biblical texts interpretations that have been overlooked or distorted by patriarchal patterns of interpretation. Scholars engaged in this second form of feminist hermeneutics of remembrance attempt to uncover countercultural understandings that are good news for the oppressed. Schüssler Fiorenza describes this second activity as reading "against the grain."[36] This entails interpreting biblical texts in ways that subvert the prevailing androcentric interpretations. This form of hermeneutics of remembrance requires a close reading of biblical texts with an eye for discovering those things that provide women and other oppressed persons with a basis for hope in the midst of their struggle for liberation.

Attention to the narrative framework of the Bible, the recognition that interpretations of biblical texts are never objective and value-neutral, interest in the role that readers' experiences play in interpreting biblical texts, and the search for the stories of women and of biblical meanings liberating for women and other oppressed persons have resulted in feminist biblical scholars' use of a hermeneutics of suspicion and a hermeneutics of remembrance, even if these terms never explicitly appear in their scholarship. Feminist biblical scholarship began with a hermeneutics of suspicion aimed at exposing the androcentric biases and patriarchal intentions operative within the Bible because these continue to contribute to the subjugation of women and of certain groups of men who are the recipients of racial or ethnic prejudice. This important exercise has paved the way for a hermeneutics of remembrance in which attention is given to how the roles of women, and of racial and ethnic minorities, have often been ignored, hidden, or misrepresented by patriarchal hermeneutics. Reconstructionist feminist scholars often propose an alternative rereading of these texts, a reconstructed meaning, by employing a variety of forms of literary analysis. These hermeneutical strategies have proven to be empowering for women and are giving women spiritual sustenance for their work of liberation today.

Women and the Bible

When I ask my students to list the women in the Bible and provide a brief sketch of their stories, nearly all of them recall Eve (the first woman, whom they describe as the one who brought sin into the world) and Mary (the mother of Jesus, who remained a virgin). A lesser number will have ***Mary Magdalene** (whom they will usually identify as the repentant prostitute who followed Jesus to the cross) and perhaps Sarah (the woman who bore Abraham a son in her old age) on their lists. Very few will know of Miriam, Rachel, Deborah, Judith, Ruth, and the other women in the Old Testament. Some will nod in recognition when Martha and her sister Mary (close friends of Jesus) are mentioned. Usually none will recognize Lydia, Priscilla (Prisca), or Thecla. Why is the knowledge of biblical women so scanty? Could it be due to patriarchal attitudes that have contributed to the neglect of women in liturgical readings and in religious instructions? This is a likely reason. To remedy the scant knowledge of women in the Bible and of texts about women, feminist biblical scholars are delving into these areas of biblical research with fruitful results.

Euro-American Feminist Biblical Scholarship

A Reconstruction of Eve's Story

We will begin our exploration of Euro-American biblical scholarship with the first woman to appear in the Bible, Eve. It is appropriate to begin with Eve, not only because she is the first woman in the Old Testament, but also because no biblical woman, except perhaps Mary the mother of Jesus, has been more of an object of patriarchal attention than she. So many people recognize Eve's name because hers is one of the first biblical stories they heard as children. On the surface, her story is a simple one. She is the first woman, made by God from the rib of the first man. She listened to a serpent, yielded to temptation, and compounded her sin by tempting her husband. The wages of Eve's and Adam's sin is death.

Phyllis Trible, a Protestant feminist biblical scholar, developed an interpretation of the Eve passage, Genesis 2–3, that went "against the grain" in the late 1970s. In many respects her interpretation of Eve's story reflects second-wave feminist goals of critiquing unchallenged patriarchal interpretations to affirm gender equality. Her interpretation of Genesis 2–3 is included in this chapter, even though it is over twenty years old, because it is widely regarded as a classic among feminist scholars, even by those who are not in full agreement with it. What it illustrates is not only a thoroughgoing application of a hermeneutics of suspicion and remembrance to a text familiar to many, but also an early example of feminist rhetorical theology. "Rhetorical" is an appropriate word to describe Trible's theological project, because she pays attention to the kinds of effects that a biblical passage and its interpretations can produce, and proposes artfully, and with considerable passion, a reconstructed alternative that seeks to convince the reader of her position.

Part of Trible's rhetorical strategy is to stress that the Adam and Eve story must be addressed by feminists because the misogynous interpretations of it over the centuries had acquired a status of canonicity and unchallenged respectability.[37] Misogyny is only one item on her list of commonly held beliefs derived from what, in her judgment, are thoroughly faulty interpretations of Genesis 2–3:

- A male God creates man first (2:7) and woman last (2:22); first means superior and last means inferior or subordinate; men are superior to women in God's scheme of things.

- Woman is created for the sake of man, a helpmate to cure his loneliness (2:18–23).

- Woman is created from the rib of man, forever dependent on him (2:21–22).

- Taken from man (2:23), woman has a derivative and not an autonomous existence.

- Man names woman (2:23) and thus has power over her.

- Woman tempted man; she is responsible for sin in the world (3:6); she is untrustworthy, gullible, and simpleminded.

- Woman is cursed by pain in childbirth for her sin (3:16).

- Man has the right, given to him by God, to rule over woman (3:16).[38]

All of these interpretations of Genesis 2–3, inaccurate in Trible's assessment, have been used to assert male superiority and female inferiority as God's will. Many Christians would find them among the familiar reasons for the subordination of women. Feminists who are post-Christian cite them as reasons for deciding to leave their churches.

Trible, in order to forge a reclamation of Eve, directs a thoroughgoing hermeneutics of suspicion to the traditional interpretations of Genesis 2–3. Scholars who use historical-critical methods of biblical interpretation agree that Gen. 2:4b–3:24 is a very ancient text — part of a tradition that possibly can be traced to the time of Kings David or Solomon (ca. 1000–950 B.C.E.). The narrative is at one and the same time a story of creation and an explanatory myth, or *etiology, responding to questions such as why people get married, why women have pain at childbirth, and why serpents lack legs. Knowing the probable historical context in which this text was written and the type of literature it represents is a helpful corrective to simplistic literal interpretations, but this information does not take one very far in remedying the many faulty interpretations of Genesis 2–3 that Trible has highlighted — interpretations that have been used for centuries to oppress women.

Trible combines a hermeneutics of suspicion and a hermeneutics of remembrance in her careful reconstruction of Eve's story. She engages in a literary analysis that is a close reading of Gen. 2:4b–3:24 by giving the words and themes careful attention. Focusing on Gen. 2:7, commonly translated "and then God formed man of dust from the earth and breathed into his nostrils a breath of life, and thus man became a living being," Trible draws attention to the Hebrew words 'ādām and hā-'adāmâ, translated in English-language Bibles respectively as "man" and "the earth." She argues that the familiar rendering of the first of these terms as "man" or "Adam" has unnecessarily contributed to patriarchal gender stereotypes of male superiority over females.

She points out that from the Hebrew it is easy to perceive that there is a word play on *hā-'ādām* and *hā-'adāmâ*. The Hebrew *hā* is simply the definite article. Its use indicates that we are dealing with nouns, not proper names. Therefore, "Adam" is inaccurate: the translation should read "the creature from the earth" or "the earth creature."[39] The translation of Gen. 2:7 should be,

> Then ***Yahweh** God formed the earth creature [*hā-'ādām*] of dust from the earth [*hā-'adāmâ*]. . . .[40]

The earth creature is neither a particular male person nor a typical human person, but is a combination of dust and the breath of God! This now breathing creature, formed from the earth, is alive but not yet complete. It is sexually undifferentiated at this stage; for this reason the pronoun "it" and not "he" is appropriate. The point Trible is making is that the creation of the human in Genesis 2 is a multistage process and not an instantaneous accomplishment. As the story unfolds, God draws attention to the incompleteness of the earth creature. God tries to make up for what is lacking by creating animals, but they prove to be unsuitable partners. So, from this sexually undifferentiated earth creature God creates two, who will be suitable companions for one another.

The word "companion" is her preferred translation of the Hebrew word *'ēzer* (Gen. 2:18) for good reason. She points out that *'ēzer* is usually translated into English as "helper." Still, the word "helper" suggests "assistant," and lends itself to the argument that women are created to help men and are therefore their subordinates. She points out that *'ēzer* is also used in the Old Testament in reference to God, who is the "helper" of Israel. God, however, is certainly not subordinate to humans! Thus, *'ēzer* is a relational term designating a beneficial relationship; "companion" captures this sense without a hint of subordination. She believes that her word choice is supported by the accompanying Hebrew phrase *k^enegdô*, "corresponding to itself."[41] Inferiority of women is neither asserted nor implied when mutual correspondence is included. Therefore, Trible believes that her translation of *'ēzer* as "companion" captures the notion that the woman is a true counterpart to the man, corresponding in every way to him as another fully human creature of God.

The divine act of creating a corresponding companion for the earth creature forever alters its nature. For, rather than make a companion from the dust of the earth, God makes the companion out of the earth creature's rib. God creates the woman by putting the earth creature into a deep sleep. God acts as a surgeon, removing a rib and building it into a woman. The androgynous earth creature, who will become a man as a result, has no active part in making the woman. He is not an active agent in her creation any more than he is in his own creation. Both the male and the female originate from God's agency.

The creature made from the rib will be called woman (*'ishah*) because from man (*'ish*) she was taken (Gen. 2:23). Trible argues that the creation of woman is a second full creation story that is necessary to the completion of the creation of the human species. Through God's activity of fashioning a creature from the first earth creature, *hā-'ādām* becomes male (*'ish*) and female (*'ishah*). The words *'ishah* and *'ish* distinguish them, but their creation is simultaneous, not sequential. Man does not precede woman in time or rank. Trible asserts,

> In the very act of distinguishing female from male, the earth creature describes her as "bone of my bones and flesh of my flesh" (Gen. 2:23). These words speak unity, solidarity, mutuality and equality. Accordingly, in this poem the man does not depict himself as either prior to or superior to the woman. His sexual identity depends on her even as hers depends upon him. For both of them sexuality originates in the one flesh of humanity.[42]

The story developed in Genesis 2:4b–23 interpreted with the help of Trible's close literary reading corrects the first four of the faulty interpretations listed above and provides a response to Elizabeth Cady Stanton's critical appraisal of the Bible's teaching on women: "woman was made after man, of man and for man, an inferior being, subject to man."[43] But it also does much more. It supplies a clear basis for a response to Stanton's negative appraisal of biblical teaching on marriage as female bondage. Marriage in Genesis 2 is not a relationship of bondage. It is partnership. The man and woman created by God from the unfinished earth creature are made to be corresponding companions. Human sexuality makes possible the experience of mutuality that the androgynous earth creature can never know in its relationship with the plants and animals in the garden. The creation of human sexuality represents the high point of the story. It signals the movement from isolation and loneliness to companionship and partnership. This is confirmed in the exclamation placed on the lips of the first male: "This one [the first female] at last is bone of my bones, flesh of my flesh" (Gen. 2:23). Sexual differentiation is for human partnership. The potential for intimate partnership is the primordial creative act of God.

Trible's hermeneutics of suspicion extends to other faulty interpretations of this passage that have contributed to women's subordination. None is more significant than the entrance of sin into the story of the first humans. Perhaps chapter 3 of Genesis was added because people recognized that the partnership, the mutually corresponding companionship, expressed in the final verses of chapter 2, was not their lived reality.

Trible's close reading of Genesis 3 draws attention to the entrance of a talking serpent in the story and the dialogue between the serpent and the woman that ensues. The interchange is about God and the directive given to the sexually undifferentiated earth creature that forbade the eating of the fruit of one of the trees in the garden. The woman acts as the spokesperson for what God requires of her and her husband. Contrary to the way in which Eve has usually been depicted, she is not dependent and passive, but rather, independent and articulate. In the conversation with Eve, the serpent challenges the logic of not eating of the tree. In the words of Trible, "The woman, then, finds the tree physically appealing, aesthetically pleasing, and, above all, sapientially transforming."[44] Three actions follow: she takes the fruit, eats it, and gives some to her husband.

Trible points out that the man, apparently there all along, remains silent. He does not speak up on behalf of obedience to the divine directive; rather, he passively accepts and eats what the woman gives him (Gen. 3:6).[45] The change in the woman and the man centers on comfort in being naked in each other's presence before they eat the fruit and shame after they eat it. At this point, God enters the garden and interrogates the pair. Trible argues that the man makes it clear that the woman God gave him was the one who gave him the fruit (Gen. 3:12). It is she who tempted him. The woman accepts responsibility for her actions after noting that it was the serpent who beguiled her (Gen. 3:13). Trible reflects, "By betraying the woman to God, the man opposed himself to her; by ignoring him in her reply to God, the woman separates herself from the man."[46] Their behavior is not due to pride, as Augustine, an early Western Christian theologian, argued. Rather, it is an expression of shattered partnership. The once mutual companionship of the pair is replaced with separation, not only from each other, but also from the other creatures of the garden. God pronounces judgment on the serpent and on them. The serpent, God curses (Gen. 3:14–15). The woman, God punishes with pain in childbearing. Of special concern are the words directed to the woman, telling her that although she will yearn for unity with her husband — the unity she first experienced at the time of their creation — he will not reciprocate her desire. Her husband will rule over her (Gen. 3:16). Trible argues that this statement is not a divine legitimation of male superiority, but rather, is condemnation because it results from sin. Through her misguided choice the woman has become property of her husband, similar to a slave. The man is corrupted also, for he has become master of his God-given equal. Where once there was mutuality in companionship, now there is a hierarchy of division.[47] God promises that man will work for his food, and his labor will not be easy.

At the time of their creation, man and woman knew the harmony and mutuality of partnership. Due to their sin, they know the discord and alienation of patriarchy, symbolized in the man naming the woman (Gen. 3:20). Although naming can be a way of establishing relationship, here it is an act of domination. The woman could have named herself, since she was able to do so. Yet here, the man names the woman and calls her "Eve," which means "mother of all the living." We do not know the name that she may have desired for herself.

Trible's rhetorical hermeneutics makes a case for a major distinction between pre-fall and post-fall understandings of woman. Pre-fall, she is the final stage in the process of human creation; she brings to perfection what was still imperfect. Post-fall, she is the temptress who caused the fall. Morally inferior to man, she is punished with subservience to him. Pre-fall Genesis 2 presents a "subversive memory" (in Schüssler Fiorenza's sense). It reminds those who read or hear this text that partnership was God's intention for human creatures. Yet, Jewish life and law would reflect the contrasting post-fall reality. Partnership between the sexes did not exist. By law, women were the property of their fathers and husbands. Yet, through the story, the Yahwist author kept alive a memory of the paradisal garden in which mutuality and equality reigned. In a sense, the story holds up "a memory of the future," an expression coined by Letty Russell to draw attention to the possibility of new life in anticipation of the fullness of God's reign that is opened up in biblical stories such as this one.[48]

A detailed summary analysis of Trible's painstaking interpretation of Genesis

2–3 has been provided here to illustrate how a hermeneutics of suspicion and remembrance can be fruitfully applied to a biblical text in a rhetorical rereading. Trible unburdens Eve's story of the heavy weight of patriarchy and puts before the reader in its stead a reconstructed interpretation with liberating potential.

The Patriarchal Paradigm Casts a Long Shadow

Trible's thoroughgoing critique of the patriarchal interpretations of Eve's story draws attention to a reality that is a recurring theme in feminist biblical scholarship: the extensive influence of patriarchy in the Bible as a whole and in many key biblical texts in which women feature strongly. So extensive is this influence that it can rightly be called a biblical paradigm. A paradigm is a symbolic framework that underlies the shared assumptions and understandings of reality of a particular society. A paradigm functions through its symbols in ways that define and limit a society's beliefs and attitudes. It establishes boundaries in a society that define the important realms of shared life, including gender roles and expectations.

The Tragedy of Sonless Women

Eve, the first woman, is a symbol for woman in a patriarchal paradigm in which women are dominated by men. To this, many biblical passages add the additional burden of value attached to the ability of a woman to produce sons for her husband and, by extension, for her tribe and nation. Attention given to childless women and son-bearing is a recurring theme in the Old Testament and is not absent from the New, especially in Luke's account of Elizabeth's conception of John the Baptist.

In Genesis, Eve is mentioned by name only once more, where it is noted that she bore two children, both sons, Cain and Abel (Gen. 4:1–2). Nevertheless, the androcentric patterns exemplified in her story continue. This is clear in the motif of neglecting daughters and highlighting sons elsewhere in Genesis, particularly in the genealogies recorded in 4:17–26; 5:1–32; 10:1–32.

The great stories that depict the extraordinary blessings of God focus on male ancestral heroes. The first of these in Genesis is the story of Abraham, who is promised at the beginning of the history of Israel that he will be the father of a great nation. The focus is on the birth of sons. In Genesis 12–18, Abraham's story is intertwined with that of Sarah, his elderly and seemingly barren wife. Because Sarah seems unable to conceive a child, Hagar, her Egyptian slave, becomes a surrogate mother for Sarah. Surrogate motherhood enabled a barren wife to maintain her status in a society in which having sons determined a woman's place and worth.

After Hagar bears Abraham a son, Ishmael, the once childless Sarah gives birth to a son of her own, Isaac, in fulfillment of God's promise. Sarah-type stories are found elsewhere in the Bible. In Genesis 30, for example, the childless Rachel cries out in anguish, "Give me children, or I shall die." After having sons through surrogates, she finally has a son of her own. When God heeds her pleading, Rachel declares, "God has taken away my reproach" (Gen. 30:23). Why "reproach"? The answer is simple: a sonless mother is not only visited with a tragic flaw, but is also inflicted with moral weakness. Rachel names her son "Joseph," with a new prayer on her lips: "May the Lord add to me another son!" (Gen. 30:23–24).

A similar story is found in the first book of Samuel. Childless Hannah, dearly loved by her husband, Elkanah, in spite of her barrenness, bitterly weeps and prays with great supplication for "a male child" (1 Sam. 1:11). Finally, Hannah conceives and bears a son, Samuel, whom, upon weaning, she gives to God's service. She visits him only once a year when she and her husband go to the temple to offer the prescribed animal offering (1 Sam. 2:19). She makes such an enormous personal sacrifice of her only son, with the willing consent of her husband, who has sons with another wife, in order to express her indebtedness to God and likely to secure her position in society. Hannah is the mother of only one son, but he is destined to play a significant role in the community. A hermeneutics of suspicion suggests that these women's stories collectively reflect a fundamental androcentric attitude: the ability to produce sons ensures a position of honor for a woman in her society and is an indication that God favored her. Without sons, a woman was without prestige and vulnerable to divorce.

Women, Property of Men

The secondary status of woman is starkly highlighted in the tenth commandment, which forbids an Israelite male to covet his neighbor's possessions: wife, slaves, cattle, or any other property (Exod. 20:17; Deut. 5:21). The paradisal vision of conjugal partnership, mutuality, and equality of Gen. 2:24 is conspicuously absent in a society in which women are listed among the possessions of their husbands.

In the book of Deuteronomy, the prohibition of adultery carries the inescapable connotation of the wife being the property of her husband (Deut. 22:13–24). The notion of wife as property provides a rationale for a divorce law that permits a man to release his wife from the marriage covenant (Deut. 24:1). However, this is not reciprocal for the wife; she cannot divorce her husband. The logic is clear: the husband, as her owner, can dispense with his property, but a wife, as property, cannot dispense with her owner.

Likewise, a minor daughter is the property of her father. He owns her and has the right to arrange for her to marry a man of his choosing without her consent. According to the law, the father is owed a bride-price from the man who marries his daughter. This bride-price is owed even from a man who rapes her before her marriage, whether or not her violator marries her (Deut. 22:28–29). The law ignores the pain of young women who have been violated and concerns itself with the father's rights over his daughter's sexuality and the bride-price by which he is compensated for the loss of her virginity. This makes a virgin daughter the father's economic asset.

The perspective of women is absent from these laws. They give no attention to the experience of the women whose lives they governed, not even of a raped young woman marrying her rapist, or a divorced woman forced from her home by her husband's writ of divorce. Although women were normally the property of their husbands or fathers, some widows, divorced women, and the rare adult daughter for whom marriage was not arranged before puberty were legally independent (Numbers 30). These cases, however, were the exception. Overall, according to law, the lives of women were in the control of men. This control is evident in laws governing uncleanness and purification set by a male priesthood. Although Leviticus 15 treats both menstrual discharges of women (15–27) and genital emissions of men (2–12) as sources of uncleanness, demanding in both cases symbolic purification and offerings of expiation, there is a highly significant subtlety about what is required of men versus women. Eight days after recovery from uncleanness, the man is instructed to "take two turtledoves or two pigeons and come before the Lord [Yahweh] to the entrance of the tent of meeting and give them to the priest" (Lev. 15:14). In contrast the woman is directed to "take two turtledoves or two pigeons and bring them to the priest at the entrance of the tent of meeting" (Lev. 15:29). The crucial phrase "before the Lord [Yahweh]" is missing for women, drawing attention to the belief that only a man may come before Yahweh directly; never a woman.[49] The difference between males and females before Yahweh is also symbolized in the rules governing a woman's purification after childbirth specified in Leviticus 12:1–5. The time of cultic impurity for giving birth to female babies is twice as long as for male babies, although in both cases the offering required is the same: "she shall bring to the priest at the entrance of the tent of meeting a lamb in its first year for a burnt offering, and a pigeon or a turtledove for a sin offering" (Lev. 12:6).

A hermeneutics of suspicion applied to these laws leads to the conclusion that the communities for whom Exodus, Leviticus, and Deuteronomy were written assume that the social systems in which they live are compatible with God's order for the universe. In fact, they are exactly what God orders. The treatment of women as property and the exclusion of women from those who may come directly before Yahweh in public religious rituals rest on unexamined presuppositions of patriarchy assumed to reflect God's will. Women are objects of the law, not its creators. In these male-defined laws, men and their perspectives on reality are at the center; women and their perspectives are on the margins.

Remembering Partnership in the Old Testament

The patriarchal treatment of women, surfaced by a hermeneutics of suspicion, leaves us with an incomplete picture unless we also remember biblical texts that present a contrasting perspective. The Song of Songs is one such text. There are several things about the Song of Songs that make it worth examining. First, the Song of Songs has a female protagonist. Not only do the imagination and words of a woman play a predominant role in this book's poems, but also the thoughts and speech of a woman are conveyed in her own voice and not by a male narrator. Second, the poetic utterances from this nameless woman's lips stand in stark contradiction to other biblical texts, where human sexuality, especially of women, is presented as requiring patriarchal control. Through the woman, a countercultural statement is made. Female sexuality is explored and celebrated, and some very specific assertions are made about it. Among the more shock- ' ing ones, considering the controls on women's sexuality required by law, is the right of a woman and a man to love whomever their heart chooses, irrespective of prevailing religious and societal norms.[50]

In the Song of Songs there is no mention of God, which prompted debates about its inclusion in the biblical canon. Yet, without this book the imagination would not be stirred to enter into a vision that beckons the reader back to God's vision for humanity in Gen. 2:24. The setting of the Song of Songs in a lush garden draws the reader back to the paradisal garden.[51] It may be that the Song of Songs is an elaboration of God's original vision for women and men. The poems describe a picture of restored mutuality between women and men, lost through sin in Genesis 3. The Song of Songs expresses the hope that the patriarchal oppression of women, associated with Eve's transgression and legitimated through laws that made women property of men and barred women from religious leadership, will end. At the same time, the lyrical lines of the love poems present a vision of ecstatic joy for women and men who are bound to one another in the equal partnership that God envisions for human creatures.

> For now the winter is past,
>   the rain is over and gone.
> The flowers appear on the earth,
>   the time of pruning has come,
> and the voice of the turtledove
>   is heard in our land.
>   (Song of Songs 2:11–12)

The Song of Songs celebrates partnership in erotic imagery. But sexuality encompasses more than genital union. Sexuality is the energy of other-directedness that makes all human relationships possible, whether or not they are expressed in spousal intimacy.

A book of the Old Testament that exemplifies the other-directed energy of human relationship in partnership even more poignantly is that of Ruth. This book presents an unlikely alliance between two widows: a Jewish mother-in-law, Naomi, and her Gentile daughter-in-law, Ruth. In an artfully constructed story, Ruth and Naomi emerge within a patriarchal milieu as women capable of making their own decisions. When widowed, the childless Ruth rejects Naomi's instruction to leave her and return to her own Moabite family (Ruth 1:8). The significance of her choice is brought into sharp relief in the light of Moab's hostile relationship with Israel (Numbers 22–24). Still, in the situation of famine, Ruth heeds the advice of Naomi about securing a spouse and financial stability (Ruth 3:1–5). She even carries out Naomi's plan for gaining the favor of Boaz, a wealthy relative of Naomi's former husband (Ruth 3:6–9). Whereas in the normal course of things men acquire wives, in this story two women conspire so that Ruth will marry and marry well. The book celebrates the relationship of a Hebrew mother-in-law and a Gentile daughter-in-law, but it does not critique the tradition that the worth of women lies in producing sons. It is noted that

Ruth's marriage to Boaz results in her conception and birth of a son, Obed. This makes her, a Gentile, the great-grandmother of David. The narrator of the story acknowledges God as granting this special blessing to Ruth.

Both continuity and change mark the Bible. Attention to the birth of a famous son is a vestige of patriarchy manifesting itself in the midst of this story of female partnership. The narrator notes, however, that the women of Bethlehem declare that God has restored the fortunes of Naomi by giving her a daughter-in-law whose love is of greater value than seven sons (Ruth 4:14–15). In a patriarchal culture, this is a startling declaration. The book of Ruth shows the biblical tradition, characterized by patriarchy and androcentrism, undergoing modification. In Ruth, women of warring tribes freely choose to bind their lives together in a partnership of mutual support and loving concern.

There are other partnerships of women in the Old Testament. In the prologue of Exodus (1:1–2:23), the combined efforts of women, at least one of whom is a non-Israelite, thwart the plans of the Egyptian pharaoh and preserve the life of Israel's future leader, Moses, the Hebrew through whom God led the Israelites to freedom. A hermeneutics of remembrance draws attention to the partnership of women who made Moses' role in the Exodus possible. Moses' life would have been cut quite short if women had heeded the command of the Egyptian pharaoh to throw into the Nile every boy born to the Hebrew slave women (Exod. 1:22). The story of the infant Moses records women who act as individuals yet form an alliance on behalf of him and the people groaning under the pharaoh's yoke of oppression. The stories of these women are accounts of defiance (Exod. 1:15–22; 2:1–2:10). The Hebrew midwives, Shiphrah and Puah, are crafty; they boldly choose not to act according to the pharaoh's edict. The defiance of Moses' mother and pharaoh's daughter is direct; they choose to oppose his command and save the child. All of the women take positions over against Egyptian authority; all make choices for life. The women do not appear to consider the consequences of their disobedience. A fear of God motivates the midwives; compassion moves the pharaoh's daughter; the determination of mother-love drives Moses' mother; quick thinking prompts the resourcefulness of his sister. All of the women work together to overcome the evil scheme of the pharaoh. In their refusal to cooperate with the oppression of the Egyptian patriarch, the liberation of the enslaved Israelites has its beginnings.

The initial chapters of Exodus provide a picture of women who defy oppression and protect human life. Later in Exodus, another woman, Miriam, is hailed a prophet and leader (Exod. 15:20). In the book of the prophet Micah she is listed along with Moses and Aaron as God's messenger responsible for the Exodus (Mic. 6:4). Miriam so listed suggests that the three formed a leadership partnership with God in making the Exodus happen.

The stories of other women leaders are found elsewhere in the Old Testament, most noteworthy of which are Deborah, a judge and prophet who collaborates with Barak in the development of plans that ensure Israel's survival (Judges 4–5); Huldah, a prophet whose counsel King Josiah sought (2 Kings 22; 2 Chronicles 34); and Judith, the woman of prayer who, when the male leaders of Israel were about to surrender their people to their enemies, declared, "Let us set an example for our kindred, for their lives depend upon us, and the sanctuary — both the temple and the altar — rests upon us" (Jdt. 8:24).[52] Women such as Miriam, Deborah, Huldah, and Judith reflect roles of strong leadership in partnership. A hermeneutics of remembrance indicates that although categorized by law with children, slaves, and property, women did not necessarily accept this categorization in how they lived their lives, nor did some of their male contemporaries. While these women may be exceptions, their public roles do suggest that women could break the boundaries set for them by patriarchy.

New Testament, Patriarchy, and Liberation in Tension

Like the Old Testament, the New Testament was composed in a patriarchal society. Extensive concrete data regarding the experience of women in Jewish and Roman society at the beginning of the Christian era is sketchy. What we do know is that women's proper roles were domestic and maternal. As already noted, up until puberty, a Jewish girl was the property of her father, after which time she was usually betrothed. With the ceremony of betrothal her father began a process of her transferal to her intended spouse. Marriage signaled her acquisition by her husband. Girls were expected to obey their fathers; likewise, women were expected to obey their husbands. The subservience of woman is symbolized by the expected public decorum: if a woman had to appear on the streets of Palestine, she was to veil her face and walk behind her husband.

In the light of this scenario, passages in the New Testament such as this one in First Corinthians should not be surprising: "In all the churches of the saints, women should be silent in the churches. For they are not permitted to speak, but should be subordinate, as the law also says. If there is anything they desire to know, let them ask their husbands at home. For it is shameful for a woman to speak in church" (1 Cor. 14:33–35). Although Corinth was a city outside of the boundaries of Palestine, the lot of most women in the Greco-Roman world was not markedly different where issues of self-determination were concerned.[53] These two verses have a theme in common with 1 Tim. 2:8–15 (already addressed in the introduction of this book). Timothy's rationale for women's silence is the "female connection" with Eve, the first to be deceived and to transgress God's order, rather than a connection to Jesus, in whom "Yahweh saves." Timothy continues: woman's key to salvation is childbearing, provided she lives a modest life (1 Tim. 2:15). These passages reflect the societal expectations for women widely shared in the broader society of the time, but they also conflict with Gal. 3:28, which directs Christians to remember that at baptism they enter a new creation, one in which "there is no longer male and female." Here, the new order for creatures ushered in by Christ is that man and woman are to experience unity and equality in Christ.

Which of the two perspectives would be the norm for the nascent Christian communities? The Gospels provide some clues. They present Jesus as associating with women in ways that contrast with the prevailing cultural norms and

Jewish religious law. To illustrate this we begin with close female friends of Jesus, the sisters Martha and Mary (Luke 10:38–42; John 11:1–5). In John's Gospel, Martha is given a role attributed to Peter in Matthew's Gospel (John 11:27, cf. Matt. 16:16). In Matthew it is Peter who rightly proclaims that Jesus is the awaited Messiah. In John, however, Martha solemnly makes the same confession. She symbolizes the fullness of faith in Jesus, the Christ, in John's Gospel, just as Peter does in Matthew's.[54] In Luke 10, a memorable interaction between Jesus and the sisters appears. The context of the passage is worthy of note. Luke speaks of Jesus sending seventy disciples to surrounding towns to preach the good news (Luke 10:1) and provides its core content: love of God and neighbor (Luke 10:25–28). In the accompanying parable he expands the message in a surprising way: the one who embodies a discipleship of love is a Samaritan who takes into his care a man — presumably a Jew, given Jesus' audience — who has been victimized by violent robbers (Luke 10:29–37). In the section that follows, the reader finds a living parable, a story involving two women friends of Jesus and a surprise turn of events that casts a new light on discipleship.

Jesus visits Martha and Mary in their home (Luke 10:38). Martha is depicted as the sister who "serves." The story notes that Martha's many tasks of service distract her. Mary, in contrast, sits at the feet of Jesus and listens to him teaching. One feasible interpretation of Mary's posture is that she was assuming a discipleship role, one usually reserved for men. "To sit at someone's feet" is a rabbinic figure of speech indicating that the one sitting was studying with that person.[55] Such a posture was reserved for males. Mary sitting at Jesus' feet suggests that she is taking the role of a disciple to Jesus, her teacher. Martha's response to Mary's choice shows that she (or some members of the Lukan community telling the story) likely thought that assuming such a posture was inappropriate for Mary. Jesus' response is affirming of Mary, who chose "the better part," a part that he (and presumably the Lukan Christian community) will not take from her or from other women (Luke 10:42). Yet, there is some ambiguity here, because the Greek verb for "serve" (*diakonein*) comes from the same root as the Greek noun for "deacon" (*diakonos*). Had Martha become a deacon in her community of Christians after Jesus' death and resurrection? This is not possible to answer with certainty.

Mary's discipleship posture suggests the position of women followers of Jesus. Although none of the Gospels count women among the twelve *apostles or formally address women as disciples, they do take note of women who followed Jesus in his ministry. In Luke's Gospel we find this summary statement:

> Soon afterwards he [Jesus] went on through cities and villages proclaiming and bringing the good news of the kingdom of God. The twelve [apostles] were with him, and also some women whom they had cured of evil spirits and infirmities: Mary, called Magdalene, from whom seven demons had gone out, and Joanna, the wife of Herod's steward Chuza, and Susanna, and many others who provided for them out of their resources. (Luke 8:1–3)[56]

This text not only associates these women with the apostles but also states that the women were supporting the ministry. It is likely that these women were important partners with the men in carrying out Jesus' mission.

The partnership of the women is not limited to providing financial support. The story of Jesus' passion makes it clear that the support of the women was embodied in a deeper fidelity. In contrast to their male counterparts, the women do not desert Jesus at the time of his arrest, nor do they betray him and deny their discipleship. All four Gospels note the presence of women near the cross as Jesus dies (Matt. 27:55; Mark 15:40; Luke 23:49; John 19:25). In the Passion Narratives, the women follow Jesus from Galilee to Jerusalem and minister to his needs. Through their fidelity the women define discipleship for Christianity, even though none of the Gospels explicitly applies the term to them. The discipleship faithfulness of the women does not end with the cross. It extends to the resurrection. In all four Gospels women go to the tomb of Jesus to minister to his body and are the first to discover the tomb empty.

Of the women numbered among those who followed Jesus, Mary from the town of Magdala[57] is most often named. In Matthew's Gospel, Mary Magdalene, along with the other Mary, is the first to see him. In the Markan addition, Mary Magdalene is the first to see the risen Jesus. In John, she comes alone to the tomb early Easter morning. She is not only the first to witness the empty tomb, but also the first to receive an appearance of the risen Jesus with the directive to tell the other disciples the good news of his resurrection (John 20:1–18).

Mary Magdalene, due to patriarchal interpretations of Luke 7:36–50 and 8:2, has been often identified as a repentant prostitute who redirected to Jesus the "love" that she formerly distributed as sexual favors to her paying customers. This interpretation has a long history in Christianity, traceable to the time of Pope Gregory the Great (ca. 540–604 C.E.), and is given a central place on stage and screen in Andrew Lloyd Webber and Timothy Rice's musical *Jesus Christ Superstar,* in Franco Zeffirelli's film *Jesus of Nazareth,* and Martin Scorsese's film version of *The Last Temptation of Christ.*[58]

Feminist scholars in applying a hermeneutics of suspicion to the Magdalene tradition draw attention to the lack of logic in the depiction of Mary Magdalene as a prostitute, the prototype of a sinful woman and the New Testament's counterpart to the sinful Eve. The woman who anointed Jesus in Luke 7 is unnamed, but she was not Mary Magdalene. Had she been, her name would have been noted, because Mary Magdalene was well known to early Christians. Surmising what Mary Magdalene's release from the seven demons signifies is difficult. There is no reason, however, to connect her release from demons with prostitution or any type of immoral behavior. It is more likely that Jesus healed her from some infirmity associated with "uncleanness" according to Jewish law. She may have suffered from epilepsy or some other physical or mental disorder. Mary Magdalene, the woman sent to proclaim the good news of Jesus' resurrection to his followers, is more appropriately remembered as the "apostle to the apostles" — in partnership with Jesus in the proclamation of Easter faith — than as a repentant prostitute. The imposition of the prostitute identity onto Mary Magdalene is a misguided patriarchal projection of male fantasy.

The presentations of feminist biblical theory and the examples of feminist reconstructionist interpretations presented above have been drawn almost exclusively from the growing body of research done by Euro-Americans. The one exception is Renita J. Weems, an African American biblical scholar cited concerning the Song of Songs. Any discussion of women and the Bible, however, is incomplete unless attention is given to the contributions of nonwhite scholars who bring perspectives that Euro-American and European feminists often overlook.

The Difference Social Location Makes When Women Interpret the Bible

To say that social location influenced the lives of people recorded in the Bible and the lives of its authors is a statement of the obvious. Consequently, social location cannot but influence the interpreters of the Bible. As already noted, feminist biblical scholarship rejects the possibility of objective, value-neutral interpretations of Scripture. There is no final "objective" or "right" reading of biblical passages. Every reading bears the mark of the one doing the reading. Why this is important emerges in especially sharp relief when considering third-wave feminist biblical scholarship. Feminist commitment to take difference seriously requires the willingness to listen to many voices, to be open to interpretations that may evoke discomfort, and to embrace the reality that no unified perspective on particular biblical texts is possible. Insistence on uniformity in the interpretation of biblical texts is a manifestation of desire for patriarchal control of biblical interpretation, which not only oppresses the persons who read the Bible from the standpoint of their specific locations, but also suppresses rich insights that might be of benefit to Christianity in the life of Christian discipleship.

Interpreting the Bible from a Womanist Perspective

African American women today read the Bible in a social location shaped by the history of slavery and the experience of racism. The term "womanist" names African American women's resistance to oppression as well as their self-affirmation and will to survive with human dignity. The Bible, which at one time was cited by European and Euro-American Christians to legitimate the enslavement of the ancestors of African Americans, is also a source of religious validation and liberation in the lives of black women.

Earlier in this chapter attention was given to the Sarah-type stories in the Bible. Still, it is not Sarah but Hagar, Sarah's Egyptian slave and concubine to Abraham (Gen. 16:1–16; 21:9–21), to whom womanist theologians turn. Why? To them, Hagar's story symbolizes the painful history of the relations of black women and white women in the United States and beyond. Economic exploitation and division characterize this history. Delores S. Williams, a theologian at Union Theological Seminary in New York, has written a book-length womanist interpretation of Hagar's story in which she emphasizes its profound connection with the stories of African American women. Rather than summarize her position on Hagar, I have chosen a quotation representative of her position. Williams stresses:

> Hagar had no control over her body. It belonged to her slave owner, whose husband, Abraham, ravished Hagar. A child Ishmael was born; mother and child were eventually cast out of Abraham's and Sarah's home without resources for survival. The bodies of African-American slave women were owned by their masters. Time after time they were raped by their owners and bore children whom masters seldom claimed — children who were slaves — children and their mothers whom slave-master fathers often cast out by selling them to other slave holders. Hagar resisted the brutalities of slavery by running away. Black American women have a long resistance history that includes running away from slavery in the antebellum era. Like Hagar and her child Ishmael, African-American female slaves and their children after slavery were expelled from the homes of many slave holders and given no resources for survival. Hagar, like many women throughout African-American history, was a single parent. But she had serious personal and salvific encounters with God — encounters which aided Hagar in the survival struggle of herself and her son. Over and over again, black women in the churches have testified about their serious personal and salvific encounters with God, encounters that helped them and their families.[59]

Hagar's story — one scarred by slavery, poverty, sexual and economic exploitation, surrogacy, rape, domestic violence, and single-parenting — exemplifies the issues and problems that black women have faced and often continue to face. But Hagar's story also gives the black woman an image of survival and defiance, a subversive memory of great power. Williams argues:

> God's response of survival and quality of life to Hagar is God's response of survival and quality of life to African-American women and mothers of slave descent struggling to sustain their families with God's help.[60]

In Williams's interpretation of the Hagar texts in Genesis, Hagar is the first female in the Bible to liberate herself from oppressive power structures. Reading her story is to evoke a "dangerous memory" of extraordinary power. Carrying the child of Abraham, dismissed by Sarah, who perceives her as a threat, Hagar flees into the wilderness, where the angel of Yahweh finds her by a spring (Gen. 16:7). This angel makes a promise similar to the one made by God to Abraham earlier (Gen. 15:2–6). Hagar's descendants will be too numerous to be counted (Gen. 16:10). The child whom she conceives will be a son, a man of strength and defiance, described as "a wild donkey of a man" (Gen. 16:12).

When Sarah finally conceives and bears a son, Isaac, Abraham, though greatly distressed, heeds the demand of Sarah that Hagar and Ishmael be dismissed (Gen. 21:10–12). The promise of a great nation from Hagar's line, however, is not revoked. Hagar and Ishmael are forced from their home and driven into the wilderness, but God is with them in their plight (Gen. 21:14–19). Hagar's life is a harsh one of a homeless single mother. But she also knows an autonomy facilitated by God's presence. This autonomy is manifested in her assumption of a role ordinarily reserved for males in the ancient Near East. It is Hagar who gets a wife for Ishmael from Egypt (Gen. 21:21). Williams reflects,

> Whatever her reasons for choosing an Egyptian wife for Ishmael, Hagar may have dealt with the problem of homelessness and poverty by founding her own "house" or tribe.[61]

Williams believes that Hagar has spoken to generation after generation of black women, because her story has been validated as true by their suffering. Hagar with her son Ishmael is a model of many African American families. A lone mother struggles to hold a family together in spite of poverty and marginalization. With only God on her side, Hagar, like many black women, goes into the wilderness of ethnic-racial prejudice to make a living for herself and her child.

Hispanic Women and the Bible

Hispanic women are divided in their opinions of the role of the Bible in doing theology from the perspective of women's experience. Ada María Isasi-Díaz, the Cuban American who coined the term *"mujerista"* to name the theology done by Hispanic women in the United States, argues that the Bible is peripheral to the daily life of most Hispanic women. Although Christianity is an essential and integral part of the Hispanic cultural heritage, the Bible is not the starting point for *mujerista* theology. The starting point is the experience of Mexican American, Cuban American, and Puerto Rican women's struggle for survival. *Mujerista* Christianity is *mestizaje* (hybrid) born, which means that it is heavily influenced by the devotional Catholicism of Spanish conquistadors and by religious practices of Native Americans and/or African slaves. In times of need, instead of turning to the Bible, the Hispanic woman draws on a rich tradition of popular religious devotions. In her struggle, she turns to God, Mary, and the saints.[62]

Isasi-Díaz points out that what most Hispanic women know of the Bible, they know from hearing it read on Sundays in their churches, but they do not know biblical texts from personal study. In times of trouble they recall what they have heard lifted up as sources of hope. Isasi-Díaz reflects:

> For Hispanic women the *palabra de Dios* ("the Word of God") is not necessarily what is written in the Bible, but refers to the unflinching belief that God is with us in our daily struggles....Such understanding [therefore] must be the critical lens through which *mujerista* theologians look at the Bible.[63]

Other Hispanic women disagree with Isasi-Díaz. Elsa Tamez, a Mexican theologian, argues that the Bible is a source of liberation for Latinas. Women oppressed by injustice turn to the Bible as a source of hope and courage. It gives to women hopeful assurance: God's action is on behalf of the poor. Like

Williams, Tamez has drawn on the story of Hagar to illustrate how Latinas look to the Bible as a source of hope in the midst of their struggle. Tamez notes that generally, when Christians speak of women in the Bible, they highlight women like Deborah, Esther, Sarah, or Mary. Rarely do they mention women who were poor, such as Hagar. But it is in Hagar's story that Hispanic women find hope. God's presence to Hagar is symbolized in the name of her son. In Hebrew, "Ishmael" signifies "God hears." In Latin America, God hears women oppressed, discriminated against, and concerned for the survival of their children, helping them in their search for a new life.[64]

This very small sample of differing opinions about the Bible could certainly be multiplied if the net were cast wider. An important piece of information about the Bible's introduction to most of the Third World, including Latin America, must be recalled. The Bible was brought to the indigenous peoples of the Third World by European colonizers. In the hands of the original missionaries, the Bible often functioned as a handbook of propaganda for a Europeanized Christ. In the postcolonial era, Third World people, including Latin American women, are in the process of inculturating Jesus Christ and the Bible in ways that free them from the colonizers' agendas.

In Latin America, biblical studies play an important role in the lives of ***basic ecclesial communities.** In these communities the Bible is being reread by women with eyes that also see the harsh realities of oppression on multiple levels, including poverty and machismo violence directed to women. More will be said about basic ecclesial communities in chapter 5.

Sub-Saharan African and Asian Women and the Bible

Women theologians in sub-Saharan Africa and Asia almost always take note in their theologies of the long-term effects of European colonial exploitation on their countries, not only to reflect to their constituencies what they already know firsthand, but also to expand the consciousness of First World persons who may read their works. The effects of colonialism are pervasive, coloring everything, including how the Bible was originally presented. For persons whose religiosity was not book-centered prior to European conquest, the Bible was often treated as a sacred object of veneration from which missionaries magically drew messages about salvation. Throughout Christianized sub-Saharan Africa and Asia, where, with the exception of the Philippines, Christianity is a minority religion, feminist theologians are engaging in a rereading of the Bible. Although many of these theologians have been educated in First World countries by their churches, their rereading is focused on the realities of their people of origin. With the exception of Japan and a few areas of Asia, that experience is marked by a persistent pattern of poverty.

While it is not uncommon for Third World women to cite First World feminist authors such as Elisabeth Schüssler Fiorenza, Phyllis Trible, and Letty Russell in their writings, they are taking the tools acquired from these Euro-American feminist theologians and adapting them to their own situations. The results are perspectives on biblical texts that are different from the biblical theologies of the First World. Although concerned about the debilitating effects of colonialism on men as well as women, women theologians of Africa and Asia are bringing to the Bible a recognition that gender questions cut across all of their other concerns in ways that do not affect men. And there is no shortage of things to be concerned about: military instability, poverty, and disease — especially HIV/AIDS — rank high among women's concerns. The struggle to find and express a voice of liberation is compounded by the attitude, voiced principally by males, that feminism is a foreign import — just one more manifestation of white colonialism.[65] This attitude is further compounded by church leaders who see any form of liberation theology, especially when it is engaged in by women, as disloyalty to Christianity.[66]

Although many have been educated in the countries of the former colonizers of their countries, African and Asian women are developing gender-focused theologies responsive to the concerns of their sisters, taking a fresh look at the Bible as a source for liberation and spiritual nurturance. The Bible is no longer a sacred object to be magically interpreted by white men, or even by their fellow seminary-educated countrymen. The Bible belongs to women as well.

Mercy Amba Oduyoye, of Ghana, acknowledges that the Bible for African women has often been a two-edged sword. On the one hand, it is used to bless women's alleged inferiority. On the other hand, it is a source of resistance against sexual violence directed toward women. She notes that as early as 1922, Presbyterian women in Kenya began a movement to resist female circumcision that gradually spread throughout Africa.[67] These women drew strength from the Bible in their promotion of the dignity of women in the face of this life-threatening and body-mutilating practice.

Oduyoye points out that often when African women read the Bible, it touches them and their situation directly. She writes,

> They see the horrors around them and gather courage to expose such horrors and struggle against them.... In the midst of patriarchy African women seek to live beyond it because they can point to women in the Bible who lived beyond the patriarchy that surrounded them.[68]

In Africa, women theologians contribute to the struggle against the death-dealing forces of their societies with a sense of hope: "In good time the fullness of God's presence will be realized in Africa."[69]

Oduyoye's words underscore the centrality given to women's experience in African and Asian feminist theology as well. Women's experiences of oppression unique to their own specific locations are brought to the biblical texts in a "reader response" approach to biblical interpretation. Historical-critical methodology, if used at all in these interpretations of the Bible, takes second place to a reading committed to eradicating oppression, especially of women. An example from Philippine scholar Judette A. Gallares illustrates this well. Gallares has written a poignant reflection on the tragic Old Testament story of Jephthah's daughter (Judg. 11:29–40), connecting it to the tragic stories of young women in her country.[70] Jephthah, a leader of the Israelites in their struggle with the Ammonites, makes a vow to God before battle:

> If you will give the Ammonites into my hand, then whoever comes out of the doors of my house to meet me, when I return victorious, shall be the Lord's, to be offered up by me as a burnt offering. (Judg. 11:30–31)

The Israelites are victorious under Jephthah's leadership. Upon his return, his daughter, his only child, is the first to rush to meet him with timbrels and dancing. Upon seeing her, he tears his clothes and says: "Alas, my daughter! You have brought me very low; you have become the cause of great trouble to me.... I cannot take back my vow" (Judg. 11:35). His nameless daughter asks for some time with her companions. At the end of two months she returns and is sacrificed. Her story ends with this remembrance: "Henceforth, for four days every year the daughters of Israel would go out to lament the daughter of Jephthah" (Judg. 11:40).

Engaging in what she calls "a re-reading of her story," Gallares points out that the lament for the sacrifice of young women continues in the Philippines. In her interpretation of the story she reflects on Jephthah's response to seeing his beloved daughter first:

> Notice that he immediately puts the blame for his misfortune on his daughter and not on himself.... He seems only to mourn for himself and not for his daughter.[71]

Drawing attention to how different this story is from that in Genesis 22 of Abraham and his plans to sacrifice Isaac, his only son, she reflects,

> Abraham's was a test of his faithfulness to Yahweh, while Jephthah's sacrifice of his only daughter is a stark demonstration of his unfaithfulness and misguided conscience.[72]

For Gallares, Jephthah's young daughter is an unfortunate prototype of the life of many young women in the Philippines who are sold by their desperately poor parents to foreign con artists. Although illegal, these recruiters openly seek out young women in the rural provinces and the slums of the urban poor of the Philippines and send them to Japan as "entertainers." Gallares notes:

> Sometimes they [agency representatives] give two hundred pesos (less than US $10) to the parents of these young women as goodwill money. Others promise heaven and earth for their future. Greed and the desire for a life of comfort goad parents to practically "sell" their daughters to these agencies.[73]

She points out that these women usually end up as prostitutes in virtual enslavement to their bosses. They are sacrificial victims of their parents' greed and of men's lust.

The story of Jephthah's daughter is open to multiple interpretations. Gallares's is clearly situation specific, yet it also speaks an inner truth that extends beyond young women of the Philippines to all young women forced into prostitution because of abject poverty, whether they live in China, Albania, Sierra Leone, or the state of Florida. The details of the story are different, but God's word of outrage speaks in the different locations of any woman inhumanly oppressed due to her gender and class.

The biblical theology of Third World feminists is concerned primarily with how a better understanding of chosen biblical passages will allow the biblical word to influence their personal lives and the lives of their readers. They do not engage in biblical theology to find erudite answers to intellectual queries, but to illustrate how the Bible helps women and men with whom they share national, ethnic, or tribal origins to address the problems people face daily. In each case, their local particularities act as a preunderstanding that enables the Bible to be read as an expression of the deep yearnings for justice of their oppressed sisters and brothers.

Conclusions

The purpose of this chapter is to provide an overview of feminist biblical scholarship, with a focus on hermeneutical theory and its application, both to the process of the Bible's formation and to specific biblical texts about or featuring women. Significant voices from each of the three waves of feminism were surveyed. The current third wave, with its attention to difference in social location, is being heard by many today as a call to partnership, rooted in beloved biblical memory, such as that of Ruth and Naomi. Desire for partnership invites solidarity among all feminists (women and men from around the globe) to achieve a common cause: end the death-dealing forces of patriarchy in our world so that all persons, but particularly women and their children, who are the most dehumanized by patriarchal systems, can flourish as human beings.

Women such as Elisabeth Schüssler Fiorenza and Letty Russell, along with many others, are facilitating solidarity among feminist scholars around the globe, focused on a rereading of the Bible. Various professional societies, including the (North American) Society of Biblical Literature (SBL), are trying to provide women of color and Third World women with forums for sharing their unique perspectives on the Bible, rising from within their own social locations. Such forums allow the freeing truth of the biblical word to he heard in new and refreshing ways. Solidarity of women with women and women with men, white and black, yellow, brown, and red, is desirable, but cannot be entered without a real commitment from each person to listen to what the other is saying. All who seek the end of patriarchy and androcentrism must be vigilant about letting the desire for a facile solidarity lead to glossing over of the difference that social location makes. Solidarity that builds bridges is but one very important and necessary step toward biblically founded justice that is in tune with God's intention to liberate and sustain life.

A Look Ahead

In this chapter on feminist perspectives on the Bible, some important questions, including perhaps the most important, how the Bible speaks about God, are bracketed. Chapter 3 addresses this question, along with the broader question of the gender of God in the Christian tradition. It is a very important issue because the Christian presumption of the masculinity of God has had and continues to have an enormous impact on the lives of women and men. What the Bible, especially the Gospels, have to say about Mary the mother of Jesus has also been bracketed. Mary, who was so highly favored by God and with whom Jesus so intimately shared his life, continues to be revered by Christians and is worthy of attention. Mary and her significance in feminist spirituality are explored in chapter 5.

NOTES

1. Elizabeth Cady Stanton, introduction to *The Woman's Bible,* 2 vols. (New York: European Pub. Co., 1895–98; reprint, Boston: Northeastern University Press, 1993), 7.

2. Stanton helped organize the first Women's Rights Convention, held in 1848 in Seneca Falls, New York, along with Lucretia Mott, a Quaker from Philadelphia. Stanton was the principal drafter of the convention's "Declaration of Sentiments" (patterned on the Declaration of Independence), which advocated female suffrage, the right of women to own property, and other rights for women, including the right of women to preach in churches and be ordained ministers. She was the editor of the suffragist journal *Revolution,* and in the 1880s helped edit the *History of Women's Suffrage.*

3. Stanton, *Woman's Bible,* 5.

4. Ibid., 7.

5. Elizabeth Griffith, *In Her Own Right: The Life of Elizabeth Cady Stanton* (New York: Oxford University Press, 1984), 212. Near the end of her life Stanton concluded that there was really very little of benefit for women in the Bible, and thus little of value for her in it and in Protestant Christianity. She died a Unitarian, a religious movement that emphasized the oneness of God, rejected Trinitarian doctrine, and generally put emphasis on rationality in the interpretation of the Bible.

6. In the introduction to *The Woman's Bible* Stanton expresses her desire for Hebrew and Greek scholars to participate in the project. She notes that unfortunately, the women scholars who were invited were afraid to engage in a project that might prove to be unpopular (p. 9).

7. Ibid., 6. This method was not unique to Stanton and her group. Martin Luther, founder of the Reformation, had done the same when writing a commentary on Paul's Epistles in the sixteenth century.

8. Carol A. Newsom and Sharon H. Ringe, eds., *The Women's Bible Commentary* (Louisville: Westminster John Knox Press, 1992).

9. Elisabeth Schüssler Fiorenza, ed., *Searching the Scriptures,* 2 vols. (New York: Crossroad, 1993–94).

10. James Hennessey, *American Catholics: A History of the Roman Catholic Community in the United States* (New York: Oxford University Press, 1981), 173.

11. "*Providentissimus Deus* ('The Study of Holy Scripture' [1893])," in James J. Megivern, ed., *Biblical Interpretation: Official Catholic Teaching* (Wilmington, N.C.: Consortium, 1978), 210. The word "magisterium" refers to the official teaching office of the Roman Catholic Church.

12. "*Divino Afflante Spiritu* ('The Most Opportune Way to Promote Biblical Studies' [1943])," in Megivern, ed., *Biblical Interpretation,* 324–28.

13. Although the word "Torah" is usually translated "law" in English, the Torah is much more than laws. Much of it is narrative that tells of the prehistory of Israel, its early ancestry, the exodus from slavery, and the journey that led to the promised land.

14. Elisabeth Schüssler Fiorenza, *In Memory of Her: A Feminist Theological Reconstruction of Christian Origins* (New York: Crossroad, 1983), 46.

15. Jouette M. Bassler, "1 Corinthians," in Newsom and Ringe, eds., *Women's Bible Commentary*, 326.

16. Bruce M. Metzger, "To the Reader," in *The New Oxford Annotated Bible*, ed. Bruce M. Metzger and Roland E. Murphy (New York: Oxford University Press, 1989), xii.

17. For an explanation of evangelical feminist perspectives on the Bible, see Rebecca Merrill Groothuis, *The Feminist Bogeywoman: Questions and Answers about Evangelical Feminism* (Grand Rapids: Baker Books, 1995).

18. Schüssler Fiorenza is among the first feminist biblical scholars to broaden the goals of reconstructionist Christian feminist theology to include men who are oppressed. See her *Bread Not Stone: The Challenge of Feminist Biblical Interpretation* (Boston: Beacon Press, 1984), xiv.

19. Among English-speaking people there is a tendency to draw a sharp line distinguishing prose from poetry and narrative from explanation. Biblical language often defies such neat categorization. It is often difficult to say whether a biblical passage in the original language is prose or poetry. Poetic language tends to be more symbolic than prose, but what was recognizable as poetry by the people for whom the biblical texts were written may not be recognized as such by translators and readers today. See Christian E. Hauer and William A. Young, *An Introduction to the Bible: A Journey into Three Worlds* (Englewood Cliffs, N.J.: Prentice-Hall, 1986), 39–42.

20. Phyllis Trible, *Texts of Terror: Literary-Feminist Readings of Biblical Narratives* (Philadelphia: Fortress, 1984), 1.

21. Elisabeth Schüssler Fiorenza, "Feminist Hermeneutics," in *Dictionary of Feminist Theologies*, ed. Letty M. Russell and J. Shannon Clarkson (Louisville: Westminster John Knox Press, 1996), 99.

22. Schüssler Fiorenza, *Bread Not Stone*, 15–20. In this section she also presents a "hermeneutics of proclamation" and a "hermeneutics of creative actualization." These are not treated here because they are less evident in feminist biblical scholarship as a whole than are a "hermeneutics of suspicion" and a "hermeneutics of remembrance." For a more in-depth treatment of these two forms of hermeneutics, see her *But She Said: Feminist Practices of Biblical Interpretation* (Boston: Beacon Press, 1992), 57–68.

23. Schüssler Fiorenza, *Bread Not Stone*, 15.

24. Ibid., 19–20.

25. Rudolf Otto, *The Idea of the Holy*, trans. John W. Harvey (New York: Oxford University Press, 1958), 12–20.

26. Schüssler Fiorenza, *Bread Not Stone*, xvii.

27. Schüssler Fiorenza, *In Memory of Her*, 226.

28. Ibid., 88; see also idem, *Searching the Scriptures*, 2:9.

29. Schüssler Fiorenza, *Bread Not Stone*, 36.

30. "Dogmatic Constitution on Divine Revelation," no. 12 (nos. 9–12 of this document echo the teaching of 2 Tim. 3:15–17).

31. Schüssler Fiorenza (*Bread Not Stone*, 40) stresses that salvation should not be understood only as saving one's soul, "but in the biblical sense of the total human salvation and wholeness. It cannot be limited to the liberation from sin, but must be understood to mean also liberation from social and political oppression."

32. Letty M. Russell, "Authority and the Challenge of Feminist Interpretation," in *Feminist Interpretation of the Bible,* ed. Letty M. Russell (Philadelphia: Westminster Press, 1985), 138.

33. Ibid., 144.

34. The positions on the canon and biblical authority of Elisabeth Schüssler Fiorenza and Letty Russell are presented here without attending to the significant differences between their positions. For Schüssler Fiorenza's assessment of Russell's position, see *Bread Not Stone,* 12–13.

35. Schüssler Fiorenza, *But She Said,* 101.

36. Ibid., 35.

37. Phyllis Trible, *God and the Rhetoric of Sexuality* (Philadelphia: Fortress, 1978), 73. For a less detailed analysis of Genesis 2–3, see idem, "Adam and Eve: Genesis 2–3 Reread," in *Womanspirit Rising: A Feminist Reader in Religion,* ed. Carol Christ and Judith Plaskow (San Francisco: Harper & Row, 1979), 74–83.

38. Trible, *Rhetoric of Sexuality,* 73.

39. Ibid., 76–77.

40. Ibid., 78.

41. Ibid., 90.

42. Ibid., 98–99.

43. Stanton, *Woman's Bible,* 7.

44. Trible, *Rhetoric of Sexuality,* 112.

45. Ibid., 113.

46. Ibid., 120.

47. Ibid., 128.

48. Russell, "Authority and the Challenge," 139.

49. This subtle difference is noted in Judith Romney Wagner, "Leviticus," in *The Women's Bible Commentary,* 42–43.

50. Renita J. Weems, "Song of Songs," in Newsom and Ringe, eds., *Women's Bible Commentary,* 156.

51. Ibid., 160.

52. The book of Judith is among the apocryphal books in Protestant Bibles.

53. For specifics on the life of a woman in the Greco-Roman world of antiquity, see Bonnie Thurston, *Women in the New Testament: Questions and Commentary* (New York: Crossroad, 1998), 18–28.

54. For more on Martha and Mary and on other women in the Gospels, especially Mary Magdalene, see Thurston, *Women in the New Testament,* 62–95.

55. Leonard Swidler, *Biblical Affirmations of Women* (Philadelphia: Westminster Press, 1979), 192.

56. The Greek behind the phrase "provided for them" is sometimes translated as "served the others." To serve does not necessarily mean that the women were subordinate to the male disciples. The Greek verb for serve (*diakonein*) is also used of Jesus. For Jesus, serving is associated with giving one's life so that the reign of God might become a reality (Mark 10:45). Schüssler Fiorenza (*In Memory of Her,* 320–21) points out that service (*diakonia*) emphasizes that the women disciples have practiced the true leadership demanded of the followers of Jesus.

57. "Magdala" likely refers to Migdal, located on the western side of the Sea of Galilee.

58. *The Last Temptation of Christ* is based on the novel of the same name by Nikos Kazantzakis, published in 1955.

59. Delores S. Williams, *Sisters in the Wilderness: The Challenge of Womanist God-Talk* (Maryknoll, N.Y.: Orbis Books, 1993), 3. Williams describes a womanist theologian as a prophetic voice that helps black women to be aware of the importance of their experience and faith for determining the character of the Christian religion in the African American community (pp. xiii–xiv).

60. Ibid., 6.

61. Ibid., 32.

62. Ada María Isasi-Díaz, "Mujerista: A Name of Our Own," in *Yearning to Breathe Free,* ed. Mar Peter-Raoul et al. (Maryknoll, N.Y.: Orbis Books, 1990), 122.

63. Ibid., 89.

64. Elsa Tamez, "The Woman Who Complicated the History of Salvation," in *New Eyes for Reading: Biblical and Theological Reflections by Women from the Third World,* ed. John S. Pobee and Bärbel Von Wartenberg-Potter (Oak Park, Ill.: Meyer-Stone Books, 1986), 5–17.

65. Mercy Amba Oduyoye, "Introduction: The Fire of the Smoke," in *Daughters of Anowa: African Women and Patriarchy,* ed. Mercy Amba Oduyoye (Maryknoll, N.Y.: Orbis Books, 1995), 3.

66. Mercy Amba Oduyoye, "Biblical Interpretation and the Social Location of the Interpreter: African Women's Reading of the Bible," in *Reading from This Place: Social Location and Biblical Interpretation in Global Perspective,* ed. Fernando F. Segovia and Mary Ann Tolbert (Minneapolis: Fortress, 1995), 44.

67. Ibid., 39.

68. Ibid., 41.

69. Ibid., 51.

70. Judette A. Gallares, *Images of Faith* (Maryknoll, N.Y.: Orbis Books, 1992), 55–76.

71. Ibid., 60.

72. Ibid., 61.

73. Ibid., 70–71.

QUESTIONS FOR REFLECTION AND DISCUSSION

1. In Elizabeth Cady Stanton's day, the Bible influenced not only religious life but also political life in the United States. Do you believe that the Bible is still influential? If so, how? If not, why?

2. Where do you locate yourself in the spectrum of opinions on the Bible? Do you believe that the Bible is beyond questioning because it is God's Word? Do you think that bringing questions to the Bible, including critical ones, can be beneficial for Christians?

3. Explain what hermeneutics is, and what reconstructionist feminists mean by the "hermeneutics of suspicion" and the "hermeneutics of remembrance." Do you have a favorite Bible story? If so, locate it in the Bible and apply a hermeneutics of suspicion or remembrance to it.

4. Why do feminist biblical scholars argue that objectivity and value-neutrality are not possible when interpreting biblical texts? Do you agree with them?

5. Take a survey among your family and friends on the women they know in the Bible. Do any of them interpret the stories of biblical women in

ways compatible with the interpretations offered in this chapter? Conduct a similar survey regarding men in the Bible.

6. Are any of the items in the list of commonly held beliefs about Eve's story in Genesis 2–3 familiar to you? What is your response to this list? Are there things that you might add to Phyllis Trible's list?

7. What are the major elements of Phyllis Trible's interpretation of Genesis 2–3 that challenge women's inferiority and subordination? Do you find her rhetorical hermeneutics persuasive?

8. Mary Magdalene has often been identified as the penitent prostitute who accompanied Jesus. Why is this interpretation seriously flawed?

9. What is your response to the treatment of patriarchy and partnership in this chapter?

10. Is attending to social location when interpreting the Bible a new concept for you? What is your response to the interpretations of biblical texts by Delores S. Williams and Judette A. Gallares? Are there ways in which you might interpret Hagar's story and that of Jephthah's daughter differently because of your social location?

AREAS FOR EXPLORATION

1. Summarize the story line of these selections in your own words: Judg. 11:1–11, 29–40; Judges 19; 2 Samuel 13; Daniel 13 (for Protestants, the book of Susanna in the Apocrypha). Then consult at least two authors' views on them. Why were these texts accepted into the biblical canon? Are there parallels to these stories in contemporary life?

2. Compare the interpretation of the following texts in at least two authors: Lev. 15:19–32; Deut. 22:13–30; Deut. 24:1–5; Num. 5:11–31. What is your response to the content of these texts and to the positions of the authors you consulted?

3. Read the genealogy of Jesus in Matthew's Gospel (1:1–17). Most of the ancestors listed are male, but a few females are included. Consult a commentary for insight into the stories of Tamar (Genesis 38), Rahab (Joshua 2), Ruth (Ruth), and Bathsheba (2 Samuel 11). Develop a position on why these women are included in this genealogy.

4. Apply a hermeneutics of suspicion to how women are depicted in one or more of the following:

   • Andrew Lloyd Webber and Timothy Rice's musical *Jesus Christ Superstar*

   • Franco Zeffirelli's TV movie *Jesus of Nazareth*

   • Martin Scorsese's film version of *The Last Temptation of Christ.*

5. Read John 4, the story of Jesus and the Samaritan woman. List those elements of the story that you believe are significant. Consult at least one commentary by a male scholar and one by a female scholar. Are there any differences in their interpretations? Does this story have relevance for life today?

6. Compare the treatment of Hagar (Gen. 16:1–6; 21:9–21) by Delores S. Williams in *Sisters in the Wilderness: The Challenge of Womanist God-Talk* (Maryknoll, N.Y.: Orbis Books, 1993) and by Phyllis Trible in *Texts of Terror: Literary-Feminist Readings of Biblical Narratives* (Philadelphia: Fortress, 1984).

RECOMMENDED READINGS

Fiorenza, Elisabeth Schüssler. *Bread Not Stone: The Challenge of Feminist Biblical Interpretation.* Boston: Beacon Press, 1984.

———. *But She Said: Feminist Practices of Biblical Interpretation.* Boston: Beacon Press, 1992.

———. "Feminist Hermeneutics." Pp. 99–100 in *Dictionary of Feminist Theologies,* ed. Letty M. Russell and J. Shannon Clarkson. Louisville: Westminster John Knox Press, 1996.

———. *In Memory of Her: A Feminist Theological Reconstruction of Christian Origins.* New York: Crossroad, 1983.

———, ed. *Searching the Scriptures.* 2 vols. New York: Crossroad, 1993–94.

King, Ursula, ed. *Feminist Theology from the Third World: A Third World Reader.* Maryknoll, N.Y.: Orbis Books, 1994.

Laffey, Alice L. *An Introduction to the Old Testament: A Feminist Perspective.* Philadelphia: Fortress, 1988.

Newsom, Carol A., and Sharon H. Ringe, eds. *The Women's Bible Commentary.* Louisville: Westminster John Knox Press, 1992.

Segovia, Fernando F., and Mary Ann Tolbert, eds. *Reading from This Place.* 2 vols. Minneapolis: Fortress, 1995.

Stanton, Elizabeth Cady. *The Woman's Bible.* 2 vols. New York: European Pub. Co., 1895–98; reprint, Boston: Northeastern University Press, 1993.

Thurston, Bonnie. *Women in the New Testament: Questions and Commentary.* New York: Crossroad, 1998.

Trible, Phyllis. *God and the Rhetoric of Sexuality.* Philadelphia: Fortress, 1978.

———. *Texts of Terror: Literary-Feminist Readings of Biblical Narratives.* Philadelphia: Fortress, 1984.

Williams, Delores S. *Sisters in the Wilderness: The Challenge of Womanist God-Talk.* Maryknoll, N.Y.: Orbis Books, 1993.

Chapter 3

Feminist Perspectives on God

> Christian theology has always recognized, theoretically, that all language for God is analogical or metaphorical, not literal.... To take one image drawn from one gender and in one sociological context as normative for God is to legitimate this gender and social group as the normative possessors of the image of God and the representatives of God on earth. This is idolatry.   — ROSEMARY RADFORD RUETHER[1]

The purpose of this chapter is to explore an important question: What are the most appropriate ways for contemporary Christians to speak about God, the ultimate reality whom Christians worship as creator, redeemer, and sanctifier/sustainer? In any religion, God imagery provides the central and integrating symbols of what believers consider to be the highest good, the greatest beauty, and the most authentic truth. In Christianity, and in the other monotheistic religions as well, the image of a male transcendent ruler who has absolute dominion over the world predominates. Christian feminist theologians find much wanting in this image, especially because Christians today tend to take male symbols for God literally. Christian feminists argue that this is not good for women, not good for men, and not true to the rich and varied Christian symbolism for God.

We begin this exploration into Christian feminist perspectives on God with the above quotation from Rosemary Radford Ruether, because she is one of the most widely known feminist theologians, not only in North America but also around the globe, to contribute to Christian feminist theology that focuses on God. In *Sexism and God-Talk,* Ruether astutely observes that "few topics are as likely to arouse such [powerful] feelings in contemporary Christianity as the question of the exclusively male image for God."[2]

Like Elisabeth Schüssler Fiorenza, whose work on the Bible we examined in the previous chapter, hermeneutics features strongly in Ruether's writings. She applies hermeneutics, in the broad sense of human interpretation and understanding of anything, especially of women's experiences and of Christian texts. In a more specific sense, Ruether's theology is characterized by the application of a hermeneutics of suspicion, especially where traditional Christian texts conflict with her own life experience. In reflecting on her experience and its effect on her personal sense of God, Ruether observes that it is the "heritage of mothers and daughters" and not "the official patriarchal heritage" that contributed to why she thinks of God "not as the paternal superego, but as the empowering matrix."[3]

Speaking of God as an "empowering matrix" may strike the reader as unusual. Ordinarily, Christians readily speak of God in more personal terms and not in abstract language. Ruether chooses the word "matrix" deliberately, however, to make a point that she believes is important. God cannot be equated with what a particular personal and therefore gendered name for God represents. She believes that God is best described as a matrix, because she envisions God to be "beneath and around us as an encompassing source of life and renewal."[4]

Early on, Ruether, like many second-wave feminist theologians, became attentive to how the masculinization of God in the Christian tradition rationalized the dehumanization of women and justified patriarchy within and outside of Christian churches. She writes, "In each case the existing social hierarchy and system of power are justified by defining them as the order of creation and the will of God."[5] Questions about God's will in particular circumstances cannot be separated from who God is, and very importantly, who (or what) persons imagine God to be. This is so because there are many meanings and images associated with the word "God" in the Christian tradition.

Over the centuries God has been experienced and understood in different ways by different people in various times and places. Although Christianity recognizes that God is "beyond" gender, the language used with reference to God has been predominantly masculine. For many, a question arises: Is God male? It may seem to many readers that the answer is "Yes! All of my life I have heard God spoken of as 'he'." Is this because the Christian God is really a male deity? Is it possible to speak of God as "she" and remain true to Christian faith? Ruether notes that speaking of God in female images and pronouns evokes strong emotions in people. These emotions have deep roots in the pattern of using the name "Father" literally and exclusively when speaking about God.[6]

Among feminists who most strongly react against God as "Father" are those who have decided that the Christian symbolism of a Father-God, the transcendent ruler of the world, makes it impossible for them to accept Christianity. These feminists, in company with Jewish feminists who share their rejection of a masculinized God, have engaged in a thorough critique of male symbols for God that has led them out of Judaism and Christianity. Arguing that a male God both reflects and supports male dominance in society, they believe that women in particular and society as a whole need a female god, a Goddess. Arguing that the emergence of a male God is fairly recent (4500 to 2800 B.C.E.),[7] these women are turning to pre-Jewish and pre-Christian traditions to develop a religion of the Goddess. There are many differences among Goddess religions, but also a common *thealogy (as opposed to a theology) that worships a Goddess figure(s), especially as the Mother(s) who gave birth to the world and continues to sustain it. Goddess thealogy also celebrates memories of societies that were matrilineal (inheritance passed through the female line) and matriarchal (women occupying positions of power in family and society).

Ruether is in sympathy with the desire of women to have a deity who is beneficent to women, but finds post-Christian Goddess religions to be romantic constructions of the feminine that do not match reality. Goddess romanticism

[margin note: Transcendence & Immanence of McFague]

ROSEMARY RADFORD RUETHER

Rosemary Radford Ruether contributed groundbreaking theological insights to feminism's second wave and continues to be an important contributor to the theology of the third wave of feminism. Her path to feminist theology was by way of Scripps College in Claremont, California, where she began undergraduate work in 1954 with the goal of working in the fine arts and perhaps becoming an artist. She soon became attracted to the humanities and the history of Christian origins. Shortly thereafter, she began to explore the intellectual and social history of late antiquity and early Christianity, and completed a doctorate in this area. In a theological career stretching over several decades, her initial interest was in liberation theology and the interaction between faith and social concerns, especially anti-Semitism in the post–World War II era and militarism during the Vietnam War years. Three highly influential events of the 1960s — the civil rights movement, the emergence of the second wave of feminism, and the Second Vatican Council of the Roman Catholic Church — were formative experiences for her. As a young adult, Ruether became actively involved in the struggle for civil rights for African Americans and in the feminist movement. Due to the Second Vatican Council, her interest in the roots of Catholicism deepened at the same time. As a result, her writings often focus on the interconnections between Christian theological questions and social action to achieve justice. A Roman Catholic, Ruether teaches at Garrett Evangelical Seminary, a Methodist seminary in Illinois, and has also taught at Howard University and Harvard Divinity School.[8] Ruether has written or edited at least thirty books and has published over five hundred articles. She contributes often to a weekly newspaper published in the United States, the *National Catholic Reporter.*

is problematic. Claiming that ancient Goddess-dominated religions were nurturing, benign, and peaceful is attractive to many women, yet highly questionable. Such claims need to be sorted out from what can be proved or not proved, from what is utopian and what is actually the case. Goddess thealogists need more than idyllic projections of a women-governed egalitarian world. They need data to provide warrants for their arguments.[9] In short, in Ruether's assessment Goddess thealogy is "historically inaccurate and ideologically distorted."[10] It inappropriately denies the possibility of positive resources in the biblical tradition for symbols for God that resonate with women's experience. To promote the reversal of a masculinized God in an absolutized feminine Goddess promotes women, most of whom are well-educated Europeans and Euro-Americans, to be the gender and social group that normatively possesses the image of God and represents God on earth. This makes Goddess thealogy worthy of being critiqued as idolatry every bit as much as an absolutized masculine God is.

Associating the divine exclusively with either masculine or feminine gender qualities puts unnecessary limits on divine reality. Christianity has long recognized that God is a mystery surpassing human understanding. Augustine drew attention to this when he pointed out that if someone believes to have understood who God is, then what that person has understood is not God.[11] A consistent tradition in Christianity is that God is a reality with such unsurpassable content that every idea about or image for God falls short of the divine reality. None of the individual names, images, symbols, or concepts for God in Christian God-talk can ever capture who or what God is. There is always more to God than can ever be put into words. When Christian feminism associates understanding with its hermeneutics, it is not speaking of comprehending God in the sense of grasping an absolute truth, but of being engaged in apprehending God in the context of meaningful relationship.

Because this is the case, Ruether stresses in the quotation cited at the beginning of this chapter that God-language must never be regarded to be literal. This is why hermeneutics is so important. God-language is intrinsically related to the world and to human experience that is "worldly," that is profoundly affected by our historical and social context. Put simply, God-language is more about relationship than definition. Because God-language is not literal, the language one uses in reference to God can never be equated with who or what God is. To promote such an equation is to make an idol of a particular concept or image for God. This is why Ruether stresses that equating a particular image drawn from one gender and one sociological context with God is idolatry. There is also more at stake, however, where women are concerned. When women imagine God to be a male deity, they tend to relate to God as "the other" but not "like me." This is one of the key problems that Goddess thealogy seeks to remedy. When women relate to God in female terms, they relate to God as more "like me." Images drawn from women's experience can strengthen the bonds of intimacy that women have with God.

Christian feminist theologians argue (in contrast to the post-Christian Goddess feminists) that drawing attention to female imagery for God need not completely negate male imagery for God. Male symbols can be a meaningful resource for helping people to relate to God. The title "Father" is an important way in which Christians have addressed God since Jesus first shared how he prayed with his followers. The "Our Father" that Christians pray is based on the prayer found in Matt. 6:9–13: "This is how you are to pray: Our Father in heaven, hallowed be your name." Yet, it is likely that Jesus' address was actually the more familiar *Abba,* meaning "Dad."[12] *Abba* expresses Jesus' special intimacy with God as a loving parent.

In the Christian tradition, God as Father plays an important role. Worship in the congregations of almost any Christian denomination is addressed primarily to God as Father. But an exclusive emphasis on speaking of God as Father can also contribute to a limited understanding of God, an understanding that has the potentiality for idolatry. For males, whether potential or actual fathers, to find in a Father-God a reflection of themselves is an instinctual response. This has resulted in a hierarchy that has long prevailed in the Christian tradition: Father-God, male, female, earth. This hierarchy creates an unnecessary distance between women and the God to whom they pray that can present difficulties for women in their spirituality.

Ruether believes that the use of parent analogues when speaking to or about God is natural for humans. The human experience of a personal relationship with a father has something in common with many people's experience of God. Our parents are the immediate source of our existence and the persons from whom most children learn fundamental trust. To "Father," Ruether adds "Mother," a less common address for God in the Christian tradition, because she believes that language for God should be gender inclusive. A deeper understanding of God is enabled by not limiting God to Father. But she also draws attention to the limitations associated with all parental God-language. Whether God is addressed as Father or Mother, it is wise to keep in mind that "parent language must be recognized as a limited language for God. It does not exhaust the way we should image our relationship to God."[13] We must balance, therefore, our parental language for God with other images.

Some have argued that the best solution for resolving the God-language problem is to use gender-neutral (nonsexist) language for God. But the use of "God" as if it were a gender-neutral name can be tedious and does not actually challenge the prevailing belief that God is male. Gender-neutral language tends to be heard as male unless the imagery or pronouns are explicitly female. At best, gender-neutral language avoids giving offense to those who object to male-only God-language. Yet, it does not help women to identify with God, as creatures made in God's own image and likeness. Put simply, gender-neutral names for God do not contribute to the full humanity of women.

In the remainder of this chapter, therefore, language for God found in the Bible and the Christian Trinitarian tradition will be explored. Feminine God-language will be highlighted with the objective of helping the reader achieve a balanced and possibly richer understanding of God. Many types of God-language are surveyed here because what is brought clearly into focus in one form may remain hidden in another. Our first task is to examine the types of God-language in the Bible. Our sources are Euro-American feminist scholarship because this was the first to make a substantial contribution to a critical analysis of biblical God-language. In this section of the chapter, attention is given to names, functional designations, narrative metaphors, and personifications for God in the Old and New Testaments. We are particularly interested in what recent feminist research has lifted up in the Christian sources that have long gone unnoticed. The core doctrine of Christian revelation, the Trinity, is also examined to further appreciate the richness of the Christian understanding of God.

It has already been noted that in the early stages of the second wave of feminism, Euro-American feminist theologians tended to ignore the realities of the lives and the perspectives on God of women outside of their own social group. In the mid-1980s, womanist theologian Delores Williams (whose interpretation of the relationship of Sarah and Hagar was presented in the previous chapter) chastised Rosemary Radford Ruether — and by implication, most Euro-American feminists — for failing to address the effects of racism and classism in their theologies. Responding to Ruether's "Feminism in the Academy,"[14] Williams writes: "Just as Christian patriarchy only makes visible and valuable the concerns of men, Ruether gives visibility and authority to the concerns of white, non-poor [well-educated] feminist women,"[15] thereby neglecting everyone else. Williams's critique, a little harsh given Ruether's personal history of involvement in civil rights for African Americans, does draw attention to Euro-American feminists' tendency to neglect the perspectives of women outside of their own social location. To focus on the theology of God being done only by Euro-American feminists would result not only in making the insights of one sociological group normative, but also in an impoverished sense of God and possibly even in idolatry. In order to have a fuller and richer sense of God, womanist, Hispanic, African, and Asian feminist perspectives on God must also be surveyed.

God-language functions in myriad ways. In the conclusions section of this chapter the implications of God-language and symbols for women's self-understanding are probed. The focus is on the connection between God symbolism and biblically rooted belief that humans, male and female, are made in the image of God (see Gen. 1:26–27). In this section the interrelationship of God images and gender attitudes is explored. Throughout, our guiding question is, What are the most appropriate ways to speak about God?

Euro-American Feminist Perspectives on Biblical God-Language

To respond adequately to this question of how to speak about God, it is important to note the early emergence of this question in Euro-American feminist thought. In 1968, Mary Daly, an American philosopher of religion, wrote a groundbreaking book, *The Church and the Second Sex,* in which she briefly drew attention to problems with how God was imaged in Christian churches. She wrote that although "no theologian or biblical scholar believes that God literally belongs to the male sex . . . the absurd idea lingers on in the minds of theologians, preachers and simple believers."[16] In 1973, Daly published *Beyond God the Father: Toward a Philosophy of Women's Liberation,* in which she argued that if women's liberation was to succeed, it must be religious in its vision.[17] Daly's books served as a catalyst for many women to decide to engage in an academic study of theology and its sources.

Much of that study has been directed to the Bible. If you read the Bible carefully, you will find that it contains many ways of speaking about God. Some are far more significant than others. God is associated with fire (Deut. 4:24), the sun (Ps. 84:11), and other inanimate objects of nature, including rocks and mountains. Animals, such as a mother bear (Hos. 13:8), a mother eagle (Deut. 32:11–12), and a mother-hen (Matt. 23:37; Luke 13:34), are used in reference to God. But none of these are as important as the personal references, especially the names and narrative metaphors, that the biblical authors use in their speaking to and about God.

Major Names for God

Biblical authors did not concern themselves with abstract definitions for God. Rather, they portray God through images and symbols in the context of stories. In these stories God is usually the subject of the narrative and not an object of thought. Because of the narrative context for talk about God, the Scriptures have numerous images, symbols, and names for God. The Old Testament has numerous narrative images for God, but none has traditionally been regarded to be of greater importance than the name God is said to have revealed to Moses in Exod. 3:14, "YHWH" (*" 'ehyeh 'asher 'ehyeh"*), consisting of the repeated verb "to be" (*hayah*). This name is revealed in the context of a story in which Moses is watching the sheep of his father-in-law on Mount Horeb. As the story unfolds, Moses comes upon a burning bush, and a conversation with God ensues.

> Moses said to God, "If I come to the Israelites and say to them, 'The God of your fathers has sent me to you,' and they ask of me, 'What is his name?' what shall I say to them?" God said to Moses, "I am who I am" [*'ehyeh 'asher 'ehyeh*]. He said further, "Thus you shall say to the Israelites, 'I am has sent me to you.'" (Exod. 3:13–14)

Except for the sheep, Moses is alone when he receives the gift of the sacred name for God. No women were present with Moses on the mountain, but some very significant women in Moses' life are in the background of this encounter. As noted in the previous chapter, without the intervention of the unnamed women who saved him in his infancy, Moses would not have been alive to have this conversation with God. To protect him from the murderous knife of the Egyptian pharaoh, his mother hid him among the foliage along the banks of the Nile. The pharaoh's own daughter sent the infant Moses back to his own mother to be nursed, and later raised Moses as part of her family. She did these things even though she knew he was "one of the Hebrew children" her father sought to kill (Exod. 2:1–10). These women not only preserved Moses' bodily existence, but also influenced his religious formation.

In chapter 3 of Exodus, the adult Moses is receptive to the mysterious manifestation of God. As is often the case in the Bible, God initiates the encounter. Although the place of the meeting is secluded and the manifestation of God in a burning bush enigmatic, it is clear that the God whom Moses meets is a "near" rather than a "distant" God. In radical proximity, God speaks to Moses. Yet, the name that God reveals to him is shrouded in mystery.

YHWH, the name that God revealed to Moses, appears frequently in the Old Testament — more than six thousand times. Although translated in most English Bibles as "I am (who I am)," it is a very complex word that defies a simple, clear-cut translation.[18] Sandra Schneiders points out that what is rendered as "YHWH" is a form of the verb "to be" and not a proper name per se. The first-person form of the verb reflects the gender of the speaker.[19] It is therefore feasible that YHWH could be interpreted to indicate that the God of Israel is either male or female, or encompasses both genders at once. Nevertheless, in the text there is evidence of the assumption that the God who calls out to Moses from the burning bush is male. A masculine pronoun is used in reference to the God whom Moses meets: "What is his name?" (Exod. 3:13).

Why is Yahweh regarded to be male? An application of a hermeneutics of suspicion brings to light the patriarchal influence on Israel's names for God. Masculine pronouns for God comply with a pattern of speech already in existence when chapter 3 of Exodus was composed. The choice of a masculine pronoun also reflects the reference, found a few verses earlier, to the God of the great male leaders of Israel — Abraham, Isaac, and Jacob (Exod. 3:15). How women — such as Sarah, Hagar, Rebekah, Rachel, and Leah — experienced God is not given the emphasis that the experience of God by certain men is given. Women's experience of God receives no public recognition. The ancestral lineage is traced through the male line. The society is patrilineal, and God symbolism leading up to Moses' unique encounter of the divine presence is patrilineal.

Because of Moses' important role in the exodus of the Hebrew people from slavery to freedom, the name for God that the Bible records being given to Moses became very important in both the Jewish and the Christian traditions. The name YHWH became so revered that it was not spoken aloud by religiously observant Jews. Out of respect for this divine name, when Jews come to YHWH in a biblical passage they substitute the Hebrew word *Adonai,* which in the Greek Septuagint is *Kyrios* and in the Latin Vulgate is *Dominus.* All are masculine nouns rendered in English as "Lord." In the recent New Revised Standard Version (1990) of the Old Testament the word LORD appears.[20] *Adonai, Kyrios, Dominus,* and LORD obscure the fact that YHWH is a name for God and not a title, wrongly suggesting that YHWH has a male identification. This word choice is all the more troublesome because "Lord" carries with it the added baggage of a term often associated with power over others. Therefore, imagery associated with "Lord" is not only male; it is also patriarchal.

What might have been Moses' primary analogue for the name YHWH? It is likely that the experiential analogue for "I am (who I am)" is God's abiding presence. The divine presence was with Moses' ancestors in the form of a promise of progeny more numerous than the stars. This presence was encountered by Moses on the mountain with the promise of freedom and a land described as a place of "milk and honey." This same presence will be ever offered to those who are receptive and will be experienced in the form in which people most need it.

As we noted, the name YHWH is extremely complex, and with the passage of time, the mysterious immanence of God that Moses recognized on Mount Horeb was recast by the practice of never pronouncing "YHWH" aloud. YHWH, the name for God that appears in Genesis 2 when God takes mud from the earth and makes the first human creature and the animals, is intimately part of the story of God's relationship to creation from the time of the earliest texts of the Hebrew Bible. Yet, paradoxically, transcendent distance and otherness became associated with YHWH. It is helpful to keep in mind that God-YHWH is wholly immanent — closer to each of us than we are to ourselves — and yet wholly transcendent. At first glance, this statement may appear to be contradictory, but actually it affirms the mysteriousness of God.

Since YHWH transcends the limitations of gender, Elizabeth Johnson, a Catholic feminist theologian, has proposed that the name be translated as "She Who Is." This feminist translation fits when one considers that in Genesis 2, YHWH is depicted as a divine relational being who gives life to the world as "pure aliveness."[21] Moreover, because this God is first encountered at the burning bush during a time of great persecution of the enslaved tribes of Israel, YHWH also functions to bring to mind a personal, compassionate, faithful God who sustains a loving relationship with a people struggling under bitter oppression. The God who is revealed in each of these narratives — the One who is — could be spoken of as She Who Is, "a robust, appropriate name for God."[22]

Persons unfamiliar with the formation of the Bible might assume that from the very beginning of their history the people of Israel were committed to belief in one God. Although the Ten Commandments do include this statement: "I am the Lord your God, who brought you out of the land of Egypt, out of the house of slavery; you shall have no other gods before me" (Exod. 20:2–3), exclusive emphasis on one God emerged only gradually among the tribes of Israel. The emergence of monotheism had a long history.

It was not until the Babylonian exile period (late 500s B.C.E.) that the Jewish people gave YHWH special status among the other deities as *the* God of land and nation. In the early history of Israel it was not uncommon for female deities to appear alongside male ones, as in the cases of Asherah (2 Kings 23:7)[23] and the Queen of Heaven (Jer. 44:25). But gradually female deities were pushed into the background. Prior to the Babylonian exile the people of Israel worshiped YHWH without explicitly denying the existence of other deities to whom homage was sometimes paid. For example, various "El" deities such as El Elyon, "God Most High" (Gen. 14:18–19); El Shaddai, "God Almighty" (Gen. 17:1); and El Olam, "Eternal God" (Gen. 21:33) were honored.

Etymologically related to El Elyon, El Shaddai, and El Olam is ***Elohim,** another Hebrew word for God frequently found in the Old Testament. Technically speaking, it is not a proper name for God; neither male nor female pronouns directly fit it. "Elohim" is a generic term for God, likely of Canaanite origin. It is probably derived from a root denoting strength or power. There is some speculation that it may have been composed of "Eloh," feminine singular for "goddess," and an added masculine plural ending, "im." If this is the case, then the word may be rendered as "god," "goddess," "gods," or simply by the generic term "deity." Where "God" appears in English Bibles, "Elohim" is most often the word in the original Hebrew. "El" words for deities occurred throughout the ancient Middle East.[24] Although at one time distinct from one another, Elohim and YHWH gradually became identified with each other, referring to the one God of Judaism.

"Spirit" is also a name for God of Old Testament origin. It is more obscure than "YHWH" and "Elohim." In Hebrew, the word often rendered as "Spirit" is *ruah,* a feminine noun, also meaning "breath" or "wind." Its Greek equivalent is *pneuma,* a neuter noun. According to Joanna van Wijk-Bos, when *ruah* and *pneuma* are linked with God, "God's vitality and power as they affect creation" are affirmed.[25] Since *ruah* is a noun of feminine gender, it may be appropriate to argue that the presence of God's Spirit in the Hebrew Bible is female, especially since it is associated with the divine work of creation, of giving life. For example, in Ps. 104:30 it is the Spirit who creates:

> You send your Spirit and they are created;
> you renew the face of the Earth.

A comparable theme is found in the opening verses of the story of creation in Gen. 1:1–2. Wijk-Bos renders these initial verses this way:

> When God began to create,
> the earth was a trackless waste;
> darkness was on the face of the deep
> and the Spirit of God, she was hovering
> on the face of the deep.[26]

Her translation with the addition of "she was hovering" makes explicit that "Spirit" is a feminine noun. While it is true that *ruah* is feminine in Hebrew, caution is required in the use of the pronoun "she" in this verse. As Johnson points out, in inflected languages a word's grammatical gender does not necessarily indicate the femaleness or maleness of the object or reality to which it refers.[27] In some languages the word for "sun" has a masculine ending and in others a feminine one, but no one thinks of the sun as a male or female star. Attributing a feminine nature to the divine Spirit in the Old Testament is not necessarily appropriate exclusively on the grounds that *ruah* is a noun of feminine gender. In the Old Testament the Spirit is also portrayed as being present in the expected Messiah (Isa. 42:1–4) and as being the agent of a new creation that will arise when the old order has finally passed away (Ezek. 36:26, 37:1–6). The ways in which the Spirit is life-giving are rich and varied.

In the New Testament, the presence of the Spirit is the occasion of two major events. The first is the *incarnation of Jesus. According to Luke, the Holy Spirit came upon Mary, making the birth of Jesus possible (Luke 1:35). The second is the presence of the Spirit at Pentecost, the "birth" of the Christian church (Acts 2:1–4). In neither of these occurrences is the presence of God explicitly male or female. When the Spirit is depicted in Christian art, the Spirit is not imaged as a male or female person, but as a dove (recalling Jesus' baptism) or fire (recalling the tongues of fire associated with Pentecost).

Functional Designations for God

Functional designations refer to specific activities attributed to God in the Old Testament.[28] Terms like "Creator," "Covenant Maker," and "Liberator" are associated with God's works revealed in the Bible. Biblical faith affirms that it was God who created all things (e.g., Gen. 1:1–2:4a), who initiated a relationship with the people of Israel in a sacred covenant (e.g., Exodus 20), and who liberated the people from slavery in Egypt (e.g., Exodus 12–14). These designations describe who God was to the people when the Bible was being formed. Although none of these designations or the activities to which they refer is inherently masculine, it is likely that the people imagined God to be male when doing these things due to the influence of patriarchy on their culture. This is the case even though these functional designations are not actually gender specific.

Analogies and Metaphors for God

God-language found in the Bible is both analogical and metaphorical. One of the things that makes language about God different from other forms of language is that God-language has a distinctive "is" and "is not" dynamic to it. In the case of analogical language, for example, when we find attributes closely associated with God, such as God is just or God is good, these affirmations also contain inherent negations: God is not just or good in exactly the same way that we experience humans being just or good. God is just and good in a superlative way. God's justice is without self-interest; God's goodness is boundless perfection.

In the case of metaphors for God, the "is" and "is not" tension is more pronounced. In a metaphor, ideas that are very different are brought together to facilitate the emergence of new understandings in a particular time and place. For example, in the Bible, God is said to be a rock (Deut. 32:15). But obviously, to assert on a literal level that God is an inanimate mineral deposit is absurd. "Rock" applied to God implies a set of qualities, particularly ones that focus on stability and reliability, that rose in the consciousness of the believing community at a particular time. Metaphors are figures of speech in which a word or phrase that ordinarily means one thing is used to express a different meaning. Sallie McFague, a Protestant feminist scholar and author of *Metaphorical Theology,* stresses that human reliance on use of metaphors is not merely poetic ornamentation. From the time we are infants we construct our understanding of the world through metaphors that are imbedded in stories.[29] A metaphor is a type of comparison in which there is an inherent tension between what would be absurd on a literal level and the reality to which it points. "All the world's a stage" is a familiar metaphor from Shakespeare's *As You Like It.* We frequently use such literary metaphors to convey a perceived similarity, while fully cognizant that literally equating our earthly environment with a stage on which a play is being enacted isn't quite logical. McFague stresses that a metaphor finds similarity in the midst of dissimilarity and therefore not only says "is not" but also "is," not only "no" but also "yes."[30]

In the Bible, metaphors play a role in the emerging story of the divine-human relationship. Metaphors for God in the Bible are figurative and should not be taken literally. "Father" is both a metaphor for God and an analogy. It has already been noted that the male parent is an important analogue for God. But the title "Father" is also metaphorical, having an "is" and "is not" tension. Viewing "Father" in reference to God as a metaphor draws more explicit attention to the inherent tension in naming God "Father." God's fatherhood is more unlike than like the fatherhood of human fathers. If the necessary "is not" element is not given due consideration, then the title "Father" may become a literalism or even a definition for God. Sandra Schneiders draws attention to the danger involved in the neglect of the "is not" element: "A literalized metaphor paralyzes the imagination."[31] It can hold the imagination captive in a conception that is too narrow to encompass the mystery of God.

Parables attributed to Jesus in the Gospels are extended metaphors, many of which convey an understanding of God that has an element of surprise. In the one known as the "parable of the prodigal son," Jesus presents a verbal picture of the kind of father God is (Luke 15:11–32). The son chose to leave home and squander his inheritance, and was reduced to tending swine, thereby making himself unclean according to Jewish law. A young man who should have been an outcast to his own family is then welcomed home with open arms by his father. The father's extravagant and unconditional love for his prodigal son sharply contrasts with his son's behavior. In the story, Jesus presents God not as a condemning patriarch but as a patient and loving parent.

In the Bible there are many additional masculine metaphors for God. One of the most popular Old Testament metaphors is "Good Shepherd," the tender caretaker concerned for the safety and well-being of the flock (Psalm 23, cf. Ezekiel 34). Shepherds, usually nomadic, were often members of the landless class, and yet Israel combined the shepherd's care with divine sovereignty in the form of a lengthy blessing bestowed on Joseph, son of Rachel, arguably the favorite wife of the patriarch Jacob:

> [B]y the hands of the Mighty One of Jacob,
> by the name of the Shepherd, the Rock of Israel,
> by the God of your father, who will help you,
> by the Almighty, who will bless you,
> with blessings of the heaven above,
> blessings of the deep that lies beneath,
> blessings of the breasts and of the womb.
> The blessings of your father are stronger
> than the blessings of the eternal mountains,
> the bounties of the everlasting hills;
> may they be on the head of Joseph,
> on the brow of him who was set apart from his brothers.
>
> (Gen. 49:24–25)

Masculine sovereignty is even more explicitly associated with God depicted as a king: "For the Lord, the Most High, is awesome, a great king over all the earth" (Ps. 47:2). The psalmists also combine the king metaphor with the metaphor of

God as a judge: "The Lord is king!... He will judge the people with equity" (Ps. 96:10). The divine king is not only judge, but also victorious warrior: "Who is the King of glory? The Lord, strong and mighty, the Lord, mighty in battle" (Ps. 24:8). The combination of king, judge, and warrior imagery can leave one with the impression that God is a judgmental and domineering ruler. But the people of Israel also attributed to the divine kings involvement with the earth:

> Yet God my King is from old,
>   working salvation in the earth....
> You opened up springs and torrents,
>   brought dry land out of the primeval waters.
> Yours the day and yours the night;
>   you set the moon and sun in place.
>   (Ps. 74:12, 15–16)

Although less prevalent, metaphors for God particular to women's realities also appear in the Bible. A maternal metaphor for God appears in conjunction with Moses in the book of Deuteronomy. According to the interpretation of the author of Deuteronomy, writing over six hundred years after the Exodus, upon Moses' completion of the task of writing the law, the people are told why they need it: "You were unmindful of the Rock that bore you; you forgot the God who gave you birth" (Deut. 32:18). The author uses the device of a "mixed metaphor" to get an important point across. In the midst of recounting the people's past misdeeds, the Deuteronomic author reminds them that they lost their way. They forgot the divine Mother, the rocklike (and breast-endowed) dependable source from whom they, and all of creation, received life. Mindfulness of the Mother who gives birth is basic to a proper relationship with God.

Motherhood metaphors appear elsewhere in the Bible. In Isa. 49:15, God's faithfulness is depicted as the steadfast love of a nursing mother. In Isa. 66:13, the people of Israel are assured that God cherishes them with a mother's love:

> As a mother comforts her child,
>   so will I comfort you;
>   you shall be comforted in Jerusalem.

In Isa. 42:14, God is depicted as a woman in the pangs of childbirth, suffering with Israel in the people's longing for a rebirth of freedom. Jesus in John's Gospel also uses the metaphor of a woman in labor to give comfort to his disciples as his death draws near:

When a woman is in labor, she has pain, because her hour has come. But when her child is born, she no longer remembers the anguish because of the joy of having brought a human being into the world. So you have pain now; but I will see you again, and your hearts will rejoice, and no one will take your joy from you. (John 16:21–22)

Elsewhere in the New Testament, Paul depicts salvation as a birthing process:

We know that the whole creation has been groaning in labor pains, but we ourselves, who have the first fruits of the Spirit, groan inwardly while we await for adoption, the redemption of our bodies. (Rom. 8:22)

Paul also used birth images in reference to his apostolic mission (Gal. 4:19).

Female Personifications

Predicating personality to God involves gender specificity. Wisdom (*Hokmah* in Hebrew, and *Sophia* in Greek — feminine-gender nouns in both languages) is being given increasing attention as an important personification for God. Wisdom is more than a feminine noun in the Old Testament; it is also a title for a type of literature. One of the objectives of *Wisdom literature is to transmit lessons that nurture life. Its broad themes can be found in the literature of other ancient Near Eastern civilizations, especially Egypt. One of the outstanding traits of biblical Wisdom literature is the personification of Wisdom as a female presence of God.

Ambiguity has long surrounded *Hokmah* and *Sophia*. Ambiguity exists because the development of the feminine Wisdom figure proceeded over several centuries and has many nuances. Sometimes, wisdom is a divine quality, not distinct from God, but not totally identified with God either. In other instances, particularly in texts focused on creation, wisdom is personified so that the figure of Wisdom appears to have taken on the status of a divine person, a female deity who is the co-creator with YHWH. In these cases, Wisdom (*Hokmah/Sophia*) is "Woman Wisdom" or "Lady Wisdom."

A careful examination of biblical texts in which *Hokmah* and *Sophia* appear is in order. Wisdom (*Hokmah*) is featured in Proverbs 1–9 and Job 28, with her role expanded further in the Wisdom of Solomon and in Sirach.[32] Although attributed to Solomon, which would mean that it was written in the 900s B.C.E., the book of Proverbs was more likely completed at least three hundred years after Solomon's death. Proverbs is a collection of sayings without a discernible unified theme. In it are several texts where a unique Wisdom figure is featured. The first is Prov. 1:20–33, where Wisdom speaks in a way that asserts divine status:

> She [Wisdom] cries out in the street...
>   at the entrance of the city gate she speaks:
> "How long, O simple ones, will you love being simple?
> How long will scoffers delight in their scoffing
>   and fools hate knowledge?
> Give heed to my reproof;
> I will pour out my thoughts to you;
>   I will make my words known to you."

More contours are given to the picture of Wisdom in Prov. 3:19 that express the special role of Wisdom in creation: "The Lord by Wisdom founded the earth." Wisdom is symbolically spoken of as the tree of life and giver of life (Prov. 3:18; 4:13). As Proverbs progresses, this Wisdom figure is depicted as a person with many of the traits of Egyptian goddesses, such as Ma'at, a champion of truth and justice for her people and protector of the right order for the universe, and Isis, a popular goddess associated with the gift of life whose symbol is the ankh. In Isis literature, the goddess is praised as the creator of the universe. She divided the earth from the heavens, set forth the path of the stars, and guided the sun and moon in their daily journeys.

In the eighth chapter of Proverbs, traits of ancient goddesses are also evident. Like the goddess Ma'at, the female Wisdom figure walks in the way of righteousness, along the paths of justice (v. 20). A few verses later the focus shifts to creation. The female Wisdom figure is said to have existed prior to creation (vv. 22–26), been present when God began the preliminary actions of creation (vv. 27–29), served as the fashioner of creation beside God (v. 30), and rejoiced in the inhabited world and delighted in the human race (v. 31). Wisdom also turns toward human creatures, soliciting their adherence to her divine ways. She declares, "Happy are those who keep my ways. Hear my instruction and be wise, and do not neglect it" (vv. 32–33).

Proverbs 8 has become the subject of considerable debate. Is Wisdom a female personification of God?[33] Is the Wisdom figure a divine hypostasis of God; that is, has what has usually been considered a personal trait of the divine — wisdom — been transformed over time in the faith of the people into a person with her own distinct existence? Many scholars today do believe this to be the case. Wisdom had a special origin, prior to creation, and an active part in the divine works of creating and promoting justice. The mystery that surrounds Wisdom is affirmed in Job 28. Here, Wisdom is presented in a preliminary stage of personification. The author of Job depicts God asking, "Where does wisdom come from?" (v. 20). The answer is that this mysterious divine figure is truly known only by God: "God understands the way to it [lit., 'her'], and knows its [lit., 'her'] place" (v. 23).

The figure of personified Wisdom reached its peak as a female divine presence late in the history of pre-Christian Judaism in the books of Sirach and the Wisdom of Solomon. Scholars believe that Sirach was written during the initial decades of the second century B.C.E., prior to 175 B.C.E. In this book, Wisdom once again appears as mysteriously produced by God. And once again she speaks, declaring her origin, status, and special role in creation:

> I came forth from the mouth of the Most High,
>   and covered the earth like a mist,
> I dwelt in the highest heavens,
>   and my throne was in a pillar of cloud.
> Alone I encompassed the vault of heaven and
>   traversed the depths of the abyss. (Sir. 24:3–5)

Woman Wisdom recalls how she searched throughout the world for a resting place and was told to pitch her tent among the people of Israel (Sir. 24:7–8). Once there, she flourished and continued to issue her invitation: "Come to me, you who desire me, and eat your fill of my fruits" (Sir. 24:19).

In Sirach, Woman Wisdom also is said to have a close connection to Torah and the sacred covenant with God (Sir. 24:23). Torah is the heart of the sacred teachings for the people of Israel. It is Sirach's Woman Wisdom who will also pour out teaching like prophecy and will leave it as a legacy for future generations (Sir. 24:33).

The teaching of Woman Wisdom is given extensive attention in the Wisdom of Solomon, another book attributed to Solomon, but, like Proverbs, having no direct connection to him. Scholars believe that the Wisdom of Solomon was written in Greek by Diaspora Jews in Hellenized Alexandria, Egypt, during the first century B.C.E., likely before the Romans conquered Palestine in 67 B.C.E. In this book, Woman Wisdom, *Sophia,* is presented as a people-loving spirit who will not enter deceitful souls (Wisd. 1:4–6). In chapter 7, *Sophia* not only acts as the Creator in the beginning, but also is part of the ongoing creative process (v. 11). She is described as the fashioner of all things (v. 22), responsible for their existence and thus aware of their secrets. *Sophia* is also a spirit who is intelligent, holy, unique, subtle, loving the good, and ever steadfast (vv. 22–23). In Wisd. 7:27, unlimited power is ascribed to *Sophia* (Woman Wisdom):

> Although she is but one, she can do all things,
> and while remaining in herself, she renews all things;
> in every generation she passes into holy souls
> and makes them friends of God and prophets.

Sophia reaches to the ends of the earth and orders all things (Wisd. 8:1). Redemption is also granted through her. It is she who gives life and immortality to the persecuted just (Wisd. 8:13). In Wisdom 9 is an impassioned prayer for the divine *Sophia,* because she knows and understands all things. In particular, she can enable those who desire her to know what is truly pleasing to God (Wisd. 9:10–11). Her role in salvation is expanded in Wisdom 10: the story of Israel's salvation history is reinterpreted from the first human being to the Exodus in the light of *Sophia*'s pervasive saving power, attributing to her the saving deeds that elsewhere are attributed to YHWH.

By way of summary, among Woman Wisdom's distinctive characteristics one finds the following:

- her divine origin: Prov. 8:22; Sir. 24:3, 9; Wisd. 7:25–26

- her existence before creation and her role in creating: Prov. 3:19; 8:22–29; Sir. 1:4, 9–11; Wisd. 7:22; 8:4–6; 9:9

- her identification with the divine spirit: Wisd. 1:6–7; 9:17

- her immanent presence in the world: Wisd. 7:24; 8:1[34]

As her tradition unfolds, Wisdom becomes more and more a female person-ification of God. It is the position of Elizabeth Johnson that "Sophia's activity is none other than the activity of God."[35] She personifies divine reality in "an expression of the most intense divine presence in the world."[36] Woman Wisdom seems, therefore, to be equivalently divine, as YHWH is divine.

In the New Testament the divine Wisdom figure is closely associated with the life and mission of Jesus. Elisabeth Schüssler Fiorenza's research has led her to conclude that the early Christians perceived the God of Jesus as divine *Sophia.*[37] To many readers such a claim may appear to be illogical, since Jesus addressed

God as *"Abba"* ("Father" [Mark 14:36]). But Jesus' use of "Father" in reference to God may have a great deal to do with the patriarchal culture of first-century Palestine. As noted in the previous chapter, women were subordinate to men. The people, no doubt, would not have been able to really hear Jesus' message if he had addressed his prayer to the divine Mother, Woman Wisdom. This could have jeopardized his mission.

Since Sirach and the Wisdom of Solomon were written relatively close to the time of Jesus, their influence on the early Christian interpreters of the life and mission of Jesus after his death and resurrection is not surprising. The figure of Woman Wisdom likely lies behind how the early Christians viewed the uniqueness of Jesus, whom they confessed to be God incarnate and the firstborn of creation. This is evident in this excerpt from an ancient hymn found in the letter to the Colossians, composed by Paul or one of his followers:

> He [Jesus Christ] is the image of the invisible God, the firstborn of all creation; for in him all things in heaven and on earth were created, things visible and invisible, whether thrones and dominions or rulers or powers — all things have been created through him and for him. (Col. 1:15–17; cf. Prov. 8:27–30)

This hymn is compared not only with Prov. 8:27–30, but also with the Prologue of John's Gospel (John 1:1–5, 10–14). In professing faith in the divinity of Jesus, John uses the masculine-gender Greek term *Logos* instead of the feminine *Sophia,* but it is clear that the ideas John expresses in the prologue are rooted in what is said about Woman Wisdom in the Old Testament's Wisdom literature. This rendition of John 1:1–4a, 14, makes the connection clear:

> In the beginning was *Sophia* [*Logos*-Word],
> *Sophia* was in God's presence,
> *Sophia* was God.
> She was present with God in the beginning.
> Through *Sophia* all things were made [cf. Prov. 3:19; 8:22–31].
> Apart from her nothing came to be.
> That which came to be in her was life.
>
> . . . .
> *Sophia* became flesh and lived among us
> [lit., "pitched her tent among us"; cf. Sir. 24:8],
> and we have seen her glory in Jesus, who is full of grace and truth.

Did John's community envision Jesus to be the incarnation of the preexistent *Sophia,* the beloved Woman Wisdom, with God from the very beginning, ever active in creation, descended from heaven to dwell on earth? The evidence lends itself to a positive response.

In sum, what the early Johannine Christians experienced in Jesus' words and deeds led them to connect him with *Sophia* and confess him to be *Sophia* incarnate, living among and for the sake of creatures. John's identification of Jesus with *Sophia,* along with the Colossian confession that Jesus Christ is the firstborn of all creation, the one in whom all things were created (Col. 1:15–16), has profound consequences for Christian faith. It enabled the early Christians to attribute cosmic significance to the crucified and risen Jesus, relating him to the whole of creation. As *Sophia* made flesh, Jesus is co-creator with the Father, and intimately and actively involved in the world.

The significance of Jesus' involvement with creation is made explicit also in a key passage in Matthew's Gospel. Jesus' role as prophetic messenger is illumined by deeds associated with divine Woman Wisdom in Matthew's Gospel. Memories of Jesus' actions no doubt led early Christians to see him as her emissary, especially to those who suffer injustice. Like *Hokmah/Sophia,* Jesus is "vindicated by her deeds" (Matt. 11:19). These words are preceded by a description of Jesus' acts of compassion for the needy he encountered: the blind receive sight, the lame walk, lepers are cleansed, the deaf hear, the dead are raised up, the poor have the gospel preached to them (Matt. 11:5). Echoing *Hokmah/Sophia*'s message, Jesus declares,

> Come to me, all you that are weary and are carrying heavy burdens, and I will give you rest. Take my yoke upon you, and learn from me; for I am gentle and humble in heart, and you will find rest for your souls. For my yoke is easy, and my burden is light. (Matt. 11:28–30; cf. Sir. 24:19)

Schüssler Fiorenza reflects that as the "child of *Sophia*," Jesus stands in a long line of prophets sent to gather the children of Israel to their gracious God. Jesus' death on the cross results from his mission as prophet of *Sophia*-God, a mission on behalf of the poor and outcasts.[38] After Jesus' execution, his disciples continue what Jesus himself had done, making the all-inclusive love of *Sophia*-God incarnate in Jesus available to others. Among these disciples are women who experienced the gracious compassion of Jesus' God. Some of these women, such as Mary Magdalene (whom we met in the previous chapter), would become leaders in the new Jesus movement.[39]

In summary, God-language in the Bible is varied and complex. Although references to God are usually made with masculine pronouns, there are many reasons why it is reductionistic to equate God with maleness. The biblical authors knew this intuitively and therefore drew upon female metaphors and personifications for God to express their developing faith.

The analogical and metaphorical nature of God-language means that God can be related to as both male and female. But the "is not" element present in analogues and metaphors requires us also to keep in mind that God is neither male nor female. God is an all-encompassing mystery and is more than any particular name, functional designation, analogue, metaphor, or personification can express. Yet, all of these language forms found in the texts of the Bible can assist people in developing a meaningful relationship to God.

The Christian God, a Trinitarian Community

The triune revelation of God in the New Testament plays such a strong role in the worship and theology of Christian churches that no theology can claim to be Christian if it focuses on God apart from Jesus Christ (his life, death, and res-

David accompanied by Wisdom on the left and Prophecy on the right
Erich Lessing/Art Resource, New York

urrection) and the Holy Spirit (the ***Paraclete**, who consoles Christians in the midst of life's struggles and challenges Christians to give prophetic witness to the God of love). When naming the three members of the community of "persons"[40] that is the incomprehensible One God of Christianity, immediately we are aware that the first two are referred to with explicitly male designations, "Father" and "Son," and the third, the Holy Spirit, is more ambiguous where gender is concerned. The hermeneutical issues associated with "Father" have already been addressed. The masculinization of God caused by taking "Father" literally is compounded by the fact that Jesus is confessed to be Son of the divine Father, and the Holy Spirit is referred to as "Lord" in the Nicene Creed. Ample reasons have already been provided to counter a depiction of the divine Trinity in exclusively male terms and symbols in our treatment of "Father" as a metaphorical name and not a literal definition, of Jesus Christ the Son as *Sophia* incarnate, and of the Holy Spirit as life-giving breath, blowing wind, flowing water, and burning fire. Maleness projected onto the triune God of Christian revelation ignores the potential for a Trinitarian theology that relates to feminist values, such as solidarity in diversity, the value of equal and mutual partnerships, and the importance of communion to being a fully human person.

An examination of the potential fruitfulness of the Christian belief in God as triune requires some attention to the historical development of Trinitarian doctrine. Although Christian churches have differently nuanced understandings of God revealed in Jesus Christ, nearly all would agree that a Trinitarian faith is at the heart of Christian belief. Entrance into a Christian church is through baptism "in the name of the Father, and of the Son, and of the Holy Spirit." In many churches, Christians profess their faith in God in a *creed, such as the Nicene and Apostles' Creeds, in which the gathered community reaffirms its shared belief in One God who is three.

During the early centuries of the church's life, the triune nature of Christianity's theology of God developed gradually. The threefold manner of speaking about God was inaugurated in the New Testament. In a sense, the Christian Scriptures provided the "raw material" from which the doctrine of the Trinity would be developed later. In the formation of Christianity, texts such as Matt. 28:19 ("Go therefore and make disciples of all nations, baptizing them in the name of the Father and of the Son and of the Holy Spirit") and 2 Cor. 13:13 ("The grace of the Lord Jesus Christ, the love of God, and the communion of the Holy Spirit be with all of you") became formative for Christian self-understanding. Matthew 28:19 is important because it became the baptismal formula and 2 Cor. 13:13 because it became a formula commonly used in liturgical prayer. But these two short texts in isolation did not constitute a doctrine or theology of the Trinity.

A well-formulated Trinitarian theology is not to be found in the New Testament. What the New Testament does provide is the basis upon which a Trinitarian theology would be developed through painstaking discernment by Christian leaders. The primary focus of the New Testament is Jesus, whose unique experience of God as *Abba* issues in the confession that Jesus is the Son of God (and is *Sophia* incarnate). The New Testament itself does not make an explicit transfer from the title "Son of God," with which the Gospel of Mark begins, to "God the Son." Nor does it explicitly attribute divine personhood to the Holy Spirit. The New Testament, however, does provide the basis for the church professing the divinity of both the Son and the Holy Spirit later as it struggled to articulate its faith in response to questions that emerged. Father, Son, and Spirit are not so much proper names for God in the New Testament as they are symbols for God emerging from experiences closely connected with Jesus. God is grasped by Jesus' disciples as transcendent (YHWH for Jesus and his followers is *Abba*, loving his children in the mode of a caring parent), as accessible in the reality of an extraordinary historical person (Jesus, the Christ, through whom salvation is offered, especially in his death and resurrection), and as immanent in the world (the life-giving Spirit who both comforts and challenges the community of Jesus' followers).

In the fourth century, questions about the identity of Jesus and his relationship to God emerged with great force. Following the conversion of the Roman

THE NICENE CREED

The core of beliefs expressed in the profession of faith known as the Nicene Creed was composed by Christian bishops in 325 in response to controversies about the identity of Jesus Christ and his relationship to the God to whom he prayed as *Abba* (Father), along with some additions and revisions made at the Council of Constantinople in 381. The official creed of the Roman Catholic and Orthodox churches, the Nicene Creed is accepted by many Protestant churches as well. It is often prayed at Sunday eucharistic liturgies as a public expression of Trinitarian belief.

We believe in one God
  the Father, the Almighty,
  maker of heaven and earth,
  of all that is seen and unseen.

We believe in one Lord, Jesus Christ,
  the only son of God,
  eternally begotten of the Father,
  God from God, Light from Light,
  true God from true God,
  begotten, not made, one in Being with the Father,
  through whom all things were made.
  For us and for our salvation
    he came down from heaven;
  by the power of the Holy Spirit
    he was born of the Virgin Mary,
    and became [hu]man.

For our sake he was crucified under Pontius Pilate;
  he suffered, died, and was buried.
  On the third day he rose again
    in fulfillment of the Scriptures;
  he ascended into heaven
    and is seated at the right hand of the Father.
He will come to judge the living and the dead,
  and his kingdom will have no end.

We believe in the Holy Spirit, the Lord and giver of life,
  who proceeds from the Father and the Son.
  With the Father and the Son he is worshiped and glorified.
  He has spoken through the Prophets.
  We believe in one holy catholic and apostolic Church.
  We acknowledge one baptism for the forgiveness of sins.
  We look for the resurrection of the dead,
    and the life of the world to come. Amen.

THE APOSTLES' CREED

According to a legend that likely began in Western Europe during the Middle Ages, the Apostles' Creed was written by the apostles listed in the Gospels shortly after the death and resurrection of Jesus. Eastern Christians appear to have no knowledge of this creed of the apostles. Today, many scholars argue that it was very unlikely that this creed was composed by Jesus' followers in the first century. In its present form, this creed is believed to have been written not earlier than the fifth century. It summarizes Christian beliefs expressed in the Nicene Creed.

I believe in God, the Father almighty,
Creator of heaven and earth.

I believe in Jesus Christ, his only Son, our Lord.
He was conceived by the power of the Holy Spirit
and born of the Virgin Mary.
He suffered under Pontius Pilate,
was crucified, died, and was buried.
He descended into hell.
The third day he rose again.
He ascended into heaven,
and is seated at the right hand of the Father.
He shall come to judge the living and the dead.

I believe in the Holy Spirit,
the holy catholic church,
the *communion of saints,
the forgiveness of sins,
the resurrection of the body,
and life everlasting. Amen.

emperor Constantine and the end of the Roman persecution of Christians, there was an enormous influx of new members into the church. Some of the new converts believed that their newly adopted Christian monotheism meant that only God the Father was truly divine. Jesus Christ was a very important mediator between God and creatures, but only the first among creatures and not fully God. Arius was the main representative of this thinking. A popular preacher, Arius offered an interpretation of Jesus Christ's identity that gained wide acceptance, not only because it preserved a monotheistic understanding of God, but also because it was a suitable counterpart to the political pattern of a strict monarchy under the leadership of the powerful emperor, Constantine.

To settle the controversy about the identity of Jesus, Constantine called for a meeting of bishops. At the Council of Nicea (325), the bishops articulated the faith of the church, affirming that Jesus Christ is "one in being with the

Father," and therefore is God the Son. A few years later at the first Council of Constantinople (381), the divinity of the Holy Spirit was affirmed. These two councils established an assured minimum of Trinitarian belief to aid new Christians in their understanding of God. The phrase "one in three persons" became the way for the church to affirm the distinctness of the Father, Son, and Holy Spirit in a manner that preserves monotheism.

Although for most of the history of Christianity the three persons of the Trinity have been spoken of as male, female imagery for the Holy Spirit can be found in hymns from early Syriac Christians. In the *Odes of Solomon,* the Spirit is compared to the mother of Christ who gives milk, like the breasts of God.[41] In other texts, such as the ***gnostic** *Trimorphic Protennoia,* God is imaged as Father, Mother, and Son.[42]

This gnostic depiction of the Trinity would not prevail in western Christianity. Augustine, whose writings are enormously influential in Western Christianity, argued that depicting the Trinity as a family consisting of father, mother, and child is unworthy of God. The reasons for his rejection of the family analogy are rooted in cultural attitudes about male-female relationships. Man is by nature superior to woman. The husband is head of the wife.[43] By implication, if the Holy Spirit is a female person, the Mother, then the Spirit would be subordinate to the Father and the Son. Because of the dominant patriarchal attitudes, Augustine believed that speaking of one of the three in the divine Trinity as a female would compromise the full equality and unity of the Trinity.

These early examples of debate about how to talk about the Trinity, especially in regard to the Holy Spirit, are worthy of note and have reappeared in the twentieth century. Some male theologians have attempted to be responsive to feminist criticisms of the tradition of an all-male Trinity by suggesting, contra Augustine, that the Holy Spirit be regarded as the feminine dimension of the divine, the dimension concerned with giving and nurturing life. An example of this type of accommodation to feminists has been argued by Yves Congar, a French theologian who in the 1980s wrote a multivolume work on the Holy Spirit. He proposed that the Holy Spirit be regarded in Christian theology as the femininity of God in the image of a kind mother.[44] Elizabeth Johnson points out, however, that there are problems with Congar's well-meaning position and that of others who locate a divine feminine presence in the Holy Spirit. It reduces women's identity to the role of mothering and reinforces patriarchal concepts of femininity.[45] While motherhood is an important role for women, it is not the only and defining role. Moreover, if only the third person is spoken of as female, that still leaves the first and second persons male. Put simply, God can be spoken of poorly even if a female dimension is included in theological discourse about the Trinity. What is needed, according to Johnson, is "the expression of the fullness of divine power and care depicted in female images."[46]

What, then, is a Christian feminist to do about the apparent maleness of the Trinity? First of all, it must be stressed that belief in God as being three in one should not be equated simplistically with the names Father, Son, and Holy Spirit. These names are not the only ways to speak to and about God. Attention to biblical metaphors for God and how they bear on women's experience is important. God has many names. Addressing God in male and female imagery will enable both women and men to develop a much richer relationship to the triune God.

Apart from the question of gender-specific persons in the Trinity, there is an important issue that transcends gender: God, for Christianity, is a triune mystery. God in Christianity is not a transcendent monad, but a living and loving community of three profoundly related to one another and to the world. Put simply, in the Trinity, God's self-revelation is in and through relationship. Patricia Wilson-Kastner, an Episcopal priest and theologian, points out that imaging God as a community of three encourages one to focus on relationship as the core of Christian belief.[47] The history of the Christian tradition shows that there has been a strong tendency in Christianity, especially in the West, to focus on God as if God were strictly a single person. This has contributed to God being imaged as "male, patriarchal and domineering."[48] A narrow monotheism neglects to take into account that in Christian doctrine God is "at heart relational, not a bare unity, or an isolated divine monarch."[49] Such a monotheism also neglects important ways in which belief in the Trinity can have practical relevance for our lives.

What could be more practical than recalling that the Christian belief in God as a Trinity of persons affirms relationship as central to who God is? Christianity's God cannot be reduced to merely one person or to three individual deities. God is a communion of three, a trinity of persons for whom being in relationship is not something extrinsic to being God. Trinity as the central symbol of Christian theology has the potential for remolding the identity of Christians as persons. From the perspective of hermeneutics, the Trinitarian symbol gives rise to thought, to a new understanding: to be a person (divine or human) is to be in relationship to others, to support and nurture life in community.

Emphasis on community relationship is not new to Christianity. In the early Trinitarian theology of the East, relatedness was the supreme characteristic of God. The Roman Catholic theologian Catherine LaCugna points out that since the eighth century, Eastern Orthodox Christians have described the Trinitarian relatedness in terms of *perichoresis,* which literally means "being in one another."[50] The notion of the total permeation of the divine persons of the Trinity corrected Eastern Christianity's tendency to locate the unity of the Trinity in the Father. The word *perichoresis* loses its static abstractness if we draw attention to the fact that closely related words signify revolving action, such as the revolution of a wheel. The verbal form, *perichoreō,* means "to encompass." It is very like another Greek verb, *perichoreuō,* which means to "dance round." If we combine these meanings, we can imagine the Trinity as three persons engaged in a circular dance, circling and encircling one another with unending energy. The Trinitarian *perichoresis,* God as the dancing three, is an example of the use of a picturesque metaphor. In this image each of the dancing three retains individuality, while affirming that collectively they are not separate. Together they exist as God in perfect harmony and unity. Like any God symbolism, *perichoresis* is only moderately helpful. Its strength lies in what it most clearly affirms about God: the relational character of God as a communion of persons. This symbol, of course, dances in opposition to the individualism, competitiveness, and isolationism of patriarchy. It reflects to the Christian its highest good and its most authentic truth: loving community.

Because feminism emphasizes equality, interrelatedness, and mutuality as the basis of the world as it ought to be, feminist theology can be greatly enriched by the image of the Trinity as three equal persons dancing together in perfect harmony. The metaphor of enacted harmony in movement and sound in a circular dance, in Wilson-Kastner's opinion, is "a far more appealing, inclusive, and revealing sign of the divine than two seated white males and a dove."[51]

In the eternal Trinitarian dance the three, though distinct, are one. Love, the foundation of divine life, creates the bond of their unity. It is the rhythm to which the three whirl and intertwine in unending motion. As the dancing three, the persons are united to each other by the bonds of love; uniqueness and unity coexist. The image of the divine *perichoresis* invites everyone, especially Christians, to join in the Trinitarian harmony. To enter into this harmony is to experience the grace of communion with the divine three. The proper response is first and foremost praise with gratitude for the abundance of God's generous and transforming love.

Praise is never meaningfully directed to God in an abstract way. Praise is offered in the midst of living because communion with the triune divine community, although ever imperfect and partial from our side, is an experience of God's steadfast fidelity. This fundamental religious experience has affirming and challenging dimensions that bring about our full personhood. It affirms our efforts to develop a community of mutuality with our sisters and brothers with respect for diversity. It supports kinship care for the creatures of the earth on which the human community depends. At the same time it challenges us to be responsive to social and ecological injustices that undermine inclusive community built on equality, mutuality, solidarity, empathy, and compassion. Our communion with other persons and our care for all of creation become aspects of our growing communion with the three-personed God. This indeed is something to dance about!

In keeping with the symbolism of the three-personed God, in addition to the perspectives of Euro-American feminists, we now turn to the perspectives on God from representative voices from around the globe, including North American womanist and *mujerista* theologians, and Latin American, African, and Asian women.

African American Womanist Perspectives on God

Alice Walker, the African American woman who coined the term "womanist," is not a theologian by academic education. Nevertheless, in her Pulitzer Prize–winning novel, *The Color Purple,* the reader finds a poignant theological conversation between two African American women about God. This is natural because Christianity has traditionally played an enormous role in the lives of African American women. In *The Color Purple,* Celie, a rural black woman friendless until Shug takes an interest in her, confesses to her friend that there

DEEP RIVER

Deep river, my home is over Jordan;
  Deep river Lord,
I want to cross over into campground,
Lord, I want to cross over into campground,
Lord, I want to cross over into campground,
Lord, I want to cross over into campground.

Oh chillin,
Oh don't you want to go to that gospel feast,
That promised land, where all is peace?
Walk into heaven and take my seat,
And cast my crown at Jesus' feet;
Lord, I want to cross over into campground,
Lord, I want to cross over into campground,
Lord, I want to cross over into campground.

Deep river, my home is over Jordan;
  Deep river Lord,
I want to cross over into campground.

Christa K. Dixon points out that one of the most uplifting experiences for pre–Civil War slaves was the camp meeting, which was held for several days after the late summer harvest. Whites and blacks from the surrounding countryside came together for the event of the year. There were picnics and songfests. The music was gospel music; blacks sang the songs that they also sang in the fields and likely made up some new ones. For blacks, the campground was a gospel feast and foretaste of the heavenly "promised land," the land of Godly freedom and unfettered joy.[52]

is no way that she can think of God and not also think that God is white, an old white man with blue eyes and a long white beard. This was the image that Celie had until Shug encourages her to liberate herself from this patriarchal God of white men. Freed from the chains that bound her, Celie comes to recognize God in her experience in a new way, including in the sheer joy of the discovery of wild flowers of the color purple.[53]

Womanist theologian and ethicist Katie Cannon, a participant in a collective of racially and ethnically mixed women known as "Mud Flower," has shared her personal reflections on God and *The Color Purple*. Recalling a time when God seemed dead to her because of her grief over the painful end of a relationship she valued, Cannon recalls that she returned home and came to see God anew as "the Creator who sustains me morning by morning, day by day." She describes how she was helped to find God:

And the resources that have helped me claim the God that I now believe in include those prayers of my family. The whole black religious tradition has been a resource for me — that strong belief in the power of prayer. All of us in my family spent every night of the month of August going to revival meetings. And we'd go all over the country. The Baptists had it one week; the Methodists the next; the Presbyterians the next.... And we learned how to pray, how to shout and clap and how to get a good beat going. And so, when I began to really believe in God, I remembered the old-time black religion experience of prayer and music.[54]

These two examples illustrate two of the major sources of womanist God-talk, story (true and fictionalized narratives reflective of black women's history in America) and the prayer life of the family, supported by soulful witness in the preaching and gospel music of black churches. Black theology does not focus on speculations about the Creeds and the nature of the Trinity. Instead, it directs its attention to the meaning of Christian faith in black people's lives: to stories of faith in times of struggle in the past and to prayer traditions from which black people continue to draw strength in the present. It is no surprise, therefore, that these memorable words have come from the pen of the African American poet Ntozake Shange: "i found God in myself...& i loved her fiercely."[55]

Like Shange, womanist theologians seek to articulate what black women finding God in their souls and hearts means. The true spiritual self of womanist theology is often closely connected with relationship to Jesus. In the prayer, preaching, and hymns of black churches little distinction is made between God, the Father, and Jesus. Jacquelyn Grant points out that there is "no difference made in the persons of the Trinity, Jesus, God or the Holy Spirit."[56] All are used interchangeably in African American prayer language. This lack of attention to the distinction of persons underscores that the African American understanding of the Trinity is not now, nor likely ever will be, identical to that of other racial groups, due to the particular exigencies of African American life in the United States.

For African Americans in the past, Jesus was the central figure. Slaves could identify with "Massa Jesus," because Jesus identified with them in his advocacy for the poor and in his own unjust suffering. An old slave woman prayed to Jesus as Lord and Master and thereby affirmed that Jesus is God and that white people, including her master, are not.

In the late 1960s the identification of Jesus with the struggles of African Americans began to focus on the "Black Christ." James Cone, one of the first theologians to write about Christ's blackness, did not propose that Jesus was ethnically sub-Saharan African. Calling Christ black was symbolic, affirming that Jesus is identified with the struggle of black people for freedom, especially from racism. Jesus is a major part of the history of God's commitment to the oppressed. For Cone, the Black Christ is a symbol that makes the good news of God's opposition to the oppression of racism contemporaneous. It logically follows, therefore, that if a person is a true follower of Jesus Christ, he or she will be "actually engaged in the task of liberating black people from the power of white racism, even at the expense of their lives."[57]

The Black Christ, although a symbol that drew attention to white racism effectively, did not address the additional burden of suffering endured by black

"Jesus of the People"
Courtesy of Janet McKenzie

women: sexism. Womanist theologians have not argued that Jesus Christ be abandoned because he was a male embodied person. For Jacquelyn Grant, black women's witness to Christ by engaging in the task of liberating black people is of central importance. Drawing from slave narratives and other early black literary sources, she finds that many of these lead her to Jesus. The freed Sojourner Truth (Belle Baumfree) not only prayed to Jesus, but also envisioned him to be the source of her Godly resolve in her struggle against slavery. When asked by a preacher if she used biblical texts as the source of her teaching, she replied, "When I preaches, I has just one text to preach from, an' I always preaches from this one. My text is, when I found Jesus."[58] And the Jesus she found is the one who forgives his oppressors publicly from the cross.

Grant argues that if Christ is the savior of all, then all of Christ's humanity is significant. For black women, the significance of Christ lies not in his maleness, but in his humanity. What does this mean for a black woman?

> For Sojourner, it meant that women could possibly save the world; for me, it means today, this Christ, found in the experience of Black women, is a Black woman.[59]

Not all womanist theologians agree with the emphasis of Grant on Christ as black woman. Kelly Brown Douglas argues that Grant's position does not sufficiently allow for the possibility of Christ being seen in the faces of black men who struggle alongside black women on behalf of their community. Christ's presence cannot be restricted to black women exclusively.[60] But in response to the question of whether Christ can be a black woman, her answer is, "Yes, when Black women are acting to establish life and wholeness for the Black community."[61] It is in these moments that Christ is seen in the faces of black women. It would seem that the primary icons for Christ are the faces of blacks involved in the struggle for liberation. Perhaps "icon" in this context is not strong enough. Perhaps God is incarnate; the Black Christ is enfleshed when black people, especially women, are claiming their power to advance wholeness for black women and men. I am led to this conclusion by the words with which Douglas ends *The Black Christ*. Citing words that Alice Walker puts on the lips of Shug in *The Color Purple,* Douglas writes,

> "Here's the thing. . . . The thing that I believe. God is inside you and inside everybody else." For a womanist Black Christ, "here's the thing," Christ is inside of my grandmother and other Black women and men as they fight for life and wholeness.[62]

Hispanic Women's Perspectives on God

The perspectives on God of North American Hispanic and Latin American women, like those of African American womanists, are deeply affected by struggles for life and wholeness. The struggle of Hispanic and Latin American women is to overcome two major forms of oppression: economic poverty and male machismo. Because of their twofold oppression, many Hispanic women find themselves with their own unique set of questions where God is concerned. Speaking primarily of Latin American women, Mexican theologian María Pilar Aquino has expressed some of the basic questions these women are raising about God. No doubt, Hispanic women who make their home in the United States have many of the same questions. She writes,

> The central questions are not about God's existence, but about how to discover God in a reality of suffering and inhumanity. How can we uncover God's true face in a context where women are reduced to insignificance? Is there any room for women in the mystery of the Trinity, the center of the Christian faith? What does it mean to speak about the God of life to people whose daily experience is being despised because they are poor women of oppressed races?[63]

These questions are being raised by women due in large measure to the conscientization process of liberation theology. The God-questions of women rise from daily experience. The answers to them do not come from Christian dogma, but from life.

An increasing number of Hispanic and Latin American women are becoming aware that the burden of their twofold oppression is not of God. Elsa Tamez points out that when women become aware of this, their God becomes the God of the oppressed.[64] They come to recognize that if one is to know God, one can find God in the faces of babies crying and old women laughing, and in the preferential love for the poor and exploited persons of the world. Tamez's way of describing where one is to find the face of God has obvious resonance with Kelly Brown Douglas finding the face of the Black Christ in the faces of those women and men who are engaged in the struggle for life.

Envisioning encountering God in the faces of the oppressed is giving faith in God new meaning for many women. Luz Beatriz Arellano, from Nicaragua, reflects,

> We [women] are ... discovering that God was different from what we had been taught. We were discovering God as the God of life, closer to us, as one who journeys with us through our journeys.... Being essentially bearers and sustainers of life, women find a new meaning in the discovery of God as God of life, and they themselves become stronger and more conscious as defenders and bearers of life, not only in the biological sense but in all of its dimensions.[65]

The certainty that God sides, not with ruling male interests, but with the oppressed challenges the view that God is a patriarchal ruler, indifferent to suffering. As Ivone Gebara, a Brazilian theologian, points out, the image of God is no longer a father to whom one owes submission. "God is basically the image of what is most human in woman and man, seeking expression and liberation."[66] What is more basic than life itself for persons for whom survival and wholeness are constant concerns? María Pilar Aquino points out that it is faith in the God of life that is the source of hope and the reason why women celebrate, not as an escape from their struggle but in anticipation of the new creation.[67]

The ability to celebrate in the midst of hardship gives a unique meaning to the words of Jesus in John's Gospel: "I came so that they may have life, and have it abundantly" (John 10:10). In womanist theologies, we have found that Jesus, especially in the image of the Black Christ, plays a central role in the faith life of African American women. Who is Jesus Christ for Hispanic and Latin American women? Responses to this question do not reflect a consensus. Ada María Isasi-Díaz, a Cuban American theologian who coined the term *"mujerista"* to describe Hispanic women's theology of liberation, indicates that the majority of Hispanic women do not relate to Jesus.[68]

In preparation for *Hispanic Women: Prophetic Voice in the Church,* Isasi-Díaz and Yolanda Tarango interviewed six Hispanic women.[69] Among the questions raised was how they describe God. These Mexican American, Cuban American, and Puerto Rican women gave a variety of responses. Jesus, although not ignored by them, was not predominant in their answers. They imaged God in a variety of ways, including a *"sentimiento"* (deep feeling),[70] "a Spirit,"[71] "a composite of qualities I admire in other people,"[72] and "the Supreme One ... who gives us life."[73] What most of the women had in common, however, was their devotion to the Virgin Mary, spoken of as the "Holy Virgin of Guadalupe," "the Virgin of Mt. Carmel," and "Our Lady of Charity," patroness of Cuba.[74]

Aquino, in contrast, is of the opinion that Christ is important to Hispanic women. Christ is the Liberator, liberating poor women and men from the chains of poverty. Since women see life as a single whole, liberation in Jesus embraces all of life. Because Jesus became flesh in the humanity of the poor and the oppressed, identifying with them, the liberation of Jesus is expressed with compassion for the poor. Because Jesus treated women as persons worthy to share in his liberating plan with men, the liberation of Jesus calls for equal relations among men and women in all facets of daily life. These features express Jesus' option for life for those who suffer poverty and dehumanization.[75]

Isasi-Díaz's critique of theologians who stress the importance of the Jesus of Scripture in their writings is applicable to Aquino, who features the New Testament in her theology. Aquino interprets the Scriptures from a liberation perspective. Isasi-Díaz argues that many academically trained theologians (such as Aquino) gloss over the fact that the great majority of Hispanic women relate very little to Jesus. In her opinion, this results, therefore, in a "new emphasis" on Jesus (by academically trained theologians) but not in a Jesus whom grassroots women have defined for themselves.[76] Isasi-Díaz's viewpoint is different from that of Aquino, possibly because she is speaking from the standpoint of a particular group of North American Hispanic women whose Catholic formation was pre–Vatican II, or at the least was not affected by the Second Vatican Council's "Dogmatic Constitution on Divine Revelation" (1965), which advocated that Catholics read and study the Bible. It is also likely that these women's lives were not directly impacted by the liberation theology that has developed in Latin America since the 1970s. In contrast, Aquino is articulating her perspective from her experience of a different group of women with whom she is acquainted, women who have perhaps discovered the Bible to be a liberating Word that speaks in their lives in the communal setting of the basic ecclesial communities, integral to Latin American liberation theology.

Differences in the emphases of Isasi-Díaz and Aquino are examples of the pluralism among Hispanic and Latin American feminist theologians and of the potential for further development as they continue the process of articulating their faith in God in the midst of their multifaceted struggles for life. Still further pluralism is evident in other parts of the world. Two examples illustrate both difference and commonality.

An African Woman's Perspective on God

Mercy Amba Oduyoye reflects on God in Africa, specifically in her native West African country, Ghana.[77] She notes that it is not always easy for African women to experience God as empowering and liberating in their churches because male clergy in Africa presume to speak for God in exclusively male terms. The maleness of God, however, is less apparent in the tribal religion of Oduyoye's origin. In the religion of the Akans, God is "Nana." Some say that Nana is father, while others say that Nana is mother, "but the sentiment is the same: human beings experience a closeness to God which they describe in terms of motherhood and fatherhood." Bringing together the two images for God is not problematic for the

MERCY AMBA ODUYOYE

A member of the Akan people of Ghana in West Africa, Mercy Amba Oduyoye is a highly respected and articulate spokeswoman for the unique contribution of African women to the development of Christian theology. A daughter of a Methodist pastor, Oduyoye earned a B.A. in the study of religion and then attended Cambridge University in England, receiving a B.A. and an M.A. in theology. During the 1990s she received several honorary doctorates in recognition of her important contributions and accomplishments. She is a founding member of the Circle of Concerned African Women Theologians and is the director of the Institute of Women in Religion and Culture at Trinity Theological College in Accra, Ghana. She was the first

Courtesy of Peter Williams/WCC

African woman to become a member of the World Council of Churches' Commission on Faith and Order and has served as the WCC's youth education secretary, deputy general secretary, and member of its "Churches in Solidarity with Women" project. She is currently the elected president of the Ecumenical Association of Third World Theologians (EATWOT).

Although Oduyoye has become an important world figure among Christian theologians, she brings to her theology a deep appreciation of her Akan heritage and a commitment to the liberation of African women. She stresses that it is as an African woman that she is a Christian theologian. Her research interests and publications reflect her concern for the liberation of African women, who are oppressed through social, cultural, and religious ideologies, and her commitment to share the oral and written traditions of the African people, demonstrating how many, although not all, are compatible with biblical understandings of God. She has written numerous articles and edited or authored several books, including *Daughters of Anowa: African Women and Patriarchy* (Orbis Books, 1995).

Akans; experiences of God vary according to the circumstances that surround people's daily life. For Christian women, the experience of God becoming increasingly articulated focuses on creation and the implications of the Christian affirmation that "God was in Christ."

Despite the sexism in the Christian church, African women readily witness to their experience of God in Christ. The Christology of Oduyoye's African sisters is centered on Jesus as friend and liberator who upholds the dignity of women. African women put a great deal of emphasis on hospitality. God in Jesus is imaged as the "Great Householder" who empowers all as children in a parent's home and around the one common table. At home with God, they experience all that is just and life-giving, because "ultimately God is on the side of the weak and the side of justice."[78]

A South Korean Woman's Perspective on God

Chung Hyun Kyung, of South Korea, reflects on the God of Christianity as source of empowerment for life and liberty in the natural and human worlds. She evokes the Holy Spirit through the spirits of the oppressed who were faithful to the struggle for life. Her perspective on the divine as a Korean woman is expressed well in these words:

> Dear sisters and brothers, with the energy of the Holy Spirit let us tear apart all walls of division and the culture of death which separates us. And let us participate in the Holy Spirit's economy of life, fighting for our life on this earth in solidarity with all living beings and building communities for justice, peace and the integrity of creation.[79]

In these diverse voices and God-images a common theme emerges: God is the God of the poor. Taking the side of the poor, God, whether in the person of a female Black Christ or the Holy Spirit who struggles for life, calls forth liberation from the effects of slavery and colonial oppression.

Conclusions

The perspectives of feminist theologians on God surveyed represent only a sample of a growing body of literature. Since imagery and symbols for God provide a focal point for understanding personal experiences, societal life, and the world as a whole, an important question remains: What is at stake for women on these multiple levels in how God is imaged? A response to this important question has been implicit in everything addressed thus far. God-symbols function as the ultimate point of reference for understanding personal experience, societal life, and the world as God's creation. They can be oppressive to women if they are exclusively male. Mary Daly has powerfully captured the oppressive results of exclusively male symbols for God in her often quoted statement "If God is male, then the male is God."[80] As "gods," the males who rule relegate women, children, and other men to roles of subjugation. Exclusively male God-language undermines the human dignity of women and is an obstacle to their human flourishing. The result is fractured community, characterized by dominance and subordination.

God images, happily, can also be liberating for women. Images such as Woman Wisdom, Black female Christ, life-empowering Spirit, and triune community of love not only help women to relate to God more intimately, but also assist women in claiming the truth: women themselves image God. Images of God that reflect female reality help to reverse inequality and promote the full human dignity of women. Drawing attention to feminine images for God as a community of mutual love resonates with these words about the creation of humanity with which the Bible begins:

> Let us make humankind in our image, according to our likeness. . . .
> So God created humankind in his image,
>   in the image of God he created them;
>   male and female he created them. (Gen. 1:26–27)

Although this passage has virtually become a central doctrine in Christian feminism, some scholars have argued that from a historical standpoint, this passage is not actually about women being equal to men or even being able to fully image God. There are historical reasons for raising these objections, but they are not insurmountable. Phyllis A. Bird, a Protestant biblical scholar, points out that Gen. 1:26–27 was likely not understood as an affirmation of the full equality of women and men when written in the 500s B.C.E. She argues that given the era in which it was composed, "male and female" should be read in the context of Gen. 1:28 and the directive "Be fruitful and multiply." Like all the other species created on the sixth day, human beings are sexual and gifted with fertility.[81] Bird's insight is all the more reasonable when one considers that evidence of patriarchal treatment of women in other texts from the same biblical tradition as Genesis 1, the Priestly tradition, abounds. It is quite likely that the Priestly writers had no experience of an egalitarian society. Genesis 1 postdates Genesis 2–3 and the story of the creation and fall of Adam and Eve by approximately four centuries. The dark shadow of women's secondary status as daughters of Eve was not removed by new light. Yet, although Gen. 1:26–27 was likely not an exception to patriarchal notions about male superiority and female inferiority when it was written and incorporated into the Torah, mutuality among the sexes in their privileged role as co-creators with God is clearly implied in this text. This mutuality resonates with the pre-fall partnership in the account of the creation of the first human pair in Genesis 2.

As already stressed in chapter 2, in feminist biblical hermeneutics the history behind a text need not take precedence over the meanings that emerge in front of it as people discern its meaning in new times and settings. The words "in the image of God he created them; male and female he created them" do more than imply egalitarian mutuality and partnership between the sexes; they inspire mutuality and partnership as truly of God. The Holy Spirit inspires the community in ever new ways, breathing new life into old words. Therefore, women's ownership of "image of God" today powerfully affirms the worth of women in the eyes of a God who is not only "he," but also "she."

Ownership by women of their creation in the image of God is affirmed also by women's full incorporation into the people of God in the rite of baptism. Christianity has consistently taught that women and men are equally redeemed by Jesus Christ, equally incorporated into the Christian community when baptized. In the rite of baptism the communitarian nature of divine love is affirmed;

all Christians are baptized in the name of the divine Three. Women and men imaging God as a triune community broadens the notion of women and men equally created and equally redeemed to women and men forming a community of equals, cooperating in loving mutuality as they work to live out the implications of their creation and redemption by promoting justice, ending violence, and advocating the health of the planet.

A Look Ahead

Ending this chapter on feminist perspectives on God with reflection on the implication of the revelation of God as Trinity for egalitarian community provides an apt link to the chapter that follows on the Christian churches and women. Chapter 4 is a multifaceted and wide-ranging story of women both denied and seeking full participation in their churches in fidelity to what they believe the example of Jesus Christ and the life-empowering Holy Spirit calls them. This chapter sketches the "big picture" of women's relationship to the church as global and ecumenical while providing examples that are specific to denomination and social location.

NOTES

1. Rosemary Radford Ruether, "Feminist Theology and Spirituality," in *Christian Feminism: Visions of a New Humanity,* ed. Judith L. Weidman (San Francisco: Harper & Row, 1984), 16.

2. Rosemary Radford Ruether, *Sexism and God-Talk: Toward a Feminist Theology* (Boston: Beacon Press, 1983), 47.

3. Rosemary Radford Ruether, *Disputed Questions: On Being a Christian* (Maryknoll, N.Y.: Orbis Books, 1989), 24.

4. Ruether, *Sexism and God-Talk,* 49.

5. Rosemary Radford Ruether, "The Development of My Theology," *Religious Studies Review* 15 (1989): 2.

6. Ruether, *Sexism and God-Talk,* 47.

7. Carol Christ, *The Laughter of Aphrodite: Reflections on a Journey to the Goddess* (San Francisco: Harper & Row, 1987), 117–31.

8. Ruether, "The Development of My Theology," 1–2.

9. Rosemary Radford Ruether, *Gaia and God: An Ecofeminist Theology of Earth Healing* (San Francisco: HarperCollins, 1992), 144–55.

10. Ruether, *Sexism and God-Talk,* 39.

11. Augustine, *Sermo* 52 (PL 38:6c).

12. "Father" appears in Mark (the earliest of the Gospels) only four times, in Luke fifteen times, in Matthew forty-two times, and in John 109 times. John was the last of the Gospels to be written, likely over twenty-five years after Mark. Perhaps with the passage of time the name "Father" grew in popularity as more people accepted the divinity of Jesus.

13. Ruether, "Feminist Theology and Spirituality," 17.

14. Ruether, "Feminism in the Academy," *Christianity and Crisis* 45 (1985): 57–62.

15. Delores Williams, "The Color of Feminism," *Christianity and Crisis* 45 (1985): 165. Jacquelyn Grant makes a similar argument, that Euro-American theologians such as Ruether and Russell ignore differences between women due to race and class, in *White*

Women's Christ and Black Women's Jesus: Feminist Christology and Womanist Response (Atlanta: Scholars Press, 1989), 144–45.

16. Mary Daly, *The Church and the Second Sex,* rev. ed. (New York: Harper & Row, 1975), 180.

17. Mary Daly, *Beyond God the Father: Toward a Philosophy of Women's Liberation* (Boston: Beacon Press, 1973), 18.

18. W. Gunther Plaut stresses the mystery that surrounds the name "Yahweh" — *"Ehyeh Asher Ehyeh"* — the most sacred name by which Jewish people call God. *Ehyeh* is the first person singular of the verb "to be." The verb's tense, however, is unclear, and it could mean "I am" or "I will be." Jewish literature offers a variety of explanations of *Ehyeh Asher Ehyeh.* The majority argues that the tense for *ehyeh* is future and interpret it as "I will be what tomorrow demands," meaning that God is capable of responding to human needs as they emerge. Others, such as S. R. Hirsch, argue that it means that God will be what God wants to be; thus, the emphasis is on the freedom of God. Plaut himself stresses that this name is surrounded in mystery. It is an aspect of God's freedom to conceal God's own essence. Therefore, *Ehyeh-Asher-Ehyeh* must remain ever elusive. See W. Gunther Plaut, *The Torah: A Modern Commentary* (New York: Union of American Hebrew Congregations, 1981), 404–6.

19. Sandra Schneiders, *Women and the Word: The Gender of God in the New Testament and the Spirituality of Women* (New York: Paulist Press, 1986), 22.

20. In some English translations, such as the Jerusalem Bible, vowels are inserted between the consonants, providing the pronounceable name "Yahweh." This removes the explicit maleness from the term but fails to honor the tradition of the Jews that forbids pronouncing this most sacred of the names for God. A possible remedy, especially in the case of English translation, would be to follow the usual New Testament practice of using "God."

21. Elizabeth Johnson, *She Who Is: The Mystery of God in Feminist Theological Discourse* (New York: Crossroad, 1992), 240.

22. Ibid., 242–43.

23. Ruether believes that Asherah was worshiped alongside YHWH in the Solomonic temple for two-thirds of its existence. The graves of Israelites show symbols for YHWH and Asherah together. See Ruether, *Sexism and God-Talk,* 56.

24. *El* has the same root as the Arabic *ilah,* which, when combined with the definite article, *al,* becomes *Allah,* the Islamic name for God found in the Qur'an.

25. Joanna W. H. van Wijk-Bos, *Reimagining God: The Case for Scriptural Diversity* (Louisville: Westminster John Knox Press, 1995), 71.

26. Ibid., 72. In Wijk-Bos's endnote for this translation she refers the reader to *Midrash Rabbah Genesis* (London: Soncino, 1951), 18.

27. Johnson, *She Who Is,* 83. This point was made also by Augustine, *The Trinity,* trans. Edmund Hill (Brooklyn: New City Press, 1991), book 12, ch. 2, no. 5, 325.

28. Schneiders, *Women and the Word,* 21. Schneiders prefers to call these functional designations "literal," meaning "matter of fact." I am using the term "functional" because I believe that it describes these designations more clearly.

29. Sallie McFague, *Metaphorical Theology: Models of God in Religious Language* (Philadelphia: Fortress, 1982), 15.

30. Ibid., 19.

31. Schneiders, *Women and the Word,* 27.

32. The Wisdom of Solomon and Sirach both are included in the Bibles of the Roman Catholic and Orthodox churches, but are found among the apocryphal books of Protestant Bibles.

33. Roland E. Murphy, *The Tree of Life: An Exploration of Biblical Wisdom Literature* (New York: Doubleday, 1990), 71. Murphy points out that the time-honored interpretation has been that Proverbs 8 provides a commentary on Prov. 3:19 ("The Lord by wisdom founded the earth"); that is, we have here a statement that wisdom is an attribute of God, a trait interior to God.

34. Ibid., 145.

35. Johnson, *She Who Is*, 91.

36. Ibid., 92.

37. Elisabeth Schüssler Fiorenza, *In Memory of Her: A Feminist Reconstruction of Christian Origins* (New York: Crossroad, 1983), 132.

38. Ibid., 125.

39. Ibid., 138–39.

40. "Persons" is in quotation marks here because when the word "person" is used of a member of the Trinity, it is not meant to refer to a distinct individual with a unique ego-identity. The unity of the three in God would be compromised by such an understanding. As Augustine points out, we use the word "person" for the three divine revelations simply because without person we would be reduced to silence. See Augustine, *On the Trinity*, book 5, ch. 9, no. 10.

41. Hymns cited in Rosemary Radford Ruether, *Womanguides: Readings in Feminist Theology* (Boston: Beacon Press, 1985), 29–31. Ruether indicates that her source is *The Odes of Solomon*, ed. James H. Charlesworth (Oxford: Clarendon Press, 1973), 82–83, 126–217. In addition, Ruether notes that some early Christian texts not accepted into the biblical canon, such as the *Gospel of the Hebrews* and the *Gospel of Philip*, also depict the Holy Spirit as female. See Ruether, *Sexism and God-Talk*, 59.

42. Ruether, *Sexism and God-Talk*, 60.

43. Augustine, *On the Trinity*, book 12, ch. 2, no. 5.

44. Yves Congar, *I Believe in the Holy Spirit*, vol. 3, *The River of the Water of Life Flows in the East and in the West*, trans. David Smith (New York: Seabury Press, 1983), 157.

45. Johnson, *She Who Is*, 52.

46. Ibid., 56.

47. Patricia Wilson-Kastner, *Faith, Feminism, and the Christ* (Philadelphia: Fortress, 1983), 122.

48. Ibid., 122–23.

49. Ibid., 124.

50. Catherine Mowry LaCugna, "God in Communion with Us: The Trinity," in *Freeing Theology: The Essentials of Theology in a Feminist Perspective*, ed. Catherine Mowry LaCugna (San Francisco: HarperCollins, 1993), 91.

51. Wilson-Kastner, *Faith, Feminism, and the Christ*, 127.

52. Christa K. Dixon, *Negro Spirituals: From Bible to Folk Song* (Philadelphia: Fortress, 1976), 89–92.

53. Alice Walker, *The Color Purple* (New York: Washington Square Press, 1982), 175–79.

54. Katie Cannon, "Kate and the Color Purple," in *God's Fierce Whimsy: Christian Feminism and Theological Education*, The Mud Flower Collective (New York: Pilgrim Press, 1985), 105.

55. Ntozake Shange, *for colored girls who have considered suicide, when the rainbow is enuf* (New York: Macmillan, 1977), 63.

56. Grant, *White Women's Christ*, 212. Her source is Harold A. Carter, *The Prayer Tradition of Black People* (Valley Forge, Pa.: Judson Press, 1976), 50.

57. James H. Cone, *Black Theology and Black Power* (1969; reprint, Maryknoll, N.Y.: Orbis Books, 1997), 41.

58. Jacquelyn Grant, "Womanist Theology: Black Women's Experience as a Source for Doing Theology, with Special Reference to Christology," in *Black Theology: A Documentary History,* vol. 2: *1980–1992,* ed. James H. Cone and Gayraud S. Wilmore, 2nd ed. (Maryknoll, N.Y.: Orbis Books, 1993), 283.

59. Ibid., 286–87.

60. Kelly Brown Douglas, *The Black Christ* (Maryknoll, N.Y.: Orbis Books, 1994), 109–10.

61. Ibid.

62. Ibid., 117; citation from Walker, *The Color Purple,* 177.

63. María Pilar Aquino, *Our Cry for Life: Feminist Theology from Latin America* (Maryknoll, N.Y.: Orbis Books, 1993), 131.

64. Elsa Tamez, *The Bible of the Oppressed,* trans. Matthew J. O'Connell (Maryknoll, N.Y.: Orbis Books, 1982), 2. She chooses to speak of the "God of the Oppressed" where women are concerned, because the proposal of Gustavo Gutiérrez, "The God of the Poor," does not adequately respond to the condition of women, who are not only economically poor, but also subjugated by males in their families and societies.

65. Luz Beatriz Arellano, "Women's Experience of God in Emerging Spirituality," in *With Passion and Compassion: Third World Women Doing Theology,* ed. Virginia Fabella and Mercy Amba Oduyoye (Maryknoll, N.Y.: Orbis Books, 1988), 136.

66. Ivone Gebara, "Women Doing Theology in Latin America," in *Through Her Eyes: Women's Theology from Latin America,* ed. Elsa Tamez (Maryknoll, N.Y.: Orbis Books, 1989), 44.

67. Aquino, *Our Cry for Life,* 134.

68. Ada María Isasi-Díaz, *En la Lucha: In the Struggle: Elaborating a Mujerista Theology* (Minneapolis: Fortress, 1993), 74.

69. Ada María Isasi-Díaz and Yolanda Tarango, *Hispanic Women: Prophetic Voice in the Church* (San Francisco: Harper & Row, 1988).

70. Ibid., 16.

71. Ibid., 26.

72. Ibid., 29.

73. Ibid., 46.

74. Ibid., and passim.

75. Aquino, *Our Cry for Life,* 142–49.

76. Isasi-Díaz, *En la Lucha,* 74.

77. Mercy Amba Oduyoye, "The African Experience of God through the Eyes of an Akan Woman," *Cross Currents* 47 (1997): 493–504.

78. Ibid., 497.

79. Chung Hyun Kyung, "Welcome the Spirit, Hear Her Cries: The Holy Spirit, Creation and the Culture of Life," *Christianity and Crisis* 51 (1991): 223.

80. Daly, *The Church and the Second Sex,* 38.

81. Phyllis A. Bird, "Sexual Differentiation and Divine Image in the Genesis Creation Texts," in *The Image of God: Gender Models in Judeo-Christian Tradition,* ed. Kari Elisabeth Børresen (Minneapolis: Fortress, 1995), 12–13. See also her " 'Male and Female He Created Them': Gen 1:27b in the Context of the Priestly Account of Creation," *Harvard Theological Review* 74 (1981): 146–47.

QUESTIONS FOR REFLECTION AND DISCUSSION

1. Complete these sentences:
   God is....
   God is not....
   Are you aware of the possible sources of what you have written from your own personal history?

2. Circle the letter for the images for God to which you feel attracted; star those to which you feel resistant.

   A. Father

   B. Mother

   C. Holy Spirit

   D. Jesus Christ

   E. Father, Son, and Holy Spirit

   F. The Dancing Three

   G. Judge

   H. Good Shepherd

   I. Friend

   J. Liberator

   K. Healer

   M. Mystery

   N. Creator

   O. Redeemer

   P. Lord

   Q. Woman Wisdom

   R. *Sophia* Incarnate

   S. Encompassing Presence

   T. Cosmic Energy

   U. Love

   V. Goddess

   W. Covenant Maker

   X. Black Christ

   Y. God of Life

   Z. God of the Poor

   Add your own image that does not appear above.

3. Which of the above that you circled are the most and least important to you? Write a few sentences explaining why.

4. What connotation do you give to YHWH, "I am (who I am)"?

5. Why are many Euro-American feminists attracted to the figure Woman Wisdom (*Hokmah* and *Sophia*)?

6. What is your response to the Euro-American feminist proposal that Jesus Christ is *Sophia* incarnate?

7. Is the depiction of the relationship of the divine Three in the Trinity in the image of *perichoresis* (the round dance of three equal persons) a helpful alternative to the presentation of God as Father Almighty, Son of God, and Holy Spirit, Lord of Life?

8. What is your reaction to the womanist image of Christ as a black female?

9. What is your response to the Latin American feminist emphasis on the God of Life?

10. Do you believe that Mary Daly's statement "If God is male, then the male is God" is valid where the issue of males and females imaging God is concerned?

AREAS FOR EXPLORATION

1. Interview three persons of different ages and from different ethnic groups, using questions 1 and 2 from the "Questions for Reflection and Discussion."

2. Look into why some women say they need Goddess religion. Can any of the things that these women find in Goddess traditions also be found in the Christian tradition's ways of talking about and to God?

3. Explore further how African, Asian, and/or Native American women are speaking about God. Reflect on the difference that social location makes in how the authors you chose speak about or to God.

RECOMMENDED READINGS

Bettenhausen, Elizabeth. "Re-Imagining: A New Stage in US Feminist Theology." Pp. 90–101 in *Women's Visions: Theological Reflection, Celebration, Action,* ed. Ofelia Ortega. Geneva: WCC Publications, 1995.

Cole, Susan, Marian Ronan, and Hal Taussig. *Wisdom's Feast: Sophia in Study and Celebration.* 2nd ed. Kansas City, Mo.: Sheed and Ward, 1996.

Douglas, Kelly Brown. *The Black Christ.* Maryknoll, N.Y.: Orbis Books, 1994.

Hilkert, Mary Catherine. "Cry Beloved Image: Rethinking the Image of God." Pp. 190–205 in *The Embrace of God,* ed. Ann O'Hara Graff. Maryknoll, N.Y.: Orbis Books, 1995.

Isasi-Díaz, Ada María, and Yolanda Tarango. *Hispanic Women: Prophetic Voice in the Church.* San Francisco: Harper & Row, 1988.

Johnson, Elizabeth A. *She Who Is: The Mystery of God in Feminist Theological Discourse.* New York: Crossroad, 1992.

Loades, Ann. *Feminist Theology: A Reader.* Louisville: Westminster John Knox Press, 1990.

Moody, Linda. *Women Encounter God: Theology across the Boundaries of Difference.* Maryknoll, N.Y.: Orbis Books, 1996.

Osiek, Carolyn. "Images of God: Breaking Boundaries." *Spirituality Today* 40 (1998): 333–44.

Procter-Smith, Marjorie. *In Her Own Rite: Constructing Feminist Liturgical Tradition.* Nashville: Abingdon Press, 1990.

Ruether, Rosemary Radford. *Sexism and God-Talk: Toward a Feminist Theology.* Boston: Beacon Press, 1983.

Chapter 4

Feminist Perspectives
on Women and the Church

> The relationship of the Church to its changing historical setting poses the thorny question of separating the relative from the absolute, peeling the onion, to use a conventional analogy. How far can the accretions of history be peeled from the core of truth? What changes can be allowed? The truth of the one Christian mystery is always embodied in human form, temporal forms, and is simply not available in its pristine essence. — ANNE E. CARR[1]

The word "church" derives from the Greek word *kyriakos,* meaning "belonging to the Lord," but is also the word used to translate the New Testament term *ekklēsia*, meaning "assembly" or "the gathered." Traditionally, the people assembled were gathered from diverse parts of society, "in Christ" (Rom. 8:1; Phil. 1:1). From the outset, even in New Testament times, although its members believed themselves to belong to Christ in a common dedication to his memory and mission, the church was not perfect. Early on, controversy swirled around "false teaching" and behavior (cf. 1 John 4:1–6; 2 John 1:9–11; 1 Tim. 4:1–5; 2 Tim. 3:1–9), as nascent Christian communities sought to "test the spirits" among them to see if they were really from God (1 John 4:1) and train each other with guidance of the Holy Spirit in "godliness" (1 Tim. 4:7).

In the quotation at the beginning of this chapter, Anne Carr, a North American Roman Catholic theologian, draws attention to the process of testing the spirits that is ongoing in most churches around the globe. The question being tested is, How are the core of Christian truth concerning women's roles in the church and the accretions about women that have developed in its history to be differentiated? Tension surrounds this question, especially because many women, and men as well, experience disparity between how the Gospels show Jesus treating women and how the churches treat women, especially where their full participation is concerned. This is the issue. Many spirits, some of which are in opposition, clamor to be tested, each claiming to be of the Holy Spirit. When authentic Godly truth is voiced, how will Christians recognize it? In the testing of spirits, feminists are employing a hermeneutical process to their experience of being church today while looking both to the church's beginnings in Jesus Christ and the early factors that set in motion its patterns of evolution.

The way in which Carr engages the feminist hermeneutical process is consonant with her basic beliefs about the church, which she speaks of as "the gift of

133

the Spirit, born of the life, death and resurrection of Jesus."[2] The church, therefore, is a sacred reality, a gift given by God through Jesus Christ and the Holy
Spirit. Her hermeneutics respects the unique nature of the church. It is not just
one organization among others. The church, however, does bear its sacred gift
"in a human vessel that has long taken many different forms in different places
and times in its long history."[3] Put simply, the church is not only a sacred reality,
but also a human one. As human, it is marked by struggle — the testing of the
spirits about which the New Testament speaks — in the midst of the complex
ambiguities of history. The church flourishes as the "body of Christ," but as the
"people of God" it also groans and travails as it awaits the fullness promised by
God through Christ (see Rom. 8:19–22).

The testing of the spirits requires attending to the travails for women in
the Christian churches, without discounting the joy that participation in Jesus'
mission also brings to women's lives. The application of a hermeneutics of suspicion leads Carr and many other feminists to conclude that the core truth of
Christianity has been misinterpreted where the roles of women are concerned.
This has resulted in decisions and practices that have been detrimental not only
to women but also to their churches. This conclusion emerges in sharp relief when one reflects on what a hermeneutics of remembrance applied to the
mission of Jesus and his proclamation of the reign of God unveils.

While proclaiming God's message, Jesus gathered followers, not only men
but also women, from all parts of society, to form a community with a mission.
In the manner in which Jesus accomplished this, he modeled that patriarchal
behavior was not of God. He welcomed marginal people among his disciples:
landless poor, outcasts, and sinners. His was an inclusive community in which
the first would be counted last and in which those who desired to be first would
give service to others. This is symbolically enacted by Jesus washing the feet
of his disciples with the directive that they do the same for one another. Put
simply, Jesus formed a community of friends, the foundation for what would develop into the church after his death and resurrection. The contemporary church,
therefore, is rooted in the mission of Jesus Christ and in the men and women
who embrace this mission as his disciples.

In chapter 2 we explored biblical stories about Jesus and the women disciples. The stories of Mary Magdalene, Martha, and Mary illustrate that women
played significant roles in Jesus' life and mission. Women were contributors to
the movement; they were among the first people gathered in Christ. There is
no reason not to argue that Jesus related to these women in an unbiased and
loving way. No doubt, they experienced themselves as belonging to his community every bit as much as the men. There are very good reasons why Elisabeth
Schüssler Fiorenza stresses again and again in her writings that the community
that Jesus formed was a "discipleship of equals."[4] There is evidence that the
pattern of women acting as disciples continued in the Christian movement after
Jesus' death and resurrection. This is apparent in the New Testament's attention to women like Lydia, a Gentile convert who offered her home as a "house
church" in Philippi (Acts 16:14–15); Phoebe, whom Paul called a "minister"
(*diakonos*) in the church (Rom. 16:1); Priscilla (Prisca), who along with her

husband, Aquila, is said to be a co-worker with Paul (Rom. 16:3); and a woman known only as Mary, esteemed for her hard work for the church (Rom. 16:6). These examples, and more besides, provide evidence that women had roles of leadership at the time of Christianity's beginnings.

Yet this is not the whole story where Paul and women are concerned. Apparently in the early 50s the Christian community at Corinth was divided about many things, including about women praying and prophesying without wearing a suitable head covering. Women were not to do this because being unveiled broke with accepted custom (1 Cor. 11:4–17). Later in the same letter, we find another issue raised. Should women be speaking in the church? The answer is that they are to be silent in the church assembly, "for they are not permitted to speak and should be subordinate as the law also says" (1 Cor. 14:34–35). Scholars have long debated whether these words directing women to be silent actually came from Paul or were added later by one of his followers. Perhaps we will never know. What we do know is that this directive is found also in the first letter to Timothy (2:11–13), which biblical scholars believe was composed by one of Paul's followers (sometime between 63 and 110).

These texts contribute to the conclusion that the patriarchal patterns of civil society overcame the discipleship of equals that Jesus had instituted. The spirits were tested and cognitive dissonance emerged between Jesus' behavior and gender roles defined by society. The churches chose to conform to the status quo as it became Romanized. This is particularly true after the Roman emperor Constantine converted to Christianity early in the fourth century and the church then underwent a transformation from a persecuted sect to a state religion. Soon, its governance became centralized in Rome, although major cities in the East would resist this centralization. As Catholic theologian Mary Hunt points out, "Everything from church architecture to the structures of decision-making, from the designs of the bishops' headgear to papal authority, was construed in a top-down way with virtually no horizontal lines. Implicit in this culture and often explicit in its teachings, was the radical inequality of men and women, of clergy and lay people."[5]

This sea change is reflected in the English word "church," which we already noted is derived from the Greek word for "belonging to the lord, the patriarch, the master." The word of choice is certainly not without significance. The preferred biblical term for church, *ekklēsia,* meaning "assembly," closely associated to the discipleship of equals, becomes less prominent. Church authority modeled after imperial Roman rule, with its well-defined hierarchy, becomes the paradigm for the Christian church. Along with it, the subordination of women becomes the norm. This sketch of the history of a Romanized Christianity begs for a more thorough treatment, but that lies beyond the purpose of the introductory section of this chapter, which is to look back to the roots of the tension in the church regarding the core of Christian truth and the accretions that developed early on. The shift in paradigms is significant, because the pattern continues to a greater or lesser degree in churches today. We have looked back into the history of the church to gain a perspective on the present, and possibly also to see with greater clarity directions for the future that are consonant with the truth of Christianity.

The Christian Church(es) Today

During Christianity's two-thousand-year history, the concrete embodiments of Christ's mission have taken many forms in communities gathered in Jesus' name. Part of the testing of what best embodies that mission has resulted in irreconcilable differences in the church. As a result, the Christian church has become a collection of churches, often called "denominations." Each must face important questions: What changes are needed now so that this church can be faithful to its charge to make the reign of God a reality for a new generation? How can the needed changes be realized in ways that honor Jesus' message and the church's revered traditions, and also contribute to its future vitality? Specifically, what role should women play in providing direction for these changes and in implementing them?

Because church is such a complex and evolving sacred human reality, how one responds to these questions is affected by how members describe their relationship to their church. These descriptions are rooted in how one conceives of church. Theologians speak of these different conceptions as "models" that describe important emphases in a person's membership in a church. These proposed models conceive of church as:

1. *A fellowship of believers, the people of God*, bound together in their shared commitment and common worship of the Trinitarian God revealed in Jesus Christ. In this model, church is an event that happens when people gather to celebrate their faith by hearing the biblical Word preached to them and, in many cases, sharing in the *sacrament of Eucharist, or Communion.

2. *A sacramental mystery* that both transcends and is visibly present in the world. The church is the mystery of God's abiding presence. It is a sacrament of salvation at all times and for all times. For persons who view the church as a sacramental mystery, participation in the sacramental worship of the church is given primacy in their expression of church membership.

3. *A prophetic voice* in a sinful world. In this model, to be church is to be committed to social justice on behalf of the oppressed. A Christian commitment calls the church to oppose societal values that conflict with Jesus' message of inclusive love.

4. *An institution,* a visible organization, hierarchically structured with clear lines of authority. This model stresses apostolic succession that can be traced to Peter and the other apostles.

5. *The presence of the reign of God* within the heart of the individual believer. This model is on the opposite end of the spectrum from the preceding model. Persons attracted to this model are likely to speak of their Christian commitment as divine election or in relationship to a "born again" experience. Persons who favor this model do not believe that any specific organizational structure is necessary for the church to be true to the gospel.[6]

It is possible for a Christian to embrace more than one of these models. They are not necessarily mutually exclusive. For example, a person can give primacy to the sacramental understanding of church and can also take a prophetic stance in response to injustice. Such an individual may celebrate the Eucharist on Sunday and protest unfair housing practices on Monday. Although these many senses of church are not particular to any one Christian denomination, a Roman Catholic is likely to identify with the church as a sacramental mystery, since sacraments play such a prominent role in the life of the Roman Catholic Church, and to think of the church as a hierarchically structured institution, since it has distinct levels of authority tied to ordination. This would be less true for Protestants. For Roman Catholic feminists, however, the institutional model is likely to be the least attractive, because women are unable to share in the church's governance and decision-making. These functions are performed by the ordained hierarchy. Many Catholic feminists would, therefore, identify more readily with the prophetic model of the church and/or the model of the people of God. Protestant feminists are also more likely to be attracted to these models than to the others. Each of these models is affected, at least to some degree, by how ordination to the ministry is conceived and by who may be ordained. Therefore, one of the thorniest questions that Christian churches must face in the era of rising feminist consciousness is, Is it appropriate for women to be ordained to church ministry? A response to this question requires some background on how ordination is understood in the Christian churches. To understand the theological meaning invested in ordination also requires an understanding of the meaning that the Christian churches give to the sacraments.

The Christian Churches and Sacraments

Every religion has certain ritual actions that its members enact publicly and communally to express their fundamental beliefs. In Christianity, some of those prayerful ritual actions are called "sacraments." Although there are different notions of what a sacrament is in the Christian churches, a generic definition for sacrament is certain specific rites or ritual actions by a particular Christian church or denomination. These ritual actions are symbolic, pointing to memorable religious beliefs associated with Jesus Christ and the offer of salvation made by God through him and through the grace of the Holy Spirit. The term "sacrament" (*sacramentum* in Latin) is usually traced to Tertullian (died ca. 220), a Western Christian theologian who applied the term "sacrament" to baptism. Soon it was applied to the Eucharist and to other religious rites and symbolic actions performed in memory of Christ. In the late fourth century, Augustine spoke of sacraments as "visible words," which have an element apparent to the senses, such as the bread and wine consecrated at a eucharistic liturgy, and a verbal element, such as the words "This is my body" and "This is my blood" said over the bread and wine.[7] Both the element apparent to the senses and the words prayed during the ritual have connections to the life and ministry of Jesus Christ.

Prior to the sixteenth century, different regions of Western Europe numbered a variety of ritual actions among their sacraments, with numbers varying from five to thirty. The sixteenth century is a significant period because this is the time in which Martin Luther, a German Augustinian monk, questioned the sacramental theology and practice of Roman Catholicism. At that time the Roman Catholic Church regarded a sacrament to be an instrumental cause of God's grace. Luther adopted an explicitly biblical approach to the sacraments, regarding them to be a special form of biblically rooted proclamation. He accepted only baptism and the Eucharist as formal sacraments, on the grounds that only these two, according to biblical witness, were instituted by Christ.

The Roman Catholic Church, in contrast, proposed a more definitive notion of sacrament at the Council of Trent in 1547, arguing that there were seven sacraments (rather than two). Not only baptism and Eucharist (the Lord's Supper) but also confirmation, penance (today called reconciliation), ordination, matrimony, and extreme unction (today called anointing of the sick) were declared to be instituted by Christ and to give saving grace to those who place no obstacle in the way.[8] The Eastern Orthodox churches have the same seven sacraments, but attach less importance to the precise number or definition. Sacraments for the Eastern Orthodox and Byzantine Catholics are the celebration of the holy mysteries that symbolically express God's initiative on our behalf to incorporate believers into the divine life revealed by Christ.

In the years following the Council of Trent, other Protestant reformers followed Luther's pattern of speaking of baptism and Eucharist as sacraments, while retaining a much broader sense of sacraments than Roman Catholics. Gradually, however, as new Protestant churches sought to divest their worship services of all things Roman Catholic, the term "sacrament" occurred less and less frequently, although baptism and the commemoration of the Lord's Supper were retained.

Since the sixteenth century there has been no full agreement among the churches regarding the number of sacraments and how they are to be understood. One finds a great diversity of positions on the sacraments not only between the Roman Catholic and Protestant churches, but also among the Protestant churches themselves. For example, the Church of England, the foundation of which can be traced to King Henry VIII's disputes with Roman Catholic authority, gives special importance to the sacraments as the visible means of God's grace. Anglicanism and the Anglican Communion churches, which developed from the Church of England, recognize baptism and Eucharist (or Holy Communion) to be sacraments because they are "certain and sure witnesses and effectual agencies of God's love and grace." The Anglican Communion churches also attribute a sacramental character to confirmation, penance, matrimony, sacred unction, and holy orders.[9] In contrast, the Baptist churches (with twenty-seven distinct church groups in the United States and more around the globe) rarely use the term "sacrament," referring to the biblically based practices of celebrating baptism and the Lord's Supper as "ordinances."[10] Of the major Christian denominations, only the Society of Friends (Quakers) and the Salvation Army make no use at all of sacraments.

Ordination and the Christian Churches

Given the diversity of approaches to ritualized actions that give a particular church its unique identity, it is obvious that understanding of ordination to ministry in the Christian churches will be equally diverse. From a historical standpoint, the term "ordination" can be traced to a public ritual in pre-Christian Rome in which free male citizens of the empire were ordained into some official governing capacity in the Roman state. After the Roman Empire became Christianized in the fourth century, church leaders appropriated the term *ordo* for the consecration of priests. *Ordo,* however, was also used for the consecration of other groups who were set apart to give service to the church, including virgins and widows. By the Middle Ages, the sacrament of holy orders was defined primarily in terms of priesthood, and with the passage of time the word "ordination" was reserved for the sacramental consecration of bishops, priests, and deacons. In keeping with the teaching of the Second Vatican Council of the Roman Catholic Church (1963–65), the pattern of sacramental ordination to the orders of diaconate, priesthood, and episcopacy continues today.

An essential part of the liturgy for priestly ordination is the laying on of hands by a bishop. The roots of this symbolic act are in the New Testament (Acts 6:6; 13:3; 1 Tim. 4:14; 2 Tim. 1:6). Priesthood, however, can be traced in the Old Testament to the priesthood of Aaron (brother of Moses) and the designation of the tribe of Levi as the tribe set apart to offer God prayer and sacrifices for sins.

The Roman Catholic and Eastern Orthodox churches maintain ordination to priesthood as a sacrament that can be traced historically to Jesus Christ and his apostles. In contrast, most of the Reformation churches, following Luther's lead, attribute no significance to the idea of apostolic succession. The exceptions among the Reformation churches are the Church of England and the Anglican Communion churches around the globe, including the Episcopal churches in the United States. The Anglican Communion holds that ordination has a sacramental character, and it affirms apostolic succession as basic to "the ministerial commission that was given as a trust from Christ."[11] Until the 1970s, only a baptized male could validly receive ordination in the churches with a sacramental priesthood.

Protestant churches, influenced by Martin Luther, do not have a sacramental priesthood, but do have public rituals for conferring the office of minister on baptized persons who meet the criteria determined by church leaders, such as bishops or elders. Influenced by the Pastoral Epistles in the New Testament, early Lutherans envisioned their local congregation as a household of God. Like any household, a congregation requires good ordering. The person ordained to public ministry is charged with "ordering" the congregation in a way that ensures that the gospel is preached effectively and that baptism and the Lord's Supper are celebrated rightly.

Following Luther's lead, ordination to public ministry in most Protestant churches is an extension or specification of baptism that requires public recognition of the special gifts, or charisms, of the person being ordained. In most ordination rituals, "laying on of hands" by others already ordained is the symbolic sign of consecration. The influential biblical text in this understanding of ordination is "I remind you to rekindle the gift of God that is within you through the laying on of my hands" (2 Tim. 1:6; cf. 1 Tim. 4:14).[12]

In the Protestant churches, somewhat different understandings of ordination emerged over time. However, most are likely to agree that knowledge of the Bible, the gift of preaching, and a generous spirit are important qualities for an ordained minister. Usually, a person is ordained only when a church calls or elects a particular person to the office of ministry. The actual rite of ordination by legitimate church authority is a public confirmation of this election and the official granting of the office.[13]

After the Reformation was underway, the Roman Catholic Church, at the Council of Trent, maintained that Christ explicitly instituted and conferred the sacrament of holy orders on the twelve apostles.[14] This sacramental ordination to priesthood was traced to the "Last Supper" that Jesus shared with his followers shortly before his death. Biblical texts indicate that Jesus, after blessing and sharing bread and wine with those gathered, said, "Do this in remembrance of me" (Luke 22:19; cf. 1 Cor. 11:25). The Roman Catholic leadership interpreted these words, attributed to Jesus, as his ordination of the apostles, all of whom were male. As successors to the apostles, bishops continued to confer the sacrament of holy orders on men.[15]

Not all of the churches that broke away from the Roman Catholic Church during the sixteenth century abandoned sacramental ordination. The worldwide Anglican Communion churches, which in the United States include the Episcopal churches,[16] retain ordination to the priesthood by bishops who are themselves lawfully ordained. Like the other churches that have a sacrament of ordination to the priesthood (i.e., Roman Catholic and Eastern Orthodox churches), the Anglican Communion churches reserved ordination to males for most of their history. However, there are now churches in the Anglican Communion that ordain women, believing that there are no theological obstacles to women being ordained as successors to the apostles. However, not every denomination within the Anglican Communion accepts the ordination of women as valid,[17] and in denominations that have accepted the ordination of women, not every local bishop is willing to ordain women to the priestly ministry.[18]

Women and the Sacrament of Priestly Ordination

During the era of the second wave of feminism, discussion regarding the ordination of women began to occur in the Roman Catholic, Protestant Episcopal, and Anglican Communion churches. In the 1970s an increasing number of women in these churches voiced their desire to be ordained because they felt a call from God to serve their communities as priests. For persons with a feminist consciousness, as Anne Carr points out, "the question of ordination to the priestly ministry represents an important symbol of the lack of presence of women in the official life of the church."[19] Canonical ordinations of women in the Anglican Communion churches took place in Hong Kong in 1971 and in Canada in

1976. This latter year was the same year in which the Episcopal Church in the United States approved the ordination of women to the priesthood at its general convention. This decision was made after the Episcopal Church had rejected the ordination of women and some retired and resigned bishops had conducted an irregular (noncanonical) ordination of women in Philadelphia.[20] These ordinations were regularized in 1977. During the same year, the first Anglican women were ordained in New Zealand.[21]

At the time when Anglican and Episcopalian women were seeking ordination in their churches, Roman Catholic women were also beginning to call for the ordination of women to priesthood in their church. New theological ideas from the Second Vatican Council (1963–65), such as the church being "the people of God," the recognition that the whole church is called to holiness, and the affirmation of the dignity and gifts of lay men and women, converged with the ideas generated by the second wave of the women's movement. Roman Catholic women began to conceive of their membership in the church differently, principally in terms of a more active participation. This participation would include different church ministries that used to be reserved only for priests or men. The call for women's equality in civil society also prompted many Roman Catholic women, especially women in the United States, to read the papal statements and Second Vatican Council documents through the lens of this experience.

In 1963, Pope John XXIII, the pope who convened the Second Vatican Council, drew attention to women's emerging consciousness in a widely read encyclical, *Pacem in Terris*. In this encyclical, John XXIII included among his list of important "signs of the times" this statement about women:

> It is obvious to everyone that women are now taking a part in public life. This is happening more rapidly in nations with a Christian tradition, and more slowly and broadly among people who have inherited other traditions or cultures. Since women are becoming ever more conscious of their dignity, they will not tolerate being treated as inanimate objects, or mere instruments, but claim, both in domestic and public life, the rights and duties that befit a human person.[22]

By drawing attention to these developments, some women were led to believe that the papacy had its finger on the pulse of the women's movement. Pope John XXIII's affirmation of the inherent dignity of women was welcomed and applauded.

In the Second Vatican Council's "Pastoral Constitution on the Church in the Modern World" (*Gaudium et Spes* [1965]), issues regarding the lack of social justice for women were addressed as part of the signs of the times. "The Church in the Modern World" stresses that "where they have not won it, women claim for themselves an equity with men before the law and in fact" (no. 9). Later in this same document the bishops noted that "every type of discrimination, whether societal or cultural, whether based on sex, race, color, social condition, language, or religion, is to be overcome" (no. 29). In addition, the fundamental personal rights of a woman "to embrace a state of life or acquire an education or cultural benefits equal to those recognized for men" are not to be denied (no. 29).

These statements about women were directed to "the modern world," meaning civil or secular societies. Left unanswered was the question about the treatment of women by the Roman Catholic Church. Since "The Church in the Modern World," the distinction between what holds true in civil society and in the Roman Catholic Church has been maintained where women's ordination is concerned. Feminists question the logic of this distinction. Since the Catholic Church was engaged in extensive internal renewal, the question was raised, How would church authorities remedy the apparent denial of women to the right and freedom to embrace a particular state of life within the church as priests? The role of the priest is to serve God by preaching and teaching, administering the sacraments, and ministering to people in times of need. The effects of the exclusion of women from these functions are far-reaching. Not only are all women and lay men dependent on a male clergy for the sacraments — especially the Eucharist, reconciliation, and the anointing of the sick — and preaching when the church community gathers to celebrate these sacraments, but the Catholic church communities also lose the talents and gifts of women who feel called to serve God as priests.

In 1974, in preparation for the United Nations Decade on Women (1975–85), the Leadership Conference of Women Religious (LCWR) in the United States (consisting of representatives from most of the Roman Catholic communities of *vowed women religious) sent a resolution to the National Conference of Catholic Bishops in United States urging them to facilitate the broader inclusion of women in ministries, including the ordained priesthood. At roughly the same time, a group of Catholic women planned the first Women's Ordination Conference. At this conference, held in 1975 in Detroit, twelve hundred women gathered to launch the call for women's ordination to the priesthood. Another five hundred had to be turned away due to lack of space. Pittsburgh Sister of Mercy Elizabeth Carroll, a former president of the LCWR, gave the keynote address.[23] At the end of the conference, female participants were asked to stand if they felt called to ordination — 280 stood. For many who attended the event, this was a prophetic moment in which they believed a Godly message was delivered.

In the same year, Pope Paul VI announced that the Papal Theological Commission and the Pontifical Biblical Commission would study the role of women in ministry, including the question of priestly ordination. Although the Pontifical Biblical Commission found the Scriptures to be ambiguous where the question of the ordination of women was concerned, the Sacred Congregation for the Doctrine of the Faith (CDF), with the approval of Paul VI, issued a declaration, "On the Question of the Admission of Women to the Ministerial Priesthood" (*Inter Insigniores*),[24] to explain why the Roman Catholic Church leadership did not consider itself authorized to admit women to priestly ordination (no. 5). The CDF likely issued the declaration at this time in response to the recent ordination of women priests in the Protestant Episcopal Church and the high visibility of the ordination movement in the U.S. Catholic Church.

The declaration contains some beautiful thoughts on the importance of women to Jesus and his ministry, but argues against the ordination of women to the sacramental priesthood on grounds rooted in a threefold argument:

1. long-held church tradition

2. the witness of sacred Scripture

3. the religious symbol *in persona Christi*

1. The argument from tradition: *Inter Insigniores* argues that church tradition provides no basis for women's ordination; the Roman Catholic Church has never held that priestly ordination could be "validly conferred" on women (no. 6). Since there is no evidence that the Roman Catholic Church ever ordained women during its long history, the document concludes that the Holy Spirit is opposed to it (no. 9). *— M. Magdalene @ Inetsgypei*

2. The argument from sacred Scripture: According to *Inter Insigniores*, the New Testament provides no evidence that Jesus considered any women for the priesthood. The apostles, all of whom were ordained by Christ, were all men. Not even Mary, Jesus' own mother, is numbered among the twelve apostles (nos. 13, 14, 19).

Anne Carr finds these two arguments to be closely related. She responds to both by drawing attention to other long-held positions that influence them, including the argument that "God is revealed in predominantly masculine imagery as father in the Scriptures."[25] She points out that God is not a sexual being; God as Spirit transcends human sexuality (this, of course, is widely held in feminist theology, as already shown in chapter 3). Carr responds also to the argument that priests must be male because Jesus is male, as were the twelve apostles he chose. In the Gospels there is a connection between the number twelve and the Old Testament regarding the twelve tribes of Israel. Twelve symbolically underscores the inclusiveness of Jesus' community. The number twelve is what matters, not the sex of the apostles. She argues that Jesus and the twelve apostles being male does not rule out women sharing very closely in the ministry of Jesus. She cites evidence already noted in this chapter and in chapter 2. Women shared in Jesus' ministry; Mary Magdalene was an apostle sent after Jesus' death to inform the other followers of Jesus that his tomb was empty.

Carr also draws attention to an additional perspective on women found in the Bible and widely shared in antiquity that underlies the tradition of the non-ordination of women. She writes, "The ancient belief in the uncleanness and temptation of their sex makes women unfit for ordination. Put simply, social and political views of female inferiority have shaped 'women's subordinate roles in the church.'"[26] Yet, this is not all that the Bible says about women as sexual creatures; because the Bible declares the creation to be good, women's sexuality is not evil but good, as a part of the created goodness.

Disputing the Vatican argument from Scripture is not unique to women scholars. Many male scholars have voiced their difficulties with the Vatican argument from Scripture. Raymond Brown, arguably the most influential American Roman Catholic biblical scholar of the twentieth century, responded to the document by pointing out that if one argues that there were no women priests in New Testament times, the claim is misleading. The term "priest" is applied to Christians only in the broad sense of the priesthood of the people (1 Pet. 2:5;

ANNE E. CARR

Anne E. Carr is a Sister of Charity of the Blessed Virgin Mary, a community of Roman Catholic women founded in the United States in 1833 by Mary Frances Clarke and four other Irish immigrant lay women. Established for the purpose of working with newly arriving Catholic immigrants, the sisters devoted their energies to education, a great need then. Carr has continued this dedication to education. A graduate of the Divinity School of the University of Chicago in 1971, Carr has taught at Mundelein College, Indiana University, and the Divinity School at the University of Chicago. She has written three books and numerous articles. In 1997 she received the prestigious John Courtney Murray Award from the Catholic Theological Society of America in recognition of her many scholarly achievements.

Rev. 5:10). Brown further points out that if one makes a claim that women did not celebrate the Eucharist in New Testament times, "there is simply no way of proving that, *even if one may well doubt that they did*."[27] We know very little about who presided at eucharistic liturgies during the period in which the New Testament was formed. Yet, there is evidence that prophets did, for prophets are said to be involved in liturgy (Acts 13:2) and to give thanks (*Didache* 10:7). The New Testament provides ample evidence that there were women who prophesied (1 Cor. 11:5; Acts 21:9). Brown is not a lone male voice; in few areas of scholarship have women found so much solidarity with male theologians as on the issue of scriptural warrants for the non-ordination of women.

3. The argument from religious symbol: The third reason cited in *Inter Insigniores* is the symbolic significance of priests acting *in persona Christi*. *In persona Christi* signifies that at the celebration of the Eucharist, "the priest acts in the role of Christ to the point of being his very image. It is required, therefore, that the priest be male" (no. 26). A common response to this interpretation of *in persona Christi* is that this is a physicalist interpretation. The physicalist interpretation ignores that the risen Christ is not limited to embodiment as a male person. It also puts limitations on the notion of a Christian acting as "another Christ," which is symbolized in the baptismal call from God to all women and

men of every age. All baptized persons are called to conform their lives to the image of Christ (Rom. 8:29).

In addition, in the Christian understanding of redemption, that Jesus was a historical male is not what is important. If the maleness of Jesus was so significant, then the salvific death of Jesus on the cross would redeem only men. Women could not be saved. What is important is that Jesus Christ was fully human. The Council of Chalcedon (451) makes this distinction explicit by confessing Jesus Christ to be truly and completely a human person and not simply a male person. The physicalist interpretation of *in persona Christi* ignores the redemptive significance for both men and women of Christ's incarnation as a fully human person and of his salvific death for all women and men.

Following the declaration "On the Question of the Admission of Women to the Ministerial Priesthood," the women's ordination question did not disappear. In 1983 the Roman Catholic Church published a revision of canon law in which it is stated, "Only a baptized male validly receives sacred ordination" (no. 1024). One of the shortest canons on record, it provides no explanation or justification. In response, the Women's Ordination Conference made posters available with words drawn from Gal. 3:28: "There is no longer male and female; for all are one in Christ."[28] By this time, these words had become a guiding axiom for American supporters of women's ordination, if not in fact a manifesto for equality for males and females in the churches. Many heard in the words from Galatians a call to the church to recognize women's full personhood and redemption in Christ through sacramental ordination to the priesthood or ministry.

Because the question has persisted among Roman Catholics, Pope John Paul II has also addressed the question of women's ordination. In an apostolic letter, "On Ordination and Women" (*Ordinatio Sacerdotalis*), he repeated Pope Paul VI's argument that the Roman Catholic Church has "no authority whatsoever to confer priestly ordination on women" (no. 4). This letter was made public in May 1994 shortly after the Church of England ordained its first women priests and just a few months before the Women's Ordination Conference in the United States celebrated its twentieth anniversary.[29] In November 1995, Cardinal Ratzinger, of the Congregation of the Doctrine of the Faith, wrote a response (*Responsum ad dubium*) underscoring that the non-ordination of women was virtually an infallible teaching, although technically, an apostolic letter is not the usual mechanism for an infallible papal pronouncement.[30]

In "On Ordination and Women," John Paul II affirms a recurring theme in many of his writings on women. He links the fundamental equality of women and men with complementarity.[31] Women are equal to men, but their roles are complementary; that is, certain gifts or qualities are unique to women because of their sex and others are unique to men. The use of complementarity as the principle for assigning church roles makes the biological differences necessary for human reproduction the determining factor. The shortcoming of the principle of complementarity is its potential for promoting hierarchical sexual dualism, rooted in long-standing gender stereotypes, as if it were part of God's will for the church.

During his pontificate, Pope John Paul II has written church documents that affirm the dignity, equality, and giftedness of women. However, what is lacking in these documents are specific recommendations to create new church roles for women that reflect what is implied in his words about males and females being equal.[32] Without these new roles for women in the church, complementarity and true equality are contradictory. The logic of complementarity requires that there be a role in the church open only to women, comparable to the role of priesthood open only to men. The roles that Pope John Paul II extols for women are motherhood and consecrated (i.e., publicly vowed) virginity. Nevertheless, the first is not a public ecclesial role, and the second is open also to males who wish to be vowed religious. A growing frustration among many Roman Catholic women leads them to call upon church leadership to provide a distinctive role for women in which they will be true equal partners in ministry.

Not all Catholic feminists support priestly ordination of women. These feminists believe that perpetuating the hierarchical distinction between ordained priests and laity exacerbates already existing problems, and conflicts with the basic goals of Christian feminism. Some believe that the goal of attaining full partnership in the church will not be achieved by ordaining women priests. Elisabeth Schüssler Fiorenza argues that a discipleship of equals that persons seek in their call for women's ordination will not happen unless there is major change in how the Catholic Church is structured as a hierarchical institution. She notes,

> To think feminist and priesthood [together] is to construct an oxymoron. According to Webster's dictionary an oxymoron is a "combination of contradictory or incongruous words." "Feminist priesthood" not only combines contradictory words but also incongruous realities and incompatible spiritual visions: the radical democratic equality of the discipleship of equals stands in contradiction to the essential religious status of hierarchical office which is conferred in and through ordination in exchange for the promise of obedience and submission.[33]

Schüssler Fiorenza does not believe that ordaining women will resolve the problems associated with patriarchy in the church. Some feminists agree. Unless substantial changes accompany the ordination of women, the church's male-defined hierarchical structure will not change. Adding a few female priests will also not change significantly male-defined ministerial priorities in dioceses or result in significant revisions of canon law. Without extensive collaboration of men and women in a spirit of true mutuality, there will be no true partnership of equals. Women presiding at Eucharist will not change currently prescribed language patterns or God imagery. Women leading prayers in which "man" supposedly includes women and God is imaged as always male will not advance the cause of women's full equality. The language must change because the experience of women acting as "another Christ," leading the community in prayer, makes the linguistic limitations currently imposed on sacramental worship incongruent with the experience of the praying community.

Despite such arguments, there are many women whose personal "testing of the spirits" leads them to believe that they are called by God to be ordained as priests. Out of frustration, some of those women are leaving the Catholic Church to join Christian denominations where they follow this call. Other women, however, support Pope John Paul II's prohibition of women's ordination. Loretta Hoffman, the head of the Alliance of Catholic Women, which has a membership of twenty-five thousand in the United States, praised John Paul II's affirmation of the ban of women's ordination. She believes that this teaching must be upheld because it has a two-thousand-year tradition. She notes that there is plenty of room for women's gifts in the church without a female priesthood. In an interview, Robin T. Edwards, of the *National Catholic Reporter,* quotes Hoffman:

> There is a place for us [women]. We are not upset that it does not include the ordained priesthood. I don't believe that we have rights per se. I believe if the church calls women to serve in a position of authority, we should consider it a privilege, not a right.[34]

Hoffman's choice to focus on "rights" reflects an implicit critique of liberal feminism that emphasizes individual rights and individual choices. There are, of course, other ways of looking at the issue of rights. For example, do Catholics have the right to expect that their local parish church will provide them with opportunities to celebrate Eucharist and the other sacraments? The number of Catholic parishes without ordained priests to preside at Sunday Eucharist in the United States and in many other parts of the world, especially Western Europe and Latin America, is growing due to the shortage of men seeking ordination to the priesthood.[35] The Catholic Church's way of being church is strongly oriented to the communal celebration of sacraments, especially Sunday Eucharist. What will the Catholic Church become in the future when large segments of it have infrequent access to the sacraments? Obviously, this is a very important question for which there is no answer at present.

The issues surrounding women's ordination in the Catholic Church are complex. Following Pope Paul VI's argument, Pope John Paul II has emphasized that the Roman Catholic Church has no authority to ordain women. He has stated that this is "a definitive teaching" of the Roman Catholic Church (no. 4),[36] and therefore is not open to further debate. Pope John Paul II has adopted this position on the grounds that this is the church's consistent position. A male priesthood is a tradition of the church, and as such, it is part of God's plan (no. 1).[37]

How one understands the term "tradition" is obviously very important. The word "tradition" (Greek, *paradosis;* Latin, *traditio*) means literally "to hand on." The handing on of the living faith can take different forms.[38] We can equate tradition with handing on the patterns established by the early church as norms to be followed by the Christian community. In this understanding of tradition, the norms are guidelines from which no member of the community should deviate, not even the pope. This appears to be the primary way in which Pope John Paul II interprets church tradition where the question of women's ordination is concerned. Tradition, however, also refers to the process of handing on the Christian faith in response to changing "signs of the times." Pope John

Paul II's contribution to the social teachings of the Catholic Church on questions related to the economy and the human dignity of workers is a prime example of this understanding of tradition.[39] Tradition in this second sense is a listening to the guidance of the Holy Spirit in the midst of the issues that Christians must face. It emerges from a testing of the spirits and is not a ready-made teaching. It remains to be seen what might develop in regard to the ordination of women if this second understanding of tradition is given more attention in the future. The "signs of the times," including the nonpatriarchal interpretation of gender roles in many parts of the world, the sense of divine call to the priesthood that many women sincerely believe is from God, and the shortage of male candidates for the priesthood may lead to more emphasis on the second understanding of tradition than is currently applied to the question of women's ordination. What is certain is that this issue will not disappear. It is central to what the Catholic Church will become in the years ahead.[40]

Women and Their Churches

The participation of women in their churches is a topic that can be adequately treated only in several volumes. Women have a centuries-long tradition of engaging in ministry as followers of Christ as a way of meaningfully living their faith. Therefore, only a few highlights can be presented as windows into a very large church in which women have prayed and ministered. We will find these windows to be rich in color and symbolism, yet works of art in process. The unfinished nature of them allows for the gentle breeze of the Spirit to continue to bring freshness to the churches and to the lives of the women who minister in them.

Euro-American Women and the Catholic Church

The first window is one that opens into the reality of Euro-American Catholic women. Historically, Catholic women of all ethnic backgrounds have been very active in their church through parish involvement. They have participated in Catholic worship in greater numbers than their male counterparts, even though they could not lead their communities in prayer as ordained priests. It is also women (many of whom were members of parish altar and rosary societies) who used their artistic talent and hard work to make the churches suitable places for worship. To further enhance their spiritual growth, provide one another with spiritual support, and provide for others in need, many Catholic women participated in societies such as the Catholic Daughters of America[41] and Ladies of Charity;[42] some women continue to participate in these societies today. Catholic women have a long tradition of giving service to their parishes and reaching out to those in need in their communities. They have provided for the poor and sick, both as members of their own societies, such as the Ladies of Charity, and as members of the auxiliaries of male-led societies, such as the St. Vincent de Paul Society.

In North America, large numbers of Euro-American women dedicated their lives to the service of the people of God as members of communities of women founded for that purpose. These communities are technically called "religious" because their members take public vows, usually of poverty, chastity, and obedience. We have already noted that Anne E. Carr is a vowed woman religious, a member of the Sisters of Charity of the Blessed Virgin Mary. This group of vowed women religious identifies its founder as Mary Frances Clarke. During the nineteenth century, the B.V.M. sisters, along with other Catholic communities of women religious, accomplished things that most women of that era could not. They were self-supporting. Most had a better education than other Catholic women. They owned and administered convents, orphanages, schools, and hospitals with considerable competence.

Since the Second Vatican Council, the number of vowed women religious in the Roman Catholic Church has dropped dramatically. Fewer women are joining religious communities of women. Yet, an increasing number of women are feeling empowered to minister to others in church- and nonchurch-related ministries. During the past thirty years there has been an enormous shift in how the term "ministry" is understood. Before the Second Vatican Council, ministry was usually reserved for ordained clergy. Not even the work done by vowed women religious was called "ministry." But when Vatican II opened to the non-ordained certain functions that had been performed only by priests, like distributing the Eucharist and visiting the sick as representatives of a parish community, the term expanded to include work done by the non-ordained. The tendency today is to apply the term "ministry" to any service that a person gives as an expression of a Christian commitment. This service may be given by paid professionals and require advanced academic degrees in theology or pastoral ministry, or be done by volunteers, many of whom also have studied theology or Christian spirituality.

There has been an enormous increase of women who are ministerial professionals on the parish and diocesan levels in the Catholic Church. Research gathered in 1997 by the Center for Applied Research in the Apostolate, a national Catholic research center that gathers social science research in response to a request of the U.S. Bishops' Committee on Pastoral Practices, indicates that there were approximately twenty-six thousand paid lay and vowed religious pastoral ministers in the United States. Of that number, 82 percent were women (75 percent lay women and 25 percent vowed women religious).[43] Since 13 percent of the parishes were without priests when this research was gathered,[44] many women serving as pastoral ministers are parish administrators who do virtually every ministry an ordained priest does, short of celebrating some of the sacraments. Unable to consecrate the Eucharist, many of these women are providing communion services on a daily and/or weekly basis.

The increase in ministries for women and non-ordained men is more than a response to the shortfall of priests. Many people are volunteering to take responsibility for the life of their parishes. They serve on committees that plan worship services, educate children, visit the sick, comfort the sorrowful, and welcome newcomers. Many ministries in which people are engaged are not limited to parish church focus. People also engage in outreach ministries in response to local,

MARY FRANCES CLARKE
(b. ca. 1804, d. 1887)

An Irish Catholic lay woman from Dublin, Mary Frances Clarke and four other women traveled to the United States to minister to Irish immigrants in North America. They arrived in Philadelphia in 1833 and formed the Sisters of Charity of the Blessed Virgin Mary with the help of Reverend Terrence J. Donaghoe, who assumed the role of priest-superior. Education became the primary work of this small group of women. Initially, that work was done in Philadelphia. Later, they relocated to Dubuque in response to a bishop's appeal for them to educate Native Americans there. That plan soon changed. Mary Frances Clarke and her sisters were assigned to teach the children of newly arrived Catholic immigrants, principally the Irish, who came to the U.S. after the 1846 potato famine. Although extreme poverty was a part of the early B.V.M. sisters' story, the numbers of sisters grew steadily, and they extended their work of teaching throughout the Midwest and as far west as San Francisco.

Mary Frances Clarke became the official superior of the B.V.M. sisters after Rev. Donaghoe's death in 1869. From the beginning of the B.V.M.s' history, all of the property of the sisters had been in his name. Shortly before he died, at Clarke's request, he willed the B.V.M. properties to her. Clarke then had the community and its property incorporated under Iowa law. She saw to the completion of the constitutions of the community, which had to be delivered to the Vatican by a priest, since women were not permitted to do so. In 1877, Pope Pius IX gave official approval of the B.V.M. and their work. Seven years later, Pope Leo XIII appointed Clarke the Superior of the community for life. She died three years later.[45]

Mary Frances Clarke was a woman of practical wisdom who enabled the B.V.M. sisters to exist as an institution. She was also a woman with a great capacity for loving people, especially her fellow B.V.M. sisters. In reflecting on Mary Frances Clarke, Kathryn Lawlor, B.V.M., writes,

> From the letters of Mary Frances Clarke we learn that she considered a religious vocation to be the participation in a community whose members, by striving to be in close relationship to one another, would, therefore, be in close relationship to God. She never viewed the community as an institution; instead she viewed it as a group of women bonded together in love of God and in love of one another — a circle of friends — a web of relationships. The charism Mary Frances Clarke brought to the church was the reality that this circle of friends, this circle of love, animates an inner freedom where the Holy Will of God is found.[46]

national, and international peace and justice issues. Many people are working together in ecumenical efforts to end racism. In their local communities they are living their commitment as Christians by providing shelter and food for the homeless or victims of domestic violence, and are giving hospice care to persons with AIDS and others who are terminally ill.

Some of these women are also participating in advocacy organizations for women, such as the Women's Ordination Conference and the Women-Church Convergence. Both have become international organizations. The Women's Ordination Conference is a Roman Catholic organization. It was formed in 1976 in the United States a few months after the meeting calling for the ordination of women was held in Detroit (1975). Over the next twenty years, many similar organizations were founded under different titles in other countries, including England, Ireland, Australia, Canada, New Zealand, and South Africa. In 1996, at the European Women's Synod in Gmundsen, Austria, the Women's Ordination Worldwide (WOW) was formed. In 1998, the first International Women's Ordination conference was held in London to coordinate a worldwide campaign for women's ordination in the Roman Catholic Church. The women who participated in this meeting were from Australia, Austria, Germany, Ireland, France, Spain, South Africa, the United Kingdom, and the United States. At that meeting a decision was made to intensify the education of the laity and clergy on the problem of the non-ordination of women, culminating in an international conference to be held early in the twenty-first century.

Women-Church Convergence has a broader agenda than addressing the non-ordination of women. This organization identifies itself as an international ecumenical movement of women's communities and networks of "justice-seeking friends" who share a common vision: the transformation of Christian churches in ways that liberate the people of God from patriarchy.[47] Women-Church emerged in the United States with a conference called "Woman Church Speaks," held in Chicago in 1983. The first conference resulted from the collaborative efforts of Roman Catholic women from the Women's Ordination Conference (WOC), the Women's Alliance for Theology, Ethics and Ritual (WATER), Las Hermanas, and the National Coalition of American Nuns, plus some smaller organizations. Although nearly 95 percent of the fifteen hundred who attended the first conference were Euro-American Roman Catholic women, the movement has become ecumenical and inclusive of women from many racial and ethnic backgrounds. For this reason, the term "Women-Church" soon replaced "Woman Church."[48]

Women-Church invites women to explore their identity as church and to articulate a guiding vision for the transformation of the Christian churches as they now exist. Women-Church has networking at the national level, but is comprised largely of women's grassroots groups. The goal of Women-Church is simple and straightforward: develop communities liberated from sexism. Women-Church has spread beyond the borders of the United States to countries around the globe.[49] In the United States, Women-Church has largely focused on providing a place where women (and men who support a discipleship of equals) can gather for ritual and prayer that express a female sense of God and repudiate the idols of patriarchy.[50] Women-Church has sponsored three major conferences: "From Generation to Generation Women-Church Speaks" (Chicago, 1983), "Women-Church Claiming Our Power" (Cincinnati, 1987), and "Women-Church: Weavers of Change" (Albuquerque, 1993).

Euro-American Women and the Protestant Churches

The second window into which we will peer is that constructed by Euro-American Protestant women. During the nineteenth century, when Mary Frances Clarke was founding the Sisters of Charity of the Blessed Virgin Mary, ideas about "true womanhood" and the literal interpretation of certain biblical injunctions in the Pauline letters of the Bible prevented women from speaking or leading religious assemblies. During the pre–Civil War period of the Protestant "Second Great Awakening," women, especially in the Northeastern states, began to participate in religious revivals in greater numbers than men. Although seldom able to participate in congregational deliberations, nor permitted to vote in church assemblies and conventions, Protestant women did regard the preservation of Christianity in the home as their special sphere. Due to the influence of the "cult of true womanhood," it was widely accepted that Protestant women would live their commitment to God by safeguarding the faith life of their husbands and children. Women did not always succeed in persuading the men of their families to attend church regularly, however. As a result, women significantly outnumbered men in active membership in Protestant churches.

The growing presence of women in Protestant churches in the mid-nineteenth century resulted, according to Elizabeth Fox-Genovese, in a gradual "feminization" of Protestantism in the industrialized northeastern United States (and in industrialized centers in Great Britain and in European countries) during the pre–Civil War period.[51] Preaching in Protestant churches by male ministers came more and more to emphasize matters important to women, especially Christian family life. This concern is a contributing reason for women supporting the abolition of slavery, believing that concubinage of black women contributed to the breakdown of the family. Concerned with the temptations of sinful worldliness, women took initiative in their churches in organizations, such as Bible, ladies' aid, and mission societies. The exact titles given to these societies differed from denomination to denomination and changed over time. However, what did not change was the wide range of services that Protestant women provided to and through their churches. Participation in these societies gave women a sense of identity as disciples of Christ and showed that they could competently carry out his mission.

In the South, on the whole, the picture was different due to the rigid hierarchy that supported the claim that white males were naturally superior to white women and slaves. Yet, diaries of southern Protestant women show that although most accepted the teaching that the Bible did not condemn slavery, they were concerned with their ability to manage the slaves in their households in a proper Christian manner. Fox-Genovese notes that a surprising number of Protestant women in slave-owning households taught their female house slaves to read the Bible, even though teaching slaves to read was forbidden by law.[52]

Protestant attitudes about women as guardians of Christian morality left an indelible mark on the experience of women in the United States. The nineteenth-century view of women as the guiding spirit of a moral home became firmly established and remains in many segments of society. This attitude transcended denominational boundaries to become the norm for all women, even if individual women did not accept it. Fox-Genovese reflects,

> The Protestant image of womanhood offered a model of womanly excellence and an internal standard of character and virtue. It also offered women a special mission and a special form of power. It promised them that they had become the moral fiber of the nation.[53]

This tradition explains in part why women (more often than men) have long been involved in service-oriented church-related projects such as tutoring, providing day care and preschool programs, and giving religious instruction to children. Through church-related outreach programs women provide services to the elderly and physically disabled, adult literacy, food banks, shelters for the homeless, job skill programs, and more.

In Protestant churches as a whole, general acceptance of ordination for women did not happen until the second half of the twentieth century. The movement toward official public roles for women was gradual. By the end of the nineteenth century, at the time in which the first wave of feminism was underway, women in Protestant churches began to argue that church leadership should be based on charismatic gifts and not on gender. The first woman on record to be ordained in the United States was Antoinette Brown Blackwell (1853), a suffragist, in a Congregationalist church in South Butler, New York. Within a year, however, she resigned her position and became a Unitarian.[54] By the end of the nineteenth century, some small church bodies such as the Pilgrim Holiness Church, the Salvation Army, and the Wesleyan Methodist Church were ordaining women.

The largest U.S. Methodist church, the United Methodist Church (UMC), formed from a merger of the Methodist Church and the Evangelical United Brethren Church in 1968, granted full ecclesiastical ordination to women that year. The way was paved for this decision in the 1950s, when the Methodist Church as a denomination granted women ordination and individual bishops of the Evangelical United Brethren Church were also ordaining women.[55] As of 1999 they had 7,370 ordained women ministers, more than any other U.S. denomination, and 37,064 clergymen. The UMC ordained its first female bishops in 1980: Leontyne Kelly, an African American, and Marjorie Matthews, a Euro-American. In 2000 it lists eleven women among its bishops in the major "episcopal areas" of the United States.

For most churches, the movement toward the ordination of women was very gradual and in stages. The Presbyterian church, a church that traces its origins to the Reformed tradition of John Calvin, provides an example. The Presbyterian Church in the U.S.A. and the Cumberland Presbyterian Church decided to admit women to the diaconate in the 1920s, but only after considerable debate.[56] Women could be deaconesses but not ministers or elders.[57] In 1953 the Disciples Committee on the Service and Status of Women of the United Presbyterian Church in the U.S.A. published a report calling for full and equal participation of women in leadership positions. Three years later this church granted women full ecclesiastical parity with men as ordained ministers and elders.[58] Statistics gathered in 1967 indicate that in spite of the fact that female membership in the United Presbyterian Church (which would become part of the Presbyterian Church in the U.S.A. in 1983) was 57.4 percent of the total membership, only .518 percent of ordained ministers were women. Among the 12,932 ministers of the United Presbyterian Church, a mere 67 were women.[59]

The United Presbyterian Church was not unique among Protestant churches prior to 1970. Before the second wave of feminism, which began in the United States in the 1960s, cultural attitudes strongly mitigated against females getting advanced theological degrees and becoming ministers. Since the 1960s and the second major wave of feminism in the United States, the vast majority of Protestant churches have officially accepted the ordination of women. In 1999 the Presbyterian Church U.S.A., of which the United Presbyterian Church is a member, had a total of 20,988 active and retired ordained ministers. Of these, 3,693 are women, and an additional 674 women are enrolled in seminaries studying for the ministry.[60]

The Lutheran Church of America and the American Lutheran Church voted to permit women to be ordained in 1970. The Evangelical Lutheran Church in America (ELCA), formed in 1988 by a merger of the Lutheran Church in America (LCA), the American Lutheran Church (ALC), and the Association of Evangelical Lutheran Churches (AELC), had approximately 5.3 million members, and as of 1993, 1,358 ordained women clergy. As of September 2000, it had seven women bishops, three in the United States and four in Europe. The first Lutheran woman elected a bishop was the Rev. Maria Jepsen, Hamburg diocese, North Elbian Evangelical Lutheran Church (Germany) on 4 April 1992. Bishop April Ulring Larson, La Crosse (Wisconsin) Area Synod, ELCA, was elected two months later. By the year 2000, seven more women had been ordained as bishops, including two additional women in the South Dakota and New England Evangelical Lutheran Synods.[61]

Nevertheless, some Protestant churches have also legislated against women's ordination. The Missouri Synod Lutherans have separated from the Evangelical Lutheran Church in their refusal to ordain women. And while sixteen hundred women serve individual Southern Baptist congregations as ordained ministers, the Southern Baptist Convention (the largest of the Baptist conventions in the United States) decided in May 2000 that although both men and women are gifted for service in the church, the office of pastor should be restricted to men. To the number of refusing churches can be added many evangelical Protestant church bodies. The usual arguments opposing women's ordination by the Protestant church bodies are based on biblical grounds, citing 1 Cor. 11:2–16; 14:34–35; and 1 Tim. 2:8–15, and the familiar directives reminding women of their proper behavior in church, including remaining silent.

Although Protestant churches are divided about women's ordination, the number of ordained women continues to grow. In 1960 there were 4,367 ordained clergywomen in the United States. In 1990 that figure had grown to 32,251; of that number 30,205 were white.[62] Trends indicate that the numbers of ordained women in Protestant churches will continue to grow in the twenty-first century. The phenomenon of growth in the number of women in the ordained ministry of Protestant churches is not unique to the United States. It is also affecting Protestant churches in many parts of the globe. Today, women may be ordained in the majority of Protestant denominations, if they and their communities believe that they are called and have gifts for this type of ministry.

The Episcopal Church illustrates the growth in the numbers of women in ordained ministry well. In 1973, there were no women priests. According to the 1998 *Episcopal Clerical Directory,* 1,955 of the priests were women; this is 13.9 percent of those ordained to the priesthood. There are also eleven female bishops worldwide, eight of whom serve in dioceses in the United States, although many of them assist male bishops as suffragan bishops. Access to ordination has not necessarily resulted in women gaining equal access to positions of authority in their churches. Ordained women tend to engage in more specialized ministries, rather than become pastors, rectors, or vicars of parishes. They are likely to serve as assistants or associates, or to be employed in hospitals, prisons, and colleges as chaplains. Paula Nesbitt, reflecting on the situation for women priests in the Episcopal Church, states,

> Though Episcopal women priests have moved upward in their careers, their attainment has fallen short of positions enabling them to exercise a significant degree of denominational influence and authority, especially when compared with the attainment levels of men within their cohorts.[63]

This may lead one to conclude that in many of the churches that permit women to be ordained, the ordained women constitute a type of "second-class" status among the ordained. Vestiges of patriarchy and androcentrism remain.

African American Women and Their Churches

Windows into the experience of African American women in their churches open us to religious realities that extend to their pre-slave history in Africa. Some elements of African religiosity would continue as the slaves became "Christianized," while others would be lost. The first African slaves in the continental United States were brought to the Spanish colony of Florida in 1565.[64] Most African Americans, however, are descendants of the slaves brought to the English colonies, the first of whom arrived in Virginia in 1619. In the late-seventeenth and early-eighteenth centuries great numbers of women and men were shipped like cargo from West Africa to the southern English colonies to work on plantations that grew tobacco and cotton. In their tribal homelands, religion had been a pervasive reality. Unlike the Christianity practiced by many of their owners, the uprooted Africans did not separate the natural and supernatural realms. In African religions animals and other aspects of nature, such as majestic mountains and trees, were regarded to be symbolic representations of the divine. The Africans also had strong oral traditions that bound them to a Supreme Being, the spirits of their revered ancestors, and the other members of their tribes. For most Africans, to live was to participate in a religious drama, one often punctuated with joyful celebration.[65] In that drama, women played many roles as diviners, herbalists, prophetesses, sages, and priests. In many tribes they were as prominent as men in the conduct of religious affairs. The religious life of Africans and the roles of women in it changed, of course, with slavery and the patriarchal values of the slave owners. The emerging religiosity among the American-born African slaves was influenced by the white slave owners. Yet, elements of African religiosity remained.

Most slave owners were at least nominally Protestant. Consequently, most African Americans who are Christians are affiliated with a Protestant church today. In the pre-Revolutionary colonies many of the owners of slaves, although having some familiarity with Christianity, were virtually unchurched. Although a black woman was baptized into a Puritan congregation as early as 1641, very few slaves were baptized before the eighteenth century. As Emilie M. Townes, a Protestant womanist theologian, points out, this did not mean that the slaves in the South and the free blacks of the North were without a religious life. She writes,

> The constant influx of Black Africans through the slave trade meant a continual renewal and revitalization of the traditions and religions of Africa in the Americas. Slaves maintained links with their African heritage through oral history, drumming at funerals and dances, preserving the art of wood carving, and making reed baskets and mats.[66]

At the turn of the eighteenth century a group of Anglican missionaries, known as the Society for the Propagation of the Gospel, came to the colonies with a special mission: preach Christianity to African slaves. Other missionaries, particularly Baptists and Methodists, followed. By the 1740s an increasing number of Africans were exposed to Christianity due to the revivalist movement known as the Great Awakening. The religious awakening of this period is considered "great" because it touched so many regions and so many aspects of daily life. Many slave owners permitted their slaves to hear the preaching of traveling missionaries, most of whom stressed an awakening to a deep sense of guilt and the need for personal salvation. Slaves were permitted to be baptized as long as all agreed that baptism would not alter the property status of the slaves. By the mid 1750s, hundreds of slaves worshiped in southern churches.

No doubt, the slave owners assumed that knowledge of the Ten Commandments would give the Africans encouragement to docility and obedience. The Ten Commandments were not all that the slaves were exposed to. They also learned of Moses' exodus from slavery and about Jesus, who preached blessings for the poor and sorrowful. Womanist theologian Katie Cannon reflects, "In the prayer meetings and song services, in the sermons and spirituals, the biblical texts provided [enslaved Africans with] refuge in a hostile world."[67] At these gatherings discontent and depression were countered by the promise of liberation and hope.

Emilie M. Townes points out that prior to the Civil War, black women converted to Christianity in greater numbers than did black men.[68] It was not uncommon for baptized slaves to be permitted to attend church services with their masters, but they sat with their children in segregated areas. A few attended newly formed black churches. In the 1770s the first black Baptist church was founded.[69] By the early 1800s dozens of others were formed; most were Baptist, but many were Methodist or Presbyterian. These churches resulted from the growth in the white membership among churches of these denominations. As larger churches were built to accommodate the white population, the older, smaller churches were often organized for slaves as adjunct missions to the parent white churches (because slaves could not legally own property).

In the early 1800s a Second Great Awakening was underway in the United States.[70] In this new wave of Protestant revivalism, some of the preachers from the northern states who took the "good news of Jesus Christ" to camp meetings were also committed to the abolition of slavery. Soon, black women were participating in the new religious abolitionism. Among the best known are Maria W. Stewart (1803–79), Sojourner Truth (1797–1883), and Harriet Tubman (1823–1913). Stewart, a member of the Boston African Baptist Church, delivered speeches in which she called for the end of slavery, arguing that to achieve this goal, violence may be necessary. Sojourner Truth, a slave in New York, was a member of the African Methodist Zion Church. She became an avid crusader, drawing attention to the plight of her black sisters. Harriet Tubman, known to her followers as "Moses," earned that name by making nineteen trips to the South between 1850 and 1857 to lead more than three hundred slaves to freedom via the Underground Railroad.

To quash the abolition movement, laws were passed throughout the South to prohibit slaves from gathering for prayer without the supervision of whites. During this period, many African slaves held their Sunday prayer in secret. An "invisible" church of enslaved Christians met clandestinely in barns and under large shade trees while their masters attended church. This experience of "being church" provided a basis for autonomy and self-determination that enabled many Africans to rise above the self-contempt that slavery inflicted upon them. The spirituals of this period, in particular, reflect the way in which African religiosity and biblical faith became intertwined in ways unique to the African American.

During the 1840s the three major Protestant denominations in the South — Methodist, Presbyterian, and Baptist — effectively broke their institutional ties with the northern churches. No longer would northern missionaries and their abolitionist proselytizing be welcome in the southern churches. After the Civil War the divisions continued.

The Civil War ended slavery, but white-controlled reconstruction offered empty promises to the former slaves. Social segregation and disenfranchisement became the norm. The majority of defeated Southerners were unwilling to respect African Americans as equal human beings with the God-given rights enumerated in the Constitution. Following the war, numerous Protestant

AIN'T I A WOMAN?
Sojourner Truth

That man over there say
  a woman needs to be helped into carriages
and lifted over ditches
  and to have the best place everywhere.
Nobody ever helped me into carriages
  or over mud puddles
    or gives me the best place....
And ain't I a woman?
  Look at me,
Look at my arm!
  I have plowed and planted
and gathered into barns
  and no man could head me....
And ain't I a woman?
  I could work as much
and eat as much as man—
  when I could get it—
and bear the lash as well....
  And ain't I a woman?
I have borne thirteen children
  and seen most sold into slavery
and when I cried out a mother's grief
  none but Jesus heard me....
And ain't I a woman?
  That man in black there say
a woman can't have as much rights as a man
  cause Christ wasn't a woman.
Where did your Christ come from?
  From God and a woman!
Man had nothing to do with him!
  If the first woman God ever made
was strong enough to turn the world
  upside down, all alone,
together women ought to be able to turn it
  rightside up again.[71]

churches for African Americans were formed in the South as white churches made the decision that it would be better for "the Colored" to have their own autonomous churches. Among them were the Colored Primitive Baptist Church (1866), the Colored Methodist Episcopal Church (1870), and the Colored Presbyterian Church (1874).[72]

After the Civil War, African American missionaries from the North, who

---

STEAL AWAY

Refrain:
>   Steal away, steal away,
>   Steal away to Jesus;
>   Steal away, steal away home,
>   I ain't got long to stay here.

1

>   My Lord, he calls me,
>   He calls me by the thunder;
>   The trumpet sounds within-a my soul,
>   I ain't got long to stay here.

2

>   Green trees a-bending,
>   Poor sinner stands a-trembling;
>   The trumpet sounds within-a my soul,
>   I ain't got long to stay here.

3

>   My Lord, he calls me,
>   He calls me by the lightning;
>   The trumpet sounds within-a my soul,
>   I ain't got long to stay here.

Christa Dixon traces this spiritual to the time of the abolitionist movement, when religious meetings and Bible readings were forbidden. "Steal Away" informed the people that a secret meeting was planned, or that guides, like the heroic Harriet Tubman, to the Underground Railroad would soon arrive. The slaves hadn't long to stay here; freedom was on the horizon and it was of God. For Jesus was calling: "Steal away, steal away."[73]

---

were free (manumitted) before the war, were sent by the African Methodist Episcopal Church (founded in 1787, denominational incorporation in 1816) and the African Methodist Episcopal Zion Church (founded in 1796, denominational incorporation in 1821) to convert the newly freed slaves. These two churches would attract the majority of African American Methodists. Since African Americans had long been affiliated with Baptist churches, the number of black Baptist churches increased. Evangelical style Methodist and Baptist churches became the major churches of the African Americans. As these churches grew in size and influence, they became a visible presence in the South.

What effect did emancipation have on African American women? After the institution of chattel slavery was destroyed, the patterns of exploitation of African American women were changed but not eradicated. These women went from being breeding stock ("brood sows") and laborers ("work oxen"), abused by their white masters and mistresses, to being field hands and domestic servants, restricted to poorly paid, menial work, and often still abused by their employers. African American women who left the South seeking employment in the industries of the North during the great migratory period (1910–30) were only rarely allowed inside the industrial manufacturing system, and when they were, it was to do work that whites did not want to do. Reflecting on this period, Townes notes that African American women began to adopt a self-defined spirituality that was different from that of most white women. The societal image of "true womanhood" portrayed white women as fragile, impressionable, and always deferring to the authority of their husbands in the home. This image was transcended as black women embraced the message of Christ. This led them to understand themselves to be ministers in their homes and to move on to a still greater call to prophesy and evangelize. Townes observes,

> This was possible through their intense evangelical spiritual drive to live a higher and better life and their concern to shape families and a society that reflected Christian morals and precepts. Black women took the images of Phoebe, Priscilla and Mary as co-workers with Paul and translated them into their own work. Their stress was on their ultimate allegiance to God and not to men.[74]

African American women have a long history of being active in their churches. Today, they make up 50 percent of the African American population in the United States but comprise more than 70 percent of the active membership of African American Protestant churches. Yet, a paradox is evident. Although the African Methodist Episcopal Zion Church ordained a woman as early as 1848, the African Methodist Episcopal Church, the oldest black church in North America, began to ordain women only in 1948. In the year 2000, the A.M.E. Church has one female bishop, the Rev. Vashti Murphy McKenzie. It was not until 1970 that the Christian Methodist Episcopal Church (called the Colored Methodist Episcopal Church until 1954) permitted women's ordination. Many black Baptist churches (the National Baptist Convention of America, Inc., which is the largest body of African American Baptists, the National Baptist Convention, U.S.A., Inc., and the Progressive National Baptist Convention) and the Church of God in Christ, the largest black Pentecostal body in North America, forbid the ordination of women on biblical grounds. Even in those churches that permit women to be ordained, men monopolize the ordained ministry.[75] According to statistics gathered in 1996, only 5 percent of the over two thousand African American clergywomen were pastoring black churches.[76]

Why is this so? One reason is that when Christianity was brought to the slaves on the plantations and to free blacks in urban areas, these preachers did not encourage leadership roles for women. Black churches, in both the South and North after the Civil War, did not cast a critical eye on the directives found in the Pauline Epistles that required women to obey their husbands and be silent in their churches.[77] The other major reason is that slavery and racism have greatly emasculated black males in devastating ways. Therefore, many black women and the vast majority of black male ministers believe that black men should hold church leadership positions.[78] A black male minister is an example to other men that human dignity is a gift bestowed by God.

Although black churches could scarcely survive without the active support of women, the offices of pastor and preacher in the historic black churches have been a male preserve. Women serve many roles in black churches, including the honorific role of "mothers of the church," reserved for the oldest and most respected female members.[79] Jacquelyn Grant points out that women in black churches are often called the "backbone" of the church. She stresses, however, that the operative word in this expression is "back." When the expression rolls off the lips of male ministers,

> What they really mean is that women are in the "background" and should be kept there. They are merely support workers. This is borne out by my observation that in many churches women are consistently given the responsibilities in the kitchen, while men are elected or appointed to the important boards and leadership positions. While decisions and policies may be discussed in the kitchen, they are certainly not made there.[80]

Grant adds that women are not only rewarded for performance in supportive positions, "they are also penalized for trying to move to head positions — leadership in their churches."[81]

Because ordained ministry is not widely open to women in the traditionally black churches, African American women have sought ordination in denominations that have been traditionally white.[82] African American women experience less resistance to ordination in United Methodist, Presbyterian, and Episcopalian churches than they do in traditionally black churches, especially the black Baptist denominations and the Pentecostal groups, such as, in particular, the Church of God in Christ.[83] Leontyne Kelly, the first African American woman to be elected bishop in the United Methodist Church, and Barbara Harris, the first African American woman to be ordained a bishop in the Episcopal Church USA, hold positions of authority in churches that are predominantly white. Even in churches where women can become bishops, full equality is not guaranteed. Harris was elected suffragan to assist Bishop David Johnson in the Boston diocese. As of 1998, no woman is on record as holding a comparable position in black churches.

Although white churches have accepted African American women for ordained ministry, the lives of these women are often marked by the subtle effects of racism and sexism. They readily admit that at times they feel that they are merely "token persons." They see themselves as being used as a "public relations piece," photographed for the news media and invited to public functions to symbolically represent their race and gender. Although their advancement to positions of real authority has been negligible, African American women are forging ahead to answer what they believe is an authentic spiritual calling from God. In the words of Pauli Murray on the occasion of her ordination to the Episcopal priesthood on 8 January 1979,

> We dare to answer this call [from God] because, in a very real sense, we have no choice in the matter. God has spoken to us through an event or

through a series of events which points us in one direction — toward full time service of God. Like the prophet Isaiah and the other prophets of the Old Testament, we are compelled to believe that sinful, rebellious, broken as we are, God is raising us as instruments of his will — not ours — to love and serve him and our fellow human beings to the greater glory of God our Creator and Redeemer.[84]

The window into the African American church through which we have peered has been constructed by Protestants. There is also a Catholic African American stained-glass window under construction. Historically, the influence of Catholicism on African Americans has not been as extensive as Protestantism. Before the Civil War, Catholics were a relatively insignificant minority in most southern states, except for Maryland, Kentucky, and Louisiana, where many Catholics lived and owned slaves. In the Catholic communities there was no major movement to evangelize slaves comparable to those undertaken by Protestants in the two Great Awakenings. Although limited in scope when compared to the Protestant effort, there were some notable developments among African American Catholics undertaken by women. Among the most noteworthy are the efforts of Mary Elizabeth Lange and the Oblate Sisters of Providence, and Henriette Delille and the Sisters of the Holy Family.[85] In the face of little support and considerable antipathy, these women educated children, cared for the sick and orphaned, and did a variety of social-work ministries among African Americans.

During the nineteenth century, Catholics would begin their own form of revival movement comparable to that of the Protestant churches, commonly known as the "parish mission," but on a smaller scale than that found among the Protestant churches. This practice would grow in popularity after the Civil War and would continue in many Catholic parishes well into the 1950s.[86] Parish missions often were annual events that lasted from one to four weeks and featured traveling priests whose preaching encouraged conversion from sin and greater devotion to Catholic practices, especially to Mary and the saints. A full history of these parish missions is yet to be written; therefore, the extent to which they affected the lives of African American women is uncertain. Catholic womanist theologian Diana Hayes points out that although Catholic church hierarchy made no special effort to evangelize blacks who were not Catholic, parish revivals did provide black Catholics with emotional experiences that resonated with their African religiosity.[87] They also provided opportunities for high-spirited social gatherings for blacks.

Like their Protestant counterparts, before and after the Civil War, Catholic churches in the South practiced segregation. African Americans occupied the rear pews designated for them. Normally, blacks were forbidden to receive Holy Communion until all the whites had. African Americans knew that these practices were not of God. From 1889 until 1894, African American Catholic laity undertook a vigorous movement to get their church to take an active interest in their concerns and held a series of national congresses. At this time, Catholics numbered about two hundred thousand in an African American population of approximately seven million.[88] Catholic womanist scholar M. Shawn Copeland points out, however, that "but for rare exceptions, ignorance, benign neglect and segregation obtained."[89] The "Congresses for Colored Catholics" abruptly ended in 1894. It is uncertain why. There is no record of women having attended these meetings; therefore, it is difficult to discern what role, if any, women played in this early movement for racial equality in the Catholic Church. What is certain is that there was a viable black Catholic lay community in the United States at the turn of the century that was composed predominantly of women. This community laid the foundation for future black Catholic movements.

From 1910 to 1930, many African Americans traveled to the northern states seeking employment in industry and a better life with more self-determination. Most moved to inner-city communities that soon became predominantly African American. The segregation of the races in southern Catholic parishes was no less blatant in northern ones. Often, black Catholics who sought to join the ethnic white parishes were viewed as intruders. Among the few African American Catholics, "Negro parishes" were founded. In most cases, the administration of these parishes was delegated to religious orders of men who were willing to take up the charge to minister to African Americans. One result of this practice was that certain religious orders attracted a few African American vocations, while most dioceses and communities of women religious attracted almost none.[90]

During the post–World War II years, when the civil rights movement began to challenge racial segregation, Catholics, either black or white, were not in the forefront. That changed when Martin Luther King Jr. called all of the nation's clergy to join him in Selma, Alabama, in 1965. Catholic priests and sisters, black and white, came in large numbers.[91] Shortly after King's death in 1968, African American priests founded the Black Catholic Clergy Caucus. A few months later, African American women religious formed the National Black Sisters' Conference. The foundation of these groups led to the National Office for Black Catholics, and an ever-present reminder that the Catholic Church in the United States has never been a white European church. To the Catholic Church, African American Christians give the "gift of blackness."[92]

Among the hallmarks of African American Christianity are these:

- the formation of communities in which the members are committed to each other's survival in a land that is often hostile to them;

- the worship of God in which biblical substance is joyfully enlivened by spontaneity;

- preaching that combines spiritual nurturance with a prophetic edge.

These hallmarks are found in Protestant and Catholic African American churches. Among black Catholics, each of these has been a point of tension. As M. Shawn Copeland points out, one of the most crucial issues is whether black Catholics should seek to be integrated into the white church that has often neglected and disregarded them, or seek out separate sites for the development of a black Catholic spiritual life.[93] Many are choosing the latter option, which makes it possible to inculturate African American religiosity into worship that is both Catholic and black. For preaching in black Catholic parishes to be meaningful to the parishioners, having African Americans in the pulpit is a high value. But the insufficient number of black priests for the 2.5 million African American Catholics makes that impossible. Many believe that the time is ripe, therefore, for the women who have long been the backbone and mainstay of African American Catholic parishes to have roles of leadership. Women are needed to build a church that is faithfully Catholic and authentically black.[94]

Hispanic Women and Their Churches

Not all Hispanic women in the United States and Latin America are Roman Catholics, but the majority are. There are historical reasons why Hispanics are likely to be baptized Catholic. From the very start of the Spanish (and later Portuguese) presence in the western hemisphere in the fifteenth century, both military conquest and evangelization of the indigenous natives were high priorities. Spain and Portugal were Catholic countries. Claims made for Spanish and Portuguese crowns were made in the name of Christ and the Catholic Church. Therefore, soon after the "New World" was conquered by soldiers, priests followed with the message of the cross. Evangelization at that time involved minimal instruction, with emphasis on baptism and the "saving of souls." Some wrongly assumed that the natives had no form of religion.[95] Therefore, they could easily stamp upon them Christian beliefs as the Spanish and Portuguese interpreted them, with very little sensitivity to the culture and religious beliefs and practices of the natives. The missionaries believed that they were doing a noble, perhaps even heroic, work: winning souls for Christ and the Catholic Church. To their credit, missionaries did challenge the assumptions of many military conquerors that the natives were not human. Some also challenged the abusive enslavement of the natives.

It is beyond our purposes here to provide a history of the Roman Catholic Church's relationship to Latin American women and North American Hispanic women. It is important to bear in mind, however, that the Latin American countries did not begin to make a break with Spain and Portugal until the 1820s. The governments of the new countries continued the pattern of a close alliance with the Roman Catholic Church, a pattern exercised by the kings and queens of Spain and Portugal. Practically speaking, this meant that the governments both supported and controlled, in varying degrees, Catholic hierarchy. That pattern gradually changed beginning in the 1930s as governments began to relinquish their control of the church. This enabled the Roman Catholics to engage in needed renewal. It also opened the door for a Protestant presence that is now growing throughout Latin America.[96]

Among Catholics in many parts of Latin America and the United States, where Hispanics are in great number, a grassroots movement of renewal is transforming the church. This movement is the creation of basic ecclesial communities, or in Spanish, *comunidades eclesiales de base* (hereafter, "CEB"). Members of CEBs gather together to support one another in their growth in faith and their work for liberation from poverty and oppression. These communities are "basic" in a sociological sense: they are comprised of people in the *barrio,* where life is lived by families, most of which are at the bottom of the economic pyramid. They are "ecclesial" in a deeply theological sense: they are communities that embody the notion of the church as a "people of God" that takes nourishment from God's Word and puts its faith into action. The CEBs are not merely subdivisions of parishes, but a new way of people being church, *una manera nueva de se iglesia.* There are thousands of CEBs throughout Latin America. Exact estimates are difficult to make because the line of demarcation between a CEB and a parish or other formal grouping of Christians is often difficult to determine.

CEBs are broadly modeled after the pedagogy that Paulo Freire developed while working with poor people in Brazil during the 1960s.[97] Freire's methodology called for teaching adults literacy skills while also raising political awareness. Because CEBs are grassroots innovations (churches of the *barrio*), they tend to vary from place to place. Depending on the location, they may be made up of a group of people, a dozen to fifty in number, accompanied by a priest or, more often, a pastoral leader. CEB members meet regularly, perhaps weekly. The meetings do not follow a rigid structure, but are likely to include a welcome, hymn singing, prayer, and reflection on people's everyday lives in the light of Bible readings. Meetings often end with more singing and sharing of food and drink (*convivencia*). Typically, the leaders teach literacy skills with Christian ideas and political analysis woven into the lessons. This combination often leads the members of CEBs to work together to improve their living conditions or to give service to people in need in their neighborhoods.

As Jeanne Gallo points out, the lay leaders, many of whom are women, are the key to the continuity and dynamism of the CEBs. The CEBs are communities whose purpose includes action, sometimes referred to as "praxis." Gallo describes the many forms that the action may take:

> The action may be in the religious domain: catechesis, Bible study, planning a prayer week. It may also be in the social arena: improvements in the neighborhood, collective works, teaching the illiterate to read, doing political and legal education, creating and strengthening trade unions, participation in political activities.[98]

What about the role of women in the CEBs? María Pilar Aquino provides a response to this question. She notes that a major characteristic of the CEBs is the quantity and quality of the involvement of women. Although women have always done much of the pastoral work in their parishes, they were not very visible. Slowly, these women are losing their anonymity. Now they are becoming "church-makers," making the church's mission present in their own way as women. They are proclaiming the gospel, giving witness, leading celebrations, and engaging in action to transform their neighborhoods and to forge unity through bridge building.[99] Aquino writes from the perspective of the Catholic Church in Latin America, a church that, due to the influential episcopal conferences in Medellín (1968) and Puebla (1979), has undertaken a renewal process in solidarity with the struggles of the poor and oppressed, a struggle that far too many women know from firsthand experience.

The increase of women's participation in ecclesial life is not unique to women in Latin America. This is verified by a study of CEBs in the diocese of Brownsville, Texas. In this diocese on the banks of the Rio Grande River, there are 417 CEBs, most of which are composed of Mexican Americans and Mexicans. In a report compiled by John E. Linnan, attention is given to the large role of women in the CEBs and in the diocese at all levels. Linnan notes that women lead several of the most innovative and most difficult of the efforts of evangelization and development in the diocese. Many pastoral administrators of mission stations are also either lay or religious women.[100]

The CEBs give their members ways of living their Christian faith as communities of purpose. For many women, these communities have become welcoming and affirming places, places in which they are for the first time emerging as actors in the church. One of the most innovative elements of the CEBs is the high level of participation, with collaboration replacing the centralization of authority in the clergy. The emphasis on collaboration is likely due largely to the wide participation and leadership of women in the CEBs. In his reflections on his experience of the CEBs that he visited, Linnan draws attention to the fact that although a CEB is

> in theory the locale of the sacramental life of the community, in fact, at least to the degree I was able to observe, such is not the case in the Diocese of Brownsville. Sacramental life is still the prerogative of the parish. It is in the parish (or the mission) that baptism, Eucharist, marriage, and reconciliation take place. This disjunction seems to threaten a separation of "real" church, which takes place in the community, from "sacramental celebration" of that life, which takes place only in the parish church or mission.[101]

Perhaps this disjunction would not exist, or at least would be less problematic, if CEBs had leaders who were ordained and could celebrate the sacraments with their people in the context of the CEB gatherings. This would mean, however, that ordination in the Catholic Church would be open to women who provide capable leadership in many CEBs. The notion of a leader, especially a woman, emerging from within an ecclesial community and having her leadership within a community authenticated by ordination, however, is an idea alien to current practice in the Catholic Church.

Tereza Cavalcanti reflects on the paradox of the leadership of women in many forms of ministry in CEBs and their exclusion from sacramental leadership:

> If women are the majority in catechesis, in biblical circles and every kind of service that prepares and builds the community, it is odd that they are set aside when the work flourishes and is transfigured into the sacraments. We recognize that this question is not yet ripe and should be analyzed seriously in the future. Nevertheless, this cannot prevent us [from] calling attention to a problem that can no longer be hidden.[102]

Cavalcanti wrote these words in 1988, seven years before Pope John Paul II declared that the church had no authority to ordain women and that this was a teaching to be definitively held. For women whose active involvement in CEBs has prompted them to own their membership in the church as the people of God, accepting this position is painful. These women are aware of the gifts and energy that they have to bring to the church. Because of their experiences, many feel a call to sacramental priesthood and to fuller participation in decision-making in the church they love and are eager to serve.

The CEB phenomenon is not confined to Latin Americans and Hispanics in the United States. In Africa, the term "small Christian communities" is used for those groups that gather to relate their Christian commitment to traditional African values of communal celebration and hospitality. Similar communities can be found in parts of Asia, especially the Philippines. Some Catholics in the United States compare the communities created in the popular parish movement known as "Renew" to CEBs.

Although the Catholic CEBs are making a "preferential option for the poor" in many parts of Latin America, many of the poor are being attracted to Protestantism, especially to Pentecostalism, widely known in Latin America as *evangélico* churches.[103] The origins of the Pentecostal movement can be traced to the margins of North American Protestantism at the turn of the twentieth century (the International Pentecostal Church was founded in 1911). Pentecostal churches look to the day of Pentecost as their spiritual birthday and the Bible, literally interpreted, as their ultimate authority. These churches emphasize repentance from sin, baptism in the Holy Spirit, and speaking in tongues (glossolalia). Worship is emotionally charged and spontaneous. Many Pentecostal churches ignore the social themes commonly addressed by the CEBs. Often among Pentecostal Christians, liberation means the expulsion of devils and freedom from evil spirits. For the Catholic CEBs it means prophetic liberation from oppression and societal sins that are the root cause of poverty.

In Latin America, a growing number of indigenous people, blacks, and *mestizo* are attracted to Pentecostal churches. In the United States, Hispanics are also joining these churches. The majority of the people joining Pentecostal churches are women. Apparently, they are finding in them spiritual and emotional benefits that they could not find elsewhere. In the *evangélico* churches, what roles do women have? They sing in choirs and are missionaries reaching out to other women. The role of greatest prestige is being the wife of a pastor. Pastors' wives participate actively in the ministry of their husbands. Women, however, usually are not pastors. The reasons given in the Bible-based *evangélico* churches combine biblical warrants (women are to be silent in the assembly [1 Tim. 2:8–15]) with those drawn from the machismo culture (it is not fitting for women to have authority over men).[104]

When compared with the practices of most CEBs, the Pentecostal churches offer women fewer decision-making roles. Yet, many women, most of whom are single mothers who are very poor and uneducated, are joining the *evangélico* churches. In these churches, the "good news" is presented in ways that these women can relate to. The message emphasized centers on personal morality, especially sexual morality. Preaching in Pentecostal churches typically attributes marital infidelity to "the work of the Devil," who is usually presented as a male figure. Addressing machismo-caused suffering in solidarity with other women is a healing experience. Having other women and men "lay hands" in rituals of healing and prayer helps the women to have a sense of Godly empowerment in their own families. Apparently, the self-esteem of women is enhanced by membership in *evangélico* churches.[105]

For many feminist theologians of Latin America who are members of older mainline Protestant churches, empowerment of women in their families is desirable but not sufficient. Women must be empowered also in their churches and the broader society. There Protestant feminist theologians speak as women who have the benefit of more education and economic security than most of the women in Pentecostal churches. Yet, women among this group, such as Methodist theologian Rosângela Soares de Oliveira, would not want their campaigns for women's liberation in their churches to be in any way "unrelated to everyday life [of poor women] with its sweat, its smells, the dishes and the children."[106] Feminist theologians from the older Protestant churches recognize that they cannot ignore the real-life issues of their poorer sisters as they struggle for greater equality in their churches.

Conclusions

This chapter began with a challenging question raised by Anne Carr about the relationship of the Christian church to its changing historical settings. To what extent can a church be responsive to the experience and desires of women and still be faithful to the "core of truth" of Christianity? How this is answered requires every church to continually "test the spirits" with openness to the guidance of the Holy Spirit and desire for "godliness" (1 Tim. 4:7). Christian feminists are bringing the exigencies of the present into dialogue with the encumbrances of the past in their search for the core of truth, revealed by God. Many envision that core of truth to be modeled by Jesus Christ and the inclusive community of men and women, gathered in a discipleship of equals. Looking for the Holy Spirit for guidance, these Christian feminists are "testing the spirits" of their own experience and of church teachings. Many are calling for and working toward the transformation of the Christian churches through their promotion of what they earnestly believe to be an authentic biblical vision of ministry for women in our time. Something new has been set in motion. Increasing numbers of women recognize that they have gifts to offer, and these gifts are being gratefully received by the people of God. A growing number of faithful Christians are becoming convinced that only a church of women and men working together to make the reign of God a reality will withstand the challenges of the future.

A Look Ahead

This survey of feminist perspectives on Christian churches by women from different social locations has made "testing of spirits" its guiding theme. This important facet of Christian feminism cannot be divorced from the more encompassing topic of feminist spirituality. Spirituality is a topic of considerable interest today. Spirituality embraces the whole of our reality as humans and invites us to be attuned to the many spirits who speak in the midst of our daily lives. Add to spirituality the further qualifiers "feminist" and "Christian," and one is invited to be attuned to the realities of women in which the spirits uniquely speak and to the voice the Holy Spirit, who in the midst of those voices invites each person to holiness. This broad perspective on Christian feminist spirituality provides a springboard for an exploration of an area of Christian feminist spirituality that is generating a great deal of energy today: reconstructed understandings of imagery for God, Mary the mother of Jesus, and her sister saints. In these reconstructions one finds both consolation and challenge from feminist images of God and from women who have tested the spirits in their own lives while searching for Godliness.

NOTES

1. Anne E. Carr, *Transforming Grace: Christian Tradition and Women's Experience* (San Francisco: Harper & Row, 1988), 25. This book has been translated into German (1990), Italian (1991), French (1993), and Portuguese (1994), and has been reprinted with a new introduction (New York: Continuum, 1996).

2. Ibid., 194.

3. Ibid.

4. See especially Elisabeth Schüssler Fiorenza, *Discipleship of Equals: A Critical Feminist Ekklesia-logy of Liberation* (New York: Crossroad, 1993).

5. Mary Hunt, " 'We Women Are Church': Roman Catholic Women Shaping Ministries and Theologies," in *The Non-Ordination of Women and the Politics of Power,* ed. Elisabeth Schüssler Fiorenza and Hermann Häring (London: SCM Press; Maryknoll, N.Y.: Orbis Books, 1999), 104.

6. For a somewhat different and often cited treatment of models of being church, see Avery Dulles, *Models of the Church* (New York: Doubleday, 1974).

7. Augustine, "Sermon on the Gospel of John," 80.3.

8. H. Denzinger, ed., *Enchiridion symbolorum: Definitionum et declarationum de rebus fidei et morum,* 37th ed. (Freiburg im Breisgau: Herder, 1991), nos. 1601, 1606.

9. Frank S. Mead, *Handbook of Denominations in the United States,* rev. Samuel S. Hill (Nashville: Abingdon Press, 1995), 134.

10. The Baptist churches usually trace their roots to the teachings of Menno Simmons in Europe and to Roger Williams in America. See Mead, *Handbook of Denominations,* 49–52.

11. John B. Webster, "Ministry and Priesthood," in *The Study of Anglicanism,* ed. Stephen Sykes and John Booty (London: SPCK; Minneapolis: Fortress, 1990), 291–92.

12. Robert W. Jensen, "The Sacraments," in *Christian Dogmatics*, ed. Robert W. Jensen, Hans Schwarz, and Paul Sponheim (Philadelphia: Fortress, 1984), 2:380–81.

13. Ibid., 2:382–83.

14. The Council of Trent declared, "If any one shall say that by the words 'Do this for a commemoration of me,' Christ did not institute the apostles priests . . . let him be anathema" (Denzinger, ed., *Enchiridion symbolorum,* no. 1752). Biblical scholar Raymond Brown points out that when interpreting this text, one must keep in mind that the

Council of Trent did not distinguish between the Jesus engaged in historical ministry and the developed christological picture of Jesus presented in the Gospel accounts of his ministry written thirty to sixty years later. They did not speak of Jesus but of Christ. See his *The Community of the Beloved Disciple* (New York: Paulist Press, 1979), 184 n. 325.

15. For more on Roman Catholic teaching about the priesthood, see *Catechism of the Catholic Church* (Collegeville, Minn.: Liturgical Press, 1994), nos. 1590ff.

16. Among the Episcopal churches in the United States are the Episcopal Church, also known as the Protestant Episcopal Church U.S.A.; the Reformed Episcopal Church; the Anglican Orthodox Church; the American Episcopal Church; and the Anglican Church of America.

17. For example, women were ordained in the Episcopal Church (Protestant Episcopal Church U.S.A.), and their ordination was regularized in 1977. After the decision to grant canonical ordination to the priesthood to women, some Episcopalians broke away to form new denominations. Although some were also reacting to changes in the Book of Common Prayer, in 1978 the Anglican Catholic Church was formed, followed by the formation of the United Episcopal Church in 1980 and the Anglican Rite Jurisdiction of the Americas in 1991.

18. Research gathered in 1997 indicates that four out of the 113 dioceses of the Episcopal Church in the United States still refuse to ordain women. In response, the Episcopal Church's general convention voted to affirm that ordination is not only permissible but mandatory. See Katie Chaired, "A Vote (Finally) Taking a Clear Stand on Women's Ordination," *The Witness* 80 (1997): 202.

19. Carr, *Transforming Grace,* 21.

20. Catherine M. Prelinger, "Ordained Women in the Episcopal Church: Their Impact on the Work and Structure of the Clergy," in *Episcopal Women: Gender, Spirituality, and Commitment in an American Mainline Denomination,* ed. Catherine M. Prelinger (New York: Oxford University Press, 1992), 291.

21. William P. Haugaard, "From the Reformation to the Eighteenth Century," in *The Study of Anglicanism,* ed. Stephen Sykes and John Booty (London: SPCK; Minneapolis: Fortress, 1990), 3.

22. Pope John XXIII, *Pacem in Terris* ("Peace on Earth"), no. 41, an encyclical reprinted in *The Gospel of Peace and Justice: Catholic Social Teaching since Pope John,* ed. Joseph Gremillion (Maryknoll, N.Y.: Orbis Books, 1976), 209–10.

23. Elizabeth Carroll, "Reaping the Fruits of Redemption," in *Midwives of the Future,* ed. Ann Patrick Ware (Kansas City, Mo.: Leaven Press, 1985), 66.

24. The declaration was officially promulgated by the CDF on 15 October 1976 (the feast of Teresa of Avila), and published in *Acta Apostolicae Sedis* 69 (1977): 98–116.

25. Carr, *Transforming Grace,* 23.

26. Ibid.

27. Brown, *Beloved Disciple,* 184–85 n. 326. See also his "The Meaning of Modern New Testament Studies for the Possibility of Ordaining Women to the Priesthood," in *Biblical Reflections on Crises Facing the Church* (New York: Paulist Press, 1975), 45–62. In this essay he predicted that the question of women's ordination would become an increasingly divisive issue in the church.

28. Galatians 3:28 is cited in the Second Vatican Council's "Dogmatic Constitution on the Church" (*Lumen Gentium,* no. 32): "Hence there is in Christ no inequality on the basis of race and nationality, social condition or sex, because there is neither Jew nor Greek."

29. Pope John Paul II, *Ordinatio Sacerdotalis* ("On Ordination and Women") (22 May 1994 — Pentecost), *Origins* 24 (1994): 50–63.

30. Congregation for the Doctrine of the Faith, "Reply to the *Dubium* Concerning the Teaching Contained in the Apostolic Letter *Ordinatio Sacerdotalis*" (28 October 1995), *Origins* 25 (1995): 401–3.

31. See especially *Mulieris Dignitatem* ("On the Dignity and Vocation of Women") (15 August 1988 — Feast of the Assumption of the Blessed Virgin Mary into Heaven), *Origins* 18 (1988): 263–83.

32. John Paul II writes, "The personal resources of femininity are certainly no less than the resources of masculinity: They are merely different." Noting the influence of the women's rights movement, the pope cautions women to avoid "masculinization," which will cause them to "deform and lose what constitutes their essential richness" (ibid., 269).

33. Elisabeth Schüssler Fiorenza, "Feminist/Womanist Priests — An Oxymoron?" *New Women, New Church* 18 (fall 1995): 10.

34. Robin T. Edwards, "Some Welcome Letter as 'Unchangeable Forever,'" *National Catholic Reporter* 30 (1994): 11.

35. See Dean R. Hoge, *The Future of Catholic Leadership: Responses to the Priest Shortage* (Kansas City, Mo.: Sheed and Ward, 1987).

36. Pope John Paul II, *Ordinatio Sacerdotalis,* 51.

37. Ibid., 49.

38. For a more in-depth treatment of different understandings of "tradition" in Roman Catholic thought and practice, see Terrence W. Tilley, *Inventing Catholic Tradition* (Maryknoll, N.Y.: Orbis Books, 2000), 7–12, 25–29, and passim.

39. See, for example, Pope John Paul II's encyclical *Laborem Exercens* ("On Human Labor") (14 September 1981), *Acta Apostolicae Sedis* 73 (1981): 577–647.

40. The poll regarding the ordination of women in the United States taken by George Gallup in 1993 showed that two out of three American Catholics favor females being ordained as priests. Among Catholics under 30 years of age, 76 percent endorse the ordination of women, compared to 67 percent of those who are 30–49 years of age, and 48 percent of those who are age 50 and older. George Gallup Jr. and D. Michael Lindsay, *Surveying the Religious Landscape: Trends in U.S. Beliefs* (Harrisburg, Pa.: Morehouse, 1999), 85.

41. The Catholic Daughters of America was founded after the Knights of Columbus rejected the supreme knight's recommendation that women be made eligible for membership in 1895. See James K. Kenneally, *The History of American Catholic Women* (New York: Crossroad, 1990), 104. The Catholic Daughters of America is a national organization with chapters in parishes. It has as its mission to embrace Catholic faith by working through love to promote justice and human dignity for all. On the national level, the C. D. of A. focuses on the legislative issues that have an impact on quality of life and family values.

42. The Ladies of Charity, USA, is a not-for-profit organization of Catholic lay women volunteers. Its primary mission is to be in direct service to the poor, in the spirit of St. Vincent de Paul, who established the first association in 1617 in France. In the United States, the first Lady of Charity was a twenty-three-year-old wife and mother named Catherine Harkins, an immigrant from Ireland, educated by the Sisters of Charity, from whom she learned about the "Ladies" as a child and later decided to form an association in her St. Louis, Missouri, parish in 1857. The national association, known as the Ladies of Charity of the United States of America (LCUSA), was established in 1960. There are organizations of Ladies of Charity in forty-seven dioceses in the United States, with a membership of approximately seventeen thousand women. Ladies of Charity visit in hospitals, nursing homes, and prisons; they serve the homeless in soup kitchens and read to the blind. In many parishes they also contribute to

the liturgical life of the parish by assisting as lectors and eucharistic ministers. See *http://www.famvin.org/LCUSA/history.html* (7 October 2000).

43. Bryan T. Froehle and Mary L. Gautier, *Catholicism USA: A Portrait of the Catholic Church in the United States* (Maryknoll, N.Y.: Orbis Books, 2000), 153–54.

44. Ibid., 121.

45. Mary de Cock, "Charting BVM History," *Salt* (1984): n.p. *Salt* is a magazine published quarterly by the Sisters of Charity of the Blessed Virgin Mary.

46. Kathryn Lawlor, "Flowing Like a Mighty River: The Development of BVM Spirituality" (unpublished paper, n.d.).

47. Mary Hunt, *Fierce Tenderness: A Feminist Theology of Friendship* (New York: Crossroad, 1991), 159–61. Hunt, cofounder of Women's Alliance for Theology, Ethics and Ritual (WATER), has provided theological leadership to the Women-Church movement in the United States.

48. In a book on the movement by Rosemary Radford Ruether, a change from "Woman Church" to "Women-Church" appears because of the possible exclusionary nature of the singular "woman." See her *Women-Church: Theology and Practice of Feminist Liturgical Communities* (San Francisco: Harper & Row, 1985).

49. For more on the Women-Church Convergence around the globe, see Schüssler Fiorenza, *Discipleship of Equals,* 326, and passim.

50. Ibid., 72.

51. Elizabeth Fox-Genovese, "Religion and Women in America," in *World Religions in America: An Introduction,* ed. Jacob Neusner (Louisville: Westminster John Knox Press, 1994), 265.

52. Ibid., 268.

53. Ibid., 270.

54. Nancy A. Hardesty, "Blackwell, Antoinette Louisa Brown (1825–1921)," in *The Dictionary of History in America*, ed. Daniel G. Reed et al. (Downers Grove, Ill.: InterVarsity Press, 1990), 164.

55. Barbara Brown Zikmund, "Winning Ordination for Women in Mainstream Protestant Churches," in *Women and Religion in America,* ed. Rosemary Radford Ruether and Rosemary Skinner Keller, vol. 3: 1900–1968 (San Francisco: Harper & Row, 1986), 341–42; 356–60. See also Holly J. Lebowitz, "Methodists Celebrate, Ponder Women's Ordination," *Religion News Service,* 22 October 1997.

56. Lois A. Boyd and R. Douglas Brackenridge, *Presbyterian Women in America: Two Centuries of a Quest for Status* (Westport, Conn.: Greenwood Press, 1983), 107–22.

57. In the Presbyterian system, each congregation has a local session made up of elders, with the pastor as moderator. The session governs the local church. Presbyteries, made up of congregations in a local district, examine, ordain, and install ministers.

58. Boyd and Brackenridge, *Presbyterian Women in America,* 152. Although women could be ordained and equality was publicly proclaimed, attitudes about women did not change overnight. Boyd and Brackenridge cite church documents in which women were cautioned to maintain their proper femininity in their ministry and not to expect to be able to do many of the things that male ministers do (p. 155).

59. Ibid., 226.

60. These statistics have been gathered by the Research Services of the Presbyterian Church (U.S.A.), 100 Witherspoon Street, Louisville, KY 40202 (*http://www.pcusa/cmd/rs*).

61. The Lutheran World Federation Department for Mission and Development (*http://umr.org/HTwomn.htm* and *http://library.northernlight.com/CK19980723040065252.html*).

62. U.S. Bureau of Census, cited by Bettye Collier-Thomas, *Daughters of Thunder: Black Women Preachers and Their Sermons, 1850–1979* (San Francisco: Jossey-Bass Publishers, 1998), 280.

63. Paula D. Nesbitt, "Feminization of American Clergy: Occupational Life Changes in Ordained Ministry" (Ph.D. diss., Harvard University, 1990), 180 (cited in Prelinger, "Ordained Women in the Episcopal Church," 292).

64. Cyprian Davis, "God of Our Weary Years: Black Catholics in American Catholic History," in *Taking Down Our Harps: Black Catholics in the United States,* ed. Diana L. Hayes and Cyprian Davis (Maryknoll, N.Y.: Orbis Books, 1998), 20.

65. For more on how the retention of African religiosity shaped African American spirituality, see Flora Wilson Bridges, *Resurrection Song: African American Spirituality* (Maryknoll, N.Y.: Orbis Books, 2001).

66. Emilie M. Townes, "Black Women from Slavery to Womanist Liberation," in *In Our Own Voices: Four Centuries of American Women's Religious Writing,* ed. Rosemary Radford Ruether and Rosemary Skinner Keller (San Francisco: HarperCollins, 1995), 155.

67. Katie Cannon, "The Emergence of Black Feminist Consciousness," in *Feminist Interpretation of the Bible*, ed. Letty Russell (Philadelphia: Westminster Press, 1985), 31.

68. Townes, "From Slavery to Womanist Liberation," 156.

69. The first black Baptist churches were founded between 1773 and 1775 in Silver Bluff, South Carolina, and Savannah, Georgia. Sydney E. Ahlstrom, *A Religious History of the American People* (New Haven: Yale University Press, 1973), 702.

70. The usual time period given for the Second Great Awakening is approximately 1795 to the beginning of the Civil War, with revivals, some of which were led by northern itinerant preachers, of varying intensity taking place in different parts of the U.S.

71. In Illona Linthwaite, ed., *Ain't I a Woman: A Book of Women's Poetry from Around the World* (New York: Wings Books, 1987), 129–30. There is no exact copy of this speech given at the Women's Rights Convention in Akron, Ohio, in 1852. The speech was adapted to poetry by Erlene Stetsen from the copy found in the frontispiece of Arthur Huff Fauset, *Sojourner: God's Faithful Pilgrim* (Chapel Hill: University of North Carolina Press, 1938), n.p.

72. Ahlstrom, *Religious History,* 707–8.

73. Christa K. Dixon, *Negro Spirituals: From Bible to Folk Song* (Philadelphia: Fortress, 1976), 81–82.

74. Townes, "From Slavery to Womanist Liberation," 159. Her source is Willie Mae Coleman, "Keeping the Faith and Disturbing the Peace: Black Women from Anti-Slavery to Woman's Suffrage" (Ph.D. diss., University of California at Irvine, 1982), 88.

75. This information is provided by Jacquelyn Grant, "Black Theology and the Black Woman," in *Black Theology: A Documentary History,* vol. 1, ed. Gayraud S. Wilmore and James H. Cone (Maryknoll, N.Y.: Orbis Books, 1979), 433 n. 23.

76. Collier-Thomas, *Daughters of Thunder,* 280.

77. C. Eric Lincoln and Lawrence H. Mamiya, *The Black Church in the African American Experience* (Durham, N.C.: Duke University Press, 1990), 276.

78. Ibid., 289–94, 300.

79. Ibid., 275. The phenomenon of "church mother" has no parallel in white churches and may be a carryover from African religious influence.

80. Grant, "Black Theology," 423.

81. Ibid., 424.

82. Lincoln and Mamiya, *African American Experience,* 298.

83. Ibid., 286–87.

84. Pauli Murray, cited in Collier-Thomas, *Daughters of Thunder,* 241.

85. Davis, "God of Our Weary Years," 29–30. See also idem, *The History of Black Catholics in the United States* (New York: Crossroad, 1996), 99–115.

86. Jay P. Dolan, *The American Catholic Experience: A History from Colonial Times to the Present* (Garden City, N.Y.: Doubleday, 1985), 226–27, 245–46.

87. Diana L. Hayes, *And Still We Rise: An Introduction to Black Liberation Theology* (Maryknoll, N.Y.: Orbis Books, 1996), 45–48.

88. M. Shawn Copeland, "African American Catholics and Black Theology: An Interpretation," in *African American Religious Studies: An Interdisciplinary Anthology,* ed. Gayraud S. Wilmore (Durham, N.C.: Duke University Press, 1989), 229.

89. Ibid.

90. Secretariat for the Liturgy and Secretariat for Black Catholics with the National Conference of Catholic Bishops, *Plenty Good Room, the Spirit and Truth of African American Catholic Worship* (Washington, D.C.: United States Catholic Conference, 1990), 36.

91. Davis, *History of Black Catholics,* 256.

92. Jamie T. Phelps, "Black Spirituality," in Hayes and Davis, eds., *Taking Down Our Harps,* 196. The reference to the "gift of blackness" is from an undocumented address of Pope Paul VI, given in Kampala, Uganda.

93. M. Shawn Copeland, "Method in Emerging Black Catholic Theology," in Hayes and Davis, eds., *Taking Down Our Harps,* 134.

94. Hayes, *And Still We Rise,* 169–80.

95. H. McKennie Goodpasture, *Cross and Sword: An Eyewitness History of Christianity in Latin America* (Maryknoll, N.Y.: Orbis Books, 1989), 12–13.

96. Ibid., 105. In 1930 the Protestant population in Latin America was less than 1 percent, roughly half a million people (p. 183). By 1960 the Protestant population was about 5 percent, and by 1985 it was nearly 15 percent (p. 222). David Lehmann points out the difficulties in establishing exact figures in Latin America due to the ways in which census data are collected and the "degrees of belonging" to the churches. See his *Struggle for the Spirit: Religious Transformation and Popular Culture in Brazil and Latin America* (Cambridge: Polity Press, 1996), 119. What he is certain of is that the number of Protestant churches is growing in Latin America.

97. For more specifics, see Paulo Freire, *The Pedagogy of the Oppressed* (New York: Herder and Herder, 1970).

98. Jeanne Gallo, "Basic Ecclesial Communities: A New Model of Church," in *One Faith, Many Cultures,* vol. 2, ed. Ruy O. Costar (Maryknoll, N.Y.: Orbis Books; Cambridge, Mass.: Boston Theological Institute, 1988), 99. Gallo is a Central American advocate.

99. María Pilar Aquino, *Our Cry for Life: Feminist Theology from Latin America* (Maryknoll, N.Y.: Orbis Books, 1993), 48–49.

100. John E. Linnan, "Basic Church Communities in the Mexican Community and Their Ecclesiological Significance," in *Dialogue Rejoined: Theology and Ministry in the United States Hispanic Reality,* ed. Ana María Pineda and Robert Schreiter (Collegeville, Minn.: Liturgical Press, 1995), 102.

101. Ibid., 108.

102. Tereza Cavalcanti, "Sobre la participación de las mujeres en el VI Encuentro Intereclesial de las CEB," in *Aportes para una teología desde la mujer,* ed. María Pilar Aquino (Madrid: Biblia y Fe, 1988), 140–41 (cited in Aquino, *Our Cry for Life,* 48).

103. Lehmann, *Struggle for the Spirit,* 117–18.

104. Ibid., 132.

105. Ibid., 133.

106. Rosângela Soares de Oliveira, "Feminist Theology in Brazil," in *Women's Visions: Theological Reflection, Celebration, Action,* ed. Ofelia Ortega (Geneva: World Council of Churches, 1995), 75.

QUESTIONS FOR REFLECTION AND DISCUSSION

1. To which of the understandings of church presented in this chapter (if any) do you find yourself drawn? If none are attractive to you, why is that the case?

    A. The church is the gathered *fellowship of believers, the people of God.*

    B. The church is a *sacramental mystery* of God's abiding presence in the world.

    C. The church is the *prophetic voice* challenging societal injustice.

    D. The church is the *visible, hierarchically structured institution* embodying an apostolic succession that can be traced to Peter and the other apostles.

    F. The church is the *invisible presence of the reign of God* within the heart of the individual believer.

2. In your judgment, are there valid theological reasons for ordaining only men to be priests and ministers? Is this judgment informed by specific biblical passages or is it influenced by historical and cultural factors?

3. What is your response to the statements of the Second Vatican Council that "every type of discrimination, whether societal or cultural, whether based on sex, race, color, social condition, language, or religion, is to be overcome" and that a woman should be able "to embrace a state of life or acquire an education or cultural benefits equal to those recognized for men" ("The Church in the Modern World," *Gaudium et Spes,* no. 29)?

4. Are you drawn to any of these positions?

    A. The ordination of women flows logically from Gal. 3:28 and the affirmation that for those baptized into Christ, "there is no longer male and female; for all are one in Christ Jesus."

    B. The ordination of women is not appropriate unless all of the manifestations of patriarchy in the churches are changed, such as clerical hierarchy, only male language for God, and noninclusive language in reference to people in prayers and hymns — for example, the use of the generic "man" rather than "men and women."

    C. The non-ordination of women must be upheld because it has a two-thousand-year tradition that began in New Testament times. Women have many opportunities to use their gifts in the church without being ordained priests.

    D. Advocacy of women's ordination is not an expression of feminist rebellion against male authority, but rather a symptom of a far-reaching cultural revolution that is not likely to be reversed.

5. There is a shortage of ordained priests in many parts of the world. Do you believe that the Catholic Church will undergo a change in identity in the future if large segments of the church have infrequent access to the sacraments?

6. What might attract a person to be a priest, ordained minister, or a vowed religious?

7. Compare and contrast Euro-American Catholic and Protestant women in regard to their relationship to their churches.

8. What is your response to the picture of black women and their relationship to their churches as it is sketched by Jacquelyn Grant? Are there elements of this picture that are also true for the relationship of Euro-American and Hispanic women to their churches?

9. Is the notion of basic ecclesial communities (*comunidades eclesiales de base*) attractive to you? Do you believe that the praxis emphasis of CEBs is appropriate for Catholic parishes and/or Protestant congregations?

AREAS FOR EXPLORATION

1. Survey at least three men and women of different generations and religious backgrounds about their preferred model of church.

2. Ask the same men and women what their opinion is of women being priests or ministers.

3. Are there any connections between how the people you surveyed answered questions 1 and 2?

RECOMMENDED READINGS

Baker-Fletcher, Karen, and Garth Kasimu Baker-Fletcher. *My Sister, My Brother: Womanist and Xodus God-Talk*. Maryknoll, N.Y.: Orbis Books, 1997. (See part 5, "Church," especially chapter 14, "Having Church: A Womanist Perspective.")

Boyd, Lois A., and R. Douglas Brackenridge. *Presbyterian Women in the United States: Two Centuries of a Quest for Status*. Westport, Conn.: Greenwood Press, 1983.

Carr, Anne E. *Transforming Grace: Christian Tradition and Women's Experience*. San Francisco: Harper & Row, 1988.

Darling, Pamela W. *New Wine: The Story of Women Transforming Leadership and Power in the Episcopal Church*. Cambridge, Mass.: Cowley Publications, 1994.

Gillespie, Joanna Bowen. *Women Speak of God: Congregations and Change*. Valley Forge, Pa.: Trinity Press International, 1995.

Hayes, Diana L. *And Still They Rise: An Introduction to Black Liberation Theology*. New York: Paulist Press, 1996.

Herder, Fran, and John Heagle. *Partnership: Women and Men in Ministry*. Notre Dame, Ind.: Ave Maria Press, 1989.

Hilkert, Mary Catherine. *Preaching and the Sacramental Imagination.* New York: Continuum, 1997.

MacHaffie, Barbara J., ed. *Readings in Her Story: Women in the Christian Tradition.* Minneapolis: Fortress, 1992.

Perlinger, Catherine M., ed. *Episcopal Women: Gender Spirituality and Commitment in an American Mainline Denomination.* New York: Oxford University Press, 1992.

Pineda, Ana María, and Robert Schreiter, eds. *Dialogue Rejoined: Theology and Ministry in the United States Hispanic Reality.* Collegeville, Minn.: Liturgical Press, 1995.

Chapter 5

Feminist Spirituality, God, Mary, and Her Sister Saints

> Saints are those who have drawn so close to the center of the circle [in which God is the center] that the Uncreated Light streams through them into the world. And the closer people draw to them, the closer they get to the divine.
> — ELIZABETH A. JOHNSON.[1]

Becoming a saint, getting close to the divine — these are goals that some people may associate with the word "spirituality." Yet, spirituality is not necessarily associated with the saints, or even explicitly with a divine being or a way of life guided by a religion. What is spirituality? Today, the term is used when speaking of programs not affiliated with a specific religion, such as the Twelve Steps of Alcoholics Anonymous, and psychological quests for sound mental health and mature personal autonomy. Spirituality is a topic of interest among athletes, entertainers, and business executives. Workshops that include "spirituality" in their titles abound. Publishers and booksellers report that works on spirituality sell well. People who associate spirituality with nonreligious programs define the goals of spirituality differently, but all seem to assume that being spiritual is a characteristic of being human. Nevertheless, spirituality is still commonly associated with the world religions, including Christianity.

Since so much ambiguity surrounds spirituality, Sandra Schneiders's description serves as the basis for our study of spirituality in this chapter. She describes spirituality as "the experience of striving to integrate one's life in terms of self-transcendence toward the ultimate value one perceives."[2] Hers is a broad yet carefully conceived description that presumes that every individual has the capacity to be a spiritual person. It also presumes that most people desire a personal integration that brings soul and body, thought and emotion, individual and social realities together. For Schneiders, personal integration and the discovery of what has ultimate value cannot be divorced from each other. The explicitly religious aspect of a person's spirituality involves a process of growth toward personal integration in a movement beyond the self, especially narcissistic self-interest, toward what or whom a person perceives to be ultimate, such as God. Since spirituality is experiential, it is not an abstract theory but a personally lived reality. Growth in spirituality doesn't magically happen. It requires conscious striving and therefore is a purposeful pursuit.

178

Christian Spirituality

What the Christian tradition understands spirituality to be incorporates the elements of personal integration and self-transcendence in relationship to the God revealed in Jesus Christ. An early source for what Christian spirituality is is found in the Pauline Epistles of the New Testament. Paul describes the influence of the Spirit of God in people's lives. He uses the term "spiritual" in reference to persons who, with the help of the Holy Spirit, are able to discern the presence and absence of God. Such persons have "the mind of Christ" (1 Cor. 2:14–15) and unique spiritual blessings (Eph. 1:3). Having the mind of Christ or being spiritually blessed does not mean that every spiritual person is the same, for among spiritual persons "there are different gifts, but the same Spirit" (1 Cor. 12:4). The Spirit, who is love poured into our hearts (Rom. 5:5), can be said to be the same for all, but the gifts by which each person manifests the presence of the Spirit are unique to each person.

Paul's notion of spirituality is closely related to the meaning he gives to the word "saint." Saints are holy women and men who are faithful Christians. Paul often addresses his letters to "the saints," to God's beloved, sanctified in Jesus Christ (Rom. 1:7; Phil. 1:1). Saints are those called to use their gifts to manifest the Spirit for the common good (1 Cor. 1:1–2; 12:7). They do so by giving witness to Christ and his message. The book of Hebrews speaks of the "cloud of witnesses" (surely what Paul means by "the saints") who have "run with perseverance the race" set before them while looking to Jesus (Heb. 12:1–2). They are also the "holy ones" who died and now are directed to rejoice in heaven (Rev. 18:20). For they are with Christ in glory.

The Christian tradition teaches that a communion exists among the holy ones of God, both living and dead. Through the saints who have gone before and have "fallen asleep," the Uncreated Light streams into the world in different hues. Drawn to their light, others in turn are drawn closer to the divine, ready themselves to run with perseverance their own race in their own time. And so, the cloud of witnesses grows.

Obviously, God, Mary, and the saints are topics of interest to Christian spirituality and theology. Although theology and spirituality are similar in significant ways, they are also different. Theology and spirituality are similar insofar as they include human experience as a source. Both can and often do focus on biblical texts and some of the same postbiblical sources. What makes them different is that Christian theology's goal is to bring faith to understanding for a Christian community. It often seeks to relate the Christian texts of the past with contemporary experience. Christian spirituality is more all-encompassing than theology. According to Anne Carr, Christian spirituality encompasses our relationships to every facet of creation.[3] In the midst of our many relationships, a spiritually attuned person listens for the call of the divine Spirit in daily events. In responding to this call, the person gains greater clarity about what is of ultimate value in her or his life and at the same time grows closer to God. This growth cannot be separated from witnessing to God's mercy and justice. In feminist theology, these characteristics associated with spirituality are rarely extrinsic to the activity of doing theology. Transformative praxis, doing justice with love, is basic to feminist theology. This is not necessarily true of all theology. Many feminists are theologians because of love for God and desire to use their gifts for the good of others, of their churches, and of the health of the Earth. The same can be said for many theologians who are not feminists. But such a life commitment is not strictly required to be an academic theologian. A person can write books on feminist theology that are more theoretical than praxis oriented.

Obviously, to become a saint does not require that a person be a theologian. Nor does sainthood require that one be an active member of a Christian church. The call to holiness can be found when and where we encounter persons of virtue. Some people feel that membership in a Christian church is not a help in their spiritual development. These people are likely attuned to the effects of human sinfulness in the Christian churches. Sin has resulted in occasions in which the churches have "missed the mark" where Jesus' authentic message is concerned. Over the centuries, churches have contributed to prejudice in its many forms: anti-Semitism, racism, sexism, and more. Institutions are prone to corruption and blind spots. Church leaders at times promote interpretations of the gospel message that contribute to their own power and control. Some church members live less-than-exemplary lives. Sometimes the cloud is not of witnesses looking to Jesus but a fog making it difficult to experience the Uncreated Light.

Although they are imperfect bearers of the good news, Christian churches, whether Roman Catholic, Eastern Orthodox, Anglican, or one of the many Protestant denominations, have succeeded in handing on elements of the message of Jesus Christ with considerable fidelity. Therefore, many women and men find them to be authentic witnesses to the triune God and rich resources for their spiritual growth. It is fitting, therefore, for a chapter on spirituality to follow the chapter on the church. Churches are more than a home for the sinner; they are communities in which people receive a call to holiness and commit themselves to virtuous lives. Institutions with human frailty, churches nonetheless have long played a significant role in the spiritual growth of their members by providing them guidance and opportunity for the expression of their gifts in ways that manifest the Spirit. Church communities have their shortcomings, but they do provide nourishment and support for saintliness that have stood the test of time. It is often difficult for an individual who is not affiliated with a church community to find social support to grow in holiness and the nourishment of shared belief about what is truly ultimate.

Just as conversation is basic to friendship, prayer is basic to Christian spirituality. Prayerful conversation with God, formal or spontaneous, falls into four major categories: (1) petition, asking God to respond to our needs or desires; (2) contrition, seeking forgiveness from God and expressing sorrow for sin; (3) praise, the outpouring of adoration of the divine; and (4) thanksgiving, expressing gratitude, for all is a gift from God.

Formalized prayer in liturgical settings helps to strengthen community bonds in a common focus — worship and love of God. Through formalized prayer, people experience "being church," being "the people of God," being "the cloud of witnesses" united in their common love for God. Spontaneous prayer, although it can take place in a church setting, such as praying for members of the community, is more individual. Spontaneous prayer, in the form of meditation, can contribute greatly to personal integration. When meditating, for example, a person may focus on a biblical story and picture herself in the situation described. The stance is one of listening for God to speak through the elements in the story that resonate with one's own life experience. In the process the person gains new insight into self, God, and the many relationships that contribute to the person she or he is. A person can also use the lives of the saints or their writings for meditation. A prayerful reading of Scripture or the writings of a spiritual writer, ancient or modern, awakens "Godward" aspirations that often lead to contemplation. *Contemplative prayer** is a prayer of open receptivity to union with God in love. Meditative and contemplative prayer can flow into one another. As a person attends to the presence of God, she or he is drawn to deeper intimacy with God in love. Praise and thanksgiving, as well as contrition and petition, can accompany experiences of deep communion with God. In prayer, especially meditative and contemplative prayer, something of the divine may be revealed. After such an experience, the person is not quite the same. An invitation to wholeness, a call to holiness has been experienced. Energy in the form of a love that seeks to contribute to the good of others often accompanies such experiences. Personal meditation also often adds depth to formalized prayer, making prayer with the church community more meaningful.

Christian Feminist Spirituality

Although Christian women since the time of Christ have sought prayerful communion with God with a desire to respond to their unique call to holiness, only since the 1970s has conversation about feminist spirituality emerged in the United States. Similar conversations began in Western Europe shortly thereafter. According to Sandra Schneiders, conversation among women about "feminist spirituality is essentially a reclaiming by women of the reality and power designated by the term 'spirit'."[4] Basic to this reclaiming of spirit is the retrieval of images and stories that empower women to be all that they can be as persons who uniquely image God. In the reclaiming of spirit for and by women, how God, Mary, and her sister saints are imagined can play an important role.

The images that one has of God, Mary, and the saints are symbolic in nature. Joann Wolski Conn, a Christian feminist who has made significant contributions to women's spirituality, emphasizes that "the importance of symbolism for spirituality cannot be overestimated."[5] Feminist scholars of spirituality are careful to draw upon symbols that have the potential of providing a dynamic, spirit-enlivened path to communion with the divine. This means that the choice of images must be made with care. Does this image resonate with my experience and help me in my prayer? Does it facilitate my spiritual journey toward authentic wholeness? Disillusionment is always possible when trying to answer such questions. Does the symbolic image present a recognizable sacred truth? Does it also inspire me, and others as well, to self-transcendence in ways that help us in our journey toward holiness? These are weighty questions that often defy simplistic answers. To answer them requires discernment, the ability to recognize the authentic presence of God.

Discernment is aided by keeping in mind that symbols that are truly sacred participate in the realities they signify, giving rise to thought and direction for action. This means that a sacred symbol, be it of God, of Mary, or of one of her sister saints, must make present authentic characteristics of the sacred for women. Wolski Conn realistically notes that religious symbolism can function for women in both life-enhancing and life-diminishing ways.[6] In her scholarship she draws upon writings of and about the saints, while ever watchful of how what her research unearths may be limiting for women's self-development and integration. Other feminists share her concern for vigilance. Anne Carr has drawn attention to the regressive and progressive potential of religious symbols.[7] She notes that some religious symbols are regressive because they do not authentically present the sacred. Regressive symbols must be abandoned if they denigrate the human dignity of women. Therefore, an important task for Christian feminists whose interest is spirituality is to apply a hermeneutics of suspicion to the symbols used for God, Mary, and her sister saints. This is a recurring theme in this book, but worth repeating. After engaging in a hermeneutics of suspicion, a hermeneutics of remembrance is the logical second step. This step enables symbols with progressive potential for women to surface. How will a person recognize a symbol with progressive potential for women? At a minimum, a progressive symbol is one that facilitates, in the words of Katherine Zappone, "the praxis of imaging wholeness" for women.[8] Personal integration is the bedrock of Christian feminist spirituality and foundational for moving through self-transcendence to union with the divine. This dynamic enables women to become women of "spirit," in Schneiders's sense of the term.

Christian Feminist Spirituality and God

Of the triad of God, Mary, and her sister saints, obviously, God is the most important. In chapter 3, hermeneutics of suspicion and remembrance were applied to imagery and symbolism for God. In Judaism and Christianity, God is understood to be personal through imagery that is predominantly male. As noted earlier, although the word "God" is not actually a gendered term, throughout the Jewish and Christian tradition God has been referred to as "he." The strong tendency to literalize male designations for God has resulted in female imagery being effectively excluded from Christian theology and spirituality. This fact of history has profoundly affected the lives of women and men.

Where God symbolism is concerned, feminist theology and spirituality flow from and to each other. In the choice of God images, feminist theology and spirituality are interdependent. Feminist spiritual practitioners are dependent on how feminist theologians interpret symbols of the divine in Scripture and in postbiblical sources. Feminist theologians are reliant on feminist spiritual practitioners for insight into whether the symbols of the sacred upon which they focus facilitate experiences of the divine in ways that contribute to women's integration and self-transcendence toward union with God. A hermeneutics of

---

RE-IMAGINING CONFERENCE

"RE-Imagining: A Global Theological Conference by Women" was held in Minneapolis in 1993. Its purpose was to provide the participants with an opportunity to re-image how they relate to God, church, and community. Two thousand woman and eighty-three men attended the three-day conference, held as part of an ongoing World Council of Churches program organized to celebrate the "Ecumenical Decade of Churches in Solidarity with Women (1988–98)." The conference closed with a worship service featuring a ritual of milk and honey (rather than the traditional bread and wine) and concluded with a prayer in which those gathered prayed, "Our sweet Sophia, we are women in your image."[9] Due largely, but not exclusively, to this ritual and its prayer to Sophia-God, there was an outpouring of criticism, especially from members of the Presbyterian Church U.S.A. and the United Methodist Church, both of which had contributed funds to support the conference. A major focus of the dispute was the question whether the Sophia to whom the participants prayed was a gnostic goddess (a pagan deity) or a personification of God's Wisdom (an authentic biblical revelation of the Holy).

The planners of the conference did not envision the emphasis on re-imagining as the establishment of Sophia as a goddess to replace the biblical God. Rather, the conference planners invited the participants to become more aware of God as female so that a meaningful connection could be made between traditional biblical language and a Christian spirituality that contributes to wholeness for women and men who find themselves diminished when God is imaged in exclusively male terms, especially as a distant and omnipotent father or king.

---

remembrance applied by feminist theologians has brought attention to imagery and symbols of the divine that have long gone unnoticed, especially to God as Sophia (Woman Wisdom), as Divine Mother, and as a triune Divine Community.

The interdependence of feminist theology and spirituality where God symbols are concerned is illustrated in gatherings of women. Perhaps none has drawn more attention than an event sponsored by the World Council of Churches in 1993, entitled "RE-Imagining: A Global Theological Conference by Women." The women gathered prayed to "sweet Sophia."[10] For many women, Sophia, Woman Wisdom, has become a meaningful biblical image, not only to correct the idolatry of an exclusively male God, but also to provide a divine guide in their spiritual journeys. Woman Wisdom empowers women, just as she empowered Jesus. For first-century Christians, Jesus was the prophet of Woman Wisdom, challenging the people he encountered to new understandings of God.[11] Thanks to the scholarship of feminist theologians, for a growing number of women and men, Woman Wisdom functions in a similar way today.

Feminists are also turning to mother imagery for God. Sallie McFague, a

Protestant theologian who has made significant contributions to feminist symbolism for God, and who was given attention in chapter 3, argues that naming God as "Mother" gives us a way of talking about the divine presence in terms of an image familiar to women and men both. The thread of similarity between God and mother helps us to know what we might not be able to talk about without the word "mother." God the Mother is the giver of life; ever on the side of the living, she wants all to flourish.[12] Of course, in spirituality, talking *about* is far less important than talking *to*. It is talking to God in prayer that facilitates self-transcendence toward union with God. The prayer on the following page, based on Psalm 139, was composed by Virginia Ann Froehle, and well illustrates the potential for a self-transcendence through loving intimacy with God.

In the introduction to the book in which this prayer is found, Froehle stresses that when she began to explore female images of God in prayer, "I leaped forward in my walk in the Spirit."[13] Many are discovering that praying with images for God such as Mother or Woman Wisdom enables their communion with God and their own personal integration to grow and deepen.

There are other ways to leap forward in one's walk in the Spirit, and they are found in feminist interpretations of the triune God. A Christian feminist spirituality does not focus on the regressive image of the three masculinized persons — Father, Son, and Holy Spirit (spoken of as "Lord" in the Nicene Creed) — existing in isolation from creatures. Rather, it seeks to recover the relational character of God, who is in all and with all. At the level of symbol, the Trinity points beyond itself to the mystery of a divine community whose ongoing relationship with creatures cannot be frozen or fixed in time. The threefold manifestations of the divine revealed in the New Testament and affirmed in the churches' creeds continue in a God who is experienced as distinctively "for us," concerned for our well-being as creatures, our salvation as sinners, and our communal ways of being human together.[14] God's threefold self-communication is connected to every aspect of our lives and reveals what it means to be a person. Personhood, whether divine or human, cannot be spoken of apart from community.

The divine community transcends the boundaries of time and place and extends beyond itself like a great circle to Mary and the other saints. Feminist spirituality is very much concerned with Mary, the mother of Jesus Christ, and women saints to discern what they, as women, can contribute to women's spiritual growth. One might ask, Isn't God enough? Certainly, God is enough! The triune God, however, is not an isolated monad. In a very real sense, no symbolization of the triune Christian God is ever adequate without attending to the broader communion of saints, living and dead, who gave witness to God in how they lived their lives.

At the outset it is important to recall that just as images and symbols for God can be regressive, so can those for Mary and the other saints. Mary and the saints, particularly women saints, have suffered under the burden of romanticism, which in our age often reduces them to the level of the trivial. The romanticizing resulted in the creation of images of Mary and women saints that are inimical to women's wholeness and holiness. When regressive linguistic and pictorial images of Mary and the saints are found, they must be set aside. Put

Mother, you have given me birth and
　　cared for me ever since;
You are familiar with all my ways.
You know all that I do, to whom I speak;
You even know what I am thinking.

Before a word jumps onto my tongue,
My God, you seem to know it.
You know my whole journey,
Every thicket and resting place along
　　my path.
You walk in front of me and behind me;
Sometimes I feel your hand resting on
　　my shoulder.

This faithfulness of your loving presence
Seems too good to be true.

Could I go away from you—or your spirit?
Is any place locked from your presence?
If I fly to the heavens, won't you be there?
If I sink to the depths of the earth,
I think I would meet you still.
If I flew on the wings of the dawn,
If I sailed to the far limits of the sea,
Your hand would still be upon me.
Guiding me, holding me safe.

You formed me before I was born.
You have created my inner self.

Thank you for making me so wonderful!
　　(All your works are wonderful!)
You always understand my spirit;
You know every cell of my body.
You have been with me in all
　　that I have done
And will be with me until the end.
Your plan is wonderful, more than
　　I can grasp;
I rest in your faith and live in your love.[15]

¹*O Lord,* you have searched me and known
me. ²You know when I sit down and when
I rise up; you discern my thoughts from
far away. ³You search out my path and my
lying down, and are acquainted with all my
ways.

⁴Even before a word is on my tongue,
O Lᴏʀᴅ, you know it completely.
⁵You hem me in, behind and before,
and lay your hand upon me.

⁶Such knowledge is too wonderful for me;
it is so high that I cannot attain it.

⁷Where can I go from your spirit?
Or where can I flee from your presence?
⁸If I ascend to heaven, you are there;
if I make my bed in Sheol,
you are there.
⁹If I take the wings of the morning
and settle at the farthest limits of the sea,
¹⁰even there your hand shall lead me,
and your right hand shall hold me fast.

¹³For it was you who formed my inward
parts; you knit me together in my mother's
womb.

¹⁴I praise you, for I am fearfully and
wonderfully made. Wonderful are your
works; that I know very well.
¹⁵My frame was not hidden from you, when
I was being made in secret, intricately
woven in the depths of the earth.
¹⁶Your eyes beheld my unformed substance.
In your book were written all the days that
were formed for me, when none of them as
yet existed.[16]

more concretely, the plaster-of-paris figurines must be smashed to make room for progressive images, ones that allow the Uncreated Light to shine in a world in which darkness abounds.

Mary, Virgin Mother of God

Contemporary Christianity exhibits a wide variety of attitudes about Mary: excessive adulation, benign neglect, and outright rejection. In the pages that follow, all of these attitudes are represented. The purpose is not so much to analyze why these attitudes exist as to explore who Mary might be if she is to be a viable resource for a feminist spirituality.

Why is Mary important for Christianity? In the *Synoptic Gospels, the mother of Jesus is identified as Mary, but beyond that she is portrayed differently. In Matthew and Luke, Mary is both the mother of Jesus and a virgin. In Matthew, we find a prophecy rooted in Isa. 7:14: " 'Look, the virgin shall conceive and bear a son, and they shall name him Emmanuel,' which means, 'God is with us' " (Matt. 1:23).[17] In Luke, we find a picture of a young Jewish virgin called to participate in God's plan of salvation. The angel Gabriel says to her, "Mary, you have found favor with God. And now, you will conceive in your womb and bear a son, and you will name him Jesus" (Luke 1:30–31).

These verses were composed after the death and resurrection of Jesus as part of the Matthean and Lukan infancy narratives. It is important to bear in mind that the primary concern of the infancy narratives was to express early Christian belief about the significance of Jesus. They are far less concerned with providing information about Mary. Perhaps to make up for the lack of information about Mary in the Gospels of the first century, in the second century an unknown author composed the "Nativity of Mary," also known as *Protevangelium of James* (attributed to James the brother of Jesus, or James the younger [see Mark 15:40]). This treatise supplies biographical information lacking in the four Gospels, including the names of Mary's parents and the choosing of Joseph as her husband.[18] The *Protevangelium,* however, is considered apocryphal, meaning of questionable authorship and authenticity. Nevertheless, its many details became a source for artistic images for Mary and of popular devotion in Marian spirituality.

A second-century development in the depiction of Mary emphasized how she, the mother of Jesus Christ, contrasted with Eve, "the mother of the living" (Gen. 3:20). Theologians such as Justin Martyr (ca. 100–165)[19] and Irenaeus, bishop of Lyons (ca. 130–200),[20] denigrated Eve, the disobedient woman responsible for the fall, and lifted up Mary as the great exception among women. Mary, through her obedience to God, "untied the knot of Eve's disobedience."[21] The biblical sources for drawing the parallel between Eve and Mary are (1) Gen. 3:15, in which a promise is made that God will put enmity between the serpent and Eve, along with her descendants, and (2) Rom. 5:14–18, in which Paul compares Adam and Christ. For Irenaeus, just as Jesus Christ is the "New Adam" and Savior, so Mary is the "New Eve," who "became to herself and to the whole human race a cause of salvation."[22] The "New Eve" symbol functioned to elevate Mary to a pedestal high above Eve and her daughters in Christian spirituality.

Mary was elevated higher still in the insistence that she was a virgin not only before but also after Jesus' birth. What is at stake in this belief involves more than the miraculous nature of Jesus' birth. Insistence on Mary's perpetual virginity was in keeping with Christian spirituality influenced by the spirit/body dualism of Greek thinking (problems associated with this pattern of thinking were addressed in chapter 1 and elsewhere). Under the influence of this dualistic thinking, it did not seem fitting for Mary, the New Eve, to be identified in any way with the realm of the body, including sexual reproduction. The spiritual realm, over which the divine reigned, was opposed to the bodily realm, in which the devil worked.

Depicting Mary as blessed by God with perpetual virginity was not the greatest honor bestowed on her. Her highest elevation into glory was the fifth-century proclamation that Mary's unique virgin-motherhood made her "God-bearer," expressed in the Greek title *Theotokos*. This lofty title was bestowed on Mary at the Council of Ephesus in 431. Although the primary concern of the Council was to affirm that Jesus Christ was fully human and fully divine, *Theotokos* symbolically presented Mary not only as the mother of the human Jesus but also as the Mother of God.

The symbolization of Mary as the Blessed Virgin and Mother of God functioned in the devotions that have sprung up to honor her. The ways in which Greeks and Romans had honored their goddesses were transposed onto her. Statues of Mary were decorated in the blue cloak and crown of the goddess and were linked to the moon and the stars. Mary was depicted as seated on a royal throne, the queen presenting her child to the world. This iconography was similar to that of the goddess Isis with her son, Horus. Prayers for mercy and praise of wisdom that had been directed to pre-Christian female goddesses were now directed to Mary, as Queen of Heaven.

During the Middle Ages, growth in devotion to Mary continued in Catholic Europe. During the era of numerous wars and many waves of plague, Christ is often depicted as a stern judge and king, distant from the people. Mary becomes the intercessor of divine mercy. To her a suffering people turned for solace. An important source of the symbolic representation of Mary during this period is the formal prayer of Christian communities. Among such prayers is the "Salve Regina," which proclaims,

> Hail, Holy Queen, Mother of Mercy,
> Hail our Life, our Sweetness and our Hope!
> To thee do we cry, poor banished children of Eve;
> To thee do we send up our sighs, mourning and weeping
>   in this valley of tears.
> Turn, then, most gracious advocate, thine eyes of mercy
>   toward us. . . .
> O clement, O loving, O sweet Virgin Mary.[23]

In this prayer, Mary is the exalted queen reigning in a world apart from the poor banished children of Eve. Yet, she is approachable. She bridges the abyss that separates male divinity from the human with her comfort, giving clemency to the afflicted. In this prayer, devotion to Mary, although called veneration, is difficult to distinguish from adoration associated with worship of God. In short, Marian symbolism functions in ways that present her as a divine being. The piety centered on her provides female imagery for God missing in the masculinized monotheism of Western Christianity.

Elizabeth Johnson has proposed that this is one of the important reasons for the amazing growth of devotion to Mary in Christian spirituality, beginning early on in the church. Mary imagery has symbolic power because she is female. Without devotion to Mary there would have been no female images in the Christian perception of the divine. Female images of God, suppressed from official theology, migrated to Mary-centered spirituality. For many Christians, Mary revealed divine love and mercy in ways in which the masculinized God did not. According to Johnson, devotions to Mary as the compassionate mother present the ultimacy of the divine with a decidedly female face.[24]

In the Protestant Reformation of the sixteenth century, enthusiastic devotion to Mary received criticism for going beyond veneration and becoming worship. Protesting the depiction of Mary in divinelike symbolism and the popular devotion directed to her, the reformers argued that Mary detracted from the attention due to Christ alone. The reformers, with their emphasis on the Scripture alone as the source of theology, noted that the New Testament provided very little information about Mary. Although sixteenth-century reformers did not dispute that Mary conceived Jesus with her virginity unimpaired, they did believe that Marian devotions detracted from the proper place a Christian should give to Jesus Christ as Son of God incarnate and the Savior of sinners. Much of this criticism was valid and needed, but it also effectively removed from Protestant prayer and spirituality all female symbolism.

In the polemical atmosphere of the sixteenth to early-twentieth centuries, Roman Catholic devotion to Mary continued and in some cases increased. Louis-Marie Grignion de Montfort (d. 1716) even proposed that one must go through Mary to reach Jesus. To Protestants this was heresy. Mary, therefore, became a line of demarcation that separated Catholics and Protestants. The line widened in the nineteenth century, when Pope Pius IX made the belief that Mary was conceived without original sin an official dogma, known as the "Immaculate Conception" (1854). In the mid-twentieth century, Pope Pius XII declared that after her death, Mary was bodily assumed into heaven, a doctrine known as the "Assumption of the Blessed Virgin Mary" (1950). During this hundred-year period shrines were built in places where Mary was said to have appeared. Places like Lourdes in France (1858) and Fatima in Portugal (1917) became popular places of pilgrimage. Popular piety was also reflected in devotions to Mary under a variety of titles, and in the establishment of communities of priests and nuns named after popular Marian titles and devotions.

To correct excesses in Marian devotion, Pope John XXIII insisted that "the Madonna is not happy when placed before her son."[25] Following John XXIII's lead, the Second Vatican Council set about locating her firmly within the Catholic Church. It emphasized that Mary's role in the church was inseparable from her union with Jesus Christ. The Council's "Dogmatic Constitution on the

Church" (1964) stressed that Mary is the "highest after Christ and yet very close to us" (no. 54). Mary is the "highest after Christ" because she is the mother of Jesus Christ, the Son of God, our Redeemer (no. 55). Yet, very importantly, Mary is close to us because she is one with all human beings in our need of salvation. She is a model for the faithful who strive to conquer sin and grow in holiness (no. 65). This new development contributed to a shift in spirituality for many Catholics from devotion to Mary to focus on Jesus and his message.

Mary in European and Euro-American Feminist Thought

Early in the second wave of feminism, feminists who were familiar with Catholic Marian devotion questioned what the Marian symbolism did for the liberation of women from patriarchy. Among the early criticism was that of Simone de Beauvoir. In 1952, she examined Christian devotion to the Virgin Mary, the queen "who reigns over all humankind,"[26] and concluded that although women rose above the sin of Eve through Mary, women do so only to bow to the will of a male God. In de Beauvoir's assessment, although the mother of Christ is exalted in glory, her virginity has a negative value for women: it is the supreme symbol of masculine victory. Mary is glorified only in accepting the subordinate role of submissive obedience assigned to her by a dominant male deity. This is made clear by the words placed on her lips: "I am the servant of the Lord" (cf. Luke 1:38).[27] De Beauvoir reflects,

> For the first time in human history the mother kneels before her son; she freely accepts her inferiority. This is the supreme masculine victory, consummated in the cult of the virgin — it is the rehabilitation of woman through the accomplishment of her defeat.[28]

In 1968, Mary Daly, in the wake of the closing of the Second Vatican Council, cited this quotation from de Beauvoir in *The Church and the Second Sex*. She posited that women's identification with Mary as the "Virgin Mother of God" has had "devastating effects."[29] It contributes to the servile condition of women in Catholic countries. Elsewhere, Daly reflected on the Eve-Mary parallel, pointing out its problems for women. Mary is glorified as the vehicle of human restoration after Eve's fall, but Mary is unique among women. "Women in the concrete did not shake off their bad reputation [as daughters of Eve] and continued to bear most of the burden of blame [for sin in the world]."[30] In Daly's opinion, a glorified Mary does not improve perceptions about "concrete, living women."[31]

During the mid-1970s and early 1980s, as feminist spirituality was emerging in the United States and Western Europe, numerous feminist scholars drew attention to the regressive nature of the Marian symbols in the lives of Christian women. Often depicted as a solitary young maiden, Mary's image smiled, eyes downcast, from church pedestals, a symbol of what women should be but could never attain. Kari Børresen, a Norwegian scholar, challenged this image of Mary: "She embodies the essential connection between femininity and sub-ordination forged by the patriarchal mind-set."[32] In a similar vein, Elisabeth Schüssler Fiorenza drew attention to what she believed had been missing from Marian symbolism: women's equality and capacity to lead.[33] Rosemary Radford Ruether critiqued the traditional exaltation of Mary. A projection by males of the feminine ideal, Mary had become the docile submissive virgin par excellence, "purified of any relation to sexual femaleness."[34]

Kari Børresen, Elisabeth Schüssler Fiorenza, and Rosemary Radford Ruether have advanced degrees in theological disciplines, but they are not the only ones to argue that Marian symbolism has functioned as an obstacle for women's spiritual development. The problematic nature of Marian symbolism for non-theologians is borne out by Sally Cunneen, who cites this quotation from an interview of a female therapist:

> For the first twenty-five years of my life Mary was very significant for me. At its worst, this influence, with its emphasis on the Virgin Birth, produced a kind of desexualization; at its best, it held up to me a symbol of loving, caring femaleness. I see most of what is presented to me as gentleness is really passivity, and her virginity a distortion of humanness.[35]

Mary in this reflection is both unattainable ideal and antithesis of female whole-ness. That Mary had become trivialized or rejected outright by many women is no surprise.

Elizabeth Johnson has taken critiques of Marian symbolism such as these very seriously. In her assessment of Mary and the reality of women, she ad-dresses three major areas. First, she draws attention to a problem noted by the others surveyed. Traditional Marian symbols simultaneously glorify Mary and subordinate women as a whole. This is particularly obvious where the Eve-Mary symbolism is concerned. Mary is glorified, while Eve is denigrated as the "cause of the fall, accomplice of Satan, the destroyer of humankind."[36] Women have far more in common with the "Devil's gateway" than with Mary. This feeds into the "Madonna-whore syndrome," which allows men to view Mary as the ideal woman to whom no other woman can ever measure up. Mary, the Madonna, is the great exception, alone of all her sex. In comparison to Mary, every daugh-ter of Eve is deficient. The Eve-Mary symbolism continues even in our own time. It can be found in the *Catechism of the Catholic Church*,[37] thereby help-ing this symbol to continue to function in the spirituality of new generations of Catholics.

Second, Johnson focuses on how the Marian tradition has dichotomized the roles of men and women. According to the traditional Marian symbolism, man modeled on male divinity, including Christ, is active; woman modeled on Mary is passive. From this pattern a conclusion is drawn regarding the proper roles of man and woman in the churches: man leads the community in prayer and preaches; woman follows and listens in silence. This dynamic results in a spiri-tuality in which men are encouraged to develop and women are admonished to take an inferior role because of their gender, "a role where she is praised for living less than her full capacity."[38]

Closely related to this second critique is the third one, in which Johnson focuses on Mary as handmaiden, virgin, and mother. These symbols taken together truncate women's development by promoting for religious reasons an ideal of woman in which the goal is to be passively obedient (handmaiden), asexual (virgin), and domestically consumed (supermother).

There are ample reasons to conclude that collectively, traditional Marian symbols have curtailed the spiritual development of women by limiting the full range of possibilities of human wholeness for women. The tendency, therefore, may be for women to reject Mary because they experience her to be thoroughly disassociated from their lived realities and goals. The problems with Marian spirituality have arisen because Mary as a person was dissolved into symbolism that abstracted her from her concrete historical life. For Mary to be a resource for feminist spirituality, she must be "a real person in human history, a woman who has more in common with the rest of womankind than she has separating prerogatives."[39]

Put simply, the abandonment of Marian symbols inimical to the flourishing of women's spirit and a quest for the historical Mary are called for. These are difficult tasks. Well-established traditions die hard. Biblical research indicates that very little is known about the Mary of first-century Nazareth. Most of the passages in which she appears are not historical reports per se, but narratives that make important theological points about Jesus. The quest is not impossible, however, if one keeps in mind that much of what can be said about Mary are things that she likely shared with other women of first-century Nazareth. Johnson summarizes what might be discovered through such a quest for Mary of Nazareth:

> What scholars find is a first-century Jewish woman, probably unlettered, living in a rural village. She is a woman whose faith was shaped by the promise of the Hebrew Scriptures and whose spirituality was centered around religious duties in the home, such as lighting the Sabbath candles. She is the wife of Joseph and the mother of Jesus, in charge of a household comprised of at least six children: James, Joses, Judas, Simon, and at least two girls called the brothers and sisters of Jesus (Mark 6:3). Where these brothers and sisters came from is the matter of some debate, but unless one holds to the unlikely proposition that they moved into the household as adults, they were in Mary's care as children. She is someone who did not at first understand her firstborn son's mission, but who after the tragedy of his execution, was a member of the circle of disciples who believed in him. Elements of this historical picture enable the historical Miriam [Mary of Nazareth] as a woman of faith, an unconventional woman, a scandal, a member of the 'anawim, a faithful disciple.[40]

An imaginative construct of Mary as a Jewish woman of a rural village locates her in a setting in which most of her fellow Jews farmed or crafted implements for farm and household. The people worked hard to sustain themselves in a political climate fraught with uncertainty. Married to a carpenter, her days were filled with the work of women, feeding and clothing the members of her household. It is reasonable to assume that she practiced Judaism in her home.

She and her husband followed Torah and observed the Sabbath and religious festivals of the time.

Johnson indicates that she was likely the mother of many children: Jesus and his four brothers listed in Mark 6:3, and perhaps at least two sisters whom Mark leaves unnamed there — something, Johnson notes, that "typically happens with women."[41] The inclusion of a household of children, who may or may not have been Joseph's from a previous marriage, possibly breaks with the traditional interpretation of Mary as a "perpetual virgin." It has already been noted that belief that Mary's virginity was perpetual and her motherhood reserved to her divine son is a fourth-century development. In the available first-century sources, no historical basis exists for arguing that Mary's virginity was perpetual.[42] Was Jesus Mary's only child? Does it make a difference in how one views Jesus as Son of God, and Mary as his mother and as wife to Joseph?

This information, meager as it is, does not yet provide a response to the most scathing critique leveled by de Beauvoir. Was Mary's yes to God that of a submissive servant girl to a dominant male deity? A hermeneutics of suspicion leads one to question this interpretation and posit one that is radically different. Mary was not a timid girl weakly expressing a yes to God out of powerlessness. Her yes was the deliberate and freely made decision of a young woman in response to a special call.[43] By that yes she became partner with God to bring about the promise of salvation.

There are important insights to be gained for feminist spirituality by reading the Marian tradition against the grain of long-held patterns of interpretation. What emerges is a woman who fully images God as a human person with dignity and strength. Mary is a woman who heard the word of God, carried it in her heart, and acted on it in her life. Mary not only gave birth to Jesus, but also was with the other women disciples when they ministered to him in his darkest hours and witnessed his moment of greatest glory. Therefore, it is reasonable to see Mary as a woman who made a free and conscious choice to participate in the reign of God, rather than as an example of passive submission to a male deity.

Apparently, Luke's community appreciated this, for Luke's Gospel puts on Mary's lips a hymn of praise, the "Magnificat," placing her in solidarity with other great women who sang God's praises: Miriam, sister of Moses (Exod. 15:21); Deborah, the prophet (Judg. 5:12); and Hannah, mother of Samuel (1 Sam. 2:1).[44]

> My soul proclaims the greatness of the Lord;
> my spirit rejoices in God my savior.
> For he has looked upon his handmaid's lowliness;
> behold, from now on will all ages call me blessed.
> The Mighty One has done great things for me, and holy is
>   his name.
> His mercy is from age to age to those who fear him.
> He has shown might with his arm, dispersed the arrogant of
>   mind and heart.
> He has thrown down the rulers from their thrones but lifted up
>   the lowly.

> The hungry he has filled with good things; the rich he has
>   sent away empty.
> He has helped Israel his servant, remembering his mercy,
> according to his promise to our fathers, to Abraham and to his
>   descendants forever. (Luke 1:46–55)

Sally Cunneen astutely points out that Luke's inclusion of the Magnificat helps the reader "to see Jesus as Mary's son in his dedication to a Jewish tradition of justice and prophecy. In his advocacy of the poor, which angered both Roman rulers and high priests, he mirrored his mother's faithfulness."[45]

The birth of Jesus, although a great joy in difficult circumstances, immediately led her to become a mother rushing with babe in arms from her homeland to become a refugee in Egypt. The sword that Simeon said would pierce Mary's heart pierced the hearts of the mothers whose sons perished at the order of Herod. She struggled to understand these things and many of the choices her exceptional son made in his ministry, even in his youth (Luke 2:29–51). At her bidding, she occasioned Jesus' reluctant choice to turn water into wine at Cana (John 2:1–11). Although she is usually in the background, there is good reason to number Mary among the faithful disciples of Jesus.

Mary's fidelity to Jesus exacted a great price, for she chose to accompany her son to his crucifixion (John 19:25). She observed in sorrow the cruel execution of Jesus by the Roman authorities, and from the cross received his broken body. In birth and in death she gives witness to the fleshly humanity of God incarnate, her son. Simply put, without Mary, Christianity would not be the Christianity that exists.

The critiques of the Marian tradition and the proposal for a reinterpretation of Mary as a self-possessed woman of decision, who did not shrink from suffering, are important for the spiritual journey of women. Medieval prayers, such as the Salve Regina, are being replaced with prayers that provide new possibilities for relating to Mary. Ann Johnson, for example, offers a prayerful meditation in which she places on the lips of Mary reflections at the time of the death of her beloved son:

> I pour myself into mourning,
>   awash in the floodtide of grief,
>   drowning . . . almost, it seems,
>   gathered . . . held to the breast of a friend,
>   one of the loved ones
>   who waited here today, preparing. . . .
>
> My arms ache with the weight of him,
>   it was just for a moment's time.
>   They left me alone holding him there,
>   alone for one kind moment,
>   His body resting, finally resting
>   heavy on my knees,
>   strange, bewildering shalom,
>   but time was short . . . the sun on its downward course.

> I prepare my mind for God . . . [the Sabbath is approaching],
>   Blessed are you, O God, Our God, . . .
>   Who has called us to be holy of heart. Amen.[46]

Others have prepared Marian litanies that draw attention to Mary's life, a mother in solidarity with those whose lives have been diminished by tragedy: "Mother of the homeless, widowed mother, unwed mother, mother of a political prisoner, seeker of sanctuary."[47]

Locating Mary "on the human side of the human-divine equation" (to borrow the words of Catholic feminist theologian Mary Hines) can facilitate a renewal of how God is imaged. The qualities traditionally applied to Mary as Virgin Mother, New Eve, and Queen of Heaven can be restored to God and Jesus Christ.[48] This also reclaims for Mary the identity of disciple, and locates her firmly among her sister saints and the communion of saints as a whole. Before turning to the saints, however, we explore how Mary is regarded in Latin America. Any treatment of feminist spirituality and Mary is seriously deficient if it does not attend to how women of Latin American origin relate to Mary in their spirituality.

Mary in Latin American Feminist Spirituality

In Latin America the spirituality of women is marked by suffering. It is important for women to see their suffering as not of God. The historical causes connected with the conquests of the indigenous people by Spain and Portugal were addressed earlier in this book and will not be revisited. The suffering of Latin American women is marked by poverty and conflict with the dominant machismo values that heap upon women burdens that rob them of human dignity. Earlier in this chapter, attention was drawn to Sandra Schneiders's emphasis on women reclaiming "spirit." María Pilar Aquino describes feminist spirituality in Latin America as women "experiencing ourselves in the power of the [Holy] Spirit."[49] The power of the Holy Spirit is one of liberation, for where the Spirit of God is there is freedom (2 Cor. 3:17). Liberating experiences of the Spirit cannot be divorced from the devotional practices that play a key role in the spirituality of Latin American women. In the devotional life of Latin Americans, Mary, the mother of Jesus, is very important. She is so important that she is frequently spoken of simply as "Our Mother."

Latin Americans have favorite images of Mary unique to each country or region, among them are ***Our Lady of Guadalupe** of Mexico, Purisima of Nicaragua, and the Black Aparecida of Brazil. Each is linked to the history and culture of the indigenous people and to their European conquerors. The one image that is frequently acknowledged to be the Mother of Latin America, however, is Our Lady of Guadalupe.[50] Therefore, focusing on her is important for understanding Latina/*mujerista* spirituality.

About a decade after the Spanish conquest of Mexico, in December of 1531, a recently converted Nahuatl, Juan Diego (also known as Cuauhtlathuac, "He Who Speaks like an Eagle" — significant because the eagle was traditionally a

ELIZABETH A. JOHNSON

This chapter has strongly featured the contributions of Elizabeth A. Johnson to feminist thought on Mary and the saints. Johnson's work is characterized by the application of a feminist critique to traditional Christian doctrines with the goal of reinterpreting them in the light of women's experience. Believing that there is value in the Christian tradition if it is interpreted in response to the "signs of our own times," she consistently brings together feminist spirituality and theology in artful and creative ways.

A Sister of St. Joseph from Brentwood, New York, Johnson was the first woman to earn a Ph.D. in theology at the Catholic University of America (1981). Upon completing her degree, she taught there for ten years and then went to Fordham University in New York, where she is Distinguished Professor of Theology. She has written numerous articles and four books, some of which have received major awards and have been translated into many languages, including French, Spanish, Italian, German, and Korean. In 1995 she served the Catholic Theological Society of America as its elected president.

sign from the Aztec gods), reported having seen Holy Mary at Tepeyac, north of Mexico City. This location was a place of pilgrimage where the goddess Tonantzin had once been worshiped. According to tradition, Mary instructed Diego to have the local bishop build a church on this site. When Diego met with the bishop, roses fell from his mantle and beneath them was the image of Holy Mary, Mother of God.

Holy Mary's face on Diego's mantle was not that of a pale Spanish woman, but of a brown-skinned Nahuatl woman. Her clothing appeared like the sun, giving forth rays. Mary identified herself to Juan Diego in ways his people associated with worship of Tonantzin: with flower and song (*flor y cantos*). She spoke to him in Nahuatl, his native language, telling him that she was the "Ever-Virgin Holy Mary, Mother of the God of Great Truth, *Totl*, of the One through whom we live, the Creator."[51] She gave him these and additional names, long associated with Tonantzin.

Word of Holy Mary's appearance to Diego on the sacred ground of Tonantzin

OUR LADY OF GUADALUPE

There are many likenesses of Our
Lady of Guadalupe. Traditional ren-
ditions of La Morenita del Tepeyac
present her as a woman of dark
skin and hair. Her eyes are downcast and her hands raised before
her in a Nahuatl gesture of offer-
tory. She wears a rose-colored shift
filigreed with gold, and over it a
cloak of blue-green, scattered with
gold stars. There is a black maternity
band at her waist, signifying someone yet to be born. Below it appears
a cross, signifying that the child she
is carrying is the Redeemer who will
change the course of history. Rays
surround her, eclipsing the Sun God
Tonatiuh. At her feet may be a phase

Courtesy of Maryknoll Photo Archives

of Venus, associated with Quetzalcoatl, the sacred plumed serpent, or the
moon, a possible reference to Revelation 1:1 of the New Testament. She is
borne by an angel, the divine messenger and intermediary between God
and humans.

The connection with the religion of Juan Diego's youth is illustrated
not only in the physical appearance of Holy Mary but also in the Nahuatl
names that Juan Diego said he received in his vision:

1. *Inninantzin in huelneli Totl Dios:*
   Mother of the True God, the God of Truth.

2. *Inninantzin inipalnemohuani:*
   Mother of the Giver of Life.

3. *Inninantzin in Teyocoyani:*
   Mother of the Creator of Humanity.

4. *Inninantzin in Tloque nahuaque:*
   Mother of the Lord of Near and Far.

5. *Inninantzin in Ilhicahua in Tlalticpaque:*
   Mother of the Maker of Heaven and Earth.[52]

spread throughout the region. The significance of the story becomes clear when
one considers how the Roman Catholic Church regards Marian appearances.
Apparition is the usual technical name for an appearance of Mary to a Christian believer. A Marian apparition is a mystical phenomenon, a symbolic vision
that is never completely open to rational interpretation. As a result, the Roman

Catholic Church exercises caution when a person claims to have had such visions. Judgment of their validity is not made lightly. Part of the criteria for their validity is whether they are a sign that encourages greater devotion and solidarity among the faithful. These criteria are clearly in evidence in the apparition of Mary as Our Lady of Guadalupe, La Morenita del Tepeyac. After the cure of Juan Diego's uncle, likely following Holy Mary's fourth appearance, Spanish authorities asked if the Virgin had given her name. The response was that she called herself Tlecuauhtlacupeuh, which for the Aztecs was a sacred place of light. To the Spaniards, Tlecuauhtlacupeuh apparently sounded like "Guadalupe" of Estremadura in Spain, original home of Cortés and a place of great devotion to Mary in a newly Muslim-free Spain. This contributed to the Spanish Catholic church authorities' recognition of her in the 1550s.

Our Lady of Guadalupe first identifying herself as "Ever-Virgin" subtly challenges the sexual abuse and rape that the Spanish conquerors inflicted on the native women. Holy Mary could understand their pain and agony, for as a young woman in Nazareth she conceived a child with no identifiable human father. Her virginity was not in opposition to conjugal intimacy but "a repudiation of one of the worst effects of the conquest: the rape of the women and the abandonment of both women and children by abusing fathers."[53]

Curiously, Holy Mary does not explicitly name herself as the mother of Jesus in the words she supposedly spoke to Juan Diego, but Spanish and baptized Nahuatls recognize her as such. She identifies herself as "Mother of the God of Great Truth, *Totl*." Part of that great truth is that she is Mother, not only to the Son of God but also to both Spanish and Nahuatls alike. The roses she bestows are more than flowers indigenous to Spain. Flowers are the Aztec symbol of truth. The truth that Mary offers to her beloved offspring, the *mestizaje* of the Americas, is that they are themselves flowers, signs of a new truth.

Jeanette Rodríguez points out that the story of Mary's appearance to Juan Diego marks the foundation of a truly Mexican Christianity because her apparition was the turning point in the conversion of the indigenous people to Christ.[54] Within six years after the apparition, nine million Aztecs were baptized. Our Lady of Guadalupe had quickly become the unifying religious symbol for the conquered and conquerors. She provides an important link between the indigenous and Spanish peoples. She is more than an apparition. She is more of an *encuentro,* a coming together of two peoples. Rodríguez reflects,

> The symbol of Our Lady of Guadalupe has had various manifestations; it affirmed the humanness of the indigenous populations, it provided a symbolic means of forging new culture and polity out of Spanish and Indian elements, and today it serves to bring together disparate groups who otherwise would never know one another.[55]

The Virgin of Guadalupe has been regarded by some as a model of servility and suffering for a conquered people. Traditionally, pilgrims to the shrine of La Virgen de Guadalupe approach her image on their knees. Prostrate, they place themselves under her protection. Such devotional practices may seem to be out of place in the twenty-first century. To test whether servility is an emphasis being internalized in the spirituality of a new generation of Mexican Americans, Jeanette Rodríguez investigated the spirituality of twenty young Mexican American mothers, ages twenty-two to thirty, in relation to Our Lady of Guadalupe.[56] From the questionnaires and interviews of these women she identified major themes. Her study provides insight into the devotional life of the women surveyed, and possibly of other Mexican and Mexican American women as well. Most of the women surveyed indicated that they had learned of Our Lady of Guadalupe from their mothers and were told to teach their children about her. Honoring Our Lady is not merely an annual December 12th feast day; her image graces their homes, usually in a place of honor. The women pray to her, light candles and place flowers before her image, and believe that she answers their prayers, but not always in the ways they hope for.

One woman interviewed called Our Lady of Guadalupe, "*La Patrona* of the Mexican faith."[57] This is not a new emphasis; it is found, for example, in the writings of Sor Juana Inés de la Cruz in her seventeenth-century poetry.[58] Mary presents the maternal face of God, a face that balances the symbolism of the all-powerful God of the Spanish conquistadors. Our Lady is the compassionate Mother of the people. She loves her offspring with a womblike love, one that manifests God's compassion.[59]

In Rodríguez's study, the highest response to characteristics of Our Lady of Guadalupe that the women affirmed is "the ideal self."[60] She is mother, *morena* (a dark one), *mestiza* (of mixed race), a woman of God with whom most of the young mothers could identify. In the interviews, the women often noted the similarities between Mary's life and their own: "Only Our Lady knows what they are going through and what their goals are."[61] Their spirituality is built on their daily conversations with her. With her help they can find a place in a world that often negates them. She symbolizes family values, enduring suffering, hope against hope, feelings of connection, a warm sense of the presence of God.

It is not possible to survey how Mary functions in the spirituality of women throughout Latin America. Jeanette Rodríguez's study has been cited because it provides a window on the actual spiritual practices of a sampling of contemporary Mexican American women. Speaking more broadly from a Latin American viewpoint, María Clara Bingemer stresses that Mary in Latin America cannot be understood apart from "the cry of the poor." To Mary the poor turn with hope. She is the "inspiration for the church that wishes to be the servant of the poor."[62]

María Pilar Aquino notes that a new figure of Mary is emerging among poor women in basic ecclesial communities in Latin America. "Mary is identified with the interests of the poor and oppressed, and her own experience of a God who is on their side."[63] Similarities between Mary's life and the lives of the poor, especially of poor women, are an important source of spirituality for women throughout Latin America. Mary is not a heavenly queen but a mother who shares the lives of poor women as a sister. Like Mary, many of them have given birth in homeless or very poor situations; have been forced to flee their homeland as a refugee with an infant in their arms; have lost a child to execution by an unjust patriarchal government. But their spirituality is about more than dwelling on the ways in which Mary is in solidarity with them in their oppression. She is also in solidarity with them in the project of creating a new societal order. She is a source of self-empowerment for the downtrodden. Aquino writes,

> Mary is prophetic and liberating, committed to the struggle for justice. . . . Mary constantly says yes to the God of life and no to an unequal socio-religious order. . . . Women's thinking about Mary gives great importance to her relationship with the reign of God, seen as a collective happening. She is not seen exclusively in terms of her role as mother of Jesus but in relation to God's reign that is bursting into history through the creative power of the Spirit.[64]

In the complex spirituality of Latin American women, the Virgin Mother, Holy Mary, is an epiphany of the divine, one that manifests an image of divine presence in the form of a great truth. God is the one through whom life is found. Mary is the creator of personhood through which a new humanity, one of human dignity, is offered to *mestizo* women and men. She is also a sister, a member of the *mestizo* people, one with them in their suffering while inspiring them to struggle for liberation from all that keeps them from being whole. As such, she is first among the saints.

Women Saints in Feminist Spirituality

A fitting way to introduce the role of women saints in feminist spirituality can be found in an aspect of Mary's story not yet given attention. This is Mary's visit to Elizabeth, her older cousin who, like Mary, is favored by God with an unexpected child (Luke 1:39–56). Over the years, scholars have speculated about why Mary made a difficult journey from Nazareth to Judah to see Elizabeth "with haste" (Luke 1:39). Was Mary trying to prevent her pregnancy from being discovered by the people of her village?[65] If she was, it is odd that she returned three months later. Surely, her pregnancy would have been more obvious. It seems more reasonable to argue that Mary made the arduous journey so that Elizabeth and she could support each other. Her decision resonates with these words from the beginning of Romans: "I long to see you, [Elizabeth], that I may share with you some spiritual gift so that you may be strengthened, that is, that you and I may be mutually encouraged by one another's faith" (Rom. 1:11). When Mary first greets Elizabeth, she feels the infant in her womb "leap." "Filled with the Holy Spirit," she responds to Mary's greeting with her own: "Most blessed are you among women" (Luke 1:39–42). Sheila Carney reflects on this meeting, surmising that Elizabeth declares Mary blessed in her ability to believe in God's promises in the midst of uncertainty.[66]

Carney's reflection on Mary's visit to Elizabeth gets at the heart of why women and men look to Mary and her sister saints in their spiritual journey. They seek strength and encouragement in their faith in God in the midst of the challenging uncertainties of life. Granted, this encouragement is not mutual in the way in which it was for Mary and Elizabeth. Yet, there is a type of mutuality involved in feminist research on women saints. Research by feminists allows women saints to step from the pages of patriarchal accounts, not as plaster likenesses, but as real, flesh and blood women. Application of a feminist hermeneutics of suspicion can bring to light how the stories of women saints have been told in ways inimical to women's wholeness. Drawing attention to these elements paves the way for a hermeneutics of remembrance that enables women saints to truly be reminders of God's promises in the midst of life's uncertainties.

SAINTS AND THEIR CANONIZATION

In a broad sense, saints are persons who manifest the holiness of God in their lives. In Judaism, the holy ones (saints) are the just who live in accord with the sacred covenant initiated by God and seek communion with God through the prayers and practices of Judaism. In Christianity and Islam, saints are those persons who have died who are memorialized for their exemplary lives, lived in fidelity to the teachings of these religions.

Quite early in the history of Christianity, perhaps as early as 100, Christians honored those who had died for the faith, and sought their intercession. The word "saint" referred to a martyr, a courageous witness to Christ who gave her or his life. Martyrs were believed to have been welcomed into heaven and could intercede with God for the earthly church members. For their heroism, they merited the honor of living Christians. When the persecutions of Christians ceased in the fourth century, the practice of honoring persons for modeling Christian fidelity to God continued. Gradually, local bishops in Roman Catholic and Eastern Orthodox churches canonized persons for being conspicuous in their holiness. In the tenth century, the authority to *canonize persons in the Roman Catholic Church was taken over by the Vatican.

Since the Reformation, Protestant churches, as a whole, have downplayed the veneration of saints as detracting from the redemptive work of Jesus Christ. As part of the Counter Reformation in the Roman Catholic Church, Pope Sixtus V established the Sacred Congregation of Rites (1588) as the agency of canonization. During the Second Vatican Council, the "Dogmatic Constitution on the Church" (1964), no. 50, and the "Constitution on the Sacred Liturgy" (1963), no. 8, discuss the saints. Recalling their memory in worship, Catholics affirm their belief in the salvific plan of Christ and in the belief that the church is more than an earthly entity — it is also part of a larger reality called "the Communion of the Saints." In 1983, Pope John Paul II clarified the canonization procedure, providing criteria for the Congregation for the Causes of Saints for the three steps to canonization: (1) a papal declaration that the candidate is "venerable"; (2) a papal proclamation that the candidate is beatified or "blessed"; and (3) papal canonization of the person in recognition of sainthood. Canonization does not "make" a person a saint. It does recognize the holiness of a person's life and the appropriateness of honoring the person for what she or he accomplished with the help of God's grace.

In the Roman Catholic and Eastern Orthodox traditions, the intercession of saints in both spiritual and temporal matters continues. As models of virtue, saints are venerated but never worshiped. As part of the liturgical calendar, saints are remembered on stipulated dates.

On the liturgical calendar of the Roman Catholic Church, 75 percent of the days honor men. This reflects the percentage of saints who are male. Of the 25 percent who are women, the least represented are married women, who remained married and did not become nuns if widowed. One is led to conclude from these statistics that being a woman, especially a sexually active one, is a liability where official recognition for holiness by male church hierarchy is concerned.

Researching the life of a saint can be a daunting task. Until recently, biographies of saints were often written as hagiography. They were a blend of facts, pious elaborations, and legendary folklore, written to inspire people to practice certain virtues that seemed stereotypically "saintly." Women saints were often romanticized, idealized figures whose feet never quite touched the ground. What was emphasized was not necessarily desirable, especially for women. Sometimes, the virtues stressed encouraged a self-effacing humility that was inimical to women's self-integration and human flourishing. Stories of women saints were told in a way that encouraged passive submission of women to male authorities.

What scholars look for in saints today is different from what was sometimes emphasized previously. They seek to unearth the historical core of a saint's life, looking to discern how this person enfleshed the gospel in the midst of the exigencies of their daily lives. The search for a "useable past" in the life of a saint can be rewarding. In such a search the focus is not so much on extraordinary asceticism but on authentic discipleship. Feminist scholarship studies those women whose lives might provide encouragement for a Christian discipleship appropriate to our age, whether those women are officially canonized or not.

Some feminist research puts the spotlight on women who were friends and fellow travelers with Jesus. These women courageously fashioned new ways for women to participate in proclaiming the reign of God. Chapter 2 gave attention to one such woman, the preeminent apostle of resurrection good news, Mary Magdalene, who accompanied Jesus in his missionary journeys, thereby going against patriarchal custom, and followed him even to the cross. Mary R. Thompson describes Mary Magdalene as a singled-minded woman. "She led others to the same kind of commitment and she demonstrated whatever courage and ingenuity were required of her."[67] This is borne out in her initiative to come to the empty tomb to minister to the dead and broken body of Jesus. Because of this single-mindedness, it was she who received the message of his resurrection and was commissioned to proclaim Jesus' triumph over death to the others in his close circle of companions (John 20:11–18).

Medieval legend identifies Mary Magdalene as the apostle who brought Jesus' message to southern France. In a thirteenth-century cathedral at Bourges, Mary Magdalene is pictured with a halo (symbol of sainthood), preaching. Portrayals of her preaching can also be found in cathedrals and churches at Sémur in Burgundy, in Florence, Lübeck, and Donaueschingen. In Lübeck she is even depicted as enthroning a bishop. Perhaps this emphasis, one that will later be suppressed, has something to do with the foundation of new convents of vowed women religious during this period and the power of the abbesses who were recognized for their leadership.[68]

The New Testament also tells of women who participated in Jesus' mission. In addition to Mary Magdalene, Luke lists "Joanna, the wife of Herod's steward Chuza, Susanna, and many others who provided for them out of their resources" (Luke 8:3). John draws attention to the sisters Martha and Mary (John 11). In Acts, female companions of Paul in his missionary journeys, such as Priscilla (Prisca), are listed (Acts 18). Priscilla, along with her husband, Aquila, a tentmaker by trade, are singled out in Paul's letter to the Romans as co-workers in Christ Jesus (Rom. 16:3–5). It is significant that Priscilla is not said to be either man's helper; in fact, her name appears before her husband's, something unusual for the time. Priscilla and Aquila traveled from Rome to Corinth to Ephesus, and possibly back to Rome again, preaching the message entrusted to them.[69] Their home in Corinth became a house church where the message of Jesus was shared in the midst of the breaking of the bread. Evidently, Christians also gathered in the home of Chloe, another prominent woman in the early church (1 Cor. 1:11). Phoebe, a benefactor, is identified by Paul as "deacon of the church" at Cenchreae (Rom. 16:1–2). Possibly, Priscilla and Chloe deserve the same title.

Among the women who were instrumental in building up the church in this early period were those said to be prophets. These women were recognized for their wisdom and courage. They traveled as itinerant missionaries, challenging the newly converted to follow Jesus' law of love. In Acts 21:9 the four daughters of Philip are said to be prophets. A woman for whom the designation "prophet" would have been appropriate was Thecla, a companion of Paul. Thecla broke the stereotype of what was proper for women of her time. Unwillingly betrothed to a man by her father, she chooses a life of celibacy and service to the mission of Christ instead. Thecla was persecuted by the authorities because virginity was not something a woman could choose on her own. The *Acts of Paul and Thecla* says that she is thrown to the lions twice, miraculously escapes, and baptizes herself after the second occasion. As a final seal of approval on her authority, Paul commissions her as an apostle.[70]

None of these women was formerly canonized, and yet, applying the title "saint" to them is appropriate, for Christianity guards their memory. Remembrance of their lives serves as a source of encouragement to those who continue to seek strength to live a commitment to give witness to the promise of God. Companions with Jesus, presiders at worship in house churches, deacons, prophets, and itinerant preachers, these women did what many women aspire to do for God today. While we cannot simplistically follow their example, because our daily reality is so different from theirs, Mary Magdalene, Martha, Mary,

Priscilla, Phoebe, and Thecla are more than figures from a Christian past; they are companions into the future.

No treatment of feminist spirituality and women saints would be complete without attention to the martyrs, the persons who gave witness to Christ by laying down their lives. To keep alive the bonds of communion with martyrs, the early Christians remembered them with an outpouring of devotion. The Age of Martyrs began early on for Christians as they refused to worship Roman deities, to pay tribute to the emperor as a divinity, or to serve in the emperor's army. Christians resisted the demand to worship the old gods and to pay tribute to the emperor, believing that such acts were idolatry. Only the God of Jesus was to be worshiped. They also resisted conscription into the army; taking the lives of others in battle was against Christ's teaching. Christ taught love, not only of one's neighbors but also of one's enemies (Matt. 5:44).

It is not known how many women were martyred during the era. What is known is that among the early martyrs are at least three women: Blandina, Perpetua, and Felicitas. All three lived in the second century. Blandina was a slave in Lyons, who, like a noble mother, encouraged her children even as she was martyred. Mary T. Malone describes her death, ca. 177, as a type of crucifixion:

> She had been hung from a post with her arms outstretched, so that her companions "saw with their outward eyes in the person of their sister, the One who was crucified for them."[71]

With the death of Blandina, women for the first time since the New Testament were raised up as exemplars for the community.

Perpetua and Felicitas died in the city of Carthage in North Africa. The *Acts of the Christian Martyrs* gives an account of their deaths (ca. 203).[72] Both are young mothers, but nothing is said of their husbands, who therefore were probably not members of the Christian community. In 202 the Roman emperor Septimus Servus issued an edict prohibiting any further conversions to Christianity. Although some aspects of the history of Perpetua and Felicitas's deaths are difficult to sort out, it is known that the emperor began to persecute members of prominent families. Perhaps believing that killing mothers would be persuasive, the emperor singled out for martyrdom Perpetua, a young mother from a prominent family. She was arrested and put in prison with her infant son and pregnant servant, Felicitas, who gave birth while imprisoned. Perpetua's diary includes accounts of visions and dreams that she shared with her companions to encourage them. Reflecting on the circumstances of their deaths, Malone writes, "This is a story about women and their bodies and the violation of these bodies in the course of imprisonment and execution.... The bodies of women carry enormous significance for the Christian community."[73]

Roman authorities martyred Christians to dissuade people from joining Christian communities and to enhance the power of Roman rule. For Christians, however, martyrdom became a way to give witness to Christ. Death, no matter how violent and unjust, does not have the final word. Telling the stories of the martyred women and men became occasions for Christians to remember with joy the heroism of those who willingly gave their lives. Elizabeth Johnson reflects,

> During the times of persecution, a sense of bondedness across the spheres between heaven and earth and across the years between martyrs and those who asked for their prayers supported those who might be called next to give the supreme witness of their lives.[74]

These prayerful bonds are the roots of the notion of the "communion of saints." Martyrs were lovingly remembered because they died for Christ, who had given his life for the salvation of all. It was believed that each martyr suffered in and for Christ and that her or his suffering, like Christ's, would bear fruit in the community. Since Christ rose from the dead, the power of his resurrection extended to the martyrs, who continued to live in Christ. By the first half of the third century, communion with the holy martyrs took the form of calling upon them for mediation before God. The intercessory prayers directed to the martyrs, such as Blandina, Perpetua, and Felicitas, flowed from the belief that those living in eternal communion with Christ continued to collaborate with him in his saving work on earth. When the final version of the Apostles' Creed was composed, perhaps in the late fourth or early fifth century,[75] the communion of saints was included. This inclusion affirmed the belief in the presence of the martyrs, and all the saints who had gone before, with the living.

In many ways, the martyrdom of Blandina, Perpetua, and Felicitas seems far removed from the contemporary experience of women. Yet, thoughts of early women martyrs and their communion with the living today come to mind when the stories of the witness given by the women martyrs of El Salvador are remembered. In 1980, four American missionaries were brutally murdered in El Salvador: Maryknoll sisters Ita Ford and Maura Clarke, Ursuline sister Dorothy Kazel, and lay missionary Jean Marie Donovan. They left the comforts of home and traveled to this small war-torn country in response to the distress of a poor and oppressed people. These courageous women were assassinated by soldiers under orders from their superiors because they were regarded to be politically dangerous, a threat to a government that intended to use any means possible to stay in power and keep the poor peasants under control. Yearly, on December 2, the anniversary of their deaths, these women are remembered in El Salvador and the United States as holy martyrs of our time.

The four North Americans were not the only women to be martyred for their public witness to the message of Christ in El Salvador. Silvia Maribel Arriola, a Salvadoran woman from a prominent family and a member of a religious order of women dedicated to ministering with the poor, volunteered to use her nursing skills to care for people in a village under siege by government forces. She was killed in 1981 and left in an open grave, along with people she had come to help.[76] Approximately four years later, another Salvadoran, Laura López, a mother of five and a lay leader in a basic ecclesial community, was also murdered. Her daughter saw this courageous woman being shot during a government attack on the village in which she ministered. Although wounded, Laura was later tied up and her skull crushed, likely by the butt of a rifle.[77] She had opportunities to flee the area but chose to stay. Her love for Christ and her dedication to her people were inseparable.

The martyred women of El Salvador, like Perpetua and Felicitas, had their lives cut short violently by civil authority to send a message to others: Don't let your love for Christ lead you to dedicate your life to the poor and oppressed people of El Salvador; abandon such thoughts or die. Ita, Maura, Dorothy, Jean Marie, Silvia, and Laura knew that persecution, even death, was a possibility when they began their ministry, yet they remained single-minded in their dedication. They "ran with perseverance the race set before them" (see Heb. 12:1). Dorothy Kazel is reported once to have said, in a moment of ecstatic joy, what she wanted on her tombstone when she died: "I am an alleluia from head to toe, because a Christian is an alleluia from head to toe."[78] Alleluia is the Easter exaltation and a fitting reminder that death for the saint is not the plunge into a cold abyss of God-forsakenness but an assent into the Uncreated Light of God's glory.

Clearly, in the life and death of these women martyrs the notion of the communion *of* the saints is transformed to communion *with* the saints, a communion characterized by solidarity in a struggle for liberating change. Although few women and men face the prospect of martyrdom for their call to holiness, a single-minded response to any form that the call takes can be costly. The search for wholeness, the journey to holiness, is rarely a "cheap grace." Remembering the heroism of the women martyrs can be a source of strength and encouragement in times of struggle. Persevere — the race is worth running. Dare to be an alleluia from head to toe.

Fortunately, in the history of Christianity, there are many women, some formally canonized as saints and some not, to whom we can look as sources of strength and encouragement. Dorothy Kazel's notion of a Christian as one who is an "alleluia from head to toe" is applicable to many if not all women who over the centuries have stood toe-to-toe with adversity of all kinds and made a difference by giving witness to Christ with integrity and courage. It is utterly impossible to delve into the lives of all of these women. Yet, it is important at least to survey some whose life stories are being retrieved from earlier eras for their liberating potential for women of our own age. Many of these stories can be rightly regarded as "dangerous memories," because they beckon women to dare to claim the power of the spirit in their own situations.

For our first bearer of "dangerous memory," we turn to Brigit of Ireland, a sixth-century saint. She is believed to have been born into slavery, yet was given the strong name of the Celtic sun goddess. Freed when she became a Christian, she devoted her life to the care of the poor and founded religious houses all over Ireland until her death in 525. Legend has it that this self-possessed abbess invited a bishop to join her community. He was so impressed with her dedication and talent that he ordained her as a fellow bishop.[79] It is not possible to know if this legend is true, but it does invite one to imagine a very differently structured church in the Ireland of old.

Our second woman is Hildegard of Bingen, a twelfth-century German woman with an exceptional spirit. Like Brigit, she was an abbess. Hildegard founded a convent for women, guided by the rule of St. Benedict. Her preparation for her role as abbess was unusual. When Hildegard was eight, her parents sent her to live with an ***anchoress** in rooms attached to a local church. She had no formal education, but did learn about prayer and a life of dedication to God from this woman. Persons often sought the spiritual advice of anchoresses, whom they also supported with food and household needs. Hildegard shared with her fellow anchoress visions that she had in prayer. Later, at the bidding of her spiritual director, she wrote down her visions. In our scientific and technological age, mystical visions might be regarded to be at best a manifestation of romantic impracticality and at worst a sign of mental illness. But during the Middle Ages, mystical visions defined reality. Visionaries were important sources of wisdom, because it was widely believed that the world of the senses was merely a veil over the more important realm of the invisible presence of God at work in creatures.

Besides being respected for her mystical visions, Hildegard was also a highly regarded composer of music and author who wrote on a wide variety of questions from doctrinal disputes to medicine. In our era, the ecological elements of her spirituality are drawing more attention than they received in her own time. Hildegard often refers to God as "Living Light" and applies the word "greenness" to God's animating energy that graciously shines forth in every creature.

Hildegard died in 1179 after a protracted dispute with the local church authorities about her decision to allow a young man who had been excommunicated to be buried in the convent cemetery. The bishop forbade the celebration of the Eucharist at the convent, but Hildegard, in failing health, remained steadfast in her decision. Near the end of what is arguably her most important work, the *Scivias*, Hildegard wrote,

> O Living Fountain, how great is your sweet compassion!
> You never lost sight of the face of your straying people,
> But saw in advance the way that You would save them....
> Rejoice that God restores you.[80]

Apparently, Hildegard took her own words about compassion to heart in this decision, a decision that cost her dearly but was a source of consolation to the young man's family.

In reflecting on Hildegard's life, Fiona Bowie and Oliver Davies muse that this self-taught woman's lack of formal instruction may have shielded her from the more "misogynistic elements" of the literature of her period. She refused to embrace the contemporary image of women as inferior to men.[81] She models the equality of women and men rarely seen in her time.

Another talented woman, remembered for her refusal to accept inferiority, is Catherine of Siena. Resisting her parents' plan that she contract a marriage advantageous to the family's interests, Catherine chose to be affiliated with the Sisters of Saint Dominic, a saint who had emphasized preaching the gospel message of Christ. At this time, religious life for women was defined as being cloistered away from the happenings of society. Desiring to preach the Word where it most needed to be heard, she dedicated her life to the mission of Jesus by entering into an alternative style of religious commitment. She became a member of what is known as the "Third Order" of Saint Dominic and was not confined to a cloistered convent.[82] She lived at home and went into the city to do the ministry that she felt compelled to do. She spoke of her "cell" (meaning a small room in a convent) as not one of stone or wood but of self-knowledge arrived at through prayer.

Catherine's self-knowledge led her to be single-minded in her commitment to the Beatitudes that Jesus preached, especially "Blessed are the peacemakers" (Matt. 5:9). During the highly contentious fourteenth century, which was ravaged by deadly plague and by political and ecclesiastical disputes, Catherine focused her energy on peacemaking. Although only in her twenties, she intervened in feuds between families in Siena. She took her peacemaking skills into conflicts involving the Catholic papacy. She mediated between the Avignon-based papacy of Gregory XI and the city of Florence, convincing the pope to return to Rome, where he could better attend to church affairs. Later, after Pope Gregory's death, she tried yet again to mediate reconciliation, this time between factions within the church's hierarchy over still another controversy over the papacy. A considerable number of the hierarchy were dissatisfied with the first man elected to be Pope Gregory's successor, so they elected a second pope. Catherine believed that having two rival popes, with the deep division in the Catholic Church that ensued, was damaging to the people. She fearlessly petitioned those behind the election of the second pope and the church's schism to a just exercise of their authority. For her efforts to heal division, even during her lifetime, she was referred to as *beata populano* — the people's own saint.[83]

Also a recipient of mystical visions, Catherine, during this time of struggle, had one of the Catholic Church as a boat buffeted by a storm. The boat was placed on her shoulders. She is said to have fallen to the ground under the great weight of it. A short time later she died; the year was 1380, and Catherine was only thirty-three years old.

For feminist spirituality, the circumstances of Catherine's death are far less important than the emphases evident in her life. Catherine had a passionate love for truth, the truth of who she was and who God is. For Catherine, God is the "gentle First truth."[84] Her commitment to the truth, to God, led her to forsake solitude and the "proper place" for the women of her era to enter a life of extraordinary activity. Love for God left no room for apathetic abandonment to the status quo. Hers was a call to prophesy, lobbying political powers for peace and challenging Catholic church authorities to reform. She did these things with an extraordinary confidence in God's love, trusting that even the most evil events can be turned to good.

Many others are worthy of exploration. Julian of Norwich, an English contemporary of Catherine, was an anchoress. She contracted the deadly plague that had struck her native England. During her illness and recovery she had numerous visions, which she called "showings," in which she experienced Christ as "our Mother from whom we are endlessly born."[85] Although she was never canonized, Julian's *Showings* have been the object of much attention in recent years.

They invite her readers to attend to the struggle that often accompanies attempts to reconcile one's own mystical experience of the divine with the content of a faith received from others, including church authorities.

At the end of the nineteenth century, we find another woman who had profound experiences of God, including during a time of terminal illness, Thérèse of Lisieux. A Carmelite nun who received special permission to enter the convent at age fifteen, Thérèse died from tuberculosis in 1897 at the age of twenty-four. During her young life she composed the *Story of a Soul,* her spiritual autobiography.[86] In this book, along with her letters and other writings, one can get a remarkably intimate picture of a young "mystic in the making." Although she traced her vocation as a Carmelite nun to her ninth year of life,[87] she also wrote of the stirring within her of the call to be a priest or to be a missionary in a far-off land, perhaps even a martyr.[88] The desire for extraordinary discipleship was tempered, however, by Thérèse's recognition that it is the ordinary occurrences of daily life that contribute to a graced relationship with God. A very profound insight guided her life: we must accept our limitations as best we can and be ever open to God's grace.

An important insight into Thérèse's spirit is revealed in one of her final conversations with her older sister Pauline, who was the prioress (mother superior) of the convent where they both resided. Near death, from her bed in the convent infirmary, Thérèse shared these thoughts, meant for her fellow sisters:

> Mother, it ["The Little Way" to holiness] is the way of spiritual childhood, it is the way of confidence and total abandon. I want to teach them the little means that have so perfectly succeeded with me, to tell them there is only one thing to do here on earth: to cast at Jesus the flowers of little sacrifices, to take him by caresses; this is the way I've taken Him, and it's for this that I shall be so well received.[89]

All of these women are Roman Catholics, but certainly there are many Protestant women of spirit as well. Many lived during the nineteenth century. Among the more notable are Angelina and Sarah Grimké, pre–Civil War Quaker women, who were raised on a slave-owning plantation in the South. As adults they traveled to the North to join the abolition movement. Soon thereafter, they became spokespersons against slavery. When condemned for preaching in New England churches, Sarah also became a spokesperson against the secondary status of women.

To any list of women of spirit in the communion of saints belongs Sojourner Truth, an antebellum slave woman whose name has appeared in this book several times. As a young woman she was known as Isabella or Belle; her surname is believed to have been Baumfree. While still in her twenties she had a powerful mystical experience in which she came to really know that Jesus loved her and had always loved her. Previously, she had heard of Jesus, but now she really knew him. She described her conversion as meeting Jesus as a friend through whom "love flowed like a fountain." So strong was this love that it rushed through her soul and enabled her to pray aloud, "Lord, Lord, I can love even the white folks,"[90] meaning the white owners who had abused and beaten her.

It is this same love that gave her the courage to change her name to Sojourner Truth and to undertake a long journey in faith for the abolition of slavery and the voting rights of women.

Others might include Amanda Berry Smith, who refused to accept the decision of the male leaders at her African Methodist Episcopal Church forbidding her to be a missionary. Although denied ordination, she led revivals known as "camp meetings" in the United States and Britain and led missionary crusades in India and Africa.[91]

On the list of twentieth-century women saints, many Protestants would likely include Anna Howard Shaw, the first woman to be ordained in the Methodist Protestant Church U.S.A. Later president of the National American Woman Suffrage Association, her vision of Christianity underlay her strong advocacy for the rights of women. Her vision of women enabled a new generation of women to allow their imaginations to conceive of themselves in new ways, including as ministers in their churches. In a sermon entitled "The Heavenly Vision," preached at the International Council of Women in 1888, she proclaimed,

> This is the hardest lesson the reformer has to learn, when with soul aglow with the light of great truth, she in obedience, turns to take it to the needy one, and instead of finding a world ready to rise up and receive her, she finds it wrapped in the swaddling clothes of error, eagerly seeking to win others to its conditions of slavery. She longs to make humanity free, she listens to their conflicting creeds and yearns to save them from the misery they endure. She knows that there is no form of slavery more bitter or arrogant than error, that truth alone can make man free, and she longs to bring the heart of the world and the heart of truth together, that the truth may exercise its transforming power over the life of the world.[92]

Shaw realistically concludes, however, that the reformer's vision will be transforming only when "the truth that she desires to teach first takes possession of herself."[93] Then, and only then, will the freeing truth "enter the hearts and transfigure the lives of all."[94]

Among twentieth-century Roman Catholic women whom many revere as a saint is Dorothy Day (d. 1980). Mother of an illegitimate child, and a Marxist socialist in early adulthood, Dorothy later combined a deep spirituality with a commitment to peace and a desire to better the condition of the homeless. She is remembered as the cofounder, with Peter Maurin, of the Catholic Worker Movement during the Great Depression. Although a social activist, one of her sources of inspiration was Thérèse of Lisieux. About Thérèse, Day wrote, "Always she was praying that she would see things as they are, that she would live in reality, not in dreams."[95] Living in reality led Day to pour her life energy into Catholic Worker Houses, where everything was shared with the homeless poor. Deeply committed to justice and nonviolence, Day participated in civil rights marches in the 1950s and 1960s. These marches were followed by peaceful protests against the Vietnam War. In the 1970s she was jailed with migrant workers who were seeking a just wage. Throughout these events she continued to write for the Catholic Worker newspaper, stressing that "all are called to be saints." In one of her many reflections she wrote,

> The world is suffering and dying. I am not suffering and dying in the Catholic Worker. I am writing and talking about it. I will not be saved alone. Wherever we are, we are with people. We drag them down or pull them up. Or we get dragged down and pulled up. In recognition of this latter fact, I recognize the need for help and counsels in the journey to God.[96]

There are many other women of spirit to whom one who is seeking a spirituality of wholeness and holiness might look for help and counsel. The limitations of time and space make it impossible to remember all of them, although all persons who have sought the truth and lived in a loving way are worth remembering as saints. We may find such persons not only among the dead written about in books, but also in our own families: grandparents, parents, aunts and uncles, sisters and brothers who have gone before us. They are our companions still, present with us wherever we are as multicolored beacons of the Uncreated Light drawing us to communion with the living God.

Conclusions

A Christian feminist spirituality emphasizes conscious involvement of women in their own personal integration through commitment to a self-transcendence that reaches toward the God revealed in Jesus Christ, through the grace of the Holy Spirit. To become a woman of "spirit," a woman must pursue her own personal wholeness, the grace-filled call to holiness. Self-integration is thoroughly life-affirming, not only in relation to oneself — although it is definitely that — but also in a world-encompassing sense. "World" here for the Christian is synonymous with God's creation. Self-transcendence is expressed in commitment to justice for all people, especially persons most in need, and concern for the good of the Earth. Such a commitment is integral to a Christian feminist spirituality.

Personal integration, wholeness, and self-transcendence in love — holiness — are very rewarding, but they don't just happen. They require conscious commitment, openness to God's self-disclosure in the context of prayer, and willingness to explore new images for God when the old ones no longer speak to one's heart. Every person desiring to make Christian spirituality a way of life can be strengthened by the example and encouragement of others. Among those others are Mary and her sister saints. Since we live in circumstances different from those of Mary and the saints who have gone before us, communion with them cannot take the form of simple imitation. Our communion with these women will necessarily be in the form of the counsel they can provide in our own discernment of directions we might take, given the times in which we live. Each age and generation must face its own problems and questions that heretofore have been unsolved or unanswered because they are new. There is no shortage of influences that can contribute to personal disintegration and loss of human dignity. For truly fruitful answers to these new challenges, women and men are discovering that they can make choices in continuity with the courageous saints of the past. Monika Hellwig describes this continuity as one "of hope, of experience, of fellowship, of prayer."[97]

Continuity made possible through a feminist hermeneutics of remembrance applied to God, Mary, and the saints facilitates a communion with them that crosses the boundaries of time and extends around the globe. Feminist scholarship offers images of God that have virtually been neglected and "dangerous memories" of Mary and her sister saints. All this can facilitate a person's becoming an authentic woman of spirit/Spirit, a hope-filled alleluia from head to toe. Such women are liberated human beings, radiating, to a world that is no stranger to darkness, Uncreated Light. Dare we allow ourselves to be drawn close?

A Look Ahead

This chapter ended with a focus on spirituality and women saints. As already noted, the early church developed a doctrine called the "communion of saints" to remind the living of their connectedness with the holy men and women who had gone before them and to follow their example and elicit their support in the midst of life's daily struggles. Curiously, the Latin term for the "communion of saints," *communio sanctorum,* is open to a second translation: the "communion of or in holy things." The latter presents to us a link between persons of holiness and the potential of all of creation to mediate the presence of the Holy One. In the age in which we live, recognizing ourselves to be part of nature as participants in a larger body of "holy things" does not come easily. Creation-centered spirituality requires a special spiritual sensitivity to our own embodiment and to our kinship with all living things. In the age of science, nonhuman nature has lost much of the sacral character that people prior to it could more easily appreciate. We have come to regard nonhuman nature as there for our use and, in many respects, to equate progress with the domination of nonhuman nature in service of human goals. Often, creatures have only instrumental value for us in our achievement of human-centered objectives. Seeing each creature as having intrinsic value, let alone a sacred character, is beyond the scope of our vision. However, what many of us can see are the ecological problems that have accompanied our loss of appreciation for the sacral character of creation.

Some participants in the third wave of feminism are very much attuned to ecological concerns and have proposed that there are connections between the domination of women and the exploitation of nonhuman nature. This form of analysis is called "ecofeminism." In the chapter that follows, the contributions of Christian feminists to ecofeminism are explored. We begin with a woman for whom "the saint of ecology" might be an appropriate title, Rachel Carson.

NOTES

1. Elizabeth A. Johnson, *Friends of God and Prophets: A Feminist Theological Reading of the Communion of Saints* (New York: Continuum, 1998), 15.

2. Sandra Schneiders, "Feminist Spirituality," in *The New Dictionary of Catholic Spirituality,* ed. Michael Downey (Collegeville, Minn.: Liturgical Press, 1993), 395. See also idem, "Theology and Spirituality: Strangers, Rivals or Partners," *Horizons* 13 (1986): 264.

3. Anne Carr, "On Feminist Spirituality," in *Women's Spirituality: Resources for Christian Development,* ed. Joann Wolski Conn (New York: Paulist Press, 1986), 49.

4. Schneiders, "Feminist Spirituality," in Downey, ed., *New Dictionary of Catholic Spirituality,* 396.

5. Joann Wolski Conn, "Women's Spirituality: Restriction and Reconstruction," in Wolski Conn, ed., *Women's Spirituality,* 24.

6. Ibid., 25.

7. Anne E. Carr, *Transforming Grace* (San Francisco: Harper & Row, 1988), 101–3.

8. Katherine Zappone, *The Hope of Wholeness: A Spirituality for Feminists* (Mystic, Conn.: Twenty-Third Publications, 1991), 46, and passim.

9. News, *Christian Century* 111 (16 February 1994): 160–61.

10. Ibid.

11. See chapter 3; see also Elisabeth Schüssler Fiorenza, *In Memory of Her: A Feminist Reconstruction of Christian Origins* (New York: Crossroad, 1983), 132, and passim.

12. Sallie McFague, *Models of God: Theology for an Ecological, Nuclear Age* (Philadelphia: Fortress, 1987), 101–9.

13. Virginia Ann Froehle, *Called into Her Presence: Praying with Feminine Images of God* (Notre Dame, Ind.: Ave Maria Press, 1992), 7.

14. Catherine Mowry LaCugna, *God for Us: The Trinity and Christian Life* (San Francisco: Harper San Francisco, 1991).

15. Froehle, *Called into Her Presence,* 45–46.

16. Ps. 139:1–10, 13–16, in the New Revised Standard Version.

17. Isaiah 7:14: "Therefore the Lord himself will give you a sign. Look, the young woman is with child and shall bear a son, and shall name him Emmanuel."

18. *Protevangelium of James,* 11:3 (cited in Luigi Gambero, *Mary and the Fathers of the Church: The Blessed Virgin Mary in Patristic Thought,* trans. Thomas Buffer [San Francisco: Ignatius Press, 1999], 39).

19. Justin Martyr, *Dialogue with Trypho* 100, cited in Gambero, *Mary and the Fathers,* 47.

20. Irenaeus, *Against the Heresies* 3.22.

21. Ibid., 4.22.

22. Ibid.

23. "Salve Regina," in *Moments with God,* ed. Edward Garesche (Milwaukee: Bruce Publishing Co., 1956), 501–2.

24. Elizabeth A. Johnson, "Mary and the Female Face of God," *Theological Studies* 50 (1989): 501–4.

25. Cited in Sally Cunneen, *In Search of Mary: The Woman and the Symbol* (New York: Ballantine Books, 1996), 9.

26. Simone de Beauvoir, *The Second Sex,* trans. and ed. H. M. Parshley (New York: Alfred A. Knopf, 1952; reprint, New York: Random House, 1974), 193.

27. Ibid.

28. Ibid.

29. Mary Daly, *The Church and the Second Sex,* rev. ed. (New York: Harper & Row, 1975), 61.

30. Ibid., 88.

31. Ibid.

32. Kari Børresen, "Mary in Catholic Theology," in *Mary in the Churches,* ed. Hans Küng and Jürgen Moltmann (New York: Seabury Press, 1983), 55.

33. Elisabeth Schüssler Fiorenza, "Feminist Theology as a Critical Theory of Liberation," *Theological Studies* 36 (1975): 624. Nevertheless, she has also noted that in Mary she found the opportunity to experience God in the figure of a woman. See idem, "Feminist Spirituality, Christian Identity and Catholic Vision," in *Womanspirit Rising: A Feminist Reader in Religion,* ed. Carol Christ and Judith Plaskow (New York: Harper & Row, 1979), 139.

34. Rosemary Radford Ruether, "Christology and Feminism: Can a Male Savior Help Women?" *Occasional Papers, United Methodist Board of Higher Education and Ministry* 1 (1976): 5–6; see also idem, "Mariology as Symbolic Ecclesiology: Repression or Liberation?" in *Sexism and God-Talk* (Boston: Beacon Press, 1983), 139–58.

35. Cunneen, *In Search of Mary,* 12.

36. Elizabeth A. Johnson, "The Marian Tradition and the Reality of Women," in *Horizons on Catholic Feminist Theology,* ed. Joann Wolski Conn and Walter E. Conn (Washington, D.C.: Georgetown University Press, 1992), 91 (first published in *Horizons* 12 [1985]).

37. *Catechism of the Catholic Church* (Collegeville, Minn.: Liturgical Press, 1994), no. 494.

38. Johnson, "Marian Tradition," 94.

39. Ibid., 99.

40. Elizabeth A. Johnson, "Mary, Contemporary Issues," in *A Handbook of Catholic Theology,* ed. Wolfgang Beinert and Francis Schüssler Fiorenza (New York: Crossroad, 1995), 460.

41. Elizabeth A. Johnson, "Mary of Nazareth: Friend of God and Prophet," *America* 182, no. 21 (2000): 11.

42. See John P. Meier, *A Marginal Jew: Rethinking the Historical Jesus,* vol. 1 (New York: Doubleday, 1991), 318–19.

43. Note the consequences of a woman's loss of virginity outside of a marriage in accord with the law in Num. 5:11–31 and Deut. 22:13–21.

44. There is no specific connection of the Magnificat to the context of Mary's pregnancy and her visit to Elizabeth. The Magnificat (with the possible exception of Luke 1:48) may have been a Jewish-Christian hymn that Luke found appropriate to insert here. If not composed by Luke, it fits in well with themes found elsewhere in Luke's Gospel: joy and exultation in the Lord; the lowly being singled out for God's favor; the reversal of human fortunes; the fulfillment of Old Testament promises.

45. Cunneen, *In Search of Mary,* 45.

46. Ann Johnson, *Miriam of Judah: Witness in Truth and Tradition* (Notre Dame, Ind.: Ave Maria Press, 1987), 100–104.

47. "Litany of Mary of Nazareth," Pax Christi, U.S.A., cited in Mary E. Hines, "Mary," in Downey, ed., *New Dictionary of Catholic Spirituality,* 644.

48. Ibid., 645.

49. María Pilar Aquino, *Our Cry for Life: Feminist Theology from Latin America* (Maryknoll, N.Y.: Orbis Books, 1993), 150.

50. To honor her significance, Our Lady of Guadalupe was declared the patroness of the Americas in 1946 by Pope Pius XII.

51. Virgil Elizondo, *Guadalupe, Mother of the New Creation* (Maryknoll, N.Y.: Orbis Books, 1997), 7, 66.

52. Ana Castillo, in *Goddess of the Americas: Writings on the Virgin of Guadalupe*, ed. Ana Castillo (New York: Riverhead Books, 1996), xvii. See also Jeanette Rodríguez, *Our Lady of Guadalupe: Faith and Empowerment among Mexican-American Women* (Austin: University of Texas Press, 1994), 40–41.

53. Elizondo, *Mother of the New Creation*, 67.

54. Rodríguez, *Our Lady of Guadalupe*, 45.

55. Ibid., 46.

56. Ibid., 94–97. The median age of the women surveyed was 26.9, slightly higher than the median age given by the U.S. Census Bureau figure of 23.5 for Mexican Americans. The mean education was 12.1 years and the mean number of children was 2.0. Eighty-five percent were second-generation Americans; the other 15 percent were born in Mexico but lived the majority of their years in the United States. All were Catholic.

57. Ibid., 106.

58. Pamela Kirk, *Sor Juana Inés de la Cruz: Religion, Art, and Feminism* (New York: Continuum, 1998), 54.

59. Rodríguez, *Our Lady of Guadalupe*, 152–58.

60. Ibid., 109.

61. Ibid., 119.

62. María Clara Bingemer, "Mary/Mariology," in *Dictionary of Third World Theologies,* ed. Virginia Fabella and R. S. Sugirtharajah (Maryknoll, N.Y.: Orbis Books, 2000), 138–39.

63. Aquino, *Our Cry for Life,* 175.

64. Ibid., 175–76.

65. Raymond E. Brown, *The Birth of the Messiah: A Commentary on the Infancy Narratives in Matthew and Luke* (Garden City, N.Y.: Doubleday and Co., 1977), 331.

66. Sheila Carney, "Women of Presence, Women of Praise," in *Claiming Our Truth: Reflections on Identity by United States Women Religious,* ed. Nadine Foley (Washington, D.C.: Leadership Conference of Women Religious, 1988), 113.

67. Mary R. Thompson, *Mary of Magdala: Apostle and Leader* (New York: Paulist Press, 1995), 120.

68. Elisabeth Moltmann-Wendel, *The Women around Jesus* (New York: Crossroad, 1982), 78–81.

69. See Acts 18:1–4, 18–19; Rom. 16:3–5; 1 Cor. 16:19–20; 2 Tim. 4:19.

70. *The Acts of Paul and Thecla,* in *New Testament Apocrypha,* vol. 2, ed. W. Schneemelcher, trans. R. McL. Wilson (Philadelphia: Westminster Press, 1965), 322–90.

71. Mary T. Malone, *Women and Christianity*, vol. 1, *The First Thousand Years* (Dublin: Columba Press, 2000), 105.

72. "The Martyrdom of Saints Perpetua and Felicitas," in Herbert Musurillo, trans. and ed., *Acts of the Christian Martyrs* (Oxford: Clarendon Press, 1972), 109–19.

73. Malone, *Women and Christianity,* 106.

74. Johnson, *Friends of God,* 78.

75. In the Middle Ages there was a legend that the Apostles' Creed was written by the original apostles shortly after the death and resurrection of Jesus. Scholars believe that it is very unlikely that this creed was actually composed in the first century. Its present form was not written before the councils of Nicea and Constantinople, both held in the fourth century.

76. Shawn Madigan, ed., *Mystics, Visionaries, and Prophets: A Historical Anthology of Women's Spiritual Writings* (Minneapolis: Fortress, 1998), 411.

77. Ibid., 407.

78. Kazel, cited in Arthur Jones, "Killers Say They Acted on 'Orders from Above'," *National Catholic Reporter* 34 (17 April 1998): 13.

79. Mary Condren, *The Serpent and the Goddess: Women, Religion, and Power in Celtic Ireland* (San Francisco: Harper & Row, 1989).

80. Hildegard of Bingen, *Scivias,* trans. Mother Columba Hart and Jane Bishop (New York: Paulist Press, 1990), 529.

81. Fiona Bowie and Oliver Davies, eds., *Hildegard of Bingen: Mystical Writings* (New York: Crossroad, 1995), 11.

82. During the Middle Ages, Roman Catholic church rules governing women's communities of vowed religious required "cloister," which meant that the sisters, with the exception of their mother superior (abbess, prioress), were shut away from the world and usually under the supervision of priests appointed by the local bishop.

83. Carol Lee Flinders, *Enduring Grace: Living Portraits of Seven Women Mystics* (San Francisco: HarperCollins, 1993), 104.

84. Catherine of Siena, *The Dialogue,* trans. S. Noffke (New York: Paulist Press, 1980), 28 and passim.

85. Julian of Norwich, *Revelations of Divine Love*, trans. M. L. del Mastro (Garden City, N.Y.: Image Books, 1977), 186.

86. Thérèse of Lisieux, *Story of a Soul: The Autobiography of St. Thérèse of Lisieux,* trans. John Clarke, O.C.D. (Washington, D.C.: Institute of Carmelite Studies, 1976).

87. Ibid., 58.

88. Cited from one of Thérèse's letters in John Beever, *Storm of Glory: St. Thérèse of Lisieux* (Garden City, N.Y.: Image Books, 1955), 146.

89. In John Clarke, trans., *Thérèse of Lisieux: Her Last Conversations* (Washington, D.C.: Institute of Carmelite Studies, 1977), 257.

90. Cited in Madigan, ed., *Mystics, Visionaries, and Prophets,* 294.

91. Emilie M. Townes, "Black Women," in *In Our Own Voices: Four Centuries of American Women's Writing,* ed. Rosemary Radford Ruether and Rosemary Skinner Keller (San Francisco: HarperCollins, 1995), 170.

92. Shaw's sermon is cited in Joanne Carlson Brown, "Protestant Women and Social Reform," in Ruether and Keller, eds., *In Our Own Voices,* 278.

93. Ibid.

94. Ibid., 279.

95. Dorothy Day, *Little by Little* (New York: Knopf, 1983), 197.

96. William D. Miller, *All Is Grace: The Spirituality of Dorothy Day* (New York: Doubleday, 1987), 1 (cited in Madigan, ed., *Mystics, Visionaries, and Prophets,* 352).

97. Monika Hellwig, *Christian Women in a Troubled World* (New York: Paulist Press, 1985), 17.

QUESTIONS FOR REFLECTION AND DISCUSSION

1. In this chapter Sandra Schneiders's description of spirituality provided the basis for our study of feminist spirituality. The major elements in her description are

    A. Experience of striving to integrate one's life

    B. Journey through self-transcendence

    C. Discovery of ultimate value as one perceives it

    Express each of these elements in your own words. Do you find Schneiders's description of spirituality helpful?

2. For Christians, the ultimate is God. The problem with masculinized symbols for God lies in the ways they have been interpreted literally and used exclusively. Do Sophia (Woman Wisdom), Divine Mother, or Trinitarian Community capture "the ultimate" in a way that may be helpful for Christian spirituality?

3. Mariology has had an important role in Roman Catholic and Eastern Orthodox spirituality. Trace the major developments in Marian symbolism. Do you agree that they locate in Marian devotion qualities that more properly belong to God? Should Marian devotions be purified of them?

4. What is your understanding of the feminist critique of Mary as "New Eve," "Blessed (Perpetual) Virgin," and "Mother of God"? Do you agree that these symbols can be an obstacle to women's wholeness?

5. Elizabeth A. Johnson and other feminist theologians have called for a "quest for the historical Mary." Is this an important development in Christian feminist spirituality? What qualities of Mary's life do you find important or attractive?

6. Our Lady of Guadalupe is very important for Latin American Christians. Latin American feminist scholars draw attention to different understandings of her in the spirituality of the people. Explain three of these understandings. Do any of them have a basis in the New Testament?

7. "Women of spirit/Spirit" could be used as a phrase that is synonymous with "women saints." Do the women saints surveyed in this chapter, most of whom lived in the past, provide any viable resources for spirituality today?

AREAS FOR EXPLORATION

1. Survey five people of different ages, religious backgrounds, and walks of life, asking each for her or his definition of "spirituality." Do any of the definitions contain elements expressed in Sandra Schneiders's description? Do any religious images and symbols carry meaning for any of the persons surveyed? What are some of them?

2. Visit several Roman Catholic churches, taking note of how Mary is depicted in each of them in statues, icons, stained-glass windows, and the like. Do these depictions reinforce the "Madonna-whore syndrome" associated with Mary as the "New Eve"? If you were asked to design a likeness of Mary for public display, what would she look like?

3. The Protestant Reformers of the sixteenth century rejected Marian devotion. Why would some Protestant women argue that this was a mistake? Survey three Protestant women of different ages to learn their opinion on the subject. Do any of them believe that honoring Mary detracts from the honor due to Jesus Christ?

4. Ask three Roman Catholic and/or Eastern Orthodox women of different generations if Mary and women saints play any role in their spirituality. Ask them to give you reasons about why or why not.

5. Every age has formed its own image of what a saint is, at least in part, according to its own needs. Survey at least five people of different ages, asking them, What qualities do you associate with a saint (woman of spirit/ Spirit) for our own time?

6. Engage in research on a saint (canonized or not) who attracts your interest. See the list of recommended readings for some helpful resources.

RECOMMENDED READINGS

Abraham, K. C., and Bernadette Mbuy-Beya, eds. *Spirituality of the Third World: A Cry for Life.* Maryknoll, N.Y.: Orbis Books, 1994.

Chittister, Joan. *A Passion for Life: Fragments of the Face of God.* Maryknoll, N.Y.: Orbis Books, 1996.

Chung Hyun Kyung. "Who Is Mary for Today's Asian Women?" Pp. 74–84 in *Struggle to Be the Sun Again: Introducing Asian Women's Theology.* Maryknoll, N.Y.: Orbis Books, 1990.

Coyle, Kathleen. *Mary in the Christian Tradition: From a Contemporary Perspective.* Mystic, Conn.: Twenty Third Publications, 1996.

Cunneen, Sally. *In Search of Mary: The Woman and the Symbol.* New York: Ballantine Books, 1996.

Elizondo, Virgil. *Guadalupe, Mother of the New Creation.* Maryknoll, N.Y.: Orbis Books, 1997.

Ellsberg, Robert. *All Saints: Daily Reflections on Saints, Prophets, and Witnesses for Our Time.* New York: Crossroad, 1999.

Flinders, Carol Lee. *Enduring Grace: Living Portraits of Seven Women Mystics.* San Francisco: HarperCollins, 1993.

Gambero, Luigi. *Mary and the Fathers of the Church: The Blessed Virgin Mary in Patristic Thought,* trans. Thomas Buffer. San Francisco: Ignatius Press, 1999.

Gebara, Ivone, and María Clara Bingemer. *Mary: Mother of God, Mother of the Poor,* trans. Phillip Berryman. Maryknoll, N.Y.: Orbis Books, 1989.

Hellwig, Monika. *Christian Women in a Troubled World.* New York: Paulist Press, 1985.

Johnson, Elizabeth A. *Friends of God and Prophets: A Feminist Theological Reading of the Communion of Saints.* New York: Continuum, 1998.

————. "Saints and Mary." Pp. 145–77 in *Systematic Theology: Roman Catholic Perspectives,* ed. Francis Schüssler Fiorenza and John P. Galvin. Minneapolis: Augsburg Fortress, 1991.

Jones, Kathleen. *Women Saints: Lives of Faith and Courage.* Maryknoll, N.Y.: Orbis Books, 1999.

Madigan, Shawn, ed. *Mystics, Visionaries, and Prophets: A Historical Anthology of Women's Spiritual Writings.* Minneapolis: Fortress, 1998.

Malone, Mary T. *Women and Christianity.* Vol. 1, *The First Thousand Years.* Dublin: Columba Press, 2000.

Paul VI, Pope. *Marialis cultus* ("True Devotion to the Blessed Virgin Mary"). Apostolic Exhortation, issued 2 February 1974 (Washington, D.C.: United States Catholic Conference, 1974).

Rodríguez, Jeanette. *Our Lady of Guadalupe: Faith and Empowerment among Mexican-American Women.* Austin: University of Texas Press, 1994.

————. *Stories We Live — Cuentos Que Vivimos: Hispanic Women's Spirituality.* New York: Paulist Press, 1996.

Chapter 6

Feminist Perspectives on Ecology

There was once a town in the heart of America where all of life seemed to live in harmony with its surroundings.... Along the roads laurel, viburnum and alder, great ferns and wild flowers delighted the traveler's eyes through much of the year. Even in winter the roadsides were places of beauty, where countless birds came to feed on the berries.... Then a strange blight crept over the area and everything began to change. Some evil spell had settled on the community: mysterious maladies swept the flocks of chickens; the cattle and sheep sickened and died. Everywhere was the shadow of death.... There was a strange stillness. The birds, for example, where had they gone? The feeding stations in the backyards were deserted. The few birds seen anywhere were moribund; they trembled violently and could not fly. It was a spring without voices.

—RACHEL CARSON[1]

An eerie "spring without voices" poignantly captures the large-scale catastrophe that Rachel Carson (1907–64) projected if farmers did not cease using harsh chemical pesticides. A tragic image of a scorched earth devoid of life is painted in her carefully chosen words. *Silent Spring* is a book written by a woman with a clear sense of mission. With passion she challenged major chemical companies who produced pesticides. She accused them of arrogance in thinking that they could control nature. She argued that there were many more effective ways to regulate the growth of insects than harsh chemicals. She stressed supporting the habitats of the natural enemies of crop-destroying insects, such as birds, which pesticides were also killing. Although she did not use the term "ecology" in *Silent Spring,* she showed that she was keenly aware that studying the interrelationships among the forms of life in ecosystems is important. She emphasized that "the predator and preyed upon do not exist alone, but in a vast web of life."[2] Consideration for the interdependence of species is therefore central to maintaining the balance that exists in an ecosystem. About the web of life Carson reflected that, on the one hand, it was "delicate and destructible," while, on the other hand, "tough and resilient, and capable of striking back in unexpected ways."[3]

Since *Silent Spring,* awareness of the hazards of environmental pollution has grown. "Ecology," from the Greek *oikos,* meaning "house, home," has itself become a household word.[4] For many people, however, ecology is privatized, focused on the home and virtually limited to recycling and perhaps choosing not to buy gas-guzzling automobiles. Although such practices are of value, an exclusive focus on them fails to take into account that ecology is concerned with so much more, namely, the interrelationships among all forms of life with which humans share a common earthly home.

RACHEL LOUISE CARSON

One of the most influential women in the area of ecology, Carson combined a gift for writing with a concern for the survival of plants and animals. In her early adult years she wrote radio scripts for the U.S. Bureau of Fisheries. Later she became editor-in-chief for the U.S. Fish and Wildlife Service. Initially, Carson found it difficult to get publishers for her books. She earned acclaim, however, for *The Sea around Us* (1951), her most comprehensive book about ocean life. It was translated into thirty-two languages. For it she won a National Book Award and election to the

On dock, Woods Hole, Mass., 1951
By permission of Rachel Carson History Project

British Royal Society of Literature. Among her books are an earlier work, *Under the Sea-Wind* (1941), a narrative of sea life that received positive reviews but limited sales, and a later book, *The Edge of the Sea* (1955), in which she focused on life forms in tidal zones.

Carson's major contribution to ecological literature, *Silent Spring* (1962), received high praise from many and resulted in numerous honors, including her election to the American Academy of Arts and Letters. It did not, however, receive accolades from chemical companies making pesticides. They leveled scientific and personal attacks against her, holding her to higher standards than many scientists doing research for them. They argued that Carson's study should be disregarded because she lacked a doctorate and was not affiliated with a major research institution.[5]

While it was true that Carson did not have a doctorate, she did have an undergraduate degree in biology from Pennsylvania College for Women in Pittsburgh (now called Chatham College), and an M.A. in zoology from Johns Hopkins University, in Baltimore, where she also taught. It was not in the artificial environment of the university laboratory but in the natural habitats of plants and animals as an employee of the Fish and Wildlife

Service that Carson formulated her scientific questions and pursued her research.

In 1963 the President's Science Advisory Committee confirmed the claims she made about her projections for ecological disaster. As its number of readers grew, *Silent Spring* galvanized public opinion and led to major legislation to control pesticide use. Stressing the importance of maintaining the habitats of birds and other animals and insects that would keep insects harmful to cash crops in check, Carson was a forerunner in organic farming long before it became popular in the United States.

Carson died on 14 April 1964 of cancer and heart disease. In 1980 she was posthumously awarded the Presidential Medal of Freedom for the contributions she made.

Some argue that talk about an ecological crisis is overblown and inimical to progress. Since Carson wrote *Silent Spring,* many disastrous trends have been reversed, particularly in the United States and Western Europe. The U.S. government no longer permits the use of the pesticide DDT. Farmers are more cautious about what chemicals they use to control crop-threatening insects. The air is cleaner in the United States due to the sanctions of the Environmental Protection Agency established in 1975, and in Europe due to the treaty on transboundary air pollution signed in 1979. Global chlorofluorocarbon emissions have dropped 60 percent from their peak in 1988, following the 1987 international treaty on ozone depletion. Issues with high emotional appeal, such as saving elephants in Africa and the bald eagle in the United States, have received media attention. Elephant slaughter has plummeted due to a 1990 ban on commercial trade in ivory. In the lower forty-eight states of the U.S., the number of bald eagles has soared from fewer than five hundred nesting pairs in 1963 to 5,700 in 1998. Yet, complacency about the survival of other species persists.

At the global level, ecological decline continues. Species loss among plants and animals is accelerating, thereby decreasing the biodiversity of the planet. Agribusinesses further challenge biodiversity by promoting certain strains of plants and animals while neglecting others that could be resistant to new pests. Deforestation is engaged in aggressively. As forestland decreases, the oxygen level on the planet decreases, and in some areas desert acreage is on the increase. Satellite pictures show that Earth's protective ozone layer continues to shrink slowly, promising an increase of skin cancer in humans and blindness in many animal species. Atmospheric carbon dioxide continues to rise, causing Earth's temperature to rise along with it. Some scientists predict that if the present global warming trend continues, the result will be an increase in sea level that could have disastrous consequences for coastal areas. In many parts of the globe, especially in Third World countries, potable water is a major concern. Lack of drinkable water along with shrinking grain supplies are contributing to an increase in malnutrition in many Third World countries. All these things, and more besides, taken together form a problem of crisis proportion.

There are ample reasons for arguing that the human species is the primary cause for the ecological crisis. The rest of nature could easily get along without us. Many plant and animal species are not surviving because of us. There are many examples of species endangerment by humans; two receiving increasing attention around the globe are the introduction by humans of alien species into new eco-systems, thereby threatening native species,[6] and the destruction of forest-based ecosystems by human-caused forest fires, destructive logging practices, collection of wood for fuel, expansion of agriculture, especially of cash crops, and creation of new human settlements.[7] On the whole, the ecological crisis, however, has not resulted from deliberate human malice; the cause is subtler, betraying an attitude that assumes that everything on Earth exists to be the building material of human life. Our language here betrays our values. We call nonhuman things "our natural resources," meaning that they do not have worth beyond what they can provide to the quality of life we desire for ourselves. This assumption results in humans treating plants and animals as "otherkind," thereby ignoring the kinship humans have not only with our closest primate relatives, such as the chimpanzee, but also with birds and fish, trees and algae. Our thought and language patterns show that most of us place ourselves in a position elevated above all of the other species with which we share a common home. Although we may appreciate a beautiful sunset, write sonnets about trees and roses, and be fascinated by the intelligence of dolphins, more often than not we regard plants and animals, if we notice them at all, as mere objects. We desire not only to understand nature, but also to control it. In the process of developing these attitudes, we have stripped the Earth of the sacredness that Christians had once attributed to it when they spoke of *communio sanctorum,* in the sense of "the holy things" of the Earth with which humans were in communion as participants in God's creation. A question is posed: How is the sacredness of creation to be reclaimed in our own time? Ecofeminism provides a distinctively feminist response that calls for a conception of feminism that explicitly takes seriously the subjugation of women and the domination of nature by patriarchal male systems to the advantage of white, upper- and middle-class males.

Ecofeminism: A Twofold Advocacy for Women and Nonhuman Nature

Ecofeminism is a term that reconceives the goals of the second wave of the feminist movement by incorporating concern for the health of the planet. During the 1970s some feminists began to apply a hermeneutics of suspicion to human destruction of nature, concluding that this was yet one more manifestation of patriarchy. They reasoned that patriarchal attitudes and systems that have diminished the human dignity of women also exploited nonhuman nature. To name the connection between the patriarchal subjugation of women and the destruction of nature, Françoise d'Eaubonne coined the term "ecofeminism" a little over a decade after Carson wrote *Silent Spring.*[8] Carson died several years before the inauguration of ecofeminism. Yet, although she never used the term "ecofeminist" to name herself, she does share with ecofeminists their critique of persons who have tried to gain mastery over nature. In *Silent Spring,* Carson attributes the destructive use of pesticides to a "need to control nature born of a Neanderthal Age of biology and philosophy" that "supposed that nature exists for the convenience of man."[9] Ecofeminists express their critique of the need for control in even stronger language than Carson did. They call it "domination."

Ecofeminism has strong ties with one of the major types of second-wave feminism analyzed in chapter 1, radical feminism, but is rightly located among third-wave feminist movements. Its connection with radical feminism lies in ecofeminists' forceful argument that the root cause of the inferior status of women and the exploitation of the Earth is patriarchy. Ecofeminism by definition refers to a connection between patriarchy's domination of women and of nonhuman nature. Ecofeminists argue that in the drive to dominate, patriarchy forgets that humans, including those in power positions, have a natural biological connectedness with all of Earth's life forms. As a movement, ecofeminism involves far more than merely adding endangered species to its list of causes. In its vision of reality it conceives of feminism in ways that are ever mindful that the domination of women and the Earth are intimately connected and mutually reinforcing. As Karen J. Warren, a North American philosopher who has made significant contributions to ecofeminist theory, points out, since eliminating the logic of domination is an essential element of feminism, feminists must include "naturism" as an integral part of any feminist movement.[10] Put simply, in Warren's opinion, every true feminist must also be an ecofeminist.

Although "ecofeminism" as a new term can be traced to French feminist theory of the early 1970s, its history as a socio-political movement is usually traced to the United States and feminist outrage at the meltdown of a nuclear power plant at Three Mile Island in Pennsylvania (1979). After that startling disaster women began to network about their common concerns about the health of the planet. In 1980, a few months after the nuclear disaster and one decade after the first "Earth Day," the first ecofeminist conference, "Women and Life on Earth: A Conference on Ecofeminism in the Eighties," was held at Amherst. At the conference, speakers made connections between feminism, ecology, and militarism, particularly the proliferation of nuclear weapons.[11] It was at this conference that Ynestra King challenged feminists to broaden their concerns to include ecology, arguing that the connections between the domination of nonhuman nature and women had to be given due attention if they were to be remedied.[12]

An important characteristic of ecofeminism as a scholarly theory is the significance of the preference for the word "ecology" over "environment." Although people at times uncritically use "environment" and "ecology" interchangeably, ecofeminists argue that the two are not synonymous. The term "environment" refers to what is apart from human beings — an object "out there" for us to study, control, or restore. The term "ecology," on the other hand, conveys a meaning that is more holistic — the study of the earthly home that humans, other living beings, matter, energy, and all life forces share. The word "ecology," therefore, explicitly includes all organic and inorganic components of an ecosystem, including ourselves, while the word "environment" does not.

Beyond its linguistic preference for "ecology," what also makes ecofeminism distinct from most environmental movements is its purpose. It does not aim to preserve the environment or conserve valuable resources primarily for their future use to achieve human desires. Ecofeminists believe that nature has intrinsic worth apart from any value that a particular group of persons attaches to it. For ecofeminists, the major goal is nothing short of a radical transformation of consciousness. In this regard, ecofeminism is similar to the "deep ecology" movement.[13] Like "deep ecologists," ecofeminists call for a radical transformation of how we view ourselves, our relationship to one another, and the Earth. Their difference lies in how each diagnoses the causes of the ecological crisis. Deep ecologists attribute the ecological crisis to anthropocentrism. The primary cause for the shape the Earth is in is the priorities that people in industrial societies give to their own self-interest. Ecofeminists further attribute the ecological crisis to an anthropocentricity that is also androcentric. They stress that ecological problems have resulted from males, particularly white males holding economic and political power, giving priority to their own interests at the expense of other persons and the Earth itself.

Early on, ecofeminists began to take a stance not only on the domination of women and nonhuman nature but also on all manifestations of patriarchy: racism, classism, and colonialism by national governments or multinational corporations. Ecofeminists argue that the exploitation of nonhuman nature to the financial benefit of a few is cut from the same cloth as discrimination based on gender, age, race, class status, and sexual orientation. Ecofeminism stresses that all of these are intertwined in different but related ways, depending on locale, in patriarchal societies. The attention to the difference that social and geographical location makes in the issues affecting people and all living things makes this movement yet another important contributor to feminism's third wave. What sets ecofeminism apart from other forms of feminism is the insight that patriarchal consciousness not only defines the hierarchy of persons, but also elevates humans over nonhuman nature with disastrous effects.

The Logic of Ecofeminist Theory

In the assessment of ecofeminists, the real cause of the ecological crisis is the system of thought and values inherent in patriarchal systems. Therefore, gender, class, race, and nature all must be theorized together if societies are to move beyond patriarchy. Ecofeminist analysis draws attention to thought patterns of patriarchy that are not only hierarchical but also dualistic. The use of hierarchical analysis is a means of analyzing things that can be benign, or at least appear to be such. A biologist, for example, classifies living species according to their complexity. A hierarchy of complexity does not necessarily posit that the more complex species are of more importance or value than the others. However, in the pervading and often subtle mindset of patriarchy, hierarchies of complexity have been usually weighted in favor of the one species designated to be at the top of the hierarchy of life forms, *Homo sapiens*. Therefore, the danger of patriarchal, hierarchical dualism is ever present. A hierarchical analysis is dualistic when it places higher value on one of the pair for arbitrary reasons —

for example, if it places emphasis on the survival needs of *Homo sapiens* to the extent that those needs override the needs of all other species. As pointed out in chapter 1, hierarchical dualisms always presume "up/down" thought patterns that arbitrarily assign higher value to what is designated as "up" at the expense of what is "down."[14] Historically, the elevation of *Homo sapiens* has been at the expense of the other species and Earth's resources. Hierarchical dualism, therefore, is at the foundation of human attempts to dominate nonhuman nature for the sake of "progress" as it is defined by a certain segment of the people. This segment — men who hold economic and political power — envisions what counts as "progress" in political and economic terms. Put simply, a hermeneutics of suspicion is in order when hierarchical language is used, even if it seems benign. In patriarchal systems, humans too easily project hierarchical values onto every facet of their experience.

In this era of ecological crisis, the culture/nature dualism is particularly dangerous. The concept of nature that we tend uncritically to accept is a product of cultural attitudes that can be traced to the scientific and industrial revolutions. Imbedded in Western consciousness is the notion that nature is discontinuous from humanity, which is the measure of all things. Nature is valued on the basis of its service to human interests, as providing enjoyable vacation spots, or as a treasury of resources with economic potential. Ecofeminism recognizes that what most people mean when they use the word "nature" is more correctly "nonhuman nature." This latter term takes into account that humans are participants in the Earth's processes and are, therefore, part of "nature." It is detrimental to the Earth's vulnerable biosphere if "nature" is treated as the external "other" of instrumental value for human use.

Since ecofeminism seeks to expose the logic of domination wherever it manifests itself, nonhuman nature cannot be treated as if it were by definition subordinate to human concerns. Ecofeminism therefore calls for replacing the notion of a hierarchy of species that contributes to dualistic thinking with holistic thinking. To capture the organic holism basic to ecofeminism, the image of the "web of life" frequently occurs in ecofeminist literature. "Web of life" captures more accurately and concretely the kinship relationship of the human species with the rest of nature. It rejects the self-appointed elevated status of human beings and calls humans to bear in mind that they are a relatively new development in the evolving Earth story. Earth is at least four billion years old, but fossil evidence indicates that *Homo sapiens* has walked on it for only approximately one hundred thousand years.[15] For most of our participation in the story of Earth, we lived in ways that were compatible with our participation in the web of life. But with each passing human generation, especially during the past three hundred years, we have magnified our own importance at the expense of other species, rendering an increasing number of them extinct.

Ecofeminism therefore presents an invitation to something radical: conversion of mind and heart from a largely unchallenged hierarchical dualism and androcentric anthropocentrism to a new egalitarian holism. Egalitarian holism may seem romantic and utopian unless we closely examine what it means for ecofeminists. Egalitarian holism is a type of consciousness that affirms that all of nature is interdependent and interconnected, an interlocking and delicate web of diversity. Every facet of each ecosystem that comprises the biosphere has inherent worth. Egalitarian holism does not promote an equality among species that reduces everything to sameness. Each has a role to play in Earth's web of life. Just as human beings have individual differences due to sex, race, ethnicity, and life experience, every plant and animal species is different from the others for a host of reasons. A human being is clearly different from an earthworm. Differences within and among species are a constant of life on Earth. It is absurd, therefore, to equate equality with sameness.

Ecofeminist egalitarian holism is not a romantic and utopian wish, as its critics sometimes argue. It is an ideal to strive for. As an ideal, it promotes the potential of living species for the optimum of life of which they are capable. This requires careful attention to the interdependent relationships needed to foster life. It does not mean that if you or I were faced with the choice of saving either a particular whale that belongs to an endangered species or a human infant on a boat that the whale is threatening, a decision in favor of the infant should not be made. Death, including killing to ensure the survival of offspring, is part of the Earth's natural processes. What it does mean is that human violence directed toward whales for the sake of economic gain is not acceptable. Species chauvinism is a manifestation of the logic of domination. It absolutizes human goals and ignores the fact that the humans are one among many threads in the delicate web of life.

The Major Strategies of Ecofeminists

The strategies of ecofeminists have taken many forms. Among the chief ones are

- creation of local grassroots movements that struggle to end human domination of nonhuman nature;
- application of a hermeneutics of suspicion to language that promotes the domination of nonhuman nature, corrected by a holistic and organic vision;
- affirmation of the sacredness of nature.

Ecofeminist Grassroots Movements

Grassroots movements promoting Earth healing in which women play leadership roles give testimony to the fundamental transformation of consciousness that ecofeminism is. Experience, not abstract principles, grounds ecofeminism. Because ecofeminism is grounded in experience, the stories of people committed to the preservation of delicate ecosystems are of interest. Maria Mies, a social scientist who teaches in Germany, draws attention to the stories of numerous local struggles against ecological destruction around the globe in which women have been instrumental. Among them are protests against atomic power plants in Germany, food pollution by chemical fertilizers in Japan, the destruction of mangrove forests in Ecuador, deforestation in the Himalayas due to chalk and limestone mining, and water pollution by industries in the northern and southern hemispheres.[16] Mies stresses that worldwide, women have felt the same anxiety and anger about ecological destruction and its long-term effects. She writes,

> Irrespective of different racial, ethnic, cultural or class backgrounds, this common concern brought women together to forge links in solidarity with other women, people and even nations.[17]

Providing detailed accounts about the grassroots strategies that women are using around the globe in response to ecological concerns would be a daunting task because each group has a unique story to tell. Still, it does seem desirable to explore at least one in some depth. Because of the role that women have played in the "Tree Huggers" movement in the Himalayan region of India, it is examined here with interest in the concrete experiences of the women involved. The Tree Huggers movement, "Chipko Andolan," can be traced to the mid-1730s when a group of women, children, and men, led by a woman called Amritha Devi, stopped the maharaja of Jodhpur's men from cutting the sacred kherjri trees of their village.[18] Willing to sacrifice themselves to the swords of the maharaja's men, they clung to the trees as an act of resistance. Recognizing the depth of the commitment of Devi and fellow resisters, the maharaja decreed that no trees would be cut in that area.

During the eighteenth century the Indian rulers curtailed the traditional rights of local villagers to glean food and fodder from the forests. This particularly affected the lives of women because gender divisions of labor meant that most of the work related to the resources of the Earth — food gathering and water collecting — fell to women. This gender-based assignment of labor remains in rural India (and other Third World countries) even today. When local resources are depleted, it is the women who travel long distances on foot in search of food and water. This has prompted village women to be the protectors of the forests. Their livelihood and the health of their families depend on them. They recognize that the survival of the forests and all the forms of life living there are profoundly intertwined with their own well-being.

Since the mid-1970s, the Chipko movement has been midwived anew. Village women of the Gharwal region took action upon learning that the trees in their local forests were being marked for felling on the grounds that it was necessary for the economic development of India. This market-based development, however, would do nothing to enhance the health of the villages affected by the forests' destruction. In fact, it threatened the survival of the villagers with far-reaching effects for the local ecosystem. The villagers viewed the forests as common property, a shared and sacred legacy. They recognized the great cost of this so-called progress. Village women began to go into the forests and hug the trees marked for felling to protect them. These women bared their backs to the axes of woodcutters, literally risking their lives.

The Chipko movement in India has an urgent task. Forests in India are disappearing. Life is threatened. Writing in 1994, Indian theologian Aruna Gnanadason notes that India at that time was losing about 1.3 million hectares of forestland per year.[19] As a result, soil conditions are deteriorating and water resources are in danger. Villages are faced with the threat of landslides and severe erosion. Animals are losing their habitats. Plants that had been part of the delicate balance in which the trees played a role are disappearing.

Vandana Shiva, an Indian scientist and feminist, tells the story of the hero-ism of a modern day "tree hugger," Chamundeyi. In 1986, Chamundeyi risked her life to protect the forest near her village, Nahi-Kala, in the Doon Valley. Limestone miners who were slowly stripping the mountains of all vegetation had cut a road through the forest. The mine quarry was in direct violation of the 1980 Forest Conservation Act. The government permit for the mining had expired in 1982, yet government officials took no action against the mine owner. A Chipko camp was set up on the road to the quarry to block the miners' access. Men hired by the mine's owner attacked the camp and nearly destroyed it. The Chipko people at the camp feared for their lives.

On 30 November 1986, Chamundeyi heard the trucks of the quarry workers who had recently attacked the Chipko camp. She was gathering fodder in the for-est and raced down the slope and stood in front of the approaching trucks. She told the drivers, "The trucks can go only over my dead body."[20] The driver re-fused to stop. After the truck dragged her for a distance, the men finally stopped and decided to turn back. In a later interview, Chamundeyi told Shiva why she was willing to risk her life to save the forest. Her answer was a description of the forest's destruction and what it meant to her.

> When I came to Nahi 17 years ago, the forests were rich and dense with ringal, tun, sinsyaru, gald, chir and banj. [Now] Gujral's mine has de-stroyed the ringal, the oak, the sinsyaru. Our water sources which are nourished by the forest have also dried up. Twelve springs have gone dry. Two years ago, the perennial waterfall, Mande-ka-Chara, ... went dry. Mining is killing our forests and streams, our sources of life.[21]

Chamundeyi also shared with Shiva that among her deepest desires was free-dom from the life-threatening oppression of the men who owned industries that destroyed the Earth in the name of progress. The mine owner had tried to bribe leaders of the local Chipko movement to end their protest. She presumes that the owner has bribed others, including government officials. She associated her desire for freedom to live the way she wished with the health of the forests. The forest is essential to good soil and clean water. Without the forest there will not be enough food to feed her family and the people of her village. Moreover, all the birds and animals that live in the forest will die. Her homeland will become a desolate place fit for neither humans nor animals.

Shiva asked another Chipko woman, Itwari Devi, who had been stoned on 20 March 1987 by thugs hired by the mine owner, about her source of strength (*shakti*) in the midst of this terrible struggle to save the forest. Itwari Devi replied, speaking not only for herself but also for the Chipko movement,

> *Shakti* comes to us from these forests and grasslands, we watch them grow, year in and year out through their internal *shakti* and we derive our strength from it. We watch our streams renew themselves and we drink their clear, sparkling water that gives us *shakti*. We drink fresh milk, we

eat ghee, we eat food from our own fields. All this gives us not just nourishment for the body but moral strength, that we are our own masters, we
control and produce our own wealth. That is why it is primitive, back-
ward women who do not buy their needs from the market but produce for
themselves, who are leading Chipko. Our power is nature's power.[22]

The words of Itwari Devi are significant. For her people, *shakti* is the dynamic
feminine principle; it is energy and power, the source and substance of everything. *Prakriti* is nature; it manifests this primordial energy and is its source.
Her words, therefore, show the deep bond between women and the Earth. When
the bond is broken, survival on many levels is at stake.

Neither of these women has any education in ecofeminist theory, nor were
they familiar with the term. Yet, Shiva believes that Chamundeyi and Itwari
Devi illustrate in a most basic way what ecofeminism seeks to accomplish.
These women are struggling to end their own oppression and the destruction
of a little piece of the Earth (a delicate local ecosystem) that is threatened. They
know that nonviolent resistance is power when they carry it out as a communal
endeavor. The story of these women and of the Chipko movement demonstrates
that women who have a deep commitment to the Earth can make a difference
using nonviolent means.

Hermeneutics of Suspicion and an Organic Vision of Nature

Grassroots movements are extremely important, because "the earth and its resources are limited, . . . our life is limited, . . . time is limited."[23] Acting locally is
very important. But so is thinking globally. The local and the global are not
in opposition. The transformation that ecofeminists pursue involves more than
stopping particular threats to an existing ecosystem. Ecofeminists believe that
they must transform human consciousness, the basic ways that people envision
and relate to reality. Changing the habits of the mind that are part of the inheritance of patriarchy requires that attention be given to the origin of the thought
patterns and language that people use to interpret reality and their place in it.
We easily miss these patterns because we tend to take them for granted as if
they describe things the way they really are. Thus, the potential destructiveness
of our thinking goes unchallenged.

One of the most significant contributors to the study of the thought and
language patterns that promote the domination of women and of nonhuman nature is Carolyn Merchant, an American historian of science. Modern science
is usually said to be a "value free" pursuit of knowledge. In her first major
book, *The Death of Nature,* Merchant questions this assumption by presenting evidence showing how the natural sciences are based on the domination of
nonhuman nature. Her study of the language patterns of early scientists reveals
that (nonhuman) nature is depicted as a woman whose secrets wait to be pene-
trated. Female nature is dissected by male scientists into her basic components,
awaiting recombination by the scientists who have now mastered her secrets.

Merchant closely examines the linguistic metaphors used by major contributors to the "Scientific Revolution" of the sixteenth through eighteenth centuries, such as Pierre Gassendi, René Descartes, Thomas Hobbes, Isaac Newton, and Francis Bacon. She is led to apply a hermeneutics of suspicion to their worldview, one that sanctions the domination of nonhuman nature and women.[24] She associates the mechanistic view of nature, which has profoundly influenced Western thinking, with René Descartes (1596–1650).[25] She points out that viewing nature as if it were a machine waiting to be fine-tuned by science replaced the earlier organic view of the Earth. The result is a dualism that wrongfully puts humans outside and over nonhuman nature, as if nonhuman nature were a mere object for study and control.

Among her strongest critiques of the logic of domination are the ones Merchant directs to the writings of Francis Bacon (1561–1626). Merchant draws attention to the extensive use of patriarchal gender metaphors in Bacon's references to nature. For Bacon, nature was not just a female, but a wild female, a witch, to be subdued by modern science. Bacon argued that just as a disorderly woman needed to be controlled by a man, so did unruly nature. Merchant notes that the witch trials in which Bacon participated likely contributed to his analogy. These trials included extensive physical examinations of the accused.[26] The practices associated with the inquisition of witches permeated his descriptions of nature and transformed Earth from nurturing mother and womb of life into a source of secrets to be extracted by any means available for economic advantage. Bacon, therefore, promoted a new ethical stance that not only allowed nonhuman nature to be controlled by humans, but also promoted the domination of nonhuman nature for human purposes.

The use of organic metaphors for the earth, such as nurturing mother, common in sixteenth-century England, was not entirely abandoned because of Bacon. The language of domination, however, did supersede organic imagery in scientific writings. Merchant concludes that the image of nature as a female to be controlled continues to subtly legitimate the exploitation of Earth's natural resources. "Nature, as active teacher and parent, has become a mindless, submissive body."[27] Not only did this new image function as a sanction for the exploitation of nature, but it also promoted norms of behavior quite different from the norms of the organic model. She concludes that these nonorganic norms, which assumed the right of humans to control the Earth through science and technology, mandated "the death of nature."[28]

To correct the mechanistic and dualistic language, ecofeminists seek meaningful alternatives by applying a hermeneutics of remembrance. Carolyn Merchant looks to the writings of Lady Anne Conway (1631–79), who challenged the mechanistic notions of the Scientific Revolution and developed a philosophy of organic holism. Conway was born just five years after Francis Bacon died. Familiar with dualistic and mechanistic thinking, she rejected these thought patterns and proposed a philosophy of organic vitalism.[29] Merchant notes that although Anne Conway (also known as Anne Finch, Viscountess of Conway) wrote *The Principles of the Most Ancient and Modern Philosophy,* in which she developed her vitalistic interpretation of the Earth's processes, her name was withheld from the original title page because in the seventeenth century scholarly writing was considered inappropriate for women. As a result, the book was originally attributed to its editor, Francis Mercury Van Helmont, who published it in 1690, more than a decade after her death. Only later was it discovered that Anne Conway was the book's actual author. Perhaps her book would have had a greater impact on Western thinking had she been alive to publish and discuss it with other scholars.

Conway was particularly critical of Descartes's thinking. Not only did Descartes depict nature as a machine, but he also promoted a rigid hierarchical dualism of mind and body. Everything apart from the rational mind was an inactive and inferior object, including a person's own body. Critical of Descartes's subject/object dualism, Conway argued that body and spirit were not contrary entities. No split between the rational mind or spirit and the body existed. An intimate bond and organic unity bound the two together.[30] Matter and spirit were two different aspects of one reality. Nature, therefore, could not be reduced to a lifeless machine, any more than the body was a machine controlled by the mind. Earth was a living body far more sublime than any mechanism. Moreover, animals should not be spoken of in mechanistic terms, as if they were merely matter. The pain that an animal experienced when dissected alive (a practice common among scientists in the seventeenth century) was far more than a mechanical response. Animals, like us, have within them knowledge, sensation, and other faculties and properties of a vital spirit.[31] In a vision of nature that depicts it as enlivened with a vital spirit, exploitation of nonhuman nature cannot be easily justified.

A devout member of the Society of Friends (Quakers), Conway no doubt was aware of the Society's belief that the experience of the inner Spirit of Christ animated the spirit of the believer. This fundamental belief likely influenced her vitalistic philosophy. Creatures were imbued with vitality, given to them by God, and were, therefore, of value. Accepting that all creatures participated in a great "chain of being" designed by God, she recognized that all creatures were interdependent and unable to live without each other. Merchant closes her treatment of Conway with these words:

> In the light of the current ecological crisis, which stems in part from the loss of this organic value system, we might regret that the mechanists did not take their vitalist critics more seriously.[32]

We can only speculate about how the relationship of Western peoples to plants and animals might have been different if a vitalistic and organic philosophical perspective had received a greater hearing. For example, what might science be like if the scientific community had adopted a holistic vision based on a subject/subject reciprocity in their research, instead of a subject/object dualism? This is a very important question for ecofeminist theorists. A clue to how we might answer this can be found in the perspectives that Barbara McClintock (1902–92), a biologist who was awarded a Nobel Prize in medicine and physiology in 1983, brought to her research.

McClintock's contribution to science was the groundbreaking discovery of the way certain genes function in plants. She was responsible for the theory of transposition, which she developed from her research into the genetics of corn plants. This theory was an important step in the discovery of DNA. From the standpoint of ecofeminism and an organic value system, how McClintock engaged in doing scientific research is of greater importance than the discovery for which she received the Nobel Prize. Evelyn Fox Keller, an American philosopher of science, has captured the essence of McClintock's research methodology in the phrase "a feeling for the organism."[33] McClintock described her work as listening to what an organism has to say by personal identification with it. To achieve this type of personal identification, the scientist must develop a capacity for an empathetic union with the plant or animal that is being studied.[34]

Integral to McClintock's unique approach to scientific research is her conception of nature. She does not view nature as a passive, mechanical object ruled by externally imposed laws, but as an alive, growing, internally ordered and resourceful reality. McClintock's understanding of nature presupposes an organic model. It resonates with Conway's vitalism. Her attitude toward nature contrasts sharply with the rigid subject/object dualism. Her approach to scientific research is built on a subject/subject model of open and empathetic willingness to be taught by the organism she studied. Keller believes that had it not been for her scientific accomplishments, McClintock may have been dismissed as a romantic woman not to be taken seriously. Instead, she discovered a different approach to genetics, one that recognizes the complexity of interacting systems and that includes the interrelationships of observer to observed, cell to organism, and organism to its environment. Her theory of transposition brought the problem of genetic inheritance into dialogue with the relationship of the organism to its ecosystem.[35] To understand the life of an organism, one must understand not only its genetic make up but also the relationship of the organism's genes to everything else in its ecosystem. Every organism is a complex interdependent relationship.

Unfortunately, McClintock's way of doing science is the exception rather than the rule. But she does illustrate that it is possible to be a scientist while being mindful that humans are part of the "nature" that a scientist studies. Although Barbara McClintock never identified herself as an ecofeminist, she, like Anne Conway, illustrates what ecofeminists mean by a transformation of human consciousness to an organic vision of nature.

Affirmation of the Sacredness of Nature

The ecofeminist organic vision of nature coupled with regarding Earth's many life forms as having intrinsic rather than instrumental value lends itself to a spirituality that affirms the sacred character of living things. Not all ecofeminists are interested in spirituality, but there are many who are engaging in re-envisioning the sacral character of nature (including humanity). These ecofeminists connect the loss of an organic sense of nature to a "desacralization" of the natural world. They associate the loss of a sense of the Earth as sacred with prevailing thought patterns that support patriarchal exploitation of the Earth, not only in the natural sciences but also in Western religions, especially Judaism and Christianity. Due to the influence of mechanistic reductionism and hierarchical dualism, people, including those who practice a monotheistic religion, do not regard the Earth as sacred. This is particularly true in First World societies. Yet, many who live in First World affluence have a sense of spiritual homelessness and alienation from the Earth.

The loss of a sense of the sacredness of the Earth has prompted many Euro-American and European women to embrace ecofeminism with a commitment to recover Earth's sacredness. Important differences exist among these ecofeminists. Many ecofeminists work from within Judaism and Christianity to recover an organic and holistic vision of the sacred. Some also look to teachings in Buddhism and Hinduism. Still others have turned to Goddess religions and therefore fit the criteria for "revolutionary feminist theology," explained in chapter 1. These ecofeminists are active in earth-centered Goddess religion, which was briefly explored in chapter 3. In that chapter the focus was largely on biblical images and symbols for God, with emphasis that images exclusively related to one gender or a single social class are idolatrous. There it was argued that merely attributing female gender traits to God is inadequate. What is needed is the recovery of female images of God, not to replace male images and thereby contribute to a new idolatry, but to enable the reconstruction of a holistic Christian theology needed for our time. The related issues of God's relationship to the whole of creation and of the sacral character of all living things were not addressed. It is to these topics that we now turn.

Ecofeminism and the Divine

Many ecofeminists are attracted to Goddess religion. It is common for ecofeminist Goddess thealogians to present the natural world as sacred, filled with "holy things" that are created by being birthed by the Goddess who continues to nurture life. The thealogy being developed by these ecofeminists goes beyond mere gender reversal to envision the divine as totally immanent in creation. In a very broad sense, their celebration of the sacral nature of the Earth's life forms resonates with the ancient Christian notion of *communio sanctorum,* when the meaning invested in the term draws attention to the "holy things" of creation of which humans as creatures are a part. A shared sense of the sacredness of the Earth and of its many life forms among Goddess ecofeminists and Christian ecofeminists creates a space for dialogue. Any dialogue requires conversation in which the participants talk through their commonalities and differences with openness to transformed understandings of the topics at hand and of their relationship to one another. Engagement in such a dialogue between Goddess ecofeminists and Christian ecofeminists is not, however, without its challenges. Many ecofeminists are participating in Goddess religion precisely because they find the maleness of the God of Judaism and Christianity and the Western Christian loss of the sacredness of the Earth among the major shortcomings of these religions.

Two examples of ecofeminist Goddess thealogians who have reacted against the biblical God and are attracting a considerable following illustrate the challenge to fruitful dialogue. Among those who look to the Goddess as a basis for ecofeminist thealogy are Charlene Spretnak and Starhawk (Miriam Simos). Spretnak is an advocate of Goddess religion of pre-Christian Europe because she finds in it the ability to symbolize the things of the Earth in the way she believes they really are. She reflects on the relationship of the Earth to the Goddess:

> All forms of being are One, continually renewed in cyclic rhythms of birth, maturation, death. That is the meaning of Her triple aspect — the waxing, full and waning moon; the maiden, mother and wise crone. The Goddess honors union and process, the cosmic dance, the eternally vibrating flux of matter/energy: She expresses the dynamic rather than static model of the universe. She is *immanent* in our lives and world. She contains both male and female, in Her womb, as a male deity cannot; all beings are *part of Her,* not distant creations.[36]

Starhawk likewise emphasizes the need for recovering a sense of the divine as immanent in the Earth's processes. She speaks of this immanence as embodiment and says that it means that "we are each a manifestation of the living being of earth; . . . nature, culture and life . . . are sacred."[37] For Starhawk, the Goddess is all that lives and serves life.[38] To immanence she adds the principles of interconnection and community. She explains interconnection as the understanding that all beings "are linked with all of the cosmos as parts of one living organism. What affects one of us affects us all."[39] She speaks of the importance of community. She emphasizes that Goddess religion is not concerned with individual salvation or enlightenment, but with the growth that comes through intimate interactions and common struggles. Among those intimate interactions are worship services conducted outdoors, under trees and sky, and accompanied by music and dancing. Starhawk's sense of community is explicitly ecofeminist. She writes, "Community includes not only people but also animals, plants, soil, air and water and energy systems that support our lives."[40]

The human communities with which Starhawk most closely identifies herself are witch covens. She speaks of witches as "benders and shapers of reality, who seek to reshape Western culture."[41] Witchcraft is one of the few ancient religions in which the leadership is in the hands of women. One element of Western culture that Starhawk seeks to reshape is its understanding of power relations. She believes that too often we uncritically equate power with "power-over," the ability to dominate. Emphasizing the importance of the recovery of the immanence of the sacred, she seeks to transform this notion to "power-from-within," the inherent ability of each thing to become what it is meant to be.[42] Power-from-within must be literally grounded, "connected to the earth, to the actual material conditions of life, for the material world is the territory of the spirit in earth-based traction."[43] Spretnak likewise stresses the importance of the reconception of power relationships and the theme of women's elemental power to grasp the holistic truths of spirituality.

Starhawk was raised a Jew, but stresses that she cannot find in Judaism resources that are compatible with her earth-bound spirituality. Spretnak was raised a Christian and identifies herself as "post-Christian." She believes Yah-weh God to be totally inimical to ecofeminism. She asserts that she is not interested in Yahweh, a thoroughly male deity, in a skirt. Adding a few feminine traits, claiming that he has a feminine side or dimension, will not change the fact that Yahweh of the Judeo-Christian tradition is a "distant, judgmental, ma-nipulative figure of power who holds us all in a state of terror."[44] Her notion of Yahweh is a major contributing factor in her uniting ecofeminism with Goddess religion. Her highly negative understanding of Yahweh challenges the reader to question, Is she right? Is the biblical Yahweh totally inimical to ecofeminism?

From the standpoint of Christian feminism, questioning the validity of Spret-nak's sweeping criticism of Yahweh God is warranted. Nevertheless, there is no reason to rule out that her description of Yahweh as a "distant, judgmen-tal, manipulative figure of power" is based on how Yahweh was presented to her.[45] No doubt, how she depicts Yahweh is based on her own experience. She is led, therefore, to conclude that the God of Christian revelation supports dom-inance, both of women and of nonhuman nature. This God, whom she argues is thoroughly transcendent, logically supports thinking that advocates human au-tonomy from the rest of nature. She is led to believe, therefore, that Christianity is a thoroughly patriarchal religion, inimical to the well-being of women and of the living Earth.[46] Christianity walks hand-in-hand with the attitudes associated with modern science and technology, and supports them. Christianity, therefore, is, at the very least, partially responsible for the plight of the Earth and the ecological crisis.

Starhawk and Spretnak are not alone in their criticisms of Judaism and Chris-tianity. Many ecofeminists find the image of a transcendent male God and of males' privileged relationship to the divine inimical to their belief in humans' intercon-nection with all of life. They believe that since Judaism and Christianity teach that only human creation is made in God's image, the human species, especially man, since God is male, is set apart from and above the rest of creation. This line of reasoning leads them to conclude that the Judeo-Christian tradition is respon-sible for human domination of the Earth and the license for male domination of females.[47] Moreover, Judaism and Christianity attribute this twofold domination to God's will. The results have been disastrous for both women and the Earth.

These passionately held assessments spark very important questions: Are the criticisms of Starhawk and Spretnak and of those who similarly reject Judaism and Christianity valid? Is it possible to find in biblical revelation and the tradi-tions of Judaism and Christianity resources for an ecofeminist Christian theology that honors the sacredness of nature, both human and nonhuman? More to the point, is it possible to find in the Bible the basis for a theology of God that is compatible with an organic vision of the Earth?

Christian Ecofeminist Theology in "Euro-America"

Christian ecofeminists answer affirmatively to questions about the possibility of finding valuable resources in the Jewish and Christian traditions and literature.

They do not accept that the Jewish and Christian traditions ignore the sacral character of the Earth and present a God who is transcendent to the point of being divorced from all living things. In chapter 3, considerable attention was given to Yahweh and the complexity of this Old Testament name for God. Yes, Yahweh is a transcendent God, the God of the mountains, but Yahweh is also an immanent God who speaks to his people on the mountain (see Exodus 3) and is described as creating the first human by scooping up mud from the earth, forming this earth creature and all animals as a "hands-on" Creator (Genesis 2). These images speak of an intimate relationship of Yahweh with creatures. Although the biblical tradition does depict Yahweh as transcendent, fidelity to biblical revelation invites this affirmation: Yahweh God is also immanent in creation.

This argument for a transcendent, yet immanent Yahweh, however, does not sufficiently resolve the issues raised by Starhawk and Spretnak. Although, technically speaking, Yahweh is a gender-neutral term, it carries with it a great deal of male baggage. A further rethinking of the God of Judaism and Christianity is required to develop a Christian ecofeminist theology for our time. Among the most significant contributors to Christian ecofeminist theology are Sallie McFague[48] and Rosemary Radford Ruether. McFague, whose insights have appeared in chapters 3 and 5, has devoted much of her writing to God-language and its connection with the ecological health of the planet. She shares with Carolyn Merchant and many other ecofeminists a strong interest in thought and language patterns that societies use to conceive of and relate to reality. McFague is especially interested in metaphorical language for God, arguing in her first book, published in 1975, that metaphor is the linguistic means humans have for "making connections, seeking resemblances, uniting body and soul — [connecting] earthly, temporal [and] ordinary experience with its meaning."[49] For her, metaphors do more than add a little spice to our communications. Metaphors are embodied language forms grounded in life experience. They have the potential of bringing the "stuff of life," including presumably the "holy things" of creation, together in ways that unite head and heart. Images and metaphors play a significant role in people's conceptions of the God-human-world relationship.

However, McFague realistically notes that God-language and its interpretation also have the potential for abuse. Spretnak's image of Yahweh as a "distant, judgmental, manipulative figure" shows how an imaginative metaphor can be harmful if given an erroneous interpretation detached from its biblical worldview. McFague associates this type of interpretation with the literalism of fundamentalism, of which she is very critical.[50] She argues that God-language in the Bible is metaphorical and expressive of relationship. Its purpose is not to provide unchangeable concepts. It has a fluidity about it.[51] The God of the Judeo-Christian tradition will be misunderstood unless this is kept in mind. Although McFague does not agree with Spretnak's interpretation of Yahweh, she is in company with Spretnak in her emphasis on the importance of a recovery of immanence in the divine. McFague attributes the loss of immanence to patriarchal idolatry. She believes that without a sense of the nearness of God, "the overwhelming sense of the way God pervades and permeates our very being," people will not find the God of Christian revelation relevant to their lives and concerns.[52]

McFague believes that the neglected immanence of God in the Christian tradition can be recovered. This is the project she undertakes in *Models of God*, which, significantly, she begins with an exploration into a "holistic view of reality." She starts with how humans envision the earth, and the effect that this imagery has on our relationship to it, ourselves, and God. She argues that we must replace the old metaphor for Earth as the "cosmic machine," if movement away from an anthropocentric worldview and toward a true solidarity with nature is to happen. She sets her own agenda by noting that few Christian feminist theologians have articulated an inclusive Christian vision that extends to the nonhuman world. She writes:

> The feminist theologians who have given attention to the nonhuman world have been, for the most part, those involved in Goddess traditions and witchcraft, for whom the body, the earth, and nature's cycles are of critical importance. Those of us from the Christian tradition have much to learn from these sources, but even these feminists have not, I believe, focused primarily on the intrinsic value of the nonhuman in a way sufficient to bring about the needed change of consciousness.[53]

Attentive to the great cosmic story being brought to light by scientists, McFague proposes an "evolutionary, mutualistic model" for understanding the relationships that make up the cosmos. In her model, all entities in the cosmos are united symbiotically and internally in levels of interdependence but are also separated as centers of action and response.[54] The theological model that she proposes to correlate with her evolutionary, mutualistic model is "the world as God's body."[55] In *Models of God* she proposes this model as a thought experiment. She makes it clear that "the world as God's body" is intended as a religious metaphor and not a literal description. Her emphasis on the metaphorical quality of "the world as God's body" is very important to her argument. If it is interpreted literally, the understanding of God she proposes would be pantheistic and not true to the Christian tradition, because "world as God's body" would reduce God to the world. Although she does not pointedly accuse ecofeminist Goddess thealogy of pantheism, this is a criticism that could be leveled against it. Immanence without transcendence collapses the divine into the world, making the world a deity. McFague does not believe that God can be reduced to the world, any more than we humans can be reduced to our bodies. Rather, she proposes that her understanding is panentheistic. By this she means that the God-world relationship is one "in which all things have their origins in God and nothing exists outside of God."[56] Obviously, the syllable "en" in "panentheistic" corresponds to her notion of the world existing *in* God. She does not equate God with the material stuff of the cosmos, because God is more than the sum of the parts of the world. God transcends the world, but nothing exists without God nurturing and sustaining it with God's gift of life.

McFague's preferred metaphor is developed further in *The Body of God*. A central theme of this book is God being "bodied forth" in the cosmic processes of an evolving universe. Critical of the neglect of the body in the Christian tradition, McFague seeks to remedy this defect by proposing a model that treats creation as the continuing, dynamic, growing embodiment of God. The sacredness of nature and the immanence of God in the world, weakened by Protestant Christianity's overemphasis on the monarchical sovereignty of God, is recovered. She is highly critical of monarchical understandings of the God-world relationship that made God so transcendent that God had no relationship to the world. God is not an abstract deity separate from the cosmos, ruling it from afar. Emphasis on God's transcendence puts unnecessary distance between God and the world. God as embodied overcomes that distance, but it does not eliminate God's transcendence entirely. Her organic model for the cosmos leads her to redefine divine transcendence in an immanent way. She writes, "Immanental transcendence or transcendent immanence is the model of the universe"[57] that the world as God's body implies.

McFague believes that the manner in which she weds transcendence and immanence is a logical position for a Christian. The foundation of Christianity is the incarnation of Jesus Christ. The Word of God is made flesh in cosmic history; the Son of God is embodied in our world, and this is itself a sign of God's involvement with creatures. In Jesus Christ, God is made available to us through the mediation of this unique embodiment. Christ is the primary symbol of the transcendent immanence she proposes. Not neglecting the Holy Spirit, McFague envisions the Spirit as the "source of the renewal of life, the direction or purpose for all bodies of the world — a goal characterized by inclusive love."[58]

About her proposal for "the body of God" as the metaphorical model needed today, McFague herself pointedly asks, Does her model help us to see some things we need to pay attention to in our era of ecological crisis?[59] A strength of her work is the evocative power of her extensive reflection on the world as God's body. Her memorable metaphor affirms the sacredness of the cosmos, because it envisions God's presence to be coextensive with the universe, encompassing everything that is in it. She also makes it clear: bodies matter to Christianity. Her book is, therefore, a valuable corrective to the hierarchical dualism that views the body as distinct from and inferior to the mind, an inferiority that has been extended to women because in patriarchal thinking women are associated with the body.

A possible limitation to "the body of God" is the fact that the body of every earthly being eventually dies and decays. Perhaps this criticism is an example of what McFague cautions her readers against: interpreting her chosen metaphor as a literal description, forgetting that no language for God can ever be taken literally without falling into idolatry. Another criticism is McFague's tendency to treat "the body" rather abstractly. Bodies consist of flesh and blood; each is unique. When she speaks of the body as a "model," her language evokes thoughts of objective and abstract scientific models that are used to explain the interaction of chemicals.

The reader will not, however, associate abstraction with her most recent book, *Super, Natural Christians*. In the vivid description she uses in this book, McFague is no disembodied and objectifying observer. She concretely illustrates her thesis: "Christian practice, loving God and neighbor *as subjects,* as worthy of our love in and for themselves, should be extended to nature."[60] She painstakingly shares with her readers a way of seeing the world. She attends to a daffodil, a butterfly on the nose, a frog splashing in the pond, and turtles basking in the sun. The inclusive love she associated with the Holy Spirit in *The Body of God* is concretely expressed in her vivid encounters with nature.

Super, Natural Christians is not simply a personal meditation on the beauty and wonder of nature. In it, McFague also develops a "subject-subjects model" of ecological knowing that resonates with the perspectives of Anne Conway and Barbara McClintock. The primary analogue for McFague's model is friendship. She stresses that the subject-subjects model is not the reverse of the subject-object model of Descartes that presumes hierarchical dualism, but merely a different model, one that underscores both radical unity and radical individuality.[61] A person enters into a subject-subjects relationship with nature by looking at nature in all its variety with eyes of love and by relating to it with an ethics of care. Such language resonates with Barbara McClintock's "feeling for the organism."

No discussion of Christian ecofeminism would be complete without giving attention to the contribution of Rosemary Radford Ruether. She first wrote about the connection between the domination of women and of nonhuman nature in 1975, insisting that women must see that there is no liberation for them and no solution to the ecological crisis within a society whose fundamental model of relationships is one of domination. She argued then that the women's movement for liberation must be united with the ecological movement for Earth healing to reshape the basic relations and the underlying values of society. Since that time, ecofeminism has been a recurring theme in her writing.[62]

In chapter 3 we examined Ruether's contribution to the feminist conversation about God. Her ecofeminist perspectives on God were not presented in that chapter because it is appropriate that they be treated here. Her ecofeminist theology of God, like McFague's, provides serious and substantive responses to post-Jewish and post-Christian ecofeminist thealogians. Our examination of Ruether's contribution to ecofeminism is limited primarily to *Gaia and God.* Ruether chose the word "Gaia" in the book's title because of its multiple meanings. In classical Greek, "Gaia" means "Goddess," specifically, "Earth Mother Goddess." Gaia also has a scientific connotation. Biologists Lynn Margulis and James Lovelock use the term when speaking about the entire planet as a living system that behaves as a unified organism. The "Gaia Hypothesis" holds that all the living matter on Earth, from whales to viruses, from oaks to algae, constitutes a single living entity or organism.[63] The book's title, therefore, expresses well her intent to present an ecofeminist vision of God that relates well to an organic — Gaia — vision of the Earth.

True to ecofeminist notions of the place of human beings in the bigger scheme of things, Ruether envisions humans to be an inextricable part of nature. She responds to a familiar critique: humans have set themselves apart from nonhuman nature and have engaged in reshaping it through domination. To rectify the problems that human domination has caused, ecological healing is a necessity. Ruether depicts this healing as a theological and psychic-spiritual process in which spirituality and ecojustice are interrelated. Her vision of healing, like her vision of the earth, is holistic.

Ruether's position is grounded in a fundamental belief she has about what it means to be a human person. She believes that human beings have an undeniable drive for transcendence. We are continually bringing forth new life and new visions of how our life should be both more just and more caring. She argues, therefore, that the human capacity for ethical reason expresses a deeper source of life beyond the biological. That source is the divine. She writes, "To believe in divine being means to believe that those [transcendent] qualities in ourselves are rooted in and respond to the life power from which the universe itself arises."[64]

Like McFague, Ruether has responded to the critiques of the understanding of the God of Judaism and Christianity by ecofeminists whose spiritual journeys have led them to Goddess religion. She writes,

> Some [ecofeminists] see the Jewish and Christian male monotheistic God as a hostile concept that rationalizes alienation from and neglect of the earth. Gaia [the Goddess] should replace God as our focus of worship. I agree with much of this critique, yet I believe that merely replacing a male transcendent deity with an immanent female one is an insufficient answer to the "god-problem."[65]

Elsewhere, she argues that Goddess religion is insufficient, not only because it is very difficult to adapt the ancient Goddess religions to contemporary life, but also because the self-blessings and emotionally charged experiences of full moon and solstice rituals can too easily become mere recreational self-indulgence for a countercultural elite.[66] She believes that Euro-American and European ecofeminist Goddess worshipers neglect to make real connections between their own reality, as privileged women, and racism, classism, and the impoverishment of nature.

Ruether is committed to developing an ecofeminist theology that looks to her Christian heritage for resources for a new vision of God. It is important to note, however, that she does not explore Christianity in isolation from other sources. She is open to a wide range of ideas, including holistic approaches to science and the cosmologies of the traditional religions of Africa, Asia, and Latin America. This is especially evident in her introductory essay in *Women Healing Earth.*

In *Gaia and God,* Ruether develops an explicitly Christian ecofeminist theology. She addresses four major themes: (1) creation, (2) destruction, (3) domination and deceit, and (4) healing. In her interpretation of the biblical story of the days of creation (Gen. 1:1–2:4b), Ruether agrees with the critics who argue that this text is anthropocentric.[67] Humans are set apart from the rest of creation as the only beings who image God and are given dominion over and charged to subdue the Earth. She argues, however, that exploitation of nature is not the intent of this passage. She notes that the reference to humans imaging God is a way of saying that humans are commissioned to be God's representatives — stewards exercising dominion (Gen. 1:26–31). About stewardship she writes,

---

GENESIS 1:24–2:4a, THE DAYS OF CREATION

Then God said, "Let the earth bring forth all kinds of living creatures: cattle, creeping things, and wild animals of all kinds." And so it happened: God made all kinds of wild animals, all kinds of cattle, and all kinds of creeping things of the earth. God saw how good it was. Then God said, "Let us make man in our image, after our likeness. Let them have dominion over the fish of the sea, the birds of the air, and the cattle, and over all the wild animals and all the creatures that crawl on the ground." God created man in his image; in the divine image he created him; male and female he created them. God blessed them, saying, "Be fertile and multiply; fill the earth and subdue it. Have dominion over the fish of the sea, the birds of the air, and all the living things that move on the earth." God also said, "See, I give you every seed-bearing plant all over the earth and every tree that has seed-bearing fruit on it to be your food; and to all the animals of the land, all the birds of the air, and all the living creatures that crawl on the ground, I give all the green plants for food." And so it happened. God looked at everything he had made, and he found it very good. Evening came, and morning followed — the sixth day.

Thus the heavens and the earth and all their array were completed. Since on the seventh day God was finished with the work he had been doing, he rested on the seventh day from all the work he had undertaken. So God blessed the seventh day and made it holy, because on it he rested from all the work he had done in creation. Such is the story of the heavens and the earth at their creation.

"This obviously means that humans are to take good care of earth, not to exploit or destroy it, which would make them bad stewards."[68]

Why does Ruether introduce the word "steward" into the conversation? The word "steward" appears nowhere in Gen. 1:1–2:4a. But biblical scholars have long interpreted the term "image of God" as royal in origin. These scholars believe that the words "image" and "likeness" echo language used of ancient Middle Eastern kings, the sovereigns who represented their gods as rulers in theocratic societies. The representatives of rulers were known as "stewards." The king represented God as God's steward. In turn, the king appointed stewards, giving them the responsibility of looking after his property in his absence. If this is the meaning implied by the symbol "image of God," then it also implies that God (the king) is represented by humans (his stewards). If this interpretation is correct, then it is extraordinary, since women as well as men are said to image God. Women, along with men, are charged with stewardship of the earth. Yet, a woman serving her king as his steward is an exception to the rule.

Ruether's "stewardian" response to those who argue that the Bible justifies the exploitation of nature has become a standard response of Christians to the ecological crisis since the 1970s. Her argument, however, strikes me to be in conflict with ecofeminism's rejection of the anthropocentrism and andro-centrism of patriarchy. By stressing stewardship, Ruether misses an opportunity to counteract the anthropocentric interpretations of this passage. Although her argument that humans act as God's stewards in caring for the earth presents a human-centeredness that is benign, it is still problematic from the standpoint of ecofeminism. Stewardship presumes that humans have a special status among creatures that gives us unique responsibilities and powers. It ensures that human power over and control of "otherkind" are preserved. As stewards, humans (historically, males) not only are to care for God's garden, but also have the God-given power to decide what will be grown in it. The latter power is par-ticularly problematic and in conflict with what most ecofeminists value. The ecofeminist emphasis on the Earth as "the web of life," with the accompany-ing emphasis on organic and egalitarian holism, rejects having any one species, including and especially humans, in charge of the others.

Good reasons exist for dismissing the criticism that Genesis is inimical to ecology without resorting to a stewardship relationship.[69] This takes us to the core of the problem with Gen. 1:24–28: the words "dominion" and "subdue." It is likely that for many North Americans, the word "dominion" conjures up images of a ruler exercising control over his domain. Why is this the case? Euro-American Christians participate in the stream of thought patterns that can be traced to the era of our colonial beginnings and back to England and Francis Bacon. Onto the biblical notion of dominion, Bacon grafted his understanding of domination through the application of science.[70] He argued that the first sin committed in the paradisal Eden was due to Eve's willful disobedience. Eve, therefore, is responsible for the human race's loss of its God-ordained domin-ion over the Earth. Before the fall, Adam and Eve were like God, sharing in God's dominion. With the fall, that wonderful Godly dominion was lost. Ba-con envisions science and its applications in new technologies as the only ways in which man can recover the original dominion lost to him through Eve's disobedience and temptation of Adam. Although woman's inquisitiveness may have caused man's fall from his God-given dominion, man's control of another female, unruly nature, could be used to regain it.

By weaving together the two stories of creation in Genesis, Bacon devel-oped a biblical legitimation for the domination of nature by educated men like himself. As Carolyn Merchant notes, his ideas provide patterns of thinking that contribute to the exploitation of nature by Western industrial and technological societies, and in other parts of the globe as well. Bacon developed an interpre-tation of the Genesis creation stories that attributed human control of nonhuman nature to God's will.[71]

Is the domination of nature that Bacon called for, and that science and tech-nology have promoted, an appropriate interpretation of the Genesis message? To respond to this question, I believe we must explore the historical influences on the Genesis creation stories. This requires that we examine the troublesome Genesis text with attention to its historical context. Obviously, it is not possible to recapture what was in the minds of the authors who wrote the first chapter of Genesis. However, examining the historical context of the formation of this passage can give us some clues into the meaning of "dominion" and "subdue." My choice of the word "clues" is deliberate. What I propose is not a fixed conclusion about what words like "dominion" and "subdue" meant. Rather, I am proposing an imaginative construct that invites the reader to enter the life experience of the people who first heard the story of the days of creation.

Although feminist biblical hermeneutics is not a form of historical-critical interpretation, there are times when looking "behind" a text to see what its history might unveil can be helpful. There is a broad consensus among biblical scholars that holds that Gen. 1:1–2:4a was composed during the era of the Babylonian exile, a time of crisis for Jews who were enslaved in a foreign land (present-day Iraq). In the midst of considerable uncertainty, the authors of this tradition (known as the Priestly tradition) reasserted their belief in God's power to order chaos in a creation narrative written for use in prayer and worship. This narrative clearly includes among its intentions the praise of God, who provides a day of rest for all of creation for this purpose. What could be more dear to slaves in a foreign land than to be at home, where they could once again freely praise God and rest in the belief that this God creates simply through the power of words?

On the same day on which God created the animals, humankind is made, and this sixth day's creation is proclaimed by God to be "very good." From an ecological standpoint, since humans do share the same day of creation with animals, there is a kinship of humankind with the animal species. Note how this kinship is affirmed later in the passage. To every beast of the earth, and bird of the air, and everything that has the breath of life — meaning humans too — God gives the green plants for food. Note that humans are not told that they may eat animals. This part of the passage affirms that humans are fundamentally connected with the other species with whom they share the sixth day of creation. Humans participate in the web of life with the other animals and with the plants. I believe that this is the ecological perspective from which dominion should be interpreted. Unfortunately, it is usually missed. Bacon's extreme anthropocentric and androcentric interpretation of dominion as domination by man over female nature has been the dominant interpretation, silencing the ecological elements in the passage.

A close reading of Genesis 1 requires that we examine the troublesome words "dominion" (Hebrew, *radah*) and "subdue" (Hebrew, *kabash*) closely. Obviously, individual words convey meaning only in the context of sentences that participate in a larger story. What might "dominion" and "subdue" mean in the context of the lives of Jews newly freed from slavery, entering their homeland once more after two generations? What might their former homeland be like upon their return? What will they have to do to make it a home?

In Gen. 1:28, the biblical authors depict God as saying to humans, "Have dominion over the fish of the sea, the birds of the air, and all the living things that move on the earth." God further says that the human creatures may eat seed-bearing plants, as may the beasts and birds (Gen. 1:29–30). God grants humans dominion over animals, but no human is permitted to kill an animal for food. Put simply, humans are to be vegetarians. A fuller meaning of "having dominion" emerges later in Genesis in the story of the great flood.

In Genesis 6, we find God deeply grieved about the extent of the wickedness of humans. Their sins result in an ecological disaster of worldwide proportions. Noah and his family alone are righteous in the sight of God. God gives Noah a mission. He is to participate in God's plan for the survival of living species. God instructs Noah to build a huge ark and directs, "Of all kinds of birds, of all kinds of beasts, two of each will come into the ark to stay alive" (Gen. 6:20). The species of the earth that were gathered included clean and unclean, domesticated and wild animals. Many of these animals were of no real use to the people. God's directive makes the meaning of having dominion clear: Noah and his family are charged with seeing to the survival of the other living creatures (not only the ones of direct benefit to humans). Human survival and that of animals are intimately related (Gen. 7:1–4). Human sin results in ecological disaster. Salvation in the sense of healing wholeness, therefore, is connected with dominion. Salvation here means deliverance from destruction to right relationship. In the context of the story that unfolds after the great flood, it also means the experience of new creation for humans, and for every kind of bird and beast (Gen. 9:1–17).

What can be said from an ecological standpoint about the more troublesome words "subdue the earth"? On the surface, subduing the earth may seem to also promote anthropocentrism with negative outcomes for the rest of creation. The Hebrew word for "subdue" is found in Num. 32:22, 29, in a passage in which Moses tells the Jews to inhabit the land that God has promised them. In Num. 32:24, the people are directed to build towns for their families and folds for their flocks. In 1 Chron. 22:17–19, David is depicted using "subdue" in reference to the land that is prepared for the construction of a temple, a suitable "sanctuary of the Lord" where God can be worshiped.[72] "Subdue," therefore, is connected with transforming land into a home where people can sustain their lives and God can be properly worshiped.

In the light of the Jews' heartbreaking loss of their homeland and temple, and their enslavement as exiles in Babylon, "subdue the earth" may simply mean that the Jews, who were returning to their former home, believed that they had a responsibility to rebuild a society in which they and their descendants could prosper with dignity in freedom and freely give Sabbath praise to God. Viewed in the historical context of the sixth century B.C.E., subduing the earth cannot be equated with a license to exploit nonhuman creation, as if it were merely of instrumental value for humans. Humans are to respect creatures; they may not kill animals for food and are to treat all living things with respect. Further, people at this time lacked the technology to exploit the earth in destructive ways. It is better interpreted as a directive to reclaim a divine gift, the original "promised land," where they could experience freedom and worship God appropriately. This land is described in Deuteronomy with the imagery of an ecological paradise. It is

> a good country, a land with streams of water, of fountains and springs welling up in the hills and valleys, a land of wheat and barley, of vines and fig trees and pomegranates, of olive trees and honey. (Deut. 8:7–8)

The above interpretations of "dominion" and "subdue" in Genesis 1 resonate with elements of Ruether's last major section of *Gaia and God,* "Healing." We now, therefore, examine how Ruether connects Earth healing with ecofeminist goals. Ruether provides a response to ecofeminists who believe that the religion of the Bible is inimical to the well-being of Earth. She believes that there are aspects of the biblical tradition and classical Christianity that provide sources for ecological values. For these sources she explores the theological notions of covenant and sacrament.

In the case of covenant, she draws attention to the sacred covenant between God and Israel that also includes nature, animals, plants, and the earth.[73] Although she does not explicitly cite Noah's covenant with God, it is her logical source. The post-flood covenant is unique. God makes it not only with Noah and his descendants but also with every living creature — "birds, cattle, and every wild beast of the earth" (Gen. 9:9–11). There is an inherent relational interdependence of humans with the rest of creation in this covenant. The Noachic covenant is a symbol of the unbreakable bond of all creatures with their Creator. The perpetual sign of this covenant is God's "bow in the clouds" (Gen. 9:13). The rainbow serves as a perpetual reminder of the special agreement that God has made, not only with humans but also with all living creatures, as well.

Ruether also draws attention to the biblical teachings on the Jubilee year as a time of renewal of God's sacred covenant with all of creation. During the year of Jubilee, Jews were required to free their slaves, cancel debts, and give the land and animals rest.[74] According to Jewish teaching, the earth itself was to be given a Sabbath rest in honor of the Creator (Lev. 25:1–7; Deut. 15:1–11). This meant that the farmlands were allowed to lie fallow. In the New Testament, Luke 4:16–19 introduces the mission of Jesus with a reminder of the Jubilee mandate. In a synagogue of Nazareth, Jesus ushers in a time of Jubilee by proclaiming glad tidings to the poor (widows and the orphans), by announcing liberty to prisoners, and by giving sight to the blind. This is a time of justice for all who are oppressed. The passage ends with a proclamation of a Sabbath year, a year of favor, in which not only were slaves freed and debts canceled, but also planting, pruning, and harvesting for storage were forbidden. The new covenant initiated by Jesus is a reminder of the ancient one in Leviticus. Allowing the land to be untilled provided it with a period of replenishment.

Sacrament is interpreted ecologically by Ruether in the broad sense of the sacramentality, the sacredness, of all of creation. She does not use the term "sacrament" in reference to particular ritual actions celebrated by the Christian community, such as Eucharist and baptism. Rather, she associates sacramentality with God's abiding presence in creation. She focuses on Christ, the Son of God incarnate in creation, as the primordial sacrament in which God is encountered. She connects the sacramentality of creation with a cosmological understanding of Christ. She recognizes that this may be a new understanding for many of her readers and notes that there has been a strong tendency, especially in modern Christianity in the West, to associate Christ only with redemption. She finds this association too limited and draws attention to the beautiful hymn in Col. 1:15–20, where Christ is declared to be the "the firstborn of all creation." She

---

COLOSSIANS 1:15–17

He is the image of the invisible God, the firstborn of all creation;
For in him were created all things in heaven and on earth,
  the visible and the invisible,
  whether thrones or dominions or principalities or powers;
  all things were created through him and for him.
He is before all things, and in him all things hold together.

---

argues that Christ is both the Creator in whom all things were created and God incarnate who participates fully and actively in creaturely life.

What is especially important about the Colossians passage from the standpoint of ecology is that Christ both holds all of creation together in cosmic unity and "reconciles all things to himself through the blood of the cross" (Col. 1:20). Reconciliation is a way of talking about the salvation offered through Christ. But it is also more. Reconciliation is a way of expressing that it is Christ who bridges the gap between nature and God, between creatures and Creator. That Jesus was historically a male person is not an impediment to incorporating the significance of God incarnate in an ecofeminist theology. In fact, Ruether believes Christ to be extremely important for ecofeminism. For her, Christ is (1) the manifestation of God in creation; (2) the immanent presence of God that creates and sustains the cosmos; and (3) the divine power that will be manifest at the end of time, healing the enmity that has divided the cosmos and reconciling the cosmos to God.[75] Because Christ is incarnate in creation, "God may be all in all" (1 Cor. 15:28).[76] It follows, therefore, that in Christ, God (Creator) and Gaia (Mother Earth) are one.

Ruether believes that the themes she has explored and newly interpreted provide a theology needed today, an ecofeminist theology. She begins the final chapter of *Gaia and God* with this carefully crafted statement:

> One speaks from the mountaintops in the thunderous masculine tones of "thou shalt" and "thou shalt not." It is the voice of power and law, but speaking (at its most authentic) on behalf of the weak, as a mandate to protect the powerless and to restrain the power of the mighty. There is another voice, one that speaks from the intimate heart of the matter. It has long been silenced by the masculine voice [of Yahweh God], but is finding again her own voice. This is the voice of Gaia. Her voice does not translate into laws or intellectual knowledge, but beckons us to communion. . . . We need both of these voices.[77]

Sallie McFague also has given attention in her writing to the cosmic Christ and the sacramentality of creation. In *Metaphorical Theology* she wrote that she found the medieval notion of a sacramental cosmos untenable in today's world.[78] Nevertheless, she believes that a revised understanding of sacrament holds great promise for ecological theology. In *The Body of God* she explores the notion of the world as the sacrament of God. She concludes that the notion of the universe as a sacrament draws attention to the presence of God that cannot be limited to particular times or places. God is coextensive with reality and present through Christ in the entire cosmos.[79]

McFague and Ruether make it clear: ecofeminists need not abandon and replace Christianity with Goddess religions. Moreover, they affirm that Jesus Christ and the God whom he reveals have significance for ecological theology and for ecofeminism. Neither theologian attaches importance to the maleness of Jesus as a historical person in her ecological theology. Neither focuses on male images of God as obstacles to ecofeminism, because they do not accept this limitation on God to be valid. Instead, they connect the cosmic significance of Jesus Christ's incarnation and the God he revealed with an earthly sacramentality in the symbols "the body of God" (McFague) and Gaia (Ruether).

A sacramental vision of material creation provides a meaningful Christian foundation for an ecofeminist theology. It helps to make the immanence of God to creatures concrete. People come to know God not only through Christ and godly humans (the saints); plants and animals are also means by which humans can know something of God. Our attitudes about nonhuman nature would likely be very different if in every creature we perceived something of the divine. In the incarnation of Christ a special kinship of God with creatures is revealed. In God, through Christ, all that exists has intrinsic value. Early Christians perhaps had some insight into this when they associated the term *communio sanctorum* not only with the saints, the holy women and men of God, but also with "holy things," the very stuff of creation. In a sense, not only Jesus Christ, but also every creature, is potentially a "sacrament" of encounter with God.

McFague and Ruether could have called upon additional biblical resources in developing their ecofeminist theologies. One worthy of attention found in the Wisdom tradition is Woman Wisdom — *Hokmah* (Hebrew), *Sophia* (Greek), already addressed in chapter 3. Woman Wisdom provides a biblical source for responding to concerns of ecofeminists who have abandoned Judaism and Christianity for Goddess religions because the God of Judaism and Christianity is transcendent to the point of complete detachment from the Earth. In the Old Testament, Woman Wisdom orders creation and pervades its every development.[80]

In Proverbs, for example, Woman Wisdom's relationship to creation is developed in ways that resonate with an ecofeminist organic vision of the Earth. Biblical scholar Claudia Camp points out that any hint of dichotomizing between God and nature, and sacred and profane, found in some Old Testament passages is overcome in Proverbs' female imagery for divine wisdom.[81]

The Woman Wisdom of Proverbs is clearly presented in ways that combine transcendence with immanence. Woman Wisdom is intimately related to the activity of creation; it is she who is the giver of life (Prov. 4:13). She has attributes that McFague associates with the Holy Spirit in *The Body of God*. In Prov. 8:22–31, Woman Wisdom transcends creation and yet is within it as the instrument of its production.[82] She participates in the activity of creation. When God established the heavens, she was there, acting as the master craftswoman (Prov. 8:27, 30). The poem concludes with Woman Wisdom delighting in the newly crafted world and in the humans who live on it. This makes Woman Wisdom the center of a threefold relationship: she spans the distance between God, the world, and human beings. She is adamantly on the side of justice and opposed to evil; she has good advice and sound wisdom, insight, and strength; she works to establish just governance of the earth; her every decree is just (Prov. 8:13–16). The proper order of creation is safeguarded by those who love her. The chapter ends with these powerful words:

> Listen to me: happy are those who keep my ways. Hear instruction and be wise, and do not neglect it. Happy is the one who listens to me, watching daily at my gates, waiting beside my doors. For whoever finds me finds life and obtains favor from the Lord; but those who miss me injure themselves; all who hate me love death. (Prov. 8:32–36)

Woman Wisdom's close relationship with creation and her commitment to justice make her a key biblical symbol for ecofeminist theology. The listening that she calls for must include the wisdom voices not only of Euro-American and European ecofeminists but also of people from around the globe whose lives are most adversely affected by ecological destruction. The organic vision of Earth and the healing needed require us to listen to many voices. Therefore, we now listen to the concerns and insights of ecofeminist theologians of the Third World.

Christian Ecofeminist Theology in the Third World

The survival struggles of women in the Third World are far more acute and urgent than many people living in the First World can imagine. That the consumption and production patterns of First World nations contribute to the poverty and ecological crisis in the Third World is undeniable. First World countries like the United States and those in Western Europe use far more energy, especially fossil fuels, than do the Third World countries. Therefore, they generate far more carbon dioxide emissions and a disproportionate share of other greenhouse gases in comparison to their populations than do Third World nations. An even more alarming concern than the consumption of energy resources is the statistics for food consumption. A study conducted by the World Watch Institute shows that in the United States, 55 percent of adults are overweight and 25 percent are obese; in Germany and Great Britain these numbers are only slightly lower, and in the rest of Europe they are 40 to 45 percent. Affluent people in the United States alone spend nearly $33 million dollars annually on the weight-loss industry. In addition, the United Sates government pays farmers not to grow crops, to keep the prices for food competitive.[83]

The World Health Organization estimates that 1.1 billion people of the 6 billion on the planet are overweight and an alarming 1.1 billion are seriously malnourished. An additional two billion are on the edge of hunger on a nearly daily basis. A study of anemia among adults in Third World countries, such as India, Bangladesh, Afghanistan, and in sub-Saharan African and Central American countries, indicates that 25 percent of the men in these countries suffer from this disease. The numbers are far higher for women: 45 percent of adult women suffer from anemia, with an alarming 60 percent of pregnant women anemic. The rate of anemia is growing, even though some of these countries are exporting "cash crops" through multinational corporations.[84] Most cases of anemia and other diseases related to malnutrition can be remedied by a proper diet, one high in grain, fruits, and vegetables. According to the experts, a healthy diet could be provided by lessening the consumption of meat and a more equitable distribution of other food sources. If a better distribution of food were undertaken by First World countries, everyone would benefit. Obviously, both hunger and obesity increase susceptibility to illness, diminish the quality of life, and shorten the human life span.

We cannot divorce the problems associated with obesity and malnutrition from the fact that the affluent life style in the so-called developed countries is connected to patterns of patriarchal colonization. Most of the people in countries where malnutrition is life-threatening were colonized by European powers centuries earlier. The colonial practices of European countries are yet another manifestation of patriarchal, hierarchical dualisms. European whites assigned an inferior status to the indigenous people of color in the southern hemisphere. At the expense of the lives of indigenous people, of animals, plants, and the land upon which they lived, colonial development was undertaken as if the Europeans were on a divine mission. Patterns that define development and progress according to Western standards begun centuries ago continue in a modified form. The resources and peoples of the southern hemisphere may no longer be controlled by foreign governments, but they are controlled in many ways by multinational corporations with their headquarters in First World countries.

Earlier in this chapter an account of the grassroots "Tree Huggers" movement, the Chipko Andolan, of India was provided. India is one among many Third World nations that suffered under the yoke of colonialism and continues to bear the burden of its long-term effects. Through Vandana Shiva we heard the stories of two Chipko women, Chamundeyi and Itwari Devi. Although these women are twentieth-century Hindus, their concerns mirror a lament sounded by the prophet Jeremiah in the sixth century b.c.e.:

> Over the mountains, break out in cries of lamentation,
>   over the pasture lands, intone a dirge:
>   They are scorched, and no one crosses them,
>   unheard is the bleat of the flock;
>   birds of the air as well as beasts,
>   all have fled, and are gone.
>   . . . .
> Attention, tell the wailing women to come,
>   summon the best of them to sound the dirge.
>
> (Jer. 9:9, 16, nab)

Chamundeyi and Itwari Devi lament what is happening to their beloved forests; they, along with many other women, are sounding a dirge. But they are also doing much more.

Chipko women are acting as prophets, reminding their fellow citizens that a definition of progress adopted from India's former colonizers is not authentic progress for India. For one thing, the privatization of lands that earlier had been communally shared has become a major source of ecological degradation. The Chipko movement, with its strong prophetic elements, is a reminder that for women in India, as in most of the Third World, ecology is an issue of livelihood and survival. The very practical concerns of women of the Third World are far removed from the romanticizing tendencies of many Euro-American ecofeminists, including Christian ecofeminist theologians.

Prophetic calls for changes that honor precolonial values of indigenous culture characterize the ecofeminism of Third World theologians. This is true of theologian Teresia Hinga, an Agikuyu from Kenya. She has drawn attention in her writing to the problems resulting from British colonization of her homeland.[85] The problems are not completely different from those found in India. The colonizers built their power and prestige by imposing their societal patterns and cultural values onto the lands they colonized. Racism, based on supremacy of whites, and classism, based on the ownership of land, converged as ways of classifying human beings and their roles in society. Not only did the colonizers have a decidedly patriarchal understanding of race, but they also projected their patterns of power associated with the ownership of land by individuals onto the Agikuyu. When the British came to Gikuyuland in Kenya, they confiscated the land that the people had farmed for generations and made it "settlers' land." They also restricted future access to unworked land, making it "Crownland," the property of the British government. Disregard for the traditional land practices of the Africans had a highly negative impact on the religious ideas and practices of the people. Theirs was a double loss. The traditional sense of how they were related to the Creator was belittled and their traditional way of life with its relationship of respect for creatures was dismantled.

Hinga draws attention to life among the Agikuyu before colonization. The Agikuyu had a belief in Ngai, the creator and provider. They understood that Ngai alone had absolute rights over creation. They viewed the lands where they lived to be gifts to enjoy by divine favor. Ngai entrusted them with the responsibility of caring for the lands given to them. The people routinely performed rituals signifying that their use of the land was a privilege. When they harvested the crops, the Agikuyu offered prayers of thanksgiving to God.

Gikuyu belief does not allow for absolute individual ownership of land. Buying and selling of land are forbidden. People may have exclusive use of land only to the extent that they cultivate it to provide food for their families and community. There are no private-property rights. Hinga argues that these attitudes and practices were, on the whole, ecologically friendly. All this changed with the colonial invasion of Africa. Colonial powers took possession of the land, claiming absolute ownership, exploiting it and its mineral resources. They decided that the Agikuyu were squatters on the land that they had long believed God had given to them to sustain their lives. Emissaries of the government decided that the best of the land would be used for cash crops, such as coffee. The coffee was exported, with the colonizers benefiting from the profits. The development of large coffee plantations led to the destruction of ecologically sound farming practices that centered on food native to the area. Delicate ecosystems suffered. The Agikuyu people suffered. Their suffering continues even though the colonizing government has withdrawn.

Hinga takes note of the effects of the colonial land policy on women. Not only did racism result in the subjugation of Africans as inferior people, but also, gender attitudes operative in British family life profoundly affected Agikuyu women and their status in society. Colonial patriarchalization disempowered women. Before colonialism, the Gikuyu society was based on mutuality between the sexes.[86] Women and men worked together to produce goods and services for the community. Agikuyu women had a significant role to play in the political, economic, and religious life of the society.

Colonial abuse of land resulted in exploitation of women. The British assumed that women were chattels of their husbands, part of the property men owned. Consequently, when the colonial representatives negotiated for land, they consulted only men. Hinga writes, "This set a deadly precedent, particularly when colonial practice eventually became law. Most laws ignored the rights of women."[87] The dignity of women was diminished. They became subjugated as inferior human beings.

Hinga pointedly challenges the notion of the right to private land ownership, because it contributes to the desacralization of the land. Land ownership reduced the land to a mere resource to be exploited rather than being a gift from God for the whole community. This exploitation cannot be separated from the denigration of women, the hunger of their families, and the destruction of delicate ecosystems. Private ownership of land exclusively in the hands of males resulted in poverty and powerlessness for women. Land devoted to cash crops compounded the struggle for survival. When cash crops fail during drought years, famine results. If indigenous and more nourishing plants were grown instead of coffee, people would still have something to eat.

According to Hinga, the oppression of Kenya's women has not prevented them from exercising moral agency in the postcolonial era. Women are coming together in a common struggle to better their lot in all spheres of life, particularly in response to the ecological crises that directly affect them and their families. They are taking initiative to reclaim their traditional values. They are struggling together for land reclamation that will reverse the ecological degradation that worsened the chances of survival of their families and communities. These women, critical of the goals of the multinational corporations controlled from First World countries, are focusing their energy on what benefits the common good, both of the people and of the ecosystems in which they live. In short, they are lifting prophetic voices on behalf of God's creation.

Ecological problems that women face in India and Kenya due to colonialism also affect the lives of Latin American women. Latin America is a major source of raw materials and cheap human labor that supports the affluent lifestyle that most North Americans and many Western Europeans take for granted. In a recent article written by Venezuelan feminist theologian Gladys Parentelli, attention is given to the effects of the affluence of a few on the many in her country. Parentelli focuses on women of Latin America who live on the periphery of societies that are the legacies of Spanish and Portuguese colonialism. She writes,

> The conquerors did not take into account the beliefs and wisdom of the indigenous peoples; they forcibly changed their ancient agricultural systems, introducing plant strains and animal species that required other ecosystems for their cultivation and continued growth. In the long run, this assault has spawned a series of ecological disasters that have become glaringly apparent in the last half of this century.[88]

Among them are massive soil erosion, desertification as the result of overgrazing, and the destruction of vast forests.

All of these things are causes of the poverty that Latin Americans, especially women, endure. Parentelli draws attention to the concrete ways in which poor women — indigenous and black women — express benevolence to the Earth, even though they are themselves often abused and disregarded. In her opinion, poor women are the region's greatest resource.[89] Most poor women of Latin America survive through their own efforts, raising their children with no support from either their children's fathers or the government. In Venezuela, for example, 50 percent of all families are headed and supported by women.[90] She describes the survival strategies of such women:

> Women take advantage of the tiniest piece of earth, an empty can or jar to plant vegetables, spices, beans, even a fruit tree.... From fruit, they use skins and pits to make juices, jams and jellies or as food for their egg-laying hens.... Rarely would poor women throw away a coat, a dress, a pair of shoes.... When a dress or suit belonging to an adult can no longer be used, the best parts of the cloth can be used to make a dress or skirt for a little girl or a pair of pants for a little boy.[91]

Such practices are not sporadic. They reveal a response, an attitude, that is very deep in women, an attitude "at every moment and in every place of fostering practical love."[92]

Through practical love the poor women of Venezuela and other Latin American countries embody a solidarity with the Earth. They live lives that honor the delicate equilibrium of the ecosystems in which they participate.

Parentelli's report of the ecologically sound patterns of poor women pointedly challenges the myth that development and progress are measured in terms of runaway consumption of the earth's resources. This understanding, common in the United States and in other First World countries, is anti-ecological. Poor women of Venezuela and other Latin American countries are living wholesome and sustainable lifestyles without overconsuming the limited resources of the Earth. They embody a respectful connectedness to nature rather than a privileged position of superiority.

The accounts of Shiva, Hinga, and Parentelli of the situations in India, Kenya, and Venezuela illustrate well that responses to the ecological crisis by eco-feminists cannot be universalized according to European and Euro-American patterns. Nor can the resolutions to particular ecological crises in India, Kenya, and Venezuela be minted by ecofeminists in the First World. The issues addressed by Shiva, Hinga, and Parentelli differ greatly from those addressed by McFague and Ruether. Third World women are far less concerned with theoretical and speculative theology of a cosmic, earth-based God than are McFague and Ruether. An earth-based spirituality is more of a given among poor women in the Third World than for First World women. Although the God that the colonizers emphasized was dichotomized from nature, many people in India, Africa, and Latin America still retain a sense of the sacredness of creation. The belief held by the Agikuyu in a divine Spirit who not only owns the Earth but also is also ever present in it is not unique to this Kenyan tribe. Nor is the belief that nature is merely entrusted to humans and that private ownership is a fallacy particular to the Agikuyu. These beliefs, along with the emphasis on practical remedies to wasteful consumption, present Euro-American and European ecofeminist theologians with important challenges to their understandings of God and their resolve to live in ways that embody the holistic global vision that they espouse.

Conclusions

Rachel Carson, in *Silent Spring,* heralded the end of another frontier — the invigorating vista of Earth's limitless bounty for humans on their own terms — and revealed it to be illusion. Euro-American ecofeminists add vision to her prophetic "voice in the wilderness" by calling for a holistic, planetary perspective in which the domination of women, people of color, and the earth play no role. If this prophetic vision is ever to become a reality, steps must be taken to ensure a sustainable future for life on Earth, especially by First World people. For the ecofeminist, the enemy of a healthy planet has been diagnosed. It is ourselves, as long as we fail to work for the end of patriarchal systems wherever we find them.

To facilitate Christian commitment to a healthy planet, Christian feminist theologians have articulated a vision of a God-world relationship needed for our time of ecological crisis. Drawing on the Christian sources, ecofeminist theologians such as Sallie McFague and Rosemary Radford Ruether have constructed the God-world relationship in radically nonpatriarchal ways, capturing the ecofeminist emphasis on an organic vision of the Earth. McFague's theological metaphor "the body of God" and Ruether's sacramental Gaia artfully retrieve invaluable insights from Christian sources about the sacredness of creation.

Holistic images of the God-world relationship, no matter how artfully conceived, do not ensure that we remember who *we* are in the choices we make in our daily life. "The body of God" and the sacramental Gaia are symbols that give rise to thought. They remind us that we cannot elevate ourselves above any of our fellow participants in creation, whether they are people from a different social location or the other forms of plant and animal life with which we share our earthly home. To do so is to forget that we are merely a part of the web of life and not its weavers. Together, all creation, and not just ourselves, live and move and have our being in God (cf. Acts 17:28).

The "body of God" and the sacramental Gaia provide only a foundation for an authentic creation-centered mindfulness of the fact that humans share the same cosmic creation story with all the "holy things" God has created. We have no legitimate power over any of God's creatures. Building the new societal structures needed for Earth healing requires sustained critique of relationships of dominance. This is a necessary step toward mutual and life-enhancing relationships with the rest of God's creatures. Ecofeminist Christian theologies not only encourage us to new thinking about our relationships to all the other forms of life, but also challenge us to embrace these new relationships as agents for healing change.

Agency for change translates into transformative praxis that reverences creatures, including ourselves, because all are of God and in God. Christian ecofeminist praxis will take many forms, depending on geographical and social location. For many, especially those of us in North America, praxis begins with repentance for the ways in which we have contributed to the damage of Earth because we failed to appreciate its intrinsic worth as a sacred gift of God. Christian ecofeminist praxis calls us also to adopt an ethics of restraint from human promotion and greed, coupled with a commitment to nurture a creation-centeredness that seeks to live in right relationship with all that inhabit our common earthly home. Commitment to praxis urges us to follow the admonitions of Woman Wisdom: live rightly and seek justice (Prov. 8:20) for all the living, especially those most endangered. Christian ecofeminist praxis calls us, therefore, to oppose evil directed to any of God's creatures, whether an abused woman in our own family, a hungry child in Kenya, or a plant species on the verge of extinction in India. These forms of Christian ecofeminist praxis are of one piece with the formation of ecocommunities in which our worship of the triune God is not separated from our devotion to the Earth so richly adorned by the divine Three with beauty and diversity.

NOTES

1. Rachel Carson, *Silent Spring* (Greenwich, Conn.: Fawcett, 1962), 13–14.

2. Ibid., 257.

3. Ibid., 261.

4. The word "ecology" was coined by Ernst Haeckel (1834–1919) in approximately 1866. It is a combination of two Greek words: *oikos,* meaning "house, home," and *logos,* meaning "word, study, reason." Haeckel used the term to refer to the interaction of living organisms (principally animals) with their environment.

5. Hilary Rose argues that the initial dismissal of Rachel Carson shows the reluctance of male scientists to surrender their domination of the field. See her "Beyond Masculinist Realities: A Feminist Epistemology for the Sciences," in *Feminist Approaches to Science,* ed. Ruth Bleier (New York: Pergamon Press, 1986), 59.

6. Donald R. Strong and Robert W. Pemberton, "Biological Control of Invading Species — Risk and Reform," *Science* 288 (2000): 1969–70.

7. Robert Bonnie, Stephen Schwartzman, Michael Oppenheimer, and Janine Bloomfield, "Counting the Cost of Deforestation," *Science* 288 (2000): 1763–64.

8. Françoise d'Eaubonne uses the terms *ecoféminisme* and *ecologie-féminisme* in *Le féminisme ou la mort* (Paris: Pierre Horay, 1974); ET, "Ecofeminism or Death," in *New French Feminisms: An Anthology*, ed. and trans. Elaine Marks and Isabelle de Courtivron (Amherst, Mass.: Amherst University Press, 1980), 64–67. According to Carol J. Adams, d'Eaubonne first introduced these terms in 1972; see *Ecofeminism and the Sacred*, ed. Carol J. Adams (New York: Continuum, 1993), xi.

9. Carson, *Silent Spring,* 261. Since *Silent Spring* was written at a time when the generic term "man" was believed to adequately include men and women, it is likely that Carson meant "human beings" when she wrote "man."

10. Karen J. Warren, "The Power and the Promise of Ecological Feminism," *Environmental Ethics* 12 (1990): 132.

11. Maria Mies and Vandana Shiva, *Ecofeminism* (London: Zed Books, 1993), 14.

12. Ibid. See also Ynestra King, "The Ecology of Feminism and the Feminism of Ecology," in *Healing the Wounds: The Promise of Ecofeminism,* ed. Judith Plant (Philadelphia: New Society Publishers, 1989), 24.

13. Arne Naess, a Norwegian philosopher, is attributed with making the distinction between "shallow" and "deep" ecology. Environmentalists are "shallow" because their motivation is self-interest. In his opinion, environmentalists have focused too much on pollution and resource depletion and not enough on saving plant and animal species because of their intrinsic value. "Deep" ecologists are dedicated to "biospherical egalitarianism." See Arne Naess, "The Shallow and the Deep, Long-Range Ecology Movements: A Summary," *Inquiry* 16 (1973): 95–100; reprinted in *Radical Environmentalism: Philosophy and Tactics,* ed. Peter C. List (Belmont, Calif.: Wadsworth Publishing Co., 1993), 19–24.

14. For more on problems associated with hierarchical language, see King, "Ecology of Feminism," 24. King argues that there is no hierarchy in nature itself, but that a hierarchy developed by patriarchy has merely been imposed on nature. There is some merit to King's position, but I believe that critical realism requires me to acknowledge a biological complexity that lends itself to the use of the analytical term "hierarchy." For example, primates are more complex than mollusks. "Hierarchy" applied to biological complexity does not necessarily connote a value judgment, but its use must always be subject to a hermeneutics of suspicion. My perspective is different from that of ecofeminists, who reject outright any valid use of the term "hierarchy."

15. Ian Tattersall, *The Human Odyssey* (New York: Prentice Hall, 1993), 139.

16. Mies and Shiva, *Ecofeminism,* 3.

17. Ibid.

18. Aruna Gnanadason, "Chipko Movement," in *Dictionary of Third World Theologies,* ed. Virginia Fabella and R. S. Sugirtharajah (Maryknoll, N.Y.: Orbis Books, 2000), 40. See also Winthrop P. Carty and Elizabeth Lee, *Rhino Man and Other Environmentalists* (Washington, D.C.: Seven Locks Press, 1992), 29–31; Pamela Philipose, "Women Act: Women and Environmental Protection in India," in Plant, ed., *Healing the Wounds,* 67–70.

19. Aruna Gnanadason, "Women, Economy, and Ecology," in *Ecotheology: Voices from South and North,* ed. David G. Hallman (Geneva: World Council of Churches; Maryknoll, N.Y.: Orbis Books, 1994), 179.

20. Mies and Shiva, *Ecofeminism,* 249.

21. Ibid., 247.

22. Ibid., 250.

23. Ibid., 52.

24. Carolyn Merchant, *The Death of Nature: Women, Ecology, and the Scientific Revolution* (San Francisco: Harper & Row, 1980).

25. Ibid., 227–35, and passim.

26. Ibid., 165; see also 138–40.

27. Ibid., 190.

28. Ibid., 193.

29. Ibid., 254.

30. Ibid., 258.

31. Ibid., 260.

32. Ibid., 268.

33. Evelyn Fox Keller indicates that Barbara McClintock often used this phrase in describing her conception of scientific research. See Evelyn Fox Keller, *A Feeling for the Organism: The Life and Work of Barbara McClintock* (San Francisco: W. H. Freeman and Co., 1983), 198. For the significance of McClintock's approach to science for Christian ecofeminist theology, see Anne Clifford, "Feminist Perspectives on Science and Their Implications for an Ecological Theology of Creation," *Journal of Feminist Studies of Religion* 8 (1992): 65–90; reprinted in *Readings in Ecology and Feminist Theology,* ed. Mary Heather MacKinnon and Moni McIntyre (Kansas City, Mo.: Sheed and Ward, 1995), 334–60.

34. Fox Keller, *Feeling for the Organism,* 198–204.

35. Evelyn Fox Keller, *Reflections on Gender and Science* (New Haven: Yale University Press, 1985), 167–72.

36. Charlene Spretnak, "Toward an Ecofeminist Spirituality," in Plant, ed., *Healing the Wounds,* 128.

37. Starhawk (Miriam Simos), *The Spiral Dance: A Rebirth of the Ancient Religion of the Great Goddess,* 2nd ed. (San Francisco: HarperSanFrancisco, 1989), 10.

38. Starhawk (Miriam Simos), "Witchcraft and Women's Culture," in *Womanspirit Rising: A Feminist Reader in Religion,* ed. Carol Christ and Judith Plaskow (San Francisco: Harper & Row, 1979), 263.

39. Starhawk, *The Spiral Dance,* 10.

40. Ibid., 11.

41. Starhawk, "Feminist, Earth-Based Spirituality and Ecofeminism," in Plant, ed., *Healing the Wounds,* 175–76.

42. Ibid., 177.

43. Ibid.

44. Spretnak, "Ecofeminist Spirituality," 128. See also idem, "Ecofeminism: Our Roots and Flowering," in *Reweaving the World,* ed. Irene Diamond and Gloria Feman Orenstein (San Francisco: Sierra Club Books, 1990), 5.

45. In an earlier essay, Spretnak draws attention to how God is talked about by the Christian Right. She quotes a representative: "Pray that God will not unleash His wrath on this nation before we, as His soldiers, have the opportunity to turn this immoral and unthinkable evil [Planned Parenthood] from His eyes" (Charlene Spretnak, "The Christian Right's 'Holy War' against Feminism," in *The Politics of Women's Spirituality: Essays on the Rise of Spiritual Power within the Feminist Movement,* ed. Charlene Spretnak [Garden City, N.Y.: Anchor Books, 1982], 471).

46. Charlene Spretnak, "Embracing the Body," in *States of Grace: The Recovery of Meaning in the Postmodern Age* (San Francisco: HarperCollins, 1991), 114–54.

47. See Marti Khell's reasons for abandoning Christianity in "Ecofeminism and Deep Ecology: Reflections on Identity and Difference," in *Covenant for a New Creation,* ed. Carol S. Robb and Carl J. Casebolt (Maryknoll, N.Y.: Orbis Books, 1991), 145.

48. Sallie McFague is the Carpenter Professor of Theology and former Dean of the Vanderbilt Divinity School of Vanderbilt University in Nashville.

49. Sallie McFague, *Speaking in Parables: A Study in Metaphor and Theology* (Philadelphia: Fortress, 1975), 16.

50. Sallie McFague, *Metaphorical Theology: Models of God in Religious Language* (Philadelphia: Fortress, 1982), 4–7.

51. Ibid., 19. For more on the metaphorical nature of God-language, see chapter 3 of the present volume.

52. Ibid., 2, 7–10.

53. Sallie McFague, *Models of God: Theology for an Ecological, Nuclear Age* (Philadelphia: Fortress, 1987), 7. Among the women whose writing on Goddess religion and witchcraft she cites is Starhawk (p. 189 n. 10); she does not mention Spretnak.

54. Ibid., 11.

55. Ibid., 68.

56. Ibid., 72.

57. Sallie McFague, *The Body of God: An Ecological Theology* (Minneapolis: Fortress, 1993), 21.

58. Ibid., 149.

59. Ibid., 157.

60. Sallie McFague, *Super, Natural Christians: How We Should Love Nature* (Minneapolis: Fortress, 1997), 1.

61. Ibid., 36–39.

62. Rosemary Radford Ruether, *New Woman, New Earth: Sexist Ideologies and Human Liberation* (New York: Seabury Press, 1975), 204. Among Ruether's other books addressing ecofeminist theology are *Ecofeminisms: Symbolic and Social Constructions between the Oppression of Women and the Domination of Nature* (Charlotte: University of North Carolina Press, 1991); *Gaia and God: An Ecofeminist Theology of Earth Healing* (San Francisco: HarperCollins, 1992); *Women Healing Earth: Third World Women on Ecology, Feminism, and Religion* (Maryknoll, N.Y.: Orbis Books, 1996), for which she is the editor.

63. See James Lovelock, *Gaia: A New Look at Life on Earth* (Oxford: Oxford University Press, 1995).

64. Ruether, *Gaia and God,* 5.

65. Ibid., 4. She cites Spretnak, *Politics of Women's Spirituality,* 273 n. 5.

66. Ruether, *Women Healing Earth,* 5.

67. Ruether, *Gaia and God,* 21. One of the first to voice this criticism against biblical creation faith was Lynn White Jr., "The Historical Roots of Our Ecological Crisis," *Science* 155 (1967): 1203–7; reprinted in *Readings in Ecology and Feminist Theology,* ed. Mary Heather MacKinnon and Moni McIntyre (Kansas City, Mo.: Sheed and Ward, 1995), 25–35.

68. Ruether, *Gaia and God,* 21.

69. See Anne Clifford, "Foundations for an Ecological Theology of God," in *And God Saw That It Was Good,* ed. Drew Christianson and Walter Grazer (Washington, D.C.: The United States Catholic Conference, 1996), 19–46.

70. Carolyn Merchant, *The Death of Nature,* 170. Merchant cites "Novum Organum," part 2 in Francis Bacon, *Works,* 4:247, and "Valerius Terminus," *Works,* 3:217, 219, ed. James Spedding, Robert Leslie Ellis, and Douglas Heath (London: Longmans Green,

1870), and "The Masculine Birth of Time," in *The Philosophy of Francis Bacon,* ed. Benjamin Farrington (Liverpool: Liverpool University Press, 1964), 62 n. 13, 317.

71. Richard J. Clifford, "Genesis 1–3: Permission to Exploit Nature?" *Bible Today* (1988): 136. Clifford's interpretation of Genesis 1 in light of the context of the first eleven chapters of Genesis reflects a belief, widely shared by Old Testament scholars, that these chapters should not be interpreted in isolation from one another.

72. Ibid., 135.

73. Ruether, *Gaia and God,* 211.

74. Ibid., 211–14.

75. Ibid., 232.

76. Ibid., 233.

77. Ibid., 254.

78. McFague, *Metaphorical Theology,* 5.

79. McFague, *The Body of God,* 184.

80. See Prov. 8:22–31; Job 38–41; Sirach 24; Wisd. 7:17–22; 8:6; 13:3–4. For a more thorough treatment of the fruitfulness of Woman Wisdom for ecofeminism, see Clifford, "Feminist Perspectives on Science."

81. Claudia V. Camp, *Wisdom and the Feminine in the Book of Proverbs* (Decatur, Ga.: Almond Press, 1985), 289.

82. As already noted in chapter 3, New Testament writings, such as the Colossians hymn cited above and the first chapter of John's Gospel, incorporate many of her traits into their understanding of Jesus Christ. Like Woman Wisdom, Christ is said to be the firstborn of all creation; like Woman Wisdom, in Christ all things in heaven and on earth were created.

83. Gary Gardner and Brian Halwell, "Escaping Excess," *World Watch* 13 (2000): 25.

84. Ibid., 26–27. Gardner and Halwell cite these statistics from a study conducted by the World Health Organization. They attribute the higher rate of anemia among women to the custom of providing food for men, for fathers and sons, before any women in the household.

85. Teresia Hinga, "The Gikuyu Theology of Land and Environmental Justice," in Ruether, ed., *Women Healing Earth,* 172–84.

86. Ibid., 179.

87. Ibid., 180.

88. Gladys Parentelli, "Latin America's Poor Women, Inherent Guardians of Life," in Ruether, ed., *Women Healing Earth,* 30–31.

89. Ibid., 29–36.

90. Ibid., 32 n. 8, 37.

91. Ibid., 33–35.

92. Ibid., 36.

QUESTIONS FOR REFLECTION AND DISCUSSION

1. Do you believe that the ecofeminist argument that a connection exists between a patriarchal domination of nature and of women is valid?

2. What are your understandings of hierarchical dualism and egalitarian holism? Give an example that illustrates each of these approaches to reality.

3. What is your response to the Chipko (Tree Huggers) movement in India? What feelings rose in you when you read words of Chamundeyi and Itwari Devi?

4. Do you agree with Carolyn Merchant that science is not "value free," and that it is important to pay attention to language patterns and the values they promote?

5. Is envisioning "Nature" as a sacred home something to which you are attracted?

6. Sallie McFague's major contribution to Christian ecofeminist theology is her metaphor of the world as the "body of God." Do you find the notion that the Earth is embodied by God thought provoking? In your opinion, does her metaphor mutually help Christian theology and feminism to recover the sacredness of the Earth?

7. How does Rosemary Radford Ruether connect Gaia with God? Explain her understandings of each. Is her sacramental approach to the Earth a helpful basis for the "earth healing" she calls for?

8. Have you ever thought about God, the Creator, as the absolute owner of the land who entrusts it to those persons who actually need it to sustain life? How might life be different if the Agikuyu understanding of land ownership described by Teresia Hinga were a worldwide practice?

9. If you are a North American, you are part of the 25 percent of the world's people whose lifestyle consumes 75 percent of all energy used. Knowing that the world's resources are limited, what is your response to this statistic? Does this statistic have any bearing on the lives of poor women of Latin America described by Gladys Parentelli?

AREAS FOR EXPLORATION

1. An important element of ecofeminism is grassroots response to ecological problems. Do an ecological audit of your local area or university. Are there ecological concerns to which you can respond?

2. An ecofeminist consciousness with its stress on an organic and sacred vision of the earth has practical, concrete implications for how we live. Rosemary Radford Ruether has shared her personal experience of a heightened awareness of the patterns of consumption in the United States that affect the lives of people and the health of an ecosystem in Mexico. In *Women Healing Earth* (p. 5), she writes,

> We must recognize the ways in which the devastation of the earth is an integral part of our appropriation of the goods of the earth whereby a wealthy minority can enjoy strawberries in winter, winged to their glittering supermarkets by a global food procurement system, while those who pick and pack strawberries lack the money for bread and are dying from pesticide poisoning.

Interview some of your friends and acquaintances about how their patterns of consumption of goods may be affecting people in distant lands, especially Third World countries. Look at the labels in your clothes to see where they are made, and consider who made them and under what working conditions they were made.

3. Ecofeminism invites Christians to rethink the Christian tradition to recover in it values that support life. Investigate religions other than Christianity for what they might contribute to a sense of human connectedness to all of creation as a web of life.

RECOMMENDED READINGS

Adams, Carol J., ed. *Ecofeminism and the Sacred.* New York: Continuum, 1993.

Clifford, Anne. "Feminist Perspectives on Science and Their Implications for an Ecological Theology of Creation." *Journal of Feminist Studies of Religion* 8 (1992): 65–90. Reprint, pp. 334–60 in *Readings in Ecology and Feminist Theology,* ed. Mary Heather MacKinnon and Moni McIntyre. Kansas City, Mo.: Sheed and Ward, 1995.

————. "When Being Human Becomes Truly Earthly: An Ecofeminist Proposal for Solidarity." Pp. 173–89 in *In the Embrace of God: Feminist Approaches to Christian Anthropology,* ed. Ann O'Hara Graff. Maryknoll, N.Y.: Orbis Books, 1995.

Diamond, Irene, and Gloria F. Orenstein, eds. *Reweaving the World: The Emergence of Ecofeminism.* San Francisco: Sierra Club, 1990.

Gaard, Greta, ed. *Ecofeminism: Women, Animals, Nature.* Philadelphia: Temple University Press, 1993.

Gebara, Ivone. *Longing for Running Water: Ecofeminism and Liberation,* trans. David Molineaux. Minneapolis: Fortress, 1999.

Johnson, Elizabeth A. *Women, Earth, and Creator Spirit.* Mahwah, N.J.: Paulist Press, 1993.

McFague, Sallie. *The Body of God: An Ecological Theology.* Minneapolis: Fortress, 1993.

MacKinnon, Mary Heather, and Moni McIntyre, eds. *Readings in Ecology and Feminist Theology.* Kansas City, Mo.: Sheed and Ward, 1995.

Merchant, Carolyn. *Earthcare: Women and the Environment.* New York: Routledge, 1995.

————. *Ecological Revolutions: Nature, Gender, and Science in New England.* Chapel Hill: University of North Carolina Press, 1989.

Ruether, Rosemary Radford. *Gaia and God: An Ecofeminist Theology of Earth Healing.* San Francisco: HarperCollins, 1992.

Smith, Pamela. "The Ethics of Ecofeminism." Pp. 19–33 in *What Are They Saying about Environmental Ethics?* Mahwah, N.J.: Paulist Press, 1997.

Warren, Karen J., ed. *Ecofeminism: Women, Culture, Nature.* Bloomington: Indiana University Press, 1997.

Epilogue

> Religion [Christianity], pure source of comfort in this vale of tears! How
> has thy clear stream been muddied by the dabblers, who have presumptu-
> ously endeavored to confine in one narrow channel, the living waters that
> ever flow towards God — the sublime ocean of existence.
>
> — MARY WOLLSTONECRAFT[1]

Mary Wollstonecraft wrote these words at the end of the eighteenth century,
yet, I find in them descriptive metaphors with the potential for describing major
elements of this introduction to Christian feminist theology. With considerable
energy, feminist theologians in almost every part of the globe have been working to release the living waters of faith from the confines of the narrow channels
in which it once flowed. Feminism is modifying Christian theology by reconstructing every facet of Christian belief in ways that are attentive to women's
experiences and voices and committed to the freeing truth incarnate in Jesus
Christ. In this book, only some of the major facets of Christian belief addressed
extensively in the second and third waves of feminism have been given attention. It seems appropriate, by way of summary, to map the major channels
of living water that feminist theologians have both discovered and constructed
during the past forty years.

In a first channel, the narrowness of theology received sustained attention
when fundamental changes in women's self-understanding led some Christian
women involved in feminism's second wave to recognize that how a woman
regards herself as a woman is interrelated with how she experiences God and
relates to the church. These women drew attention to the virtual invisibility
of women in Christianity and pursued advanced degrees in theology to give
women's perspectives on Christian beliefs an opportunity to be heard. Women
were long ignored in Christian theology. The silence imposed on them was not
of God. This realization spread quickly among Christian women during feminism's second wave. Adrienne Rich's words capture the dynamic of Christian
feminism in the mid-1970s: "The sleepwalkers are coming awake, and for the
first time this awakening has a collective reality."[2]

A second channel of living water, closely related to the first, was the collective recognition among feminist theologians that when women are included,
especially when they are the specific focus of biblical and Christian texts, they
are often treated in ways that diminish their human dignity. This led women to
the question, Were these texts of God? This line of criticism soon flowed into
a new and third channel: the search for a useable past, not only to add women

261

to the all-male theological "hall of fame," but also to draw attention to those sources that support the full human dignity and equality of women with men.

In company with these channels, methodological concerns about how to navigate in already existing and new waters emerged. Not all Christian feminists find the issue of theological method attractive or important. Some have even dismissed it as a manifestation of "masculine thinking" in which feminists should not participate. I disagree with that position, and in this book I have consistently addressed and applied methodologies developed by feminist scholars. Clarity about the methodology guiding theological reflection not only enables Christian feminist theology to stand against accusations of naivety, but also challenges those who seek to suppress feminist theology to provide valid reasons for their positions.

Of particular methodological concern to Christian feminist theology is language. Through language, humans create powerful symbols, and in turn, human attitudes and values are created and perpetuated by these symbols. Language conditions how we think and often what we think. Of particular importance for Christian feminist theology is language about God, which is why a whole chapter and substantial sections of additional chapters were devoted to imagery and symbols of God. There is no question of greater importance in Christian feminist theology today. As Elizabeth Johnson often repeats, "The symbol of God functions."[3] It gives rise to thought that either supports or discourages human flourishing, and either encourages or stymies agency for justice.

Understanding which God symbols function best to promote positive transformation requires "testing the spirits." From a methodological standpoint, a logical way to weigh the pros and cons of important feminist concerns, whether they involve God-language, biblical teaching, church participation, Marian spirituality, or ecological wholeness, is to apply feminist hermeneutics. Throughout this book, hermeneutics of suspicion and of remembrance have been extensively applied with the hope that their repeated use might encourage its readers to adopt them as "habits of the mind."

This brings us to an additional channel with multiple branches: recognition and celebration of the diversity of the third wave of feminism. This channel is itself a methodological challenge to Christian feminist theology because it requires broadening goals and widening the circle of discourse. It calls all feminists to work to end patriarchy in all of its manifestations, not only with women but also with men. It means working toward solidarity and seeking remedies to end not only sexism but also racism, classism, ageism, heterosexism, and naturism.

In writing this book, I have discovered that it is much easier to speak of taking diversity into account in social location than it is to actually do it. Throughout the book's composition, I have agonized over how to appropriately include the voices of non-Euro-American women. Should I simply provide the reader with extensive quotations? At times I have done just that. Should I try to provide very careful summaries of positions of my nonwhite colleagues and hope that they will be sufficiently adequate to encourage my readers to seek out the primary sources? This has also been a recurring pattern. At the risk of treating non-Euro-American contributions inadequately, I chose not to be silent about them. My neglect of women from social locations other than my own would only contribute to their invisibility and result in making me complicit in their continued oppression. Let me be clear about one thing, however: incorporating the voices of womanist, *mujerista,* Latina, African, and Asian voices at the end of each chapter does not mean that I value them less than Euro-American and European voices, but that treating them in this order was dictated by my prior decision to give the history of Christian feminist theology priority over other possible organizing themes.

I end this book with a very simple hope that Christian feminist theologians in every locale around the globe will continue the work already begun in fidelity to the freeing truth of the gospel. In fidelity to this freeing truth, may these theologies channel faith's living waters toward God for the sake of the full human flourishing of all people and for the good of the Earth and its many living creatures.

NOTES

1. Mary Wollstonecraft, *A Vindication of the Rights of Women* (1792; reprint, London: J. M. Dent; Rutland, Vt.: Charles E. Tuttle, 1995), 184.

2. Adrienne Rich, "When We Dead Awaken: Writing as Re-Vision," in *Adrienne Rich's Poetry,* ed. Barbara Charlesworth Gelpi and Albert Gelpi (New York: W. W. Norton, 1975), 90.

3. Elizabeth A. Johnson, *She Who Is: The Mystery of God in Feminist Theological Discourse* (New York: Crossroad, 1992), 38.

Glossary

The terms in the glossary are indicated with an asterisk and bold type in the text on the first significant appearance.

abolitionist: Someone who seeks the termination of slavery. Abolitionists have often condemned slavery on religious grounds with a commitment to emancipate those who have been sold into slavery.

Adam: Hebrew for "human earth creature." Its roots lie in Genesis 2 and God creating the first human creature from the soil or dust of the earth. It is the name by which the Bible identifies the first male human.

anchoress: A woman who chooses to live a solitary life of prayer in small rooms attached to a church. During the late Middle Ages people visited anchoresses for spiritual guidance.

androcentrism: Literally, it means "man- or male-centered." Androcentrism results in making what is associated with being male central in every facet of life; being male is regarded as normative, while being female is regarded as the exception to the norm.

apocalyptic: From the Greek for "uncover." Used in reference to the Bible it denotes crisis literature that uncovers the secrets of the end of time and the beginning of a new age.

Apocrypha: From the Greek for "concealed" or "hidden," refers to those books not part of the canon of Hebrew Scriptures but found in early Christian versions of the Old Testament (based on the Greek Septuagint). The Apocrypha includes 1 and 2 Esdras, Tobit, Judith, Wisdom of Solomon, Sirach, Baruch, 1 and 2 Maccabees, the Letter of Jeremiah, and additions to Esther and Daniel. During the Reformation, Protestants set aside a special section for them in their Bibles, following Martin Luther's decision to incorporate only books written in Hebrew into the Old Testament canon. The Roman Catholic and Eastern Orthodox churches regard these books to be "deuterocanonical," meaning secondarily canonical, and do not locate them in a special section of their Bibles. To them Eastern Orthodox churches add additional books, such as 3 and 4 Maccabees.

apostles: From the Greek for "one sent." In the New Testament it is used in reference to the circle of friends who worked closely with Jesus in his ministry.

baptism: A ritual blessing using water modeled after Jesus' own blessing by John (Mark 1:9–11); according to Christian belief, through this ritual action or sacrament a person is incorporated into the Christian community, bringing with membership in the church the forgiveness of sin and the grace of salvation. Although the Christian churches have different perspectives on the sacraments, there are no fundamental disagreements on baptism among the Christian churches.

basic ecclesial communities: In Spanish, *comunidades eclesiales de base,* and in Portuguese, *comunidades eclesias de base.* Small groups of Christians, especially poor families at the bottom of the socioeconomic pyramid, who gather regularly to pray, to read the Bible, to celebrate their faith, and to plan actions to be taken by the community that will benefit the poor.

Bible: From the Greek for "books." Composed over a span of many centuries, it is a library of books in two major divisions: the Old Testament and the New Testament. This collection is often referred to as the Word of God, Sacred Scripture, or the canon.

canon: From the Greek for "measuring rod." Used of the Bible it refers to the books that the Christian churches agree to accept into their sacred libraries as divine revelation.

canonize: To publicly recognize the holiness of a person's life and appropriately honor the person for what she or he accomplished with the help of God's grace. Canonization of a saint in the Roman Catholic Church is a gradual process: (1) papal declaration that the candidate is "venerable"; (2) papal proclamation that the candidate is beatified, or "blessed"; and (3) papal canonization of the person as a saint. Roughly 75 percent of the canonized saints are men; the remaining 25 percent are women.

catechism: A handbook of religious beliefs expressed in question and answer form.

communion of saints: From the Latin *communio sanctorum,* meaning "fellowship of holy persons" (also, depending on the context, referring to "sacred things"). In the Roman Catholic Church, the communion of saints includes the canonized saints, the blessed dead, and the church as the people of God.

conscientization: The first step in liberation theology, it is the process of raising awareness and analyzing the causes of oppression.

contemplative prayer: Derived from the Latin word *templum,* referring to time and space; it is a form of communing with God in which one places oneself in the presence of God to become more deeply united with God in love. Such communing with God may be facilitated in a formal way by imaginatively entering a biblical narrative, placing oneself in the time and place of the unfolding story, while being attentive to how it touches one's mind and heart. In a less formal way, contemplative prayer is an awareness of the presence of God in creation and in the midst of the events of daily life.

Council of Trent: The nineteenth ecumenical council of the Roman Catholic Church, which met intermittently between 1545 and 1563. It was called to clarify issues raised by Protestant Reformers, particularly Martin Luther. Among the major decrees are those that deal with the number and nature of sacraments.

creed: Derived from the Latin *credo,* meaning "I believe." A creed summarizes the beliefs agreed upon by a particular church.

cultural feminism: The form of feminism that seeks to humanize society by emphasizing the special contribution that women can make to create a better world because women tend to be more nurturing, less competitive, and more collaborative than men.

denomination: Derived from the Latin word *denominare,* meaning "to name." It is used in reference to a specific Christian group or church whose members have the same or similar beliefs and social organization and engage in similar practices. A denomination acknowledges that it is one expression of a larger whole, a greater unity shared by others. In the annual *Yearbook of American and Canadian Churches* over two hundred denominations are listed. Similar religious groups, like the many Baptist bodies in the United States, constitute a denominational family; the largest denomination within the Baptist family is the Southern Baptist Convention.

disciples: Those who follow Jesus and carry out his mission. Some Christian feminists envision the church as a "discipleship of equals."

dualism: From the Latin *duo,* meaning "two." It is a construction of the world in terms of binary oppositions: male/female; white/black; rational/emotional.

ecclesiology: The name given to the study of the Christian church with focus on doctrine (teaching) about its organization and lines of authority.

ecofeminism: Specifies the connection between the domination of women and other forms of social domination (e.g., racism and economic classism) and the exploitation of nonhuman nature.

Elohim: Hebrew for "God" or "gods."

Epistles: From the Greek for "letter." In the New Testament, Epistles are letters of instruction; of the twenty-seven books of the New Testament, twenty-one are letters.

etiology (also aetiology): In the context of the study of literary genres of the Bible, an explanatory story, rich in symbolism, that provides responses to questions about the basic causes of the present experience of the people. In the case of Genesis 2–3, responses are provided to questions regarding why animals are not suitable companions for humans, why men and women leave the homes of their parents and enter conjugal relationships, and why there is good and evil.

Eve: The first woman (Gen. 2:21–22). The meaning of the name is somewhat obscure, but its resemblance to the Hebrew word for "living" relates to the identification of Eve as the "mother of all the living" (Gen. 3:20).

femicide: The killing of women and female children because a particular society attaches very little value to the life of female persons.

feminism: In the broadest sense, a theory about women. It is used commonly to describe the discontent of women about the many manifestations of sexism directed to them and the struggle by women for social, political, and economic equality. As used in this book it refers to a coordinated set of ideas and a practical plan of action rooted in women's critical awareness of how a culture controlled in meaning and action by men, for their own advantage, oppresses women and dehumanizes men.

first wave of feminism: Traceable to the mid-nineteenth century in Western Europe and North America; in the United States the first event of major significance was the Women's Rights Convention, held in Seneca Falls, New York, in 1848. It continued until women gained the right to vote, which in the United States occurred in 1920 with the passage of the Nineteenth Amendment to the Constitution.

First World: A common name for those countries that have higher levels of average per capita income, access to education, and technology. In these countries, nutrition levels are high and infant mortality low. These countries are located in North America (Canada and the United States) and Europe, and also include Japan, Australia, and New Zealand.

gender: Socially acquired roles designated as appropriate to either males or females by a society at a given time in its history. The association of traits such as aggressiveness and competitiveness with males and nurturing and passivity with females is due to cultural gender stereotyping and is not biologically determined.

gnostic: From the Greek *gnōsis,* meaning "knowledge." A variety of religious movements of the early Christian period that claimed to have special knowledge from which came salvation.

gospel: English translation of the Greek for "good news." In the New Testament it refers to the message proclaimed by Jesus and his followers. Capitalized, it refers to the books in the New Testament called Matthew, Mark, Luke, and John.

Gospels: *See* gospel.

hermeneutics: A word derived from the name of the mythological Greek messenger Hermes. It refers to interpretation, especially the principles and methods of interpreting literature such as the Bible. Feminist hermeneutics is the theory and art of interpretation in the interest of women's full humanity.

incarnation: The Christian doctrine that teaches that the second person of the Trinity assumed flesh and shared our human history in Jesus, the Christ, as both fully divine and fully human.

liberal feminism: The form of feminism that holds that female subordination is rooted in legal constraints that exclude or block women's full and equal participation in the so-called public world. Liberal feminism tends to emphasize women's rights and individual freedoms.

liberation theology: Theological response to social oppression guided by the gospel message of Jesus, who proclaimed liberty to captives. It is also reflection on liberating praxis, concrete actions undertaken to transform society. Liberation theology arose first in Latin America and now has a plurality of forms: black (U.S.), womanist (U.S.), *mujerista* (U.S.), *minjung* (Korea), and liberation theologies in most Third World countries (e.g., South Africa) and of indigenous peoples (e.g., Native American and Australian aboriginal).

liturgy: The form of public worship of God by believers, especially the celebration of the Eucharist.

Mary: The mother of Jesus. The Gospels of Matthew (ch. 1) and Luke (chs. 1–2) depict her as a young, unmarried woman blessed by God with the conception of the divine Son, Jesus. Early Christian doctrine called her a "virgin" and "Mother of God" (Greek, *theotokos*). A major element of critique for feminist theology today is the Marian symbol of the obedient "New Eve," who contrasts sharply with the first Eve.

Mary Magdalene: A woman who accompanied Jesus in his missionary journeys, accompanying him even to the cross. On the third day after Jesus' death, she found his tomb empty and was sent to the other disciples with the message. She is regarded as the first apostle of the good news of Jesus' resurrection (see John 20:11–18).

misogyny: Male hatred of females, often involving male violence directed to women.

Moses: Leader of the Jewish people to whom God revealed the divine name YHWH (Yahweh) and gave the law of the covenant on Mount Sinai. Under his leadership the Jews were liberated from slavery in Egypt.

mujerista: Coined by Ada María Isasi-Díaz, it refers to a Hispanic or Latina woman who struggles to liberate herself not only as an individual, but also as a participant in a Hispanic community.

nativism: An extreme form of American nationalism that expresses itself as intense opposition to an immigrant minority on the grounds that it is foreign. In the nineteenth century it focused on European immigrants, most of whom were Roman Catholic.

New Testament: Means "new covenant"; it is the second collection of sacred books of the Christian Bible. The use of the term can be traced to Tertullian (160–230 C.E.) in the West and Origen (185–254 C.E.) in the East. Although there are some disagreements about what books should be included in the New Testament, most Christian churches accept the twenty-seven books listed by

Athanasius of Alexandria in the fourth century. The major types of literature in the New Testament are Gospels and Acts, Epistles (Letters), and Revelation.

Old Testament: Means "old covenant"; it is the first major collection of sacred books of the Christian Bible. The use of the term can be traced to Tertullian (160–230 C.E.) in the West and Origen (185–254 C.E.) in the East. The Protestant pre-Christian Scriptures include the same thirty-nine books of the Bible of Judaism (the Hebrew Tanakh); the Roman Catholic Old Testament includes several other books and additions to books found in the Greek Septuagint; the Eastern churches' Old Testament is similar to the Roman Catholic Old Testament, with some Eastern churches including additional texts such as 3 and 4 Maccabees. The major types of literature of the Old Testament are law, narrative, prophecy, wisdom reflections, poetry, proverbs, and apocalypses.

ordination: The sacrament of orders by which ministers of the church are appointed in a sacramental manner, usually by the laying on of hands by a bishop or church authority, for permanent ministry within a Christian church.

Our Lady of Guadalupe: The apparition of Mary, the mother of Jesus, to an indigenous Native American in Mexico. Mexican and Mexican American feminists envision her to be the representative of oppressed women. She is associated with the biblical preferential option for the poor and is the basis for a spirituality of liberation from all forms of injustice. (Comparable apparitions can be found elsewhere in the Third World — for example, Purisima of Nicaragua, the Black Aparecida of Brazil, and the Black Madonna of the Philippines.)

paradigm: A symbolic framework that underlies the shared assumptions and understandings of reality of a particular society.

Paraclete: The Gospel of John's name for the Holy Spirit, the third person in the Blessed Trinity; the English noun form of a Greek verb *parakaléo* (meaning I exhort, I comfort). In John's Gospel Jesus promises his disciples that when he departs he will send them another Paraclete (NRSV "Advocate") to remain with them (John 14:16–17, 26; 16:7).

paternity: The state of being a father.

paternalism: Governing in a fatherly way; a male relating to his adult children or other persons over whom he has authority without respect for their autonomy and equality with him.

patriarchy: Literally, "the rule of the father." It is a system of legal, economic, and political relations that legitimate and enforce relations of dominance in a society. Historically, it has resulted in a hierarchically ordered society in which men have power. Patriarchy is commonly regarded as male dominance over women, but it is also manifested in the dominance of certain males over other males, and certain females over other females, particularly when the persons dominated are from a racial or ethnic minority and/or from a lower economic class.

praxis: A word used in liberation theologies, usually referring to transformative action, guided by the example of Jesus, taken in response to oppression. Its goal is the achievement of social justice and freedom from those things that dehumanize people.

radical feminism: That form of feminism that argues that patriarchy is the root cause not only of women's oppression but also of all forms of hierarchical dualism that result in women's secondary status in society.

reconstructionist Christian feminist theology: Theology done by Christian feminists who draw attention to patriarchal influences on Christianity that result in oppression and injustice. In this theology, the Bible and the Christian tradition are studied with interest in uncovering their manifestations of patriarchy and androcentrism ("hermeneutics of suspicion") and also as sources that support the struggle for liberation of women and other oppressed groups ("hermeneutics of remembrance").

reformist Christian feminist theology: Theology that reflects a commitment to the Bible and Christian tradition, opposition to gender bias, and a desire for greater participation in existing church structures.

revolutionary feminist theology: Influenced by radical feminism, this is a type of theology that rejects the Hebrew and Christian Scriptures and their male deity as sources of patriarchal oppression, and centers its reflection on Goddess traditions and the celebration of women's unique talents and abilities.

sacrament: Translates the Latin *sacramentum* and the Greek *mysterion.* It is (1) a significant symbol or religious rite through which participants experience the Paschal mystery of Jesus Christ and the offer of salvation (e.g., baptism and Eucharist); (2) the mystery of the kingdom of God fulfilled in the church of Jesus Christ.

saints: Persons who manifest the holiness of God in their lives. In Judaism, saints are persons who live in accord with the sacred covenant with desire for communion with the living God. In Christianity and Islam, saints are persons who respond to God's call to holiness (Christians) or submit to Allah's will (Islam) by loving God (Allah) and creatures. They are also those persons who have died who are memorialized and/or venerated by Christians and Muslims for their exemplary lives of holiness. Roman Catholics, Eastern Christians (Orthodox and Byzantine), Anglican Communion churches, and most Lutherans venerate saints; all the Protestant churches influenced by Calvin and the Anabaptist traditions do not.

Second Vatican Council: Commonly known as Vatican II. An international assembly of Roman Catholic bishops and theologians, called by Pope John XXIII, that met in Rome from 1962 to 1965. During the council, sixteen documents were written that articulated the Catholic Church's self-understanding and mission in the world.

second wave of feminism: Traceable to the adoption by the United Nations in 1967 of the "Declaration of the Elimination of Discrimination against Women"; in the United States its beginnings are closely associated with Euro-American women's advocacy for equal rights in conjunction with the civil rights movement of the 1960s and early 1970s. Among the earliest significant theological works was Mary Daly's *The Church and the Second Sex* (1968), read widely in the United States and Western Europe.

Septuagint: The translation into Greek of the Hebrew and Aramaic Jewish Scriptures between 250 and 100 B.C.E. The texts of the Septuagint were incorporated into the Christian Bible as the Old Testament and the deuterocanonical/apocryphal books.

sexism: The erroneous belief, conviction, or attitude that one sex, female or male, is superior to the other by the very nature of reality. Although it is possible for either females or males to be treated as inferior, historically, women have been more negatively affected by sexism than men.

socialist feminism: That form of feminism which uses Marxist and feminist analysis in tandem to argue that economic class and gender definitions work together in capitalist societies to oppress women.

sola scriptura: Latin for "scripture alone." Luther coined this term as an axiom to emphasize that the Bible is the authority for understanding and for living faith.

spirituality: Striving to integrate one's life in terms of self-transcendence toward what one perceives to be the ultimate value or good. Christian spirituality is striving for personal integration and self-transcendence in relationship to God as revealed in Jesus Christ.

Synoptic: "To see together"; the term is used in reference to the Gospels of Matthew, Mark, and Luke. If printed in parallel columns with similar materials located side by side, it becomes clear that their accounts of the public life of Jesus are similar in content and order.

Tanakh: An acronym for the Hebrew Scriptures created from the Hebrew names for the three sections of the Hebrew Bible: Torah (Law), Nebi'im (the Prophets), and Ketubim (the Writings).

thealogy: Coined by Canadian Jewish feminist Naomi Goldenberg, it refers to reflection on the divine in feminine terms, especially when this reflection is associated with Goddess religion.

third wave of feminism: Traceable to the "International Women's Year" (1975), which launched the "UN Decade for Women" at a conference held in Mexico City. During this decade it became increasingly clear that European and Euro-American women's experience of discrimination was different from that of other racial and ethnic groups whose history included slavery and colonization. Since the early 1980s increasing attention has been given to the difference that social location makes in the lives of women, especially in the degree and kinds of struggles women face daily. During this period theologies that are location specific have emerged; among them are Christian feminist (European and Euro-American), womanist (African American), and *mujerista*/Latina (Hispanic and Latin American).

Third World: A name for countries, most of which are in the southern hemisphere, that have low levels of literacy and per capita income, and high levels of malnutrition and infant mortality. It can also be applied to poor persons, usually minorities, who live on the margin in societies of great wealth (e.g., the United States, Japan, Australia, New Zealand).

tradition: From the Latin *traditio* and the Greek *paradosis,* meaning "to hand on." The basic Christian meaning is the handing on of beliefs, doctrines, rituals, and revered sources, such as the Bible, by a church in ways that are responsive to the concerns of the time.

Trinity: A central doctrine of Christianity that affirms that there are three divine "persons" existing in one God. This mystery is rooted in the biblical belief in God as creator, redeemer, and sanctifier, and in the teachings of Jesus about God as "Father" and the promise of Jesus Christ, the Son of God, to send the Holy Spirit after his earthly life had ended.

vowed women (and men) religious: Persons who live their Christian faith by belonging to a religious institute in which they make a permanent commitment to the evangelical counsels of voluntary celibacy, poverty, and obedience.

Wisdom literature: The body of biblical literature that is concerned primarily with the pursuit of God's proper order for life.

womanist: Coined by Alice Walker, and related to the term "womanish," it names the unique struggle of African American women to overcome the oppression of racism, sexism, and classism, and affirms the contributions that black women make to the well-being of African Americans, female and male.

Yahweh: A name for God (YHWH), which, according to the Old Testament book of Exodus, was revealed to Moses. In Jewish tradition, it is considered a name too holy to be pronounced aloud and is replaced by *Adonai* (NRSV "LORD").

Index